To

F...
Mom
'10

think on these things

think on these things

NORVAL F. PEASE

Chairman,
Department of Religion, Loma Linda University
Riverside Campus

Author of

AND WORSHIP HIM

BY FAITH ALONE

This book is published in collaboration with
the Missionary Volunteer Department as an enrichment of the Morning Watch devotional plan.

REVIEW AND HERALD PUBLISHING ASSOCIATION
WASHINGTON, D.C.

Dedication

To my wife, Blanche, who helped gather material for this book, who typed the manuscript, and who made many valuable suggestions.

THE NEW YEAR

A great door and effectual is opened unto me, and there are many adversaries. 1 Cor. 16:9.

The statement in 1 Corinthians 16:9 occurs toward the end of Paul's first letter to the church at Corinth. He is writing from Ephesus, near the close of his long ministry in that city. He had been successful in Ephesus, but this very success had made bitter enemies.

Acts 19 tells of one of the adversaries who had confronted Paul at Ephesus. The apostle's teaching against idol worship had hurt the business of the silversmiths. A representative of their guild, Demetrius by name, stirred up a riot so violent that "the whole city was filled with confusion" (verse 29). This incident was apparently only a sample of the problems Paul met in Ephesus, for in recalling those days he said, "For we would not, brethren, have you ignorant of our trouble which came to us in Asia, that we were pressed out of measure, above strength, insomuch that we despaired even of life" (2 Cor. 1:8).

But despite the problems, Paul did not lose sight of the opportunities. "A great opportunity has opened for effective work," he said, "and there is much opposition" (N.E.B.).

How appropriate for the beginning of a new year! The future holds great opportunities. Advances in communication and transportation have shrunk the globe until messages encircle it in moments, and men in hours. Diseases that once terrorized whole populations have been conquered. Knowledge has increased in every field. Rewarding careers are beckoning millions of youth.

But, as Paul said, "there are many adversaries." War, famine, hate, fear, have not been overcome. Cities are increasingly restless and dangerous. God is forgotten in the quest for material things.

The apostle might have said fearfully, "*But* there are many adversaries." Instead he exclaimed, "*And* there are many adversaries." We may look upon the new year as a threat; or, like Paul, we may consider it a challenge. Which shall it be? Whether 1970 is a happy and successful year depends to a great extent on our attitude toward the crises that lurk among its days, weeks, and months.

5

WORSHIPFUL SEEKERS AFTER TRUTH

When Jesus was born in Bethlehem of Judaea in the days of Herod the king, behold, there came wise men from the east to Jerusalem, saying, Where is he that is born King of the Jews? for we have seen his star in the east, and are come to worship him. Matt. 2:1, 2.

Christmas cards often picture three camels and three robed philosophers of the East. In the hands of these men are their precious gifts— gold, frankincense, and myrrh.

The Magi speak to us of searchers for truth throughout the world. Scattered everywhere are honest men and women who are sensitive to spiritual values, and who see stars in their skies that others do not see. These people may come from varied backgrounds and may adhere to different creeds; but their minds reach out beyond the ordinary experiences of daily living to the meaning of life. Divine providence often leads such people to Christ, because they are willing to be led. The Magi traveled far in their search for Christ. Their concern was not merely casual; they were willing to invest something in their quest for the One "that is born King of the Jews."

The Magi also teach us the lesson of a worshipful attitude. When they approached Herod regarding Jesus, they said that they had come to worship Him. When they reached the manger they presented their gifts as expressions of homage. Their motive in seeking the newborn King was not curiosity, personal gain, intellectual satisfaction, or adventure. They came to worship. They may not have sensed the full meaning of His birth, but they were ready to bow their knees before Him. The wise men of today would discover more at the end of their quest if they sought wisdom that they might worship.

The search for truth and the will to worship—are not these two of the primary ingredients in the meaningful life? These two factors complement each other. When men search for truth without recognizing God, they limit their outreach. When men try to worship without searching for truth their worship can become sentimental and superficial. The world is looking for worshipful seekers after truth.

TURNING STONES INTO BREAD

When the tempter came to him, he said, If thou be the Son of God, command that these stones be made bread. But he answered and said, It is written, Man shall not live by bread alone, but by every word that proceedeth out of the mouth of God. Matt. 4:3, 4.

It has often been said that this temptation represents the clamor of appetite, and in a sense this is true. But the Master's situation is not comparable to that of the average person who is tempted to indulge appetite. Jesus was not like the alcoholic reaching for the bottle, or the glutton unable to resist the appeal of food. In Jesus' case, the problem was not a problem of indulgence, but of survival. For forty days He had fasted, and His strength was spent. Food was not available. The smooth stones that lay on the desert ground may have looked like loaves of bread, but they merely mocked His hunger. Without strength to secure food, what should He do?

At this desperate point the devil enters the picture. "I have a solution," he says. "Use your divine power, if you are the Son of God. Turn these stones to bread." But Jesus could not accept the devil's solution to His problem. He came to earth as man, and He must meet the problems of human existence in the ways open to man. No man could turn stones to bread, so He could not permit Himself that privilege.

But any man in a similar situation could call upon God for help. Jesus quoted Deuteronomy 8:3, where Moses refers to Israel's experience with the manna. With no food in sight, they too faced the question of survival. Believing, Jesus depended on the care and grace of His Father, and "angels came and ministered unto him." He met the crisis in the same way that any follower of God can meet a similar crisis.

This temptation was a variation of the age-old excuse, "A man has to live." Every manner of wrongdoing has been rationalized on this pretext. Jesus set us an example when He refused to compromise His mission in a circumstance that seemed to threaten His very survival. A man does *not* have to live, but he must be loyal to his God.

7

JUMPING FROM A CHURCH STEEPLE

The devil taketh him up into the holy city, and setteth him on a pinnacle of the temple, and saith unto him, If thou be the Son of God, cast thyself down. Matt. 4:5, 6.

Jesus stood at a point of crisis in His life. He had been the carpenter's son at Nazareth. Now He was to go throughout the towns and villages preaching the gospel of the kingdom. He had a great mission, but would anyone listen to Him? How could He reach the confused and unresponsive hearts of the multitudes? This question troubles every evangelist, and Jesus was an evangelist.

At this point the devil appeared with a plausible answer to His problem. He took the Saviour to Jerusalem and placed Him on a pinnacle of the Temple. He could look down upon the city and the throngs in the Temple area below. There were the people He needed to reach with His gospel. "It's simple," the devil whispered. "Just jump into the crowd. Sail down from the sky. If you are the Son of God, your Father will not let you get hurt. When the people see this, they will listen!"

But Jesus knew that this was not the answer. He Himself must not use any power that would not be available to those whom He was about to send into the world. Furthermore, His gospel must not be tarnished by sensationalism. Instead of sailing down from the pinnacle of the Temple, Jesus "began to preach, and to say, Repent: for the kingdom of heaven is at hand" (verse 17).

In resisting this temptation Jesus taught a lesson to all of His followers. Sensational tricks may awaken curiosity, but they will never convert sinners. Jesus chose to preach by the lakeside, in the synagogues, in the fields, and in the Temple courts. He appealed to the loyalty and intelligence of His hearers, not to their credulity. His miracles were performed to heal people, not to appeal to their superstitions. Faith is not presumption, and God is not the author of magic. The simple recital of the acts of God's power is not enhanced by the bizarre and spectacular. Preaching is more effective—and safer—than jumping from steeples!

THE WORLD FROM A MOUNTAINTOP

The devil taketh him up into an exceeding high mountain, and sheweth him all the kingdoms of the world, and the glory of them; and saith unto him, All these things will I give thee, if thou wilt fall down and worship me. Matt. 4:8, 9.

A tremendous lesson emerges from this confrontation between Jesus and the devil, and that lesson is to be found in Jesus' answer to the devil's temptation: "Thou shalt worship the Lord thy God, and him only shalt thou serve" (verse 10). Jesus declared emphatically that God is the one legitimate object of worship in the universe, and that we are to serve Him.

In giving His law from Sinai, God began with the command "Thou shalt have no other gods before me." He revealed Himself to Israel as a "jealous God" who would not permit any of His creatures to worship any being or thing other than Himself. Jesus revealed His understanding and acceptance of this principle when He refused to bend His knee to the devil, even for the whole world.

Many Christians have given their lives for this principle. In the early Christian centuries the worship of the Roman emperor was a symbol of loyalty. The subject was asked to recognize the sacredness of the emperor by performing an act of worship, such as offering a bit of incense. This he could not do as a Christian, even though his refusal to do so might jeopardize his life.

The question in the modern world is not Shall we worship God or the emperor? God or an idol? God or Baal? Rather, the question is Do we live as if there were no God? Standing on his high mountain and looking on all the kingdoms of the world, modern man says, "What do I need with God? I don't need to pray for health, I have medicine. I don't need to pray for rain, I irrigate. I don't need to pray, 'Thy kingdom come,' I have one of my own."

Jesus' answer to the devil, "Thou shalt worship the Lord thy God, and him only shalt thou serve," is as important in the asphalt jungle as it was in the wilderness of Judea. Too often modern Christians give the same homage to materialism that Jesus *refused* to give.

9

FISHERS OF MEN

He saith unto them, Follow me, and I will make you fishers of men. Matt. 4:19.

One day Jesus found Simon Peter and his brother Andrew "casting a net into the sea," and used their occupation as an illustration of the work He called them to do. A few eventful years later Peter cast his gospel net into the sea at Pentecost, and his marvelous catch amounted to "about three thousand souls." He had followed his Lord, and he truly became a fisher of men.

If this analogy teaches anything, it reminds us that the Christian, to fulfill his mission, must bear his witness where the people are. He cannot wait for people to come to him. One successful evangelist has put it this way: "Suppose I built a beautiful fishhouse down by the side of the lake, designed it after the Gothic pattern, placed stained glass windows in it, burned candles in it at noonday, carpeted its floors, ornamented its walls, and placed outside its doors an electric sign that read: 'Fishhouse. All fish invited. Fishing hours 11:00 A.M. and 7:30 P.M.' How many fish would I catch?"—BOB SHULER, *What New Doctrine Is This?* p. 138.

When Peter preached his great sermon he was where "the multitude came together." He took his message to the people of his day. And what was his message? "This Jesus hath God raised up, whereof we all are witnesses. . . . God hath made that same Jesus, whom ye have crucified, both Lord and Christ." The message that touched the hearts of so many people was the simple story of the Son of God, crucified, resurrected, ascended, and coming again.

There are many "fishers of men" in the world, some with worthy motives and some with selfish motives. People are having every type of bait dangled before them, and are feeling the mesh of a variety of nets. The Christian message, now as in Peter's time, must be none other than the "new old story" of Jesus and His love. Christ's teaching leaves no room for philosophies that would reduce the gospel to social uplift. The purpose of the gospel is the salvation of men.

"IMMEDIATELY"

And going on from thence, he saw two other brethren, James the son of Zebedee, and John his brother, in a ship with Zebedee their father, mending their nets; and he called them. And they immediately left the ship and their father, and followed him. Matt. 4:21, 22.

Jesus had just called Peter and Andrew, who responded "straightway" to His invitation. Now He approached two other brothers with the same call, and they also responded. Peter, Andrew, James, and John had been part-time followers of Jesus since His baptism, but they were still fishermen.

The time had come for these four men to leave the sea, their boats, and their nets and become full-time followers of Jesus. This was a crucial decision. It is hard for most people to tear away from a life that is familiar and strike out into the unknown. Risk is involved.

But in both cases the response was wholehearted. Peter and Andrew "straightway left their nets" and James and John "immediately left the ship." The words "straightway" and "immediately" are translations of the same Greek word, which expresses the idea of no delay. Jesus knew the right time to call these men to a new vocation, and they sensed that the time had come to answer the call.

One modern philosopher is quoted as saying, "If I ever become seriously Christian, I shall be ashamed of having tried everything else first." How many Christians should share his shame. Jesus comes to their home, office, workshop, or place of business and says, "Follow me," just as He did to Peter, Andrew, James, and John. He wants their full-time service. Instead of responding "immediately," they say, "I'll think it over," "Not now," "When conditions are different." Delay causes them to lose opportunities that might add great meaning to their lives. And too long a delay may mean eternal loss.

Many a person is mending nets who ought to be preaching Christ —others, like Zebedee, need to stay with the ship. Happy is the person who recognizes the call of Christ and responds "immediately." This is especially true in an age that is facing catastrophe. There is no longer time to put off responding to Christ's invitation.

11

TEACHING—PREACHING—HEALING

And Jesus went about all Galilee, teaching in their synagogues, and preaching the gospel of the kingdom, and healing all manner of sickness and all manner of disease among the people. Matt. 4:23.

Jesus was a teacher. Mark gives an example of Jesus' "teaching in their synagogues." After Jesus had called a little group of followers, the record says, "They went into Capernaum; and immediately on the sabbath he entered the synagogue and taught. And they were astonished at his teaching, for he taught them as one who had authority, and not as the scribes" (Mark 1:21, 22, R.S.V.). A hint as to the content of Jesus' teaching is found in Luke 4:16-21, which tells of Jesus' visit to His home town synagogue at Nazareth, and His application of Isaiah 61:1, 2 to Himself. Part of Jesus' mission was to give instruction.

Jesus was a preacher. The word translated "preach" means literally "to proclaim." The word refers to ancient heralds' going through the streets of the cities shouting information of interest and importance to the inhabitants. Jesus' message was the "gospel of the kingdom." Everywhere He went Jesus uttered this proclamation, declaring that it would eventually reach all nations. He sent His disciples to the world with the same message of deliverance and salvation.

Jesus was a healer. While remembering the needs of men's minds and souls, Jesus did not forget the needs of their bodies. He revealed His love and kindness by exerting divine power to heal afflictions for which the people had no remedies. This healing activity was dependent on the faith of the people; those who believed on Jesus were healed—those who disbelieved were not. In this respect the healing of the body was an object lesson revealing how Christ works in the healing of the soul. The miracles of Jesus were among His best methods of revealing His love.

Jesus' followers were called to be teachers, preachers, and healers. The purpose of this activity, at all times and places, was to communicate the love of God and to redeem man. Methods may change with changing cultures, but the teaching, proclaiming, and healing functions of the gospel are ever the same.

12

THE FIRST REQUIREMENT FOR HAPPINESS

Blessed are the poor in spirit: for their's is the kingdom of heaven. Matt. 5:3.

Each of the Beatitudes pronounces a blessing on something difficult. It isn't easy to be "poor in spirit," for this means humility, and humility is not a popular virtue. In the *New English Bible* this Beatitude reads, " 'How blest are those who know that they are poor.' " It calls for a self-understanding that is foreign to most people.

"It is reported of Francis of Assisi that he had a simple and effective way of keeping himself humble. Whenever anyone praised his virtues, he would ask a fellow monk to sit down with him and tell him his faults. It might facetiously be said that if Francis had been married, he would have had that service rendered him at home!"—RALPH W. SOCKMAN, *The Higher Happiness*, p. 28.

It is so much easier to be proud of our accomplishments, our nationality, our belongings, our family connections, than it is to admit that we are weak and faulty. It takes real Christian grace to acknowledge our weakness and seek strength from God sufficient to meet our needs. It is interesting that Jesus listed this virtue first among the Beatitudes.

"He who feels whole, who thinks that he is reasonably good, and is contented with his condition, does not seek to become a partaker of the grace and righteousness of Christ. Pride feels no need, and so it closes the heart against Christ and the infinite blessings He came to give."—*Thoughts From the Mount of Blessing*, p. 7. The person who recognizes his spiritual poverty is not happy *because* he is poor and weak. He is happy because, through Christ, he can become wealthy and strong. This recognition of his need makes it possible for God to supply his need.

Billy Graham has said, "I have searched the world over in my travels for contented and happy men. I have found such men only where Christ has been personally and decisively received. There is only one permanent way to have peace of soul that wells up in joy, contentment, and happiness, and that is by repentance of sin and personal faith in Jesus Christ as Savior."—*The Secret of Happiness*, p. 14.

HAPPY MOURNERS

Blessed are they that mourn: for they shall be comforted.
Matt. 5:4.

Does this Beatitude place a premium on gloom and sorrow? Does it mean that God does not want us to be happy? No. It does mean that the way to happiness is often by way of sorrow.

It is often only when health is severely impaired that we learn how to live temperately, and thus find it again. The loss of wealth can lead us to develop habits of thrift and industry. It is often when the blessings of life can no longer be taken for granted that we learn lessons of permanent happiness. Out of tragedy and loss often come insights that enable us to recognize the real values of life.

One of the most important aspects of mourning is the sorrow that results from sympathy for others. Abraham Lincoln is quoted as saying, "I am sorry for the man who can't feel the whip when it is laid on the other man's back." Jesus wept at the opening of a tomb, and when He looked upon a doomed city. He could not be indifferent to human sorrow and tragedy.

How can we but mourn when we think of the millions who go to bed hungry every day—if they have a bed? How can we be indifferent when we think of the bereaved, the homeless, the victims of war? It is not good to be able to live in a world like this and be unconcerned. Nothing will be gained by becoming morbid over the world's ills, but no follower of Christ can be indifferent to the sufferings of others. Concern must find expression in actions. To mourn over the world's ills, yet do nothing, is futile.

" 'Happy are they that mourn.' They are happy because they know that their pain, their distress, and their privation are the travail of a new creation, the birth pangs of a better world. They are happy because they are aware that the Master Artist—God—is employing both light and shadow to produce a masterpiece worthy of divine artistry.

"They are also made to glory in their infirmities, to smile through their tears, and to sing in the midst of their sorrow because they realize that in God's economy 'if we suffer, we shall also reign with him.' "
—BILLY GRAHAM, *The Secret of Happiness,* pp. 27, 28.

14

THE TAMED LIFE

Blessed are the meek: for they shall inherit the earth. Matt. 5:5.

It has been suggested that the Greek word translated "meek" was once used of wild animals that had been tamed. If so, this use throws interesting light on the text. Many people fail to see meekness as a virtue. They think of the meek man as a spineless creature lacking strength and manhood. Surely this type of person will never "inherit the earth"!

But suppose we think of the meek man as a normal person with selfish impulses, an aggressive nature, and a bad temper, but in whom these instincts have been tamed. There is no lack of strength, but the strength is under control. To change the figure, the person is a dynamo of energy—but the result is light and power, not destruction.

In other words, Christian meekness is gentle power, controlled aggressiveness, directed energy. Is it not true that this type of person often gains position and respect in the world? The Christian gospel is a taming influence, and only after the Christian has submitted to this process, often called "sanctification," can God share His world with him.

Christ was actually quoting from Psalm 37:11, "The meek shall inherit the earth," and this psalm is our best commentary on Jesus' statement. Here the psalmist says, "Fret not thyself because of evildoers." It takes a tamed spirit to obey this command. It is also this psalm that says, "Commit thy way unto the Lord; trust also in him; and he shall bring it to pass." This is not an easy thing to do, but when a person ceases striking out at life, and puts his trust in God, in a very real way he inherits the earth. Life takes on new meaning, and he becomes heir to great spiritual riches.

"Meekness," says Ralph W. Sockman, "is not apathy, or lack of spirit, or weakness, or timidity. It is power blended with gentleness. It is the soul in the majesty of self-possession, lifted above impulsiveness and irascibility. It is that high and radiant state of mind in which all the faculties function under the sway of their divine Master."— *The Higher Happiness,* p. 66.

FOOD FOR THE HUNGRY

Blessed are they which do hunger and thirst after righteousness: for they shall be filled. Matt. 5:6.

The meaning of this passage is hard for moderns to understand, because the word "righteousness" is seldom used except in prayers or sermons. To speak of a person as "righteous" is not considered a compliment. The righteous person bears the image, in the modern mind, of a holier-than-thou Pharisee. But this was far from Jesus' meaning. The righteousness of which He spoke is conformity to the divine will, and the person who hungers and thirsts after righteousness is a person who deeply desires to be in harmony with God.

This Beatitude informs us that the blessing of being Godlike is not gained by "painful struggles or wearisome toil, not by gift or sacrifice, . . . but it is freely given to every soul who hungers and thirsts to receive it" (*Thoughts From the Mount of Blessing,* p. 18). This is the gospel. Goodness is a gift, a free gift, bestowed upon those who reach out for it in faith.

Certain attitudes and practices ruin the appetite for goodness. What are these things that keep us from hungering and thirsting for righteousness?

Just as children aren't hungry at mealtime when they have eaten too much candy between meals, so preoccupation with the follies and pleasures of the world may ruin our appetite for the things God has for us. Sensational fiction may cause us to reject the Bible. The theater may dampen our desire for the church. Excessive concern with sports may make serious Christian service unappetizing. Only when we keep our appetites healthy will we desire the things we need most. Dishonesty, immorality, hatred, and self-centeredness will likewise so distort our sense of values that sacred things become repulsive.

For what are we hungering and thirsting? For pleasure, fame, comfort, security? These things, though not necessarily bad, are not the real answer in life. Someone has said, "Be careful what you set your heart on, for it will probably be yours." If our hunger is for the things of this world we *may* receive them. If our hunger is for righteousness we *shall* be filled.

16

THE QUALITY OF MERCY

Blessed are the merciful: for they shall obtain mercy. Matt. 5:7.

"There are many to whom life is a painful struggle; they feel their deficiencies, and are miserable and unbelieving; they think they have nothing for which to be grateful. Kind words, looks of sympathy, expressions of appreciation, would be to many a struggling and lonely one as the cup of cold water to a thirsty soul."—*Thoughts From the Mount of Blessing,* p. 23.

One reason for being merciful is that we all need mercy. There is an often-repeated story regarding John Wesley and Governor Oglethorpe of the Georgia Colony. It seems that a servant had drunk several bottles of the governor's rare wine. Wesley was interceding for the frightened servant, urging the irate governor to forgive. "Sir," he shouted, "I never forgive." "Then," replied Wesley, "I hope you never offend."

Being merciful is not only a blessing to the recipient of mercy—it reacts upon the person who is merciful. Shakespeare wrote:

"The quality of mercy is not strain'd;
  It droppeth as the gentle rain from heaven
  Upon the place beneath: it is twice bless'd;
  It blesseth him that gives and him that takes."

It takes a big man to be merciful. The story is told that when William E. Gladstone was chancellor of the exchequer he asked his statistician to prepare some figures for his budget speech. The statistician made an error. Without verifying the figures, Gladstone made his speech before the House of Commons.

The newspapers immediately called attention to glaring inaccuracies, much to Gladstone's embarrassment. He immediately called for the statistician, who was certain that he would lose his job. Instead, Mr. Gladstone said, "I know how much you must be disturbed over what has happened, and I have sent for you to put you at your ease. For a long time you have been engaged in handling the intricacies of the national accounts, and this is the first mistake you have made. I want to congratulate you and express to you my keen appreciation."

17

THE HEART GOD CLEANSES

Blessed are the pure in heart: for they shall see God. Matt. 5:8.

Ellen G. White, in *Thoughts From the Mount of Blessing,* suggests a deeper, more inclusive interpretation of this Beatitude than is generally recognized. To be pure in heart means more than to be "free from that which is sensual, pure from lust." It means to be true in the hidden purposes and motives of the soul, free from pride and self-seeking, humble, unselfish, childlike. . . . Unless you accept in your own life the principle of self-sacrificing love, which is the principle of His character, you cannot know God."—Page 25.

How can we achieve purity of heart, so that nothing in our lives will eclipse our vision of God? "E. Stanley Jones tells us that while he was visiting Gandhi a Sadhu came eight hundred miles to ask Gandhi two questions. The questions were these: 'How can I get rid of sin, and how can I find God?' Having asked Ghandi, the seeker after God came to ask Jones the same questions. He said to the inquirer: 'Before I answer you, would you mind telling me what Gandhi told you?' 'No, I don't mind telling you,' he answered. 'He told me to sit down in one place and not roam about as the Sadhus do, but stay in one place till I had conquered my senses and my passions and worn them out; then I might find release.' 'Was there no offer of immediate relief?' Jones asked. 'O, no,' was the reply. 'He said it would take a long, long time.' And then he turned to Jones and said, 'Now what do you say?' and this radiant missionary told him what had happened to himself. He said: 'My yearning was exactly your yearning. I needed to know how to get rid of sin, and I needed to know God. But I did not need to stay in one place till I had worn out my passions; I simply turned over a bankrupt soul to Jesus Christ, and, lo, as I gave my all He gave me his all. It did not take ages, it took surrender. It did not take time, it took me.' "—CLOVIS G. CHAPPELL, *The Sermon on the Mount,* pp. 85, 86.

It is only after I have been thus cleansed that I can see God. I can see Him in His Word, in His world, and especially in His Son. I can see His hand guiding in the affairs of my life and, finally, I hope to see my Pilot face to face. This will be the final reward.

PEACE

Blessed are the peacemakers: for they shall be called the children of God. Matt. 5:9.

"There is a peace of mind which we can understand the world may give to a man. A family is gathered for the evening meal in a comfortable home. The hush of eventide has quieted the day's activities. Bodies which have been healthily exercised are now restfully relaxed. No danger lurks to disturb the thoughts. No financial worries threaten the morrow. In such a delicious sense of physical well-being and mental contentment, we can understand the father or mother looking around the family circle and saying, 'Now this is what I call peace.'

"But when Jesus says, 'My peace I give unto you,' he is speaking out of a totally different setting. He is met in an upper room with the comrades who have weathered with him the attacks of adversity and ridicule. The air of the city is electric with the gathering storm which is to break around him in all its fury on the morrow. He knows the pain which is being prepared for him. His sensitive imagination can feel in advance the excruciating torture of the cross. Treason has entered the ranks of his most trusted friends, and one is already on the way to plot his arrest. Out of such a situation come the words, 'My peace I give unto you.' Surely it was hardly necesary for him to add, 'Not as the world giveth, give I unto you.' For whatever peace Jesus felt at that moment was beyond the power of the world to give or take away."—RALPH W. SOCKMAN, *The Higher Happiness,* pp. 151, 152.

In the past four thousand years, it is said, there have been fewer than three hundred years of peace. The efforts of men and nations to stop war have failed. Two thousand years of Christianity have not succeeded in taming the beast in man. The future is admittedly dark, with the atomic cloud hanging over our planet. In a world like this, "Blessed are the peacemakers." Happy are those who have learned what real peace is—peace with God and with their fellow men. Happy are those who are able to live at peace with themselves, with their neighbors, and with God, whatever conditions may exist. The Christmas message was "Peace on earth." The only way this hope can be fulfilled is for peace to dwell in the heart, in the family, in the church, in the community.

19

SUFFERING FOR CHRIST

Blessed are they which are persecuted for righteousness' sake: for their's is the kingdom of heaven. Blessed are ye, when men shall revile you, and persecute you, and shall say all manner of evil against you falsely, for my sake. Rejoice, and be exceeding glad: for great is your reward in heaven: for so persecuted they the prophets which were before you. Matt. 5:10-12.

One of the most thought-provoking passages I have read in recent years is a statement by John R. W. Stott, a well-known London pastor:

"Supposing we raised our standards and stopped our compromises? Supposing we proclaimed our message and tightened our discipline with love but without fear? I will tell you the result: the Church would suffer. There would be an outcry. We should be called puritanical, Victorian, old-fashioned, unpractical, rigid. Indeed, every imaginable derogatory epithet would be called into the service of the unbelieving world, and the Church would again find itself where it belongs—outside the gate, and in the wilderness.

"I am not advocating a harsh lovelessness towards the weak, the sinful or the penitent. Nor am I recommending that we court opposition with rash and foolish indiscretion. I am simply suggesting that we should not compromise on clear, moral and spiritual issues. I am just saying that we should face this fact, namely, that if we do not suffer it is probably because we compromise and that if we do not compromise we certainly shall suffer."—*What Christ Thinks of the Church,* pp. 44, 45.

It seems strange to the Christian that living a life motivated by Christian love should cause him to be shunned, scorned, and possibly hated. This is true because Christians' lives are a rebuke to those who reject the Christian gospel.

A workman was chiseling a piece of stone at the base of a tall church. He explained, "See that little opening up there? I'm shaping this down here so it will fit up there." This is what God does for us through persecution, trial, and hardship. Let us not be impatient. God is shaping us down here so we will fit up there.

THE SALT OF THE EARTH

Ye are the salt of the earth: but if the salt have lost his savour, wherewith shall it be salted? it is thenceforth good for nothing, but to be cast out, and to be trodden under foot of men. Matt. 5:13.

"You are like salt for the earth" (T.E.V.). It has often been suggested that Jesus compared His church to salt because salt is a preservative and adds flavor and palatability to food. While this interpretation of Jesus' figure of speech is apt, another dimension of our Lord's meaning is suggested in a comment from *Thoughts From the Mount of Blessing:*

"Salt must be mingled with the substance to which it is added; it must penetrate and infuse in order to preserve. So it is through personal contact and association that men are reached by the saving power of the gospel. They are not saved in masses, but as individuals. Personal influence is a power. We must come close to those whom we desire to benefit."—Page 36.

In a European country a group of Catholic priests tried the experiment of accepting jobs at common labor so they could work alongside ordinary people day after day, and thus exert religious influence upon them. Several years ago a family of our missionaries on an American Indian reservation lived in a primitive hogan for many months in order to establish a close personal contact with the people on the reservation. Some years ago a group of adherents to a religious denomination sold their homes and moved to a community where their faith was not well known. They bought homes and accepted employment in the community in order that they might communicate their faith. If Christians are to be salt for all mankind they must break down the walls of isolation between themselves and their neighbors and communicate their faith by personal witness. They must be where their neighbors are.

But what if, after they have done this, "the salt loses its taste" (T.E.V.)? Suppose so-called Christians mix freely with their fellow men but radiate no love and exhibit no faith. They have muted their witness. Be *where* you are needed and also be *what* is needed.

THE NEW HYPOCRISY

Ye are the light of the world. A city that is set on an hill cannot be hid. Neither do men light a candle, and put it under a bushel, but on a candlestick; and it giveth light unto all that are in the house. Let your light so shine before men, that they may see your good works, and glorify your Father, which is in heaven. Matt. 5:14-16.

With natural grace the Christian's light should shine in the world. It should be neither a flickering nor a blinding light, but a soft, steady glow—dependable, warm, and assuring. Darkness suggests depression, fear, insecurity. Light suggests happiness, confidence, hope. In this context we can understand what Jesus meant when He said, "You are like the light for the world" (T.E.V.).

This idea is especially needed in today's world. Dr. Clovis G. Chappell points out this need in challenging words:

"We are not to be afraid to be openly Christian. We are not to be afraid to be ourselves. Dr. Sockman spoke recently of 'The New Hypocrisy.' He declared that there was a day when the Church was strong and dominant in the life of the people; that, in that day, to win popularity men often sought to appear better than they were. That was the old hypocrisy. Today, when the church does not loom so large in the public eye, there are those who seek to appear worse than they are. That is the new hypocrisy.

"And this new hypocrisy is altogether too common. How many are afraid to appear as good as they actually are! . . . They are ashamed of the ideals that are the very glory of their manhood and womanhood."—*The Sermon on the Mount,* p. 133.

This insight is especially applicable to young people. The scorn that is heaped upon the "square" is a formidable deterrent to letting one's light shine. It is much easier to compromise a little, to hide the light, to avoid ridicule. It is well to remember that this compromise is aptly described as "the new hypocrisy."

Notice, Jesus does not say, "You *have* the light." He says, "You *are* the light." This light will shine if we let it. It is the Christlike life of the Christian that interprets God to the world.

THE HIGHER RIGHTEOUSNESS

For I say unto you, That except your righteousness shall exceed the righteousness of the scribes and Pharisees, ye shall in no case enter into the kingdom of heaven. Matt. 5:20.

This verse contains the theme of the Sermon on the Mount. The "righteousness" of the scribes and Pharisees was well known to Jesus' listeners. These men were meticulous, highly religious, and dedicated. They occupied positions of honor and trust. They were generally accepted as authorities on religious matters, and as patterns for conduct. But Jesus said, "Your righteousness must exceed theirs."

He made His meaning very clear. "They" were deeply concerned about the legalities of religion. They were experts on definition and codification. They knew all the implications of the law that said, "Thou shalt not kill," except the one that named unjustified anger as a violation of that law. They had interpretations of the law that said, "Thou shalt not commit adultery," but somehow their codes had never condemned lust. They were agreed on loving their neighbors, but they had never caught the idea that their enemies were also to be loved. Eight times in the fifth chapter Jesus repeats the statement "But I say unto you." In each case He is contrasting their limited interpretation of divine law with His "higher righteousness."

Commenting on this text, Ellen White says: "A legal religion is insufficient to bring the soul into harmony with God. The hard, rigid orthodoxy of the Pharisees, destitute of contrition, tenderness, or love, was only a stumbling block to sinners. . . . The disciples of Christ must obtain righteousness of a different character from that of the Pharisees, if they would enter the kingdom of heaven."—*Thoughts From the Mount of Blessing,* pp. 53-55.

A modern version translates this verse, "For I tell you, if your virtue goes no deeper than that of the scribes and Pharisees, you will never get into the kingdom of heaven" (Jerusalem Bible). The righteousness of the disciple of Christ exceeds that of the modern Pharisee because it is based on fellowship with Him who alone completely fulfilled the law. No one but Jesus can impart this "higher righteousness."

ANGER

Ye have heard that it was said by them of old time, Thou shalt not kill; and whosoever shall kill shall be in danger of the judgment. But I say unto you, That whosoever is angry with his brother without a cause shall be in danger of the judgment, and whosoever shall say to his brother, Raca, shall be in danger of the council: but whosoever shall say, Thou fool, shall be in danger of hell fire. Matt. 5:21, 22.

The New English Bible has an interesting translation of verse 22: "Anyone who nurses anger against his brother must be brought to judgement. If he abuses his brother he must answer for it to the court: if he sneers at him he will have to answer for it in the fires of hell." This translation seems to define three levels of hatred a person may harbor against his brother. First, there is the level of nursing anger. How common is a smoldering hostility, never extinguished and occasionally bursting into flame.

Then there is the person who "abuses" his brother. He never misses an opportunity to downgrade him. He minimizes his accomplishments, perhaps by faint praise. He compares him, always unfavorably, with others. He admits his virtues, but underscores his weaknesses. He is always present to publicize his mistakes.

Finally, there is the man who "sneers" at his brother. The reason a sneer is the most wicked of all is that the one who sneers holds his brother up to contempt with no effort to explain why. When one person criticizes another the victim may be defended by himself or others, but what defense is there against a sneer? It is the most damaging, devilish form of personal assault imaginable. For this reason, the person who sneers is, according to the text, headed for destruction.

There is a justifiable anger. The King James Version of our text levels God's judgment against those who are angry "without a cause." Some ancient manuscripts do not have this phrase, but it is certainly in harmony with the teaching of Jesus. Jesus Himself became angry when weak people were being mistreated by those who were strong, when human values were being disregarded. Anger is defensible when it is caused by a concern for people.

LIFE AND WORSHIP

If thou bring thy gift to the altar, and there rememberest that thy brother hath ought against thee; leave there thy gift before the altar, and go thy way; first be reconciled to thy brother, and then come and offer thy gift. Matt. 5:23, 24.

Watch the man on his way to the place of worship with a gift that represents his dedication to God. Perhaps he has saved for a long time to fullfill his heart's desire to make a substantial contribution to the cause of God. He is almost to the altar where the gift is to be delivered. The climactic moment is at hand. Suddenly he remembers that his next-door neighbor hasn't spoken to him for a long time. There was a disagreement over a line fence, and the neighbor felt that he was cheated in the settlement. The neighbor had "something against" him. There were hard feelings; the bond of friendship had been broken.

What should he do? He had been taught that a person should be clean when coming into the presence of God. But could he not see the neighbor tomorrow? This was his big day. Why delay the ceremony?

No, Jesus said, "Leave the gift before the altar"—check it, have someone watch it, hide it somewhere—go back and make things right with the neighbor. Then come and offer your gift.

Throughout the Bible, God teaches that worship must be ethical. Lips that have spoken lies, unkind words, falsehood, profanity, and smut during the week cannot acceptably praise God on Sabbath. Hands that have grasped dishonest dollars during the week cannot be blessed as they place an offering in the plate at church. Eyes that have looked unnecessarily at scenes of wickedness—on the television screen, at the theater, or anywhere else—cannot see God at church. Ears that have listened to the music of the devil cannot appreciate sacred melodies in the hour of worship.

The psalmist says, "Who shall ascend into the hill of the Lord? or who shall stand in his holy place? He that hath clean hands, and a pure heart; who hath not lifted up his soul unto vanity, nor sworn deceitfully" (Ps. 24:3, 4). What we are determines the meaningfulness of our worship.

25

AMPUTEES FOR CHRIST

*If thy right hand offend thee, cut it off, and cast it from thee:
for it is profitable for thee that one of thy members should
perish, and not that thy whole body should be cast into hell.*
Matt. 5:29.

A pastor in a large city church once preached a sermon on this
text. One of his listeners, who was suffering from mental illness,
went home from church and literally obeyed the command—she cut
off her right hand. Such a reaction to Jesus' statement fills us with
horror, and rightly so. What *did* Jesus mean?

The answer is given in *Thoughts From the Mount of Blessing:*
"To prevent disease from spreading to the body and destroying life,
a man would submit to part even with his right hand. Much more
should he be willing to surrender that which imperils the life of the
soul."—Page 60. Frequently we see amputees who would not be living had they not given up an arm or leg.

To some people who are being ruined by their money their Lord
has come as He did to the rich young ruler, saying, "If you would live,
you must part with your excess wealth. It is a cancer that is destroying
your soul." The wise person, under such circumstances, will submit
to the surgery, painful though it be.

Christ has confronted others with His claims while they were engaged in a profession or business that is intrinsically contrary to Christian ideals. Suppose an owner of a gambling house should decide to
become a Christian. To part with his lucrative business would be like
losing his right hand, but there would be no other way.

Or perhaps a person might discover his obligation to keep the
Sabbath while engaged in a legitimate occupation, but one that would
not permit Sabbath observance. To readjust his life might be traumatic,
but to refuse to do so would imperil the life of his soul.

Others may be called upon to give up cherished friends for Christ,
or deeply entrenched habits, or popularity. Their decision may be a
hard one, but to fail to make the sacrifice will mean eternal loss.

"Amputees for Christ" might figuratively describe many dedicated
people. But from their suffering they receive life.

"RESIST NOT EVIL"

Ye have heard that it hath been said, an eye for an eye, and a tooth for a tooth: but I say unto you, that ye resist not evil: but whosoever shall smite thee on thy right cheek, turn to him the other also. And if any man will sue thee at the law, and take away thy coat, let him have thy cloke also. And whosoever shall compel thee to go a mile, go with him twain. Matt. 5:38-41.

The *Pulpit Digest* of December, 1967, published a sermon in which the preacher made the following statement: "During the First World War, the Society of Friends printed the Sermon on the Mount as a separate pamphlet without comment for distribution among the Allied armies. Both the British and French governments banned it, and forbade its distribution among their troops on the grounds that it was subversive of national policy."—Page 48 (Frank Holliday Ferris, "Food for the Full-Grown").

If true, this illustrates the dilemma of the Christian. His Lord calls upon him to accept and practice a philosophy of nonresistance in a world that operates on the philosophy of survival through retaliation. Can there be no resolution of the frustration that comes from trying to harmonize Christian ethics with the practices of men and nations? There is no aspect of life that more eloquently proclaims that the Christian is a "stranger and a pilgrim" in this world. Despite compromises and rationalizations by Christians, Jesus' teaching still stands, "Resist not evil."

If Christians through the centuries had observed the ideal of non-resistance *among themselves,* their influence on the affairs of the world would have been much greater. From church board meetings to religious wars, Jesus' followers have violated this principle. Witness the factions in churches, all the way from Corinth to today. Witness the bitterness between religious groups. Witness the political ambitions of Christian leaders who try to gain position and prestige. Here are areas where we *can* follow the precepts of our Lord.

We cannot prevent the wars of the world, but we can prevent the wars that rend churches and Christian homes. If we are to practice Jesus' principles of nonresistance, this is the place to begin.

WHAT ABOUT PERFECTION?

Be ye therefore perfect, even as your Father which is in heaven is perfect. Matt. 5:48.

Several years ago, a subscriber addressed the following question to the religion column of a California newspaper: "There is a passage in the Bible that asks Christians to be perfect. It is my contention that it is impossible for anyone to live a perfect life. Please give your opinion." This problem has puzzled many Christians. They want to do right, but when they look honestly at their own lives they see how far short they come from perfection. An inner conflict develops that is likely to cause discouragement and despair. Or they may react like the woman who approached Spurgeon. "I have not sinned for some time," she said. "You must be very proud," he replied. "Indeed, I am!"

Matthew 5:48 must be understood in reference to its context. An analysis of verses 43 to 48 reveals Jesus' line of thought running something like this:

"Your Father in heaven makes His sun to shine on the evil and on the good.

"Your Father in heaven sends rain on the just and on the unjust.

"You love only those who love you.

"You salute only your brethren.

"Be like your Father in heaven. Love your enemies. Bless them that curse you. Do good to them that hate you. Pray for them that misuse you. *This is what I mean by being perfect or mature."*

This analysis of the text is confirmed by noting the parallel text in Luke. Where Matthew says, "Be ye therefore perfect, even as your Father which is in heaven is perfect," Luke says, "Be ye therefore merciful, as your Father also is merciful" (Luke 6:36). Comparing these two passages we note that to be merciful is to be perfect. The word translated "perfect" literally means "full-grown," "mature." Is maturity better manifested than in an attitude of love and mercy toward friends and enemies alike? Jesus is saying that in loving his enemy, the Christian is becoming like his God. This is not an easy attainment, but it is the goal of the Christian. And it is a goal that is not reached in a day.

TALKING TO GOD

But thou, when thou prayest, enter into thy closet, and when thou hast shut thy door, pray to thy Father which is in secret; and thy Father which seeth in secret shall reward thee openly. Matt. 6:6.

"And when you pray, do not be like the show-offs! They love to stand up and pray in the meeting houses and on the street corners so that everybody will see them. Remember this! They have already been paid in full. But when you pray, go to your room and close the door, and pray to your Father who is unseen. And your Father, who sees what you do in private, will reward you" (T.E.V.).

Jesus does not teach here that there should be no public prayers. There are too many examples of public prayer in the Bible to admit this interpretation. He does teach that prayer must never be offered to impress people, and that prayer, at its best, is a personal encounter with God.

There is much disparagement of personal religion. Many seem to feel that religion is an ecclesiastical and social function but not a personal relationship to God. But what could be more personal than an individual, alone in his room on his knees, talking to God? And what could be more personal than the activity of God in leading, comforting, and directing such a one in the details of his life? This is real religion. At this point a man comes in closest contact with his Maker.

Dr. Clarence Macartney, a minister for many years, tells of a student who had been urged to do something that was very wrong, and had come to him for counsel. Amazed that the student should feel the need of advice as to the right or wrong of the suggested action, Macartney asked, "How does it seem to you when you pray about it?" "Oh, then," came the quick answer, "it seems to be wrong." Commenting on this experience, Macartney stressed one of the greatest blessings of private prayer: "It strips the mask from the face of temptation."—*Macartney's Illustrations,* p. 271.

There is no substitute for the experience of talking to God when no one else is listening or watching.

LESS WORDS!

*When ye pray, use not vain repetitions, as the heathen do:
for they think that they shall be heard for their much speaking.
Be not ye therefore like unto them: for your Father knoweth
what things ye have need of, before ye ask him.* Matt. 6:7, 8.

"Not so many words" is the essence of our Lord's counsel. There
are several ways in which this counsel applies to Christians in the
twentieth century.

First, when we pray privately or in family worship, are our prayers
mere repetitions of the words we have used over and over again, without thinking? Have we picked up certain clichés, and do we repeat
them, *ad infinitum?* This is not to say that every prayer will be a literary masterpiece. Such is not necessary. But if we were to go to the house
of a friend each day and repeat a series of well-worn statements, we
would soon wear out our welcome. Prayer demands freshness, spontaneity, naturalness—not a mere repetition of clichés.

Second, those of us who pray in public must avoid "vain repetitions." How often prayers offered in church never vary from a trite
pattern. We criticize religious leaders who read formal prayers, but often our prayers are more repetitious and less meaningful than those
that might be found in a prayer book! Think before you pray.

One minister asked: "What would happen to our members if . . .
they heard some genuine, urgent, expectant praying? If each week they
had a heart-searching experience of the confession of sin, who can say
that they would not go home and spend more time on their knees?
If in public prayer each Christian were led to see anew the fulness
of God's grace and to pour out his gratitude to him, would it not be that
in time he would be characterized by the grateful heart so that he would
eventually, as Paul says, 'in everything give thanks'?"—ROBERT L.
WILLIAMSON, *Effective Public Prayer,* p. 139.

May God help us learn to pray, not in flowery words or in
repetitious phrases, but in simple, heartfelt expressions of praise, confession, thanksgiving, and petition. May deadening formality give way
to inspiring warmth and reality. May we really talk with God.

"OUR FATHER"

After this manner therefore pray ye: Our Father which art in heaven, Hallowed be thy name. Matt. 6:9.

Seventeen times in the Sermon on the Mount, God is spoken of as "Father." In John 14 the title is used twenty-three times. One reason Jesus came to earth was to teach men that God is not a cruel tyrant or an impersonal deity, but a loving Father. He reinforced the teaching by suggesting that, when we pray, we address Him as "Father."

Leonard Griffith pictures God as Father with the following story:

"In his Yale Lectures of 1910, Frank Gunsaulus told of a time when Abraham Lincoln as President of the United States was sorely troubled with affairs of state. One day his little boy Tad came to Secretary Chase and said, 'I want my father.' Tad had been fighting with another boy and had come off second best. At this point the Yale lecturer asks us to use our imagination. Suppose Chase, with his Olympian forehead, had said patronizingly and cruelly, 'My little fellow, I will tell the Chief Executive of the nation . . . that you wish to see him.' It would have been a true statement, but the boy would have said again to the Secretary of the Treasury, 'I want my father.' Then little Tad encounters Seward with a cry straight from his heart, 'I want my father.' Suppose Seward had said, 'I will get for you the most remarkable diplomatic mind who ever warded off from a young nation in sore straits the attack of the British Empire. The Secretary of State would have told the truth. The boy, however, wipes away the blood and dirt and cries, 'I want my father.' Then the proud Stanton, Secretary of War, hears the boy's appeal and tells him, 'I will get for you the Commander-in-Chief of the Armies of the United States.' Stanton knew the president in that capacity. He also was telling the truth about Lincoln, but it was not the truth of Lincoln's child. Tad's truth expressed itself in the sob, 'I want my father.' "—*God's Time and Ours,* p. 151.

The most important truth about God is that He is our Father. He is interested in us. He loves us. He is concerned about the things that concern us. He is committed to our eternal salvation. Surely we can say to such a Father, "Hallowed be thy name."

31

"THY KINGDOM COME"

Thy kingdom come. Thy will be done in earth, as it is in heaven. Matt. 6:10.

What did Jesus mean when He taught His disciples to pray, "Thy kingdom come"? What is meant by the frequently used term "the kingdom of God"?

The psalmist gives a good answer to the question in Psalm 103: 19: "The Lord hath prepared his throne in the heavens; and his kingdom ruleth over all." This text describes the extent of God's kingly authority. He rules over "all." Psalm 145:13 reveals the duration of His authority, "Thy kingdom is an everlasting kingdom, and thy dominion endureth throughout all generations." Not only is God's kingdom everywhere, it is always.

But into this universal, eternal kingdom there came a rebel. He said, "I will exalt *my throne* above the stars of God: . . . *I* will be like the most high" (Isa. 14:12-14). Eventually rebellion centered in the corner of the universe we know as Earth. This posed a problem for God, humanly speaking. He could neither ignore the rebellion nor crush it by force, for neither course of action would be in harmony with His character. He decided to send His representative—Jesus, His only Son —in an effort to win back the loyalty of those who had followed the rebel. Jesus was to pay the ultimate price of submitting to death at the hands of the rebel's followers, in order that He might break the power of the enemy's influence on the minds and hearts of men.

It is the ultimate objective of God and His Son that their will be done "on earth as it is in heaven." This objective will be fully realized when God again reigns in a universe where there is no rebellion. In the meantime, "The kingdom of God's grace is now being established, as day by day hearts that have been full of sin and rebellion yield to the sovereignty of His love."—*Thoughts From the Mount of Blessing,* p. 108.

This is another way of describing the gospel. That is why Jesus used the term the "gospel of the kingdom." It is good news to know that there is a King who will ultimately prevail, and that He will share His victory with His loyal subjects.

"OUR DAILY BREAD"

Give us this day our daily bread. Matt. 6:11.

"The first half of the prayer Jesus has taught us is in regard to the name and kingdom and will of God—that His name may be honored, His kingdom established, His will performed. When you have thus made God's service your first interest, you may ask with confidence that your own needs may be supplied. If you have renounced self and given yourself to Christ you are a member of the family of God, and everything in the Father's house is for you. . . . The world, with everything in it, is yours so far as it can do you good."—*Thoughts From the Mount of Blessing,* p. 110.

Paul's statement "All things are your's" (1 Cor. 3:21) is a strange idea to many Christians. They have never discovered the great truth that God wants them to be happy, healthy, and prosperous. They have somehow equated poverty and anxiety with Christian experience.

When Jesus instructed His followers to pray for their daily bread He thereby expressed the divine concern about the material needs of His children. God is aware that we need food, shelter, and clothing comparable to that enjoyed by other people in the culture in which we live. He also wishes us to enjoy some of the other good things of life—the things that feed the soul. While He warns against materialism, secularism, and extravagance, it is not His will that His children should be subjected to want, privation, and worry.

"Give us today the food we need" (T.E.V.), is a good translation of this text. When we pray this prayer we assume a responsibility. If there are those about us who, through no fault of their own, are without the necessities of life, it may be God's plan to use us to answer their prayer. "God gives to us in trust, that we may feed the hungry."—*Ibid.,* p. 112.

God will guide in the choice of a vocation, in securing a job, in meeting the pressures and competition of modern life. God's care for us is not limited to the Sabbath; it is a daily affair. The actual distinction between the secular and the sacred may not be as sharp as we sometimes make it. All needful and legitimate activities of life are, in a sense, sanctified for a Christian.

FORGIVENESS

Forgive us our debts, as we forgive our debtors. . . . For if ye forgive men their trespasses, your heavenly Father will also forgive you: but if ye forgive not men their trespasses, neither will your Father forgive your trespasses. Matt. 6:12-15.

Jesus took great pains to teach the requirement of forgiveness. Our text records His emphasis on this subject in the Sermon on the Mount. He made it clear that sinners will be forgiven in proportion to their willingness to forgive.

Jesus once told a story illustrating the principle on which forgiveness works. A man owed his king "ten thousand talents"— "millions of dollars," as another translation puts it. The king forgave his enormous debt. But the same man insisted on collecting from a fellow servant who owed him only one hundred pence. The king's wrath was formidable. The lesson is spelled out in Matthew 18:35: "So likewise shall my heavenly Father do also unto you, if ye from your hearts forgive not every one his brother their trespasses."

At the close of Jesus' ministry, during the final week before His crucifixion, He said, "And when ye stand praying, forgive, if ye have ought against any: that your Father also which is in heaven may forgive you your trespasses."

During the same eventful week He illustrated what He meant by forgiveness. As He hung on the cross He prayed, "Father, forgive them." To whom did He refer? This prayer was a sincere petition in behalf of Judas, who betrayed Him; of the Pharisees and priests who hated Him; of Pilate and Herod, who could have delivered Him; of the soldiers who tormented Him; and of all mankind, whose sins helped place Him on the cross. Jesus, who needed no forgiveness, was willing to forgive.

This doctrine is intensely practical. It is easy to repeat in church the words, "Forgive us our debts, as we forgive our debtors," but the real test comes in human experience. Suppose someone cheats *me* out of everything I own. Suppose someone lies about *me*. Suppose someone harms *my* child. In circumstances like these, could I forgive?

TEMPTATION

Lead us not into temptation but deliver us from evil. Matt. 6:13.

Dietrich Bonhoeffer comments: "Many and diverse are the temptations which beset the Christian. Satan attacks him on every side, if haply he might cause him to fall. Sometimes the attack takes the form of a false sense of security, and sometimes of ungodly doubt. But the disciple is conscious of his weakness, and does not expose himself unnecessarily to temptation in order to test the strength of his faith. Christians ask God not to put their puny faith to the test, but to preserve them in the hour of temptation."—*The Cost of Discipleship*, p. 144.

The same idea is presented in *Thoughts From the Mount of Blessing:* "It is not safe for us to linger to contemplate the advantages to be reaped through yielding to Satan's suggestions. Sin means dishonor and disaster to every soul that indulges in it; but it is blinding and deceiving in its nature, and it will entice us with flattering presentations. If we venture on Satan's ground we have no assurance of protection from his power. So far as in us lies, we should close every avenue by which the tempter may find access to us."—Page 118.

To pray, "Lead us not into temptation," is to ask that God will keep us from the places, books, and people that would influence us to do wrong. We are asking for God's help in the unequal battle against the tempter. And God has promised that He "will not suffer you to be tempted above that ye are able; but will with the temptation also make a way to escape, that ye may be able to bear it" (1 Cor. 10:13).

There is a legend that Augustine, after he was converted, met a former mistress on the street. She endeavored to get his attention, but he turned and went the other way. Surprised, she shouted, "Augustine, it is I." Continuing in the opposite direction, Augustine replied, "Yes, but it is not I." He was a different Augustine after his conversion, and he was not about to place himself in the devil's line of fire.

It is important that we constantly pray that our puny faith be not put to the test, and that we cooperate with God in answering this prayer.

TREASURE IN HEAVEN

Lay not up for yourselves treasures upon earth, where moth and rust doth corrupt, and where thieves break through and steal: but lay up for yourselves treasures in heaven, where neither moth nor rust doth corrupt, and where thieves do not break through nor steal: for where your treasure is, there will your heart be also. Matt. 6:19-21.

Treasures are usually considered in terms of such things as bank accounts, stocks and bonds, homes, jewelry, furniture, automobiles, and business investments. These things are valuable, but their duration is limited. Death, depression, devaluation, destruction, are the thieves that "break through and steal."

At Newbold College in England is a fine old building that was once the mansion of a prosperous exporter. But hard times came, business crashed, and the owner died destitute—on charity. The relics of former affluence seem to say with great fervor, "Lay not up for yourselves treasures upon earth, where moth and rust doth corrupt, and where thieves break through and steal."

But there are treasures that survive. Parents' treasures will be children whose companionship they may enjoy throughout eternity. The teacher's treasures will be students whose lives and characters have been shaped for service here, and survival hereafter. The minister's treasures will be souls won to Christ and nurtured in Christian faith. The philanthropist's treasures will be people who found life as a result of his gifts. Every Christian can build an account in heaven as he witnesses for Christ and influences others to make a full Christian commitment.

Notice that Jesus is talking about treasures *in heaven*. There are good people who endow worthy enterprises, and thereby leave significant monuments of their concern about things of worth and beauty. But the Taj Mahal, the Sistine Chapel, the Roman Colosseum—all the great secular monuments of mankind—are subject to decay and ultimate ruin. Real treasure resides in persons, and they will be of ultimate value only as they are recreated to live forever.

GOD AND MONEY

No man can serve two masters: for either he will hate the one, and love the other; or else he will hold to the one, and despise the other. Ye cannot serve God and mammon. Matt. 6:24.

"You cannot be the slave both of God and of money" (Jerusalem Bible). Why is this true? There are several good reasons:

First, the slave of money is self-centered. Every decision in life is based on selfish considerations. The slave of God is not supremely concerned about his own interests; his wish is to know and do the will of God.

A man with a problem once visited a famous English preacher. The preacher knew that the man was money mad, so he endeavored to teach him a lesson. He opened his Bible, and pointed to the word "God." "Can you see that word?" he asked. Then he took a coin from his pocket and covered the word. "Can you see it now?" he asked. It is undeniably true that slavery to money can hide God. People who place their trust in money and in the things money can buy do not feel the need of God. They are secularists, who live as if God did not exist.

Second, the slave of God can have no other master. "Thou shalt have no other gods before me." God must come first. Money, friends, work, family—all are important, but God transcends all. If God calls a man to a responsibility that involves the loss of friends and money, it is his duty to respond, regardless of the sacrifice. Thus the slave of money is not capable of wholehearted service for God.

Third, the person who tries to serve both God and money is extremely unhappy. His service to God is curtailed by his materialism, and his service to money brings him qualms of conscience. He is like the church member of whom it was said, "He has too much religion to be happy at a dance and not enough to be happy at a prayer meeting." The person who tries to serve both God and money will lose both worlds!

Yet many are trying to gain both. You cannot "run with the hares and chase with the hounds." Those who serve God must place His service first. No compromise is acceptable.

37

WORK WITHOUT WORRY

Seek ye first the kingdom of God, and his righteousness; and all these things shall be added unto you. Matt. 6:33.

Jesus had been warning His listeners against anxiety. In verse 25 He said, "Be not anxious regarding food and clothing." As an example of God's keeping power He referred to the birds of the air and the flowers of the field, emphasizing that man is not without a helper in his battle for bread. There is One who cares and who provides for his needs. Then, in the words of our text, He points to man's basic reason for living—to be a subject of God's kingdom and to reflect His righteousness. Temporal blessings will not be denied if spiritual goals are sought.

Luther explained this passage: " 'Now mark ye, no beast worketh for his sustenance, but each hath his proper function, according to which he seeketh and findeth his own food. The bird doth fly and sing, she maketh nests and beareth young. That is her work, but yet she doth not nourish herself thereby. Oxen plough, horses draw carts and fight, sheep give wool, milk, and cheese, for it is their function to do so. But they do not nurture themselves thereby. Nay, the earth bringeth forth grass, and nurtureth them through God's blessing. Likewise it is man's bounden duty to work and do things, and yet withal to know that it is Another who nurtureth him: it is not his own work, but the bounteous blessing of God. It is true that the bird doth neither sow nor reap, yet would she die of hunger if she flew not in search of food. But that she findeth the same is not her work, but the goodness of God. For who put the food there, that she might find it? For where God hath put nought, none findeth, even though the whole world were to work itself to death in search thereof.' "—Quoted in DIETRICH BONHOEFFER, *The Cost of Discipleship,* p. 154.

Thus we have a balanced view of life's responsibilities. God does not necessarily package and deliver the necessities of life, but He assures us that our work will not be in vain. He does not stigmatize work, but He does find fault with anxiety. He is urging us to work without worry, recognizing that we serve a loving and dependable God.

RELAX

Take therefore no thought for the morrow: for the morrow shall take thought for the things of itself. Sufficient unto the day is the evil thereof. Matt. 6:34.

John Sutherland Bonnell, former pastor of the Fifth Avenue Presbyterian church in New York City, tells this story:

"A little time ago I rode in a taxi up Fifth Avenue at the rush hour. We were caught in a traffic jam, and for fifteen minutes I experienced that exquisite torture that comes to any one possessed of Scotch blood when seeing the cash indicator steadily spinning and the wheels of the taxi not making a single turn. Just as we began to move, another taxi shot through a small opening between us and a bus and moved in front of us. My driver pulled up alongside the other taxi and very slowly and deliberately opened the window beside him. He addressed what he considered to be appropriate remarks to the driver of the other taxi. The adjectives were especially impressive. When we resumed our journey he became more and more jittery, muttering all the while to himself and cursing the other driver. He was burning up energy like a furnace while just sitting at the wheel of his car. Finally I said: 'Driver, I have an important appointment right now with an out-of-town psychiatrist, and I wanted especially to be there right on the dot, and I am already twenty minutes late.' He broke in: 'I am sorry, Mister, but I can't help it. I am going just as fast as I can.' 'I know that,' I said; 'you don't understand me. I mentioned this fact only to remind you that I am the one who ought to be doing all the worrying in this taxi. You are the one who is making money now. Some time ago I saw that I was going to be late and that there wasn't a thing that I could do about it. I just relaxed and left the outcome in the hands of God. Why don't you try that some time?' He made no reply. Later, as I was leaving the taxi, the driver said to me very quietly: 'I am sorry, Mister, that I got so excited out there on the Avenue. I have learned something today that I am not going to forget.'"—"Living Without Inner Tension," in CHARLES F. KEMP, *Life Situation Preaching,* pp. 178, 179.

Why not try this method *today?*

JUDGE NOT

Judge not, that ye be not judged. For with what judgment ye judge, ye shall be judged: and with what measure ye mete, it shall be measured to you again. Matt. 7:1, 2.

"The effort to earn salvation by one's own works inevitably leads men to pile up human exactions as a barrier against sin. For, seeing that they fail to keep the law, they will devise rules and regulations of their own to force themselves to obey. All this turns the mind away from God to self. His love dies out of the heart, and with it perishes love for his fellow men. A system of human invention, with its multitudinous exactions, will lead its advocates to judge all who come short of the prescribed human standard. The atmosphere of selfish and narrow criticism stifles the noble and generous emotions, and causes men to become self-centered judges and petty spies.

"The Pharisees were of this class. They came forth from their religious services, not humbled with a sense of their own weakness, not grateful for the great privileges that God had given them. . . .

"The people partook largely of the same spirit, intruding upon the province of conscience and judging one another in matters that lay between the soul and God. It was in reference to this spirit and practice that Jesus said, 'Judge not, that ye be not judged.' That is, do not set yourself up as a standard. Do not make your opinions, your views of duty, your interpretation of Scripture, a criterion for others and in your heart condemn them if they do not come up to your ideal. Do not criticize others, conjecturing as to their motives and passing judgment upon them."—*Thoughts From the Mount of Blessing,* pp. 123, 124.

A celebrated Persian writer tells how it was always his custom in his youth to arise from sleep during the night to read the Koran, meditate, and pray. One night his father awoke and saw him at his religious exercises. He said to his father, "Behold thy other children are lost in irreligious slumber, while I alone am awake to praise God." "Son," answered the father, "it is better to sleep than to awake to remark about the faults of thy brethren."

"Judge not, that ye be not judged."

THE MOTE AND THE BEAM

Why beholdest thou the mote that is in thy brother's eye, but considerest not the beam that is in thine own eye? Or how wilt thou say to thy brother, Let me pull out the mote out of thine eye; and, behold, a beam is in thine own eye? Thou hypocrite, first cast out the beam out of thine own eye; and then shalt thou see clearly to cast out the mote out of thy brother's eye. Matt. 7:3-5.

Various translations have tried in different ways to make clear the meaning of "mote" and "beam." One version says, "speck" and "log." Another says "speck of sawdust" and "great plank." Another says "splinter" and "plank." The idea is clear. Why should we alarm ourselves about a little sin in another man's life when we have a big sin in our own!

Too often we are like the little girl who was heard praying for her brother. She said, "O Lord, bless Johnny, and make him as good as I am." We see ourselves through different eyes than the ones with which we see others. We look at others' faults through a magnifying glass, but we turn the glass around when we look at our own!

Church members are especially susceptible to this sin. We are very zealous for the traditions and good name of our church. We want to be looked up to and respected. If a fellow member does something that is questionable, we become upset, not because the sin is so reprehensible to us, but because we want to protect our reputation. But we may be rationalizing conduct of our own far worse than that of our neighbor. We may be able to excuse deep-seated hatred, lust, or selfishness in our own lives, while we are intensely critical about how our neighbor dresses, what he eats and drinks, or what entertainment he chooses. Perhaps he *does* need the "speck of dust" removed from his eye, but how about the "great plank" in our own eye?

Religious persecution has always been the ultimate argument of the man with a "great plank" in his own eye, who tries by force to remove the "speck of sawdust" from the eye of another. This persecution is not limited to physical torture. It may manifest itself in the intolerance, the criticism, the faultfinding that all too often finds its way into churches.

41

ASKING AND RECEIVING

Ask, and it shall be given you; seek, and ye shall find; knock, and it shall be opened unto you: for every one that asketh receiveth; and he that seeketh findeth; and to him that knocketh it shall be opened. Matt. 7:7, 8.

Too often this text is interpreted superficially. Some people look at God as a celestial Santa Claus who will satisfy all of their desires. When their so-called prayers do not seem to be answered, they find themselves shaken with doubt. They forget that the person who comes to the place where he can prevail with God in prayer will *know* Him.

In his book *For God and C.M.E.,* Dr. Merlin Neff tells of an experience in the early life of Dr. P. T. Magan, veteran Adventist educator. Dr. Magan had an offer from W. K. Kellogg, of Battle Creek, to join the expanding food factory. In a letter written to a friend many years later, Dr. Magan recalled: " 'He offered me a block of stock, $10,000 worth at par value. He wanted me to take charge of stock sales and offered me a commission on all I sold with a permanent place in the company when this work was done. That $10,000 of stock would be worth today somewhere in the neighborhood of $1,000,000 and, of course, trading on that I could have made it probably $3,000,-000 or $4,000,000. The offer in a way was tempting. But I remember well spending the greater part of the night under a maple tree at old Berrien, then in the process of its own birth, and talking the whole matter over with the Master. And as the morning light broke I had decided that in spite of all difficulties with brethren I must stick to this message and give whatever time and talent I had to the making of Adventists rather than to the making of cornflakes.' "—Pages 103, 104.

Magan was known in his later years as a man whose prayers God heard. But behind his dynamic, highly successful career of service to God were experiences such as the night under the maple tree.

Would we like to reach the spiritual maturity where we can ask and receive, seek and find, knock and enter? Such accomplishments are not for careless, prayerless opportunists. Only as we learn to make right decisions in the presence of God can we expect to be entrusted with great experiences and responsibilities.

THE GOLDEN RULE

All things whatsoever ye would that men should do to you, do ye even so to them: for this is the law and the prophets. Matt. 7:12.

W. E. Sangster was one of the great ministers of England. From 1939 to 1955 he served as pastor of Central Hall, Westminster. In 1940 the bombing of London began. The large basement of his church was reinforced, and Dr. Sangster threw it open to the homeless folks from the slums. "Sangster and his family insisted on making their home there also and in occupying only one cramped room. This they shared for five long years. It was typical of Sangster's realism and compassion."—HORTON DAVIES, *Varieties of English Preaching, 1900-1960,* p. 207.

Wrote Ellen White:

"The standard of the golden rule is the true standard of Christianity; anything short of it is a deception. A religion that leads men to place a low estimate upon human beings, whom Christ has esteemed of such value as to give Himself for them; a religion that would lead us to be careless of human needs, sufferings, or rights, is a spurious religion. In slighting the claims of the poor, the suffering, and the sinful, we are proving ourselves traitors to Christ. It is because men take upon themselves the name of Christ, while in life they deny His character, that Christianity has so little power in the world. . . .

"Search heaven and earth, and there is no truth revealed more powerful than that which is made manifest in works of mercy to those who need our sympathy and aid. This is the truth as it is in Jesus. When those who profess the name of Christ shall practice the principles of the golden rule, the same power will attend the gospel as in apostolic times."—*Thoughts From the Mount of Blessing,* pp. 136, 137.

This means that we as Christians owe a debt to the starving multitudes of India, to the underprivileged in our own country, to those who need help in our own communities, and to the weaker members of our own church and families. We are to treat them as we would wish them to treat us were our situations reversed. Have we caught the idea of unselfish Christian service?

43

THE TWO WAYS

Enter ye in at the strait gate: for wide is the gate, and broad is the way, that leadeth to destruction, and many there be which go in thereat: because strait is the gate, and narrow is the way, which leadeth unto life, and few there be that find it. Matt. 7:13, 14.

"There is a magnificent skyscraper being built in our city. Do you suppose that the architect who planned this building went about the task in a careless and slipshod manner? Did he draw all sorts of pictures and make numerous blueprints just as the mood of the moment led him, without any regard to whether they were accurate or not? No, he found the way exceedingly narrow. His drawings and his calculations could not be made at random. They could not be only approximately correct, they had to be exactly correct. And the contractor who is undertaking to make the dream of the architect into a reality is also having to travel a narrow road. He cannot follow any set of blueprints that chances to fall into his hands. He is shut up to only one. No more can he presume to change those drawn by the architect according as the whim strikes him. He must build exactly as planned. Truly, 'narrow is the way.' . . .

"Here is a young couple that has decided to share life with each other in the marriage relationship. It is a high adventure, full of possible romance and poetry. How may they hope to succeed? How may they find the fullest and deepest joy? How shall we instruct them? We must tell them that narrow is the way. 'John, wilt thou have Mary to thy wedded wife, to live together after God's ordinance in the holy estate of matrimony? Wilt thou love her, comfort her, honor and keep her, in sickness and in health; and forsaking all other, keep thee only unto her, so long as ye both shall live?' 'It is a narrow way, indeed!' you say. 'Yes, but it is the only way that leads to a successful wedded life. All other roads end in tragic failure.' "—CLOVIS G. CHAPPELL, *The Sermon on the Mount,* pp. 209-211.

If worthy earthly goals can be reached only by a narrow way, should we be surprised that heaven is approached by a steep, rugged incline? The few who choose the narrow way are earth's great people.

FALSE RELIGIOUS TEACHERS

Beware of false prophets. Matt. 7:15.

A false prophet is more than a person who makes incorrect predictions. This verse is probably more correctly translated, "Be on your guard against false religious teachers" (Phillips).

What are the marks of "false religious teachers"? Jesus reveals their most prominent characteristic—they aren't what they seem to be. Outwardly they wear "sheep's clothing," but inwardly they are "greedy wolves" (Phillips). They are trying to gain something for themselves—money, position, recognition, a following. They appear harmless like sheep, but they are actually grasping like wolves.

Jesus suggests that such people are to be judged by the fruitage of their lives. Thorns do not bear grapes and thistles do not bear figs. Anyone who purports to be a religious teacher must submit himself to the "fruits" test. What are the results of his influence and teaching?

"What message do these teachers bring? Does it lead you to reverence and fear God? Does it lead you to manifest your love for Him by loyalty to His commandments?"—*Thoughts From the Mount of Blessing,* p. 145.

What is the spirit of these teachers? Are they fair and kind or are they hostile and critical? Are they constructive or destructive? Are they forgiving or are they rigid? Are they like Christ or like His enemies, the Pharisees?

What are the results of their work? Do they edify the church and improve its effectiveness? Do they enhance the evangelistic thrust of the church? Do they support and strengthen the institutions of the church? Do they promote loyalty to the church? Recognizing the weaknesses of the church, are they constructive in their search for remedies?

Are these teachers true to the Bible and its great message? Do they stand firm on such great truths as the incarnation, the resurrection, and the second coming of Jesus?

One additional observation: It is dangerous to accept a *false* religious teacher, but it is cruel to reject a *true* religious teacher. Let us be equally concerned that we reject the false and accept the true. And let us remember that even a true servant of God is imperfect.

DOERS, NOT TALKERS

Not everyone that saith unto me, Lord, Lord, shall enter into the kingdom of heaven; but he that doeth the will of my Father which is in heaven. Matt. 7:21.

"Religion consists in doing the words of Christ; not doing to earn God's favor, but because, all undeserving, we have received the gift of His love. Christ places the salvation of man, not upon profession merely, but upon faith that is made manifest in works of righteousness. Doing, not saying merely, is expected of the followers of Christ. It is through action that character is built."—*Thoughts From the Mount of Blessing,* p. 149.

Yes, salvation is by faith alone, but the saved person accepts a responsibility that results in good works. The person who has been redeemed by the grace of God has a new motivation to be obedient to the will of God. Conversely, the person who is willfully disobedient to God reveals that he has no concept of God's love and grace.

The dilemma between faith and works is well expressed by Maude Frazer Jackson:

"What if I say
        That Jesus Christ is Lord divine;
        Yet fellow-pilgrims can behold
        Naught of the Master's love in me,
        No grace of kindly sympathy?
        If I am of the Shepherd's fold,
        Then shall I know the Shepherd's voice
        And gladly make his way my choice.
We are saved by faith, yet faith is one
With life, like daylight and the sun.
Unless they flower in our deeds,
        Dead, empty husks are all the creeds.
        To call Christ, Lord, but strive not to obey,
        Belies the homage that with words I pay."

Real faith is total response to God, and this response implies obedience.

ROCK AND SAND

Whosoever heareth these sayings of mine, and doeth them, I will liken him unto a wise man which built his house upon a rock: and the rain descended, and the floods came, and the winds blew, and beat upon that house, and it fell not: for it was founded upon a rock. Matt. 7:24, 25.

In one edition of *Thoughts From the Mount of Blessing* is an artist's illustration that tells the story of this passage of Scripture. A foaming torrent of water is raging down a ravine, carrying with it trees, rocks, and a partially destroyed home. In the background are dark clouds indicating the source of the calamity. Upon a hillside is a palace upon a rock cliff, seemingly impervious to the storm.

Jesus leaves no one in doubt as to what He means. The wise man who built his house on the rock was like the person who lived in harmony with the teachings of Jesus, and the foolish man who built on the sand was like the person who refused Jesus' way of life.

"We are building all the time, whether wisely or foolishly. We are building by everything that we do. We are building by every thought that we think. We are building by every word that we speak, every dream that we dream, every picture that we hang upon the walls of our imagination, every ambition that we cherish. . . .

"Some of us are putting some shoddy stuff into our buildings. We are putting material that cannot stand the test of the storm. The oath that you swore, that thoughtless blasphemy that you flung from your lips, that was poor material. That foul story that you told, that unclean thing that you did, that, too, was shoddy. That time that you ran with the multitude to do evil out of sheer cowardice; that time when you should have spoken—that, too, was poor stuff to put into your soul temple. . . .

"Then some are building staunchly and beautifully. . . . That was rugged and substantial stuff that Joseph used when he fled his temptation, even though his escape cost him the horrors of a dungeon. That is fine material you are using as you walk life's common ways in loving loyalty to your duty as God gives you to see your duty."
—CLOVIS G. CHAPPELL, *The Sermon on the Mount*, pp. 218-220.

STRANGERS IN THE KINGDOM

And I say unto you, that many shall come from the east and west, and shall sit down with Abraham, and Isaac, and Jacob, in the kingdom of heaven. Matt. 8:11.

A centurion had come to Jesus at Capernaum, asking Him to heal his servant who was "sick of the palsy." Jesus replied, "I will come and heal him." The centurion's answer revealed a remarkable insight into the character and power of Jesus. He said, "I am not worthy that thou shouldest come under my roof: but speak the word only, and my servant shall be healed. For I am a man under authority, having soldiers under me: and I say to this man, Go, and he goeth; and to another, Come, and he cometh; and to my servant, Do this, and he doeth it."

When Jesus heard this remarkable testimony from the lips of a Roman centurion, "he marvelled, and said to them that followed, Verily I say unto you, I have not found so great faith, no, not in Israel." Then, as Jesus looked with prophetic eyes across the centuries, He uttered the words of our text. He looked forward to the ingathering of those who were not Jews, who would be "fellow-heirs, and of the same body, and partakers of his promise in Christ by the gospel" (Eph. 3:6). Through the centuries there have been gathered into His kingdom people of every nation and kindred. And this process will continue until the work of the gospel is completed.

There is yet another facet of Jesus' statement. Paul speaks of Gentiles "which have not the law, [but] do by nature the things contained in the law." These people, Paul says, "shew the work of the law written in their hearts." Of such was the centurion whose servant Christ healed.

There are millions of descendants of this centurion in the world today—people who have never been confronted with the claims of Christ, but who live under the direction of an inward motivation that God placed in their hearts.

May we as Christians be sensitive enough to recognize the many ways in which God works for the salvation of men. May we always be thankful that we serve a God who is generous with His love.

PEACE AND WAR

Think not that I am come to send peace on earth: I came not to send peace, but a sword. Matt. 10:34.

All of us crave security. We like the idea of a comfortable salary, an ample bank account, a sound retirement plan, and a lovely home where we can sit by the fireside in an armchair. There is nothing wrong in these aspirations, but they are often unrealistic for the dedicated Christian.

"But where has God had his dealings with men? By the fireside? Open your Bible and what do you find? It is on the wind-swept hill that the bush burns. It is on Sinai, amid thunder and lightning, that the word is spoken and the command given. It is on a stony pillow that men have dreamed of the ladder of communication between earth and heaven. Not when all was going well with them but when they were up against odds, contending against adversaries without and within has God come mightily in renewal of life to men. Which perchance explains the prayer entry in George Whitefield's *Journal:* 'When Thou seest me in danger of nestling,—in pity—in tender pity—put a thorn in my nest to prevent me from it.' "—R. J. MC-CRACKEN, *Questions People Ask,* p. 85.

Our text suggests that the gospel will cause conflict. Unfortunately, this is true. There is something about the purity and dedication of the Christian faith that tends to arouse violent hostility on the part of those who do not share this purity and dedication. At the trial of Jesus the record says "the servants did strike him with the palms of their hands" (Mark 14:65). Ignorant, base men slapped Jesus out of sheer hostility for one who was obviously better than they.

Jesus explains, in the verses following our text, that this conflict will often be of the most heartbreaking kind—within the family. "A man's foes shall be they of his own household." What can exceed the animosity often revealed in families where one member departs from the religious—or irreligious—tradition of the home?

So Christ may not bring security, but conflict. Nevertheless, above the conflict we hear the voice of our Lord saying, "Fear none of those things which thou shalt suffer" (Rev. 2:10).

MARTYRS

He that findeth his life shall lose it: and he that loseth his life for my sake shall find it. Matt. 10:39.

Many years ago a French philosopher received a message from friends in Paris who were overthrowing the Bourbons. "A terrible game is being played here," they wrote; "our heads are in danger; come and add yours."

This has been the spirit of Christianity from the time of the apostles until now. Millions have risked—and lost—their lives because of their loyalty to Christ. But Christ assures us that those who lose life for Him will find it. How does this principle work?

First, those who are willing to give their lives for Christ live on in the memory of their fellow men. A few years ago I visited the martyrs' monument in Oxford, England. This monument commemorates three Protestant martyrs, Bishops Ridley and Latimer who died in 1555, and Archbishop Cranmer who followed them to the stake in 1556. The flames in which these men died lighted a fire that burned throughout the world.

But immortality of influence in this world is not the only way in which martyrs gain immortality. John the revelator tells of a "great multitude" before the throne of God of whom it was said, "These are they which came out of great tribulation, and have washed their robes, and made them white in the blood of the lamb" (Rev. 7:14).

But why talk about martyrs? Modern people are seldom burned at the stake for their faith. In a literal sense this may be true but in another sense people are giving their lives for Christ every day. Missionaries, who renounce the comforts of home to preach the gospel in undeveloped countries, are giving themselves in a very real way. People who sacrifice brilliant careers in order to render humble service to God and their fellow men are, in a sense, martyrs.

In our world a terrible "game" is being played. Christ and Satan are competing for the souls of men. This battle, like all battles, is hazardous. Our Master asks us to take the risks involved, and He promises that those who lose their lives will find them again.

"Our heads are in danger; come and add yours."

JESUS ILLUSTRATES HUMILITY

And Jesus called a little child unto him, and set him in the midst of them, and said, Verily I say unto you, Except ye be converted, and become as little children, ye shall not enter into the kingdom of heaven. Matt. 18:2, 3.

Jesus did things so differently! Most folks would have said to the little children, "When you grow up, try to be like Peter or John or one of the other disciples." Instead, Jesus said to the disciples, "Become as little children."

Why did Jesus give this counsel? The disciples were much concerned about their positions in the new kingdom their Master had announced. Apparently they were not fully satisfied with their great commission to heal, to cast out devils, and to preach the gospel. They wanted status positions where they could exercise authority. How human they were!

Jesus reminded them of the lack of status consciousness of a little child. Small children of all races, economic backgrounds, and religions can play together with no sense of difference. Only when they grow older and learn these distinctions from their elders do they become concerned.

Man instinctively likes to feel that he is better, more intelligent, more talented, more prosperous, more powerful than his contemporaries. It would be well for every Christian to give frequent attention to this counsel:

"By all that has given us advantage over another—be it education and refinement, nobility of character, Christian training, religious experience—we are in debt to those less favored, and, so far as lies in our power, we are to minister unto them."—*The Desire of Ages,* p. 440.

When Solomon took over his kingdom he prayed, "I am but a little child: I know not how to go out or come in." Jesus was trying to teach His disciples this attitude, but they learned slowly.

In an age when much emphasis is placed on status, education, position, and power, how important it is that every Christian maintain the humble spirit of a little child.

51

CAESAR AND GOD

Then saith he unto them, Render therefore unto Caesar the things which are Caesar's; and unto God the things that are God's.
Matt. 22:21.

The Pharisees decided to push Jesus into a corner. They sent a committee to Him to ask Him a question. The committee prefaced their question with insincere words of flattery: "Master, we know that thou art true, and teachest the way of God in truth, neither carest thou for any man; for thou regardest not the person of men" (verse 16). Then they posed their question: "What thinkest thou? Is it lawful to give tribute unto Caesar, or not?" If Jesus should say Yes, He would be in trouble with the Jews; if He should answer No, He would be in trouble with the Romans.

Jesus asked that they bring Him a coin and He pointed out to them the face and name of Caesar on the coin. Then He made the pronouncement that has been the basis of the attitude of Christians toward government through the centuries: "Pay to the Emperor what belongs to him, and pay to God what belongs to God" (T.E.V.).

Some of Jesus' hearers were probably disappointed. They would have felt much more comfortable if Jesus had said, "Resist Caesar, burn your draft card, protest your taxes, demonstrate in the streets!" Instead, Jesus consistently recognized the duty of His followers to reverence and obey God, and also to respect their civil obligations.

Two extremes must be avoided—first, the extreme of renouncing secular society. If Christians withdraw themselves from the world and break off communication with their fellow men, they can never be leaven to bring blessing to the world.

On the other hand, Christians must not be controlled by the viewpoint of secular society. The Christian cannot influence the worldling by becoming a worldling. He cannot witness for his Lord by trying to be a good fellow at any price.

The Christian is in the world, and he must remain in the world to accomplish his mission. The world needs what he has to give. But when he becomes "of the world," and loses his distinctiveness, he has betrayed his Lord.

JESUS REBUKES THE SCRIBES AND PHARISEES

Then spake Jesus to the multitude, and to his disciples, saying, The scribes and the Pharisees sit in Moses' seat: all therefore whatsoever they bid you observe, that observe and do; but do not ye after their works: for they say, and do not. Matt. 23:1-3.

The Jews had a great tradition. Abraham, Isaac, and Jacob were their forefathers and Moses was their lawgiver. The prophets—Isaiah, Ezekiel, Daniel, and all the rest—had made a great contribution to their heritage. God had spoken to them on many occasions, most notably from Sinai.

But no amount of glorious tradition could excuse or condone sin and selfishness on the part of those who inherited the tradition. In the words of Paul, "Thou therefore which teachest another, teachest thou not thyself? thou that preachest a man should not steal, dost thou steal? Thou that sayest a man should not commit adultery, dost thou commit adultery? thou that abhorrest idols, dost thou commit sacrilege? Thou that makest thy boast of the law, through breaking the law dishonourest thou God?" (Rom. 2:21-23).

During the third century B.C., a fourteen-hundred-mile wall was built across the north border of China. This wall was twenty feet high, fifteen feet wide on top, and had watchtowers every three hundred feet. Despite this stupendous effort to protect her borders, China was invaded several times during succeeding centuries. It has been said that the invaders never scaled the walls or attacked the towers—they merely walked through the open gates after bribing the gatekeepers.

Just as no wall is stronger than the character of its gatekeepers, so no religious movement is stronger than the character of its leaders and laymen. A rich tradition of encounter with God in the past will not make up for disregard for God in the present. Sacred writings must be interpreted into life. Law must be reflected in integrity. Religion must produce spiritual stature.

No lesson of the past is more frightening than the tragedy of outward conformity without inner commitment. Jesus pointed to the scribes and Pharisees as examples. May every professed Christian learn this lesson well.

PREPARATION

Watch therefore, for ye know not what hour your Lord doth come. But know this, that if the goodman of the house had known in what watch the thief would come, he would have watched, and would not have suffered his house to be broken up. Therefore be ye also ready: for in such an hour as ye think not the Son of man cometh. Matt. 24:42-44.

This world is moving toward the greatest crisis of its history—the second coming of Christ. Thoughtful men recognize the imminence of this event.

In the October 13, 1967, issue of *Christianity Today,* was a report of an interview between Carl F. H. Henry, the editor, and Dr. Kenneth Scott Latourette, Sterling Professor of Missions and Oriental History emeritus at Yale University. In the course of the interview, Dr. Henry asked:

"If you were to venture a guess about the year 2000 . . . how would you position Christianity among the world religions and ideologies at the end of this century?"

Dr. Latourette replied: "Well, as you know, I believe that our Lord may return at any time and bring the present stage of history to an end. That may well come between now and the year 2000."

It would be a great tragedy if those who have proclaimed the second coming of Christ for years should lose their concern and make it necessary for others to fill the gap. Long familiarity with the message of the coming Christ sometimes makes us indifferent to the reality.

The fact of the coming of Christ implies preparation for that event. "Be ye also ready," the Lord said. General Foch, of World War I fame, is quoted as saying, "The battle is won the day before." Men must come to Christ *now.* Wrong patterns of living must be given up *now.* The work of God must be done *now.* To wait until Christ comes will be too late.

The person who knows God, who has accepted the claims of Christ, and who is dedicated to Christian service, need have no fear of the coming day of judgment. To him it will be deliverance. His battle will have been won long *before* his Master comes.

"HE SERVETH BEST WHO LOVETH BEST"

The King shall answer and say unto them, Verily I say unto you, Inasmuch as ye have done it unto one of the least of these my brethren, ye have done it unto me. Matt. 25:40.

The scriptural measure of service to Christ is loving service to men and women. This reveals to us how closely our Lord identifies Himself with His children.

"But of him who serves another in Christ's name it may actually be said, his life touches Christ. Tolstoy has brought this out in his story, *Where Love is, God is.* Martin, an old cobbler, is reading about Christ and half wishes Christ would visit him. He falls asleep musing, and is startled by a voice which says, 'Martin, Martin, look into the street tomorrow! I will come!' the old cobbler cannot make up his mind whether the voice is real or whether it is just a dream. The next day he finds himself continually going to the window: 'Will He indeed come, I wonder? It is too much to expect, and yet such things have happened.' During the day the old man brings in a sweeper from the street, gives him tea, and invites him to warm his hands by the stove. Then he brings in a soldier's wife whom he sees from the window trying to wrap up her baby in a piece of old sacking, and he gives her food and drink and comfort. Then he brings into his little room an apple-woman and the boy who had run away with one of her apples. As he talks to her, her anger disappears, and, when he dismisses them, the boy is helping her to carry her load.

"The last scene shows Martin sitting at the table on which burns a solitary candle. 'The day is nearly over and He hasn't been. It must have been a dream after all. Yet His voice seemed so real.' But, as the old man sits there, the figure of the snow-sweeper rises up before his eyes, and a voice says, 'Martin, Martin, do you not know me? This is I.' . . . Then follows the figure of the apple-woman, and the Voice says, 'And this also is I.' And the great truth dawns upon the old cobbler that God has come near to him in man, that in loving service to men and women he has actually served the Christ."—LESLIE D. WEATHERHEAD, *The Transforming Friendship,* pp. 131, 132.

JESUS INSTITUTES THE LORD'S SUPPER

As they were eating, Jesus took bread, and blessed it, and brake it, and gave it to the disciples, and said, Take, eat; this is my body. And he took the cup, and gave thanks, and gave it to them, saying, Drink ye all of it; for this is my blood of the new testament, which is shed for many for the remission of sins. Matt. 26:26-28.

As Jesus approached the cross, He must have asked Himself the question, "What can I do to ensure that man will always remember the event of Calvary?" Using symbols to aid comprehension and memory, Jesus chose two simple objects, food and drink—symbols that are universal in their appeal—and He clothed these elements of daily living with profound meaning. "The love of Jesus, with its constraining power, is to be kept fresh in our memory. Christ has instituted this service that it may speak to our senses of the love of God that has been expressed in our behalf."—*The Desire of Ages,* p. 660.

There is no substitute for the communion service. Dr. Clarence E. Macartney tells of a church where the pastor distributed flowers rather than bread and wine. "The idea of Atonement, of substitution, of the Broken Body and the shed Blood of our Lord, was repugnant to him. Hence, he gave the congregation flowers instead of the sacred elements! A sad picture that is; and all the more so because it is a picture of how in many places the sublime, central, inspiring, and creative fact that Christ died for us has been passed over, and in its place the people have been given flowers and fancy and rhetoric."—*Great Nights of the Bible,* p. 20.

The bread and the wine not only point *backward* to Calvary—they point *upward* to the same Saviour who ministers in our behalf today, and *forward* to the day when He will come again. "For as often as ye eat this bread, and drink this cup, ye do shew the Lord's death till he come" (1 Cor. 11:26). This sacred service also points *inward* to our own experience—"Let a man examine himself" (verse 28). Never has so much meaning been packed into a single, simple service! The communion service gives us an opportunity to relive the scenes of Calvary and to rededicate ourselves to our Redeemer.

JESUS PRAYS IN GETHSEMANE

He went a little farther, and fell on his face, and prayed, saying,
O my Father, if it be possible, let this cup pass from me: never-
theless, not as I will, but as thou wilt. Matt. 26:39.

Prayer was no new experience for Jesus. Dr. John Sutherland Bonnell reviews Jesus' prayer life as follows:

"We find that Jesus prayed with special concentration before taking each important step in his life. When the time came to select from
among his followers the twelve men who would become his disciples
and apostles, he spent the entire previous night in a mountain alone
with God. He gave himself to prayer at the commencement of his
ministry in the hour of baptism. He was in the midst of prayer with
three of his disciples on a mountaintop when he was transfigured with
the reflected glory of heaven, and just before he informed his disciples
that he was going to Jerusalem to suffer and die, he turned aside for
prayer. In the Garden of Gethsemane, beneath the olive trees, occurred
what was perhaps the bitterest conflict in his whole life, and through
prayer he gained the victory. Finally, on Calvary with its blasphemies
and tortures, he breathed out his life in prayer to his Heavenly Father.
The practice that prevailed throughout his life was strong in the hour
of death and brought to him an unbroken peace that not all the enmity
of evil men could take away."—*The Practice and Power of Prayer,*
pp. 74, 75.

In a unique way the humanity and the divinity of Jesus shone
through in this prayer. The human desire to be spared from suffering
was balanced against the divine willingness to do the will of God, and
the latter won. It was, however, no easy struggle. Three times He
prayed the prayer, and, as Luke describes it, "He was in agony and
prayed even more intensely so that his sweat was like great drops of
blood falling to the ground" (Luke 22:44, Phillips).

After the battle was won, Jesus faced the mob and His betrayer with
great calm. Never once did He flinch during the long and bitter trial,
nor on Calvary. He was in perfect command of Himself, and He met
His death with dignity. All of this came as a result of His communion
with His heavenly Father.

TEARS

He went out, and wept bitterly. Matt. 26:75.

"Dick Sheppard used to tell a story about a man who sat drinking in a bar. He had been drinking for a long time. He had swallowed considerable quantities of liquor. And as he drank, he wept. He wept because he had wasted his life. He wept because he had failed to do his duty to his family. He wept because he had never appreciated his wife properly. He wept because somehow his good intentions always went wrong. But never mind, he told himself, this time it would be different. He would redeem the past and make up for everything. All, he resolved, would yet be well. He felt uplifted and noble at the very thought. His mind glowed with a genial assurance of virtue. Just then the bartender said, 'Time, gentlemen, please'—*and he went home and swore at his wife."*—ROBERT J. MCCRACKEN, *Questions People Ask,* p. 104.

The tears of this poor weakling were quite different from those of Peter. Peter wept because he had denied his Lord, and by the grace of God he never denied Him again. The alcoholic wept because he recognized his depravity, but he lacked the character and the motivation to do anything about it.

So there are two kinds of tears—those that acknowledge failure and mark the dawn of victory, and those that merely express weak despair. Paul speaks of these two varieties of tears: "For godly sorrow worketh repentance to salvation not to be repented of: but the sorrow of the world worketh death" (2 Cor. 7:10).

The people of our generation, despite the billions they spend in search of pleasure, seem to be carrying a burden of sorrow. Much of the literature of the day is marked by a spirit of gloom and pessimism. Much of the pleasure seeking and loose living reflects an effort to escape fear and depression. Psychologists and psychiatrists are besieged with worried, maladjusted, frightened patients who face life with panic and whose tears are like the screams of a cornered animal.

But one day "God shall wipe away all tears from their eyes" (Rev. 21:4) if, like Peter, they seek their Lord in sincerity.

THE RESULT OF INSINCERITY

Then Judas, which had betrayed him, when he saw that he was condemned, repented himself, and brought again the thirty pieces of silver to the chief priests and elders, saying, I have sinned in that I have betrayed the innocent blood. And they said, What is that to us? see thou to that. And he cast down the pieces of silver in the temple, and departed, and went and hanged himself. Matt. 27:3-5.

In his book *What New Doctrine Is This?* Bob Shuler cites the story of a chainmaker who produced a chain no one could break. Later, he committed a crime for which he was sentenced to be chained to a large rock in a dungeon and left to die.

This sentence caused the criminal no grief because he thought he knew all about chains and could easily escape. "The chain maker would be the chain breaker. He slept soundly, determined to awaken at midnight and free himself. He did awaken. The moon was shining through the bars of his dungeon. He smiled at the embarrassment of the keeper of the prison and the chagrin of the judge when the news of his flight would break. He moved his shackled limbs. He examined the chain. And horrors! It was the chain of his own forging!"— Page 77.

For months Judas had been forging a chain that eventually proved impossible to break. He had schemed, he had misappropriated funds, he had criticized, he had sought personal preferment over his colleagues. All of these activities he had rationalized as means to desirable ends. He had adopted a "new morality" that he considered far more sophisticated than the simple faith of his fellow disciples. And, despite all of this insincerity, he managed to hold the confidence of his peers. Only Jesus sensed the direction in which Judas was headed.

His theories crashed when he saw the One whom he had betrayed flogged, bound, and condemned. He tried repentance, but it was too late to repent. He threw the thirty pieces of silver on the floor of the Temple, but the clanging of the metal on the pavement mocked him. He acknowledged himself a sinner, but no one on earth or in heaven offered him pardon. He lacked complete commitment.

"BUT SOME DOUBTED"

When they saw him, they worshipped him: but some doubted.
Matt. 28:17.

Before His death and resurrection, Jesus had made an appointment to meet His followers on a mountain in Galilee. At the appointed time and place about five hundred believers were gathered together, "eager to learn all that could be learned from those who had seen Christ since His resurrection. From group to group the disciples passed, telling all they had seen and heard of Jesus, and reasoning from the Scriptures as He had done with them. Thomas recounted the story of his unbelief, and told how his doubts had been swept away. Suddenly Jesus stood among them. No one could tell whence or how He came. Many who were present had never before seen Him; but in His hands and feet they beheld the marks of the crucifixion; His countenance was as the face of God, and when they saw Him, they worshiped Him."—*The Desire of Ages,* pp. 818, 819.

"But some doubted." How could anyone disbelieve in the presence of such convincing evidence? No doubt some of the five hundred hung around the edges of the crowd, never getting close enough to Jesus to feel the impact of His life and His message. If they had pressed in toward the center, they might have believed. Others, perhaps, did not want to believe. They knew that belief would change their manner of life, and they were not ready for this transformation. Still others may have let dislike for people who believed stand in the way of faith.

Whatever may have motivated the doubters among that crowd, think what they missed! This was Jesus' only post-resurrection appearance to a large group. Here was the resurrected Lord, soon to return to His home in heaven. What an opportunity! But some of those present were unable to grasp the significance of what was going on.

God reveals Himself today in various ways. A man is converted from sin to righteousness. The change in his life should convince anyone. But some doubt. The miracle of life goes on all around us. But some doubt. The revelation of God through Christ and in the Bible is clear and convincing. But some doubt.

May we not let doubts cloud our spiritual skies.

JESUS COMMISSIONS HIS DISCIPLES

Go ye therefore, and teach all nations, baptizing them in the name of the Father, and of the Son, and of the Holy Ghost: teaching them to observe all things whatsoever I have commanded you. Matt. 28:19, 20.

The setting was a mountain in Galilee. The resurrected Christ was speaking to His eleven shaken, but faithful, disciples. He prefaced His commission with the statement, "All power is given unto me in heaven and in earth" (verse 18). What a spirit of awe must have gripped those eleven men as the meaning of this sentence reached their minds. They were in the presence of unlimited power.

Then He outlined their mission in the world. They were to go to *all* nations with the gospel of Him who possessed *all* power. They were to teach the people of the world *all* things He had taught them. And He promised to be with them through *all* time.

"We are told that Napoleon in his best days would, on the eve of every great battle, send for his marshals and have them come one by one to his own tent. There in silence he would clasp each man's hand, look into his eyes for a moment and let him go. He had not uttered a word, but it was enough. Every man of them went out ready to do and to dare and to die, if need be, next day for Napoleon. His shadow had fallen upon them, healing them of any lurking remnant of cowardice or any lingering uncertainty touching the victory they were to win. They felt as if they were all Napoleons and that their stars were in the ascendant."—CHARLES R. BROWN, *Yale Talks,* p. 87.

How much greater must have been the eagerness of Peter and John and the rest as they listened to the challenge of their risen Lord. Is it any wonder that they turned their world upside down?

Can we as Christians, many centuries removed from Galilee, recapture the wonder of that great hour? To do so would add new life to our witness for Christ. It will help us if we remember that the risen Christ who appeared that day in Galilee still lives. It will encourage us to remember that He completed His statement with the assurance, "Lo, I am with you alway, even unto the end of the world."

THE EVER-PRESENT JESUS

Lo, I am with you alway, even unto the end of the world.
Matt. 28:20.

The occasion was a meeting of Jesus with His followers after the resurrection. It was there in Galilee that Jesus gave them His great commission, "Go ye therefore, and teach all nations," and His great promise, "I am with you alway."

This promise encouraged Livingstone to endure illness, loneliness, and danger in the heart of Africa. After years of missionary service, gaunt from thirty fevers, and crippled as the result of an encounter with a lion, he quoted this text, it is said, to a convocation of students at the University of Glasgow as his source of strength.

The glory of this promise is that it is always up to date. It presents a living Christ, who is beside His followers every day.

"Leonardo da Vinci in his painting of the Last Supper depicts the Saviour as a present Christ. The landscape which can be seen through the window in the background of the picture is like that near Milan rather than Palestine. The table and chairs, the cloth and dishes are not like those used in Jerusalem in the first century but the kind that were to be found in Italy when the picture was painted. The men sit around the table in European, rather than Oriental, style. Probably the artist copied the objects that were actually being used in the monastery where the picture was painted. He wanted people to know Jesus as a contemporary, one who was actually in their midst, blessing them with His comradeship, and calling them to unselfish loyalty."—WALTER DUDLEY CAVERT, *Remember Now,* pp. 17, 18.

This promise is not limited to great missionaries or great artists. It means that a humble Christian, engaged in the most menial tasks, can claim the companionship and guidance of his Lord. This great truth is the answer to feelings of futility. How can life be meaningless if the risen Christ is by our side?

The Christian faith has its roots in the past and its hope in the future, but it is essentially a "now" religion. The ever-present Christ is the center of the Christian's life.

A MANIAC ASPIRES TO BECOME A MINISTER

When he was come into the ship, he that had been possessed with the devil prayed him that he might be with him. Howbeit Jesus suffered him not, but saith unto him, Go home to thy friends, and tell them how great things the Lord hath done for thee, and hath had compassion on thee. Mark 5:18, 19.

A maniac had been tamed by the gospel. The devils that once tormented him had entered a herd of hogs that, amid squeals and splashes, had plunged "violently down a steep place into the sea." The hog tenders took a look at the restored maniac, considered their drowned hogs, and begged Jesus to leave the country. After all, weren't hogs more valuable than maniacs?

After the excitement had subsided, we see Jesus and the man whom He had made whole talking on the deck of the fishing boat. The man is very earnest. It is obvious that he is asking for something that means much to him. He is begging for the privilege of remaining with Jesus. He wants to join the group of disciples and dedicate himself completely to his new-found Friend. It is not hard to understand why he was reluctant to leave his Benefactor.

But Jesus is shaking His head. How strange! He had invited others to follow Him, some of whom had refused. Why should not this man realize his deep desire? Listen to what Jesus is saying to him: "Go home to thy friends, and tell them how great things the Lord hath done for thee, and hath had compassion on thee." There was something greater for this man than joining the twelve. He could go and tell the story of what Jesus had done for him—not in some far-off city, but to his friends. None of the twelve could fulfill this assignment as well as he. The reality of his experience would be more persuasive than any logic or argument that might be presented.

Commenting on this very experience, Ellen White remarks, "This is the witness for which our Lord calls, and for want of which the world is perishing."—*The Ministry of Healing,* p. 99. No amount of logic, no eloquence, no learning, will so effectively persuade men to follow Jesus as the simple testimony of a person who has been transformed by the gospel.

FAITH AND HEALING

Jesus said unto him, If thou canst believe, all things are possible to him that believeth. And straightway the father of the child cried out, and said with tears, Lord, I believe; help thou mine unbelief. Mark 9:23, 24.

At the foot of the Mount of Transfiguration, the nine disciples are in trouble. A man has brought his demon-possessed son to them for healing, and they are having no success. An excited crowd is milling about, and hostile scribes are asking embarrassing questions.

The Master, with Peter, James, and John, arrives at the scene. The father makes an agonizing appeal to Jesus, describing the distressing symptoms of his afflicted son. "If thou canst believe, all things are possible to him that believeth." At this, the father utters one of the most touching responses to the divine challenge to believe: "Lord, I believe; help thou mine unbelief." The story has a happy ending. Jesus casts out the spirit, takes the boy by the hand, and lifts him to his feet. All of the symptoms are gone. The father receives his son, restored from a condition worse than death.

What does this incident teach us who live in the twentieth century? It is not often that we see cases of demon possession like those of Jesus' time. Satan has devised ways of controlling men more in keeping with contemporary culture. But the great truth still remains that all things are possible to the believer. Faith is as much the gateway to life today as it was nineteen centuries ago.

Modern man, like the distraught father, can well pray the honest, forthright prayer, "Lord, I believe; help thou mine unbelief." We are aware of our doubts. They result from the inadequateness of our minds, and our ignorance of God and His ways. They also stem from the secularism of the world in which we live. But belief—faith—is like a beam of light dissipating the darkness of doubt. Faith is stronger than doubt and is the secret of a radiant, effective life. Faith is not belief in spite of evidence, but trust in spite of fear. "Faith is the victory, . . . that overcomes the world."

JESUS CALLS A RICH YOUNG RULER

Then Jesus beholding him loved him, and said unto him, One thing thou lackest: go thy way, sell whatsoever thou hast, and give to the poor, and thou shalt have treasure in heaven: and come, take up the cross, and follow me. And he was sad at that saying, and went away grieved: for he had great possessions. Mark 10:21, 22.

On the left side of his painting, *The Rich Young Ruler,* Hofmann portrayed a cripple and his daughter. To the right, in the picture, is the richly dressed young man. Jesus appeals to him to go and look after the needs of people such as the cripple and his daughter, and then to come and follow Him. The young ruler would gladly have accepted new legal obligations; he would gladly have made substantial contributions to the Temple; he would, no doubt, have contributed to established charities; but Jesus asked more than he was willing to give.

Jesus asked him to turn his resources into cash, and with his own hands distribute to the needs of the poor. Having done so, he could join Peter and John and the other disciples in their itinerant life. "Follow me," Jesus said. This was too much. This meant complete dedication, which he was not yet willing to give. If he had been willing, his name, which we do not know, might have come down to us with the names of Peter and John as one of the great apostles of the Lord. This young man was conscientious regarding the observance of the law; he really wanted eternal life, but he could not make the decision to break with his affluent way of life.

Will the Lord always have to depend on the weak and dispossessed to witness for Him? A few possessors of wealth and influence are willing to follow Jesus, but not many. Could they but realize it, nothing makes a rich man richer than to identify himself with Christ. Conversely, nothing makes a rich man poorer than to become enslaved by his riches.

So far as we know, the rich young ruler never returned. When he turned his back on Jesus, he turned his back on life. As we watch him retreating into the distance, do we see ourselves?

3   65

THE WIDOW AND THE LITTLE BOY

There came a certain poor widow, and she threw in two mites, which make a farthing. And he called unto him his disciples, and saith unto them, Verily I say unto you, That this poor widow hath cast more in, than all they which have cast into the treasury: for all they did cast in of their abundance; but she of her want did cast in all that she had, even all her living. Mark 12:42-44.

"When Alaska experienced a terrible earthquake a few years ago, the Governor's wife said that many phone calls came to the Governor's Mansion. She answered most of them, and usually they were demands that she do something for some relative or some friend. But she received a letter from a ten-year-old boy in the Midwest who sent her two nickels. 'If you need any more,' he wrote, 'please let me know.' There is faith in all its shining splendor! Two nickels are not much, but they were probably all the boy had. He was one of those persons who thought it was better to do his best even if it was small."
—GERALD H. KENNEDY, *Fresh Every Morning*, pp. 125, 126.

The widow and the little boy illustrate a facet of human life that is disturbing. Wealthy people seldom give their all, though occasionally a poor widow may do so. Mature people didn't give their last two nickels to the governor's wife—it was a little boy. So-called liberals are not often liberal when the collection plate is passed.

Generally speaking, churches do not depend on the liberal gifts of wealthy donors but on the multiplied small gifts of common people. In other words, an ordinary person often seems more willing to risk something for God than does a person endowed with greater wealth and ability. Most church pastors will verify this observation.

Is it not time to seek a change in this trend? In the affluent parts of the world it is time that some people become so aware of the needs of God's church that they give much. Occasionally a person accepts this challenge. More often Christians fail in this respect.

Our gifts to God are not counted, they are weighed. He is concerned about our motives, and He is aware of how much we have left after we have given.

"WHAT SHALL WE DO?"

He came into all the country about Jordan, preaching the baptism of repentance for the remission of sins. **Luke 3:3.**

John the Baptist was an evangelist. He called his hearers to repentance and baptism, and he reminded them of the coming Saviour, who "shall baptize you with the Holy Ghost and with fire."

Successful evangelist that he was, he brought conviction to the hearts of his hearers. The people said, "What shall we do?" John answered, "He that hath two coats, let him impart to him that hath none; and he that hath meat, let him do likewise."

The publicans asked, "What shall we do?" John answered, "Exact no more than that which is appointed you."

The soldiers asked, "What shall we do?" John said, "Do violence to no man, neither accuse any falsely; and be content with your wages."

It is true that John did not have the whole gospel which would soon be preached by "one mightier than I, . . . the latchet of whose shoes I am not worthy to unloose." But John did understand the responsibilities of the gospel. He saw clearly that self-sacrificing love, honesty, concern about others, and lack of envy and jealousy were truly the fruits of the Spirit. Jesus taught the same truths, as have His followers through the centuries.

John's message to his day underscores the fact that Christianity is a practical, ethical faith. The prophets emphasized this truth. John was teaching the same truth as did Micah when he said, "And what doth the Lord require of thee, but to do justly, and to love mercy, and to walk humbly with thy God?" This emphasis reached its height in Jesus' Sermon on the Mount.

Some people confuse Christian responsibility with salvation by works. When folks asked, "What shall we do?" John didn't reply, "My dear people, you don't have to *do* anything—only believe." While it is true that salvation is the result of divine grace and human faith, it is also true that the saved person has a new attitude toward his fellow man and toward God. His spirit of love inspires him with a desire to express that love by loving actions.

67

JOHN THE BAPTIST QUESTIONS JESUS

And John calling unto him two of his disciples sent them to Jesus, saying, Art thou he that should come? or look we for another? . . . Then Jesus answering said unto them, Go your way, and tell John what things ye have seen and heard; how that the blind see, the lame walk, the lepers are cleansed, the deaf hear, the dead are raised. . . . And blessed is he, whosoever shall not be offended in me. Luke 7:19-23.

How could John the Baptist ask a question like this? Had he not recognized Jesus at the Jordan and baptized Him? Had he not heard the voice from heaven, "This is my beloved Son, in whom I am well pleased" (Matt. 3:17)? Had he not observed the ministry of Jesus since the time of the baptism? Did he not have the testimony of the prophets regarding the coming Saviour?

We can only understand John's doubt in view of the weakness of human nature. He was in prison, and there seemed to be no prospect of his release. His former life of activity was gone, his followers were scattered, the days and nights were long. It is no wonder he doubted.

"Throughout the centuries numberless individuals—and fine individuals too—have been assailed by sudden moods of doubt and fear. Listen to this pitiful confession: 'Though God has often visited my soul with a blessed disclosure of Himself, yet afterward I have been so filled with darkness that I could not even conceive the God or the comfort by which I had been refreshed.' Who said that? John Bunyan, author of *Pilgrim's Progress.* Or study this letter, 'Pray for me! Sometimes God doth visit me with His comfort: sometimes I am so afraid I could creep into a mouse-hole. So God cometh and goeth. Pray for me, I beg you.' Who wrote that? Hugh Latimer, the English bishop who in 1555 suffered martyrdom at Oxford."—J. G. GILKEY, *When Life Gets Hard,* p. 2.

It is a source of encouragement for us ordinary mortals to know that the best of men have had their dark days. Jesus responded to John the Baptist's doubt by supplying him with additional proofs that He really was the one "that should come." He is equally willing today to strengthen the faith of His confused, groping followers.

"THE OVERWHELMING MINORITY"

Therefore said he unto them, The harvest truly is great, but the labourers are few: pray ye therefore the Lord of the harvest, that he would send forth labourers into his harvest. Luke 10:2.

In his book *The Christian Persuader,* Leighton Ford tells of a Scottish minister who was having a hard time awakening a spirit of evangelism in his congregation. "Then one day, at the depth of his discouragement, he was riding the subway. His eye was caught by an advertising sign for a fashion magazine: VOGUE IS READ BY THE OVERWHELMING MINORITY. . . . 'The overwhelming minority!' Has God's work not always moved forward by the growing edge, the cutting edge of overwhelming minorities—Gideon's band, Jesus' twelve disciples?"—Page 51.

In every age of man's history, the destiny of the race has been shaped by minorities—political, religious, or social. A few people with vision, wealth, power, ideas, or just plain determination, have often made the world in which they lived. This situation has not always been desirable. The minority may have been ruthless and indifferent to human welfare—nevertheless, they have exerted the power.

In today's world dedicated Christians represent a small minority of the total population. May they be an *overwhelming* minority! In today's church those who are highly motivated in witnessing for Christ are a small minority. May they also be an *overwhelming* minority. This is what Jesus meant when He compared the kingdom of heaven to yeast. Just a little bit of yeast in a large pan of dough could leaven the whole lump.

We have no basis for hoping that the dedicated followers of Christ will ever be other than a minority—but let them be an *overwhelming* minority. May their influence be felt in every land and every community.

Charles Spurgeon prayed, it is said, "Give me twelve men, importunate men, lovers of souls who fear nothing but sin and love nothing but God, and I will shake London from end to end." An overwhelming minority could shake the world of our time also.

THE KIND SAMARITAN

A certain Samaritan, as he journeyed, came where he was: and when he saw him, he had compassion on him, and went to him, and bound up his wounds, pouring in oil and wine, and set him on his own beast and brought him to an inn, and took care of him. Luke 10:33, 34.

The familiar story of the good Samaritan depicts a man who was helpful in a situation in which there was no possibility of repayment. This kind of love was rare in his day, and is in ours.

After the wounded man recovered, do you suppose he studied for the priesthood? Probably not. The image of the priesthood had been badly marred by the experience on the way to Jericho. Or do you suppose his regard for Levites was high from that time on? Probably not. But he never again felt the same nationalistic prejudice against Samaritans—of that we can be assured. He probably retold the story hundreds of times, to anyone who would listen.

Leslie D. Weatherhead relates the following story:

"Not far from my home lives a little family of a mother and four children. The eldest, a little boy of ten, is partly paralysed. He cannot walk. . . . They had all been members of a certain church. I will not even name its denomination, but when her husband fell ill with tuberculosis, no one visited the home, and although all the children at that time went to the Sunday School, no one heeded. The father died of tuberculosis unvisited by his minister whose house is less than five minutes' walk away. 'Then,' said the woman, 'some Roman Catholics heard about us and they have been wonderful to us.' Materially, they had been generosity itself, and for the semi-paralysed laddie they had done all sorts of things. Then, looking at me, the woman spoke the sentence that has lived with me ever since. She said it with a kind of half-frightened look in her eyes as though she were afraid of some rebuke of mine. 'I hope you won't think we have done wrong,' she said, 'but we have become Roman Catholics.' And then she added quickly, without waiting for me to reply, 'They never said a word about religion. They were just unceasingly kind to us.' "— *That Immortal Sea*, p. 79.

MARY SITS AND LISTENS

It came to pass, as they went, that he entered into a certain village: and a certain woman named Martha received him into her house. And she had a sister called Mary, which also sat at Jesus' feet, and heard his word. Luke 10:38, 39.

The Revised Standard Version says that Mary "listened to his teaching." While Martha was doing the things that had to be done by a hostess, Mary was listening to what Jesus had to say. Long after the meal was forgotten, Mary would carry in her mind the lessons she had learned as a listener.

There is a time to serve Christ, as Martha did; and there is a time to listen .to Christ, as Mary did. Ultimately, which is the more important? Jesus answers the question: "Mary hath chosen that good part, which shall not be taken away from her."

Every pastor is acquainted with good people who, like Martha, are diligent in their service for Christ. They pay their tithe and offerings, they solicit mission funds, they help in welfare work, they are active in Sabbath school and MV work, they are always present and on time wherever they are needed. Such people are a great asset to any church. But some of these people, like Martha, never take time to sit and listen. They are activists, restlessly looking for something to do. The art of meditation and creative listening they have never learned.

It has been reported that the late John Charles Thomas, popular radio soloist, devoutly spent the half hour before his broadcast in a little anteroom of the studio in quietness, meditation, and prayer. No doubt this half hour was much better spent than if he had used the time practicing his solos. Meditation gives depth and meaning to activity. Listening helps to make communication more meaningful.

It is in the world of the spiritual that life is lived at its best. The Marthas who devote their entire attention to activity, however good it may be, never really live as do the Marys who concern themselves with the things that matter most.

71

MARTHA DOES THE HOUSEWORK

But Martha was cumbered about much serving, and came to him, and said, Lord, dost thou not care that my sister hath left me to serve alone? bid her therefore that she help me. And Jesus answered and said unto her, Martha, Martha, thou art careful and troubled about many things: but one thing is needful: and Mary hath chosen that good part, which shall not be taken away from her. Luke 10:40-42.

Jesus' counsel to Martha should not be interpreted as a lack of appreciation for her diligence in looking after the material welfare of her guests. Rather, Jesus was telling her that there were things even more important than being a good hostess.

Martha is a type of millions of wonderful women who devote their best energies to their homes and their social obligations. Such women deserve honor. James Gordon Gilkey tells of a young mother who left her husband at home to take care of three small children. When she returned, she found the house in chaos and the children out of hand. Her husband, a statistician, listed his activities:

"Tied the children's shoes 14 times.
Dried their tears 16 times.
Served 22 drinks of water.
Arbitrated 26 fights.
Told the children not to cross the street 34 times.
Children crossed the street 34 times.
Toy balloons inflated—4 per child.
Average life of balloon—6 seconds."
—*When Life Gets Hard,* p. 60.

Let us not depreciate the Marthas who carry crushing burdens and keep life running smoothly. It is interesting to note that at the death of her brother, Lazarus, it was Martha who went out to meet Jesus—"Mary sat still in the house." It was Martha who expressed her faith in Jesus' life-restoring power.

The record says, "Now Jesus loved Martha, and her sister, and Lazarus." Jesus still loves the Marthas.

LEARNING HOW TO LIVE

He said unto them, Take heed, and beware of covetousness: for a man's life consisteth not in the abundance of the things which he possesseth. Luke 12:15.

A news columnist told the following story:

"In 1923, a group of the world's most successful financiers met at the Edgewater Beach Hotel in Chicago. Present were: the president of the largest independent steel company, the president of the largest utility company, the greatest wheat speculator, the president of the New York Stock Exchange, a member of the President's cabinet, the greatest 'bear' in Wall Street, the president of the Bank of International Settlements, the head of the world's greatest monopoly. Collectively, these tycoons controlled more wealth than there was in the United States treasury, and for years newspapers and magazines had been printing their success stories and urging the youth of the nation to follow their example. Twenty-five years later, let's see what happened to these men.

"The president of the largest independent steel company lived on borrowed money the last five years of his life and died broke. The greatest wheat speculator died abroad, insolvent. The president of the New York Stock Exchange had been recently released from Sing Sing. The member of the President's cabinet was pardoned from prison so he could die at home. The greatest 'bear' in Wall Street committed suicide. The head of the world's greatest monopoly committed suicide.

"All of these men had learned how to make money but not one of them had learned how to live."

Strangely enough, every generation seems to have to learn this lesson anew. Young people often evaluate success in materialistic terms, and plan their lives accordingly. When it is too late to change their course, they discover that they have not learned how to live. Jesus gave the positive answer to the question of how to live when He said, "Seek ye first the kingdom of God, and his righteousness; and all these things shall be added unto you" (Matt. 6:33).

JESUS DEFINES A FOOL

God said unto him, Thou fool, this night thy soul shall be required of thee: then whose shall those things be, which thou hast provided? So is he that layeth up treasure for himself, and is not rich toward God. Luke 12:20, 21.

The fool of this parable was an intelligent, hard-working, thrifty, forward-looking man. He was a fool because he was more interested in social security than in soul security. When prosperity overtook him he failed to face up to the question, "What is my duty to God in view of my increased resources?"

Many years ago Dr. Frank Crane published an essay entitled "The Fool." This is how the fool's creed read:

"I believe in Now. I believe appetites were made to be gratified and not to be controlled. I believe in having a good time, for I'll never be young but once. I believe in mortgaging every acre of the future and using the money now. I believe in picking all the blossoms and never caring for the fruit. I believe in looking out for number one. I believe in other people being thrifty, self-restrained, and temperate, for my benefit. I believe in luck. I believe no one ever really got on by hard work, but that success is a throw of the dice. I believe the rich are happy. I believe I do not need advice. I believe in always being kind, thoughtful, liberal, and charitable—to myself."— *Four Minute Essays,* vol. 8, p. 136.

If the above observations are true, there never was a time when there was as much danger of becoming a fool as now. The modern glorification of *things* makes of many a man a rich fool. The current prejudice against a man who makes religion central in his life has encouraged materialism, and has not made men "rich toward God." The ease with which wealth may be accumulated in the more prosperous countries of the world contributes toward the proliferation of the type of fools the parable describes.

Jesus told this story to illustrate the truth that "a man's life consisteth not in the abundance of the things which he possesseth" (verse 15). The fool believes it does. The wise man seeks deeper satisfactions, more lasting values.

ABLE TO FINISH

Which of you, intending to build a tower, sitteth not down first, and counteth the cost, whether he have sufficient to finish it? Lest haply, after he hath laid the foundation, and is not able to finish it, all that behold it begin to mock him, saying, This man began to build, and was not able to finish. Luke 14:28-30.

Speaking on "The Temptations of Maturity," a prominent preacher once made the following statement:

"The temptations of maturity are as real and as ruinous as the temptations of youth. More obituaries than one likes to think, if they were honest, would say: 'This man began to build, and was not able to finish.' A good beginning never implies a good ending, for the qualities which enable a man to start well are not the same qualities which enable him to carry on well to the end. A man can start on any enterprise if he is eager, ardent, hopeful, enthusiastic, susceptible to the thrill of a new adventure; but, if the enterprise lasts a long time and faces difficulty, as all worth-while enterprises do, he must have other attributes if he is to come to a fine finish—constancy, patience, perseverance, courage, steadfastness. How many good starters there are in comparison with good finishers!"—HARRY EMERSON FOSDICK, *What Is Vital in Religion,* p. 212.

This explains why the world is full of promising young people, when there are so few outstanding successful people of middle age. What happens to all the bright young men who march down the aisle on Commencement day, clutching their diplomas? Some of them make good, many more are not "able to finish." They settle for lives of mediocrity when they might have done something worth while.

What happens to the thousands of young people who are baptized into the church? On their baptismal day they mean to be true to their commitments, but the rains come and the winds blow and the once-eager Christians lose their motivation. They are unable to finish.

When Paul faced death he was able to say, "I have *finished* my course, I have *kept* the faith." We honor the great apostle, not merely because he responded to the call of his Lord on the way to Damascus but also because he was able to finish his course with strength.

JESUS REMEMBERS HUMBLE PEOPLE

Then said he unto the disciples, It is impossible but that offences will come: but woe unto him, through whom they come! It were better for him that a millstone were hanged about his neck, and he cast into the sea, than that he should offend one of these little ones. Luke 17:1, 2.

What strong language Jesus used to express His concern about "little" people. To whom was He referring? He was thinking of the millions of ordinary people—peasants, outcasts, humble workmen, the "common people" of all ages. He was thinking of the starving millions of overcrowded, underdeveloped countries, and of the millions whose ordinary talents and training fit them only for menial tasks.

Harry M. Tippett tells the following story:

"Some years ago a great soprano of national reputation was helping her home church choir in an eastern city to present a great oratorio. In justifiable pride she had often told of the important people she had entertained, including European royalty. But one night she was leaving the church after a rehearsal when the scrubwoman cleaning the vestry timidly touched her and said, 'Please, ma'am, I love your beautiful voice. Could you—would you sing for me sometime my favorite hymn, "Someday the silver cord will break"?'

"The singer smiled and promised to do so, but as she stepped into the chill of the night something prompted her to go back right then and sing for the woman. She returned to the church, and finding the organist still there, beckoned for the janitress to come down front. Then with all the skill of her training she sang blind Fanny Crosby's famous hymn, 'And I shall see Him face to face, and tell the story— Saved by grace.' The countenance of the woman with the dustcloth was transformed with spiritual rapture, and the soloist declared that it was a greater inspiration than when she had sung before kings, for she felt the blessing of Christ's 'Inasmuch' and the unseen accompaniment of angelic choirs."—*My Lord and I,* p. 18.

May we never lose the common touch. May education and position and wealth never cause us to disregard those who have not enjoyed our opportunities.

A PHARISEE CONGRATULATES HIMSELF

The Pharisee stood and prayed thus with himself, God, I thank thee, that I am not as other men are, extortioners, unjust, adulterers, or even as this publican. I fast twice in the week, I give tithes of all that I possess. Luke 18:11, 12.

A minister tells of preaching a sermon at a Sabbath morning service, on the story of the Pharisee and the publican. After the sermon was over, the person who offered the closing prayer said, "Lord, we thank Thee that we are not like the Pharisee in this parable." Dr. Harry Emerson Fosdick tells of a chaplain who offered the following prayer before a genealogical society, where all were congratulating themselves on being the descendants of their ancestors: " 'Justify, O Lord, if it be possible, the high esteem in which we hold ourselves.' "—*On Being a Real Person*, p. 262. Unfortunately, that isn't possible.

In this letter to the Romans, Paul pieces together a series of Old Testament statements, mostly from the Psalms, that graphically describe man's predicament:

"None is righteous, no, not one;
no one understands, no one seeks for God.
All have turned aside, together they have gone wrong;
no one does good, not even one."
"Their throat is an open grave,
they use their tongues to deceive."
"The venom of asps is under their lips."
"Their mouth is full of curses and bitterness."
"Their feet are swift to shed blood,
in their paths are ruin and misery,
and the way of peace they do not know."
"There is no fear of God before their eyes."

Rom. 3:10-18, R.S.V.

This is the picture of man as God sees him. Man's solution to his predicament is not in himself and his own attainments. The publican in the parable recognized this when he said, "God be merciful to me a sinner" (Luke 18:13).

77

CHRIST AND THE CITY

When he was come near, he beheld the city, and wept over it. Luke 19:41.

It has become commonplace for those of us who live in the country and in small towns to look upon the cities with a certain degree of contempt. After returning from a few hours on the busy streets, we sigh and exclaim, "I surely wouldn't want to live there!" We extol the more wholesome atmosphere of the country and congratulate ourselves that we are not caught in the asphalt jungle.

All this is understandable, but have we paused to think that it is in the cities where people are?

> "Cities are more than steel and stone
> or humming wheels and towers a-drone;
> or busy shops and boulevards,
> or parks, or homes with well-kept yards.
> Cities are more than block-long stores
> with neon-signs and countless doors.
> Cities have eyes afire with tears
> and hearts that flee the mocking years;
> ears that hear no sound of song,
> feet that stumble on streets of wrong.
> Cities are full of children crying,
> cities are full of people dying.
> Cities are more than stone-steel towers
> proudly proclaiming this time of ours.
> Cities are men for whom Christ died;
> cities are souls for whom He died."

—LON WOODRUM, quoted in *Minister's Manual, 1968,* pp. 119, 120.

When Jesus looked at His city, His heart responded to the sordidness, the selfishness, the suffering, and the shame that He saw there, and He wept. If He were to look at our cities—London, New York, Los Angeles, Tokyo, Paris, Calcutta—would not His tears flow again? Should we consider them as off-bounds areas to be shunned, or should their needs challenge us to find ways to reach them with the gospel?

JESUS SEES PETER'S FUTURE

The Lord said, Simon, Simon, behold, Satan hath desired to have you, that he may sift you as wheat: but I have prayed for thee, that thy faith fail not: and when thou art converted, strengthen thy brethren. Luke 22:31, 32.

At the time Jesus spoke these words, Peter was a confused and unpromising man. He was much concerned about his place in the kingdom he thought would soon be established; he was about to do some rash things; and in a few hours he would be guilty of basely denying his Lord.

But Jesus' viewpoint of Peter was not based on Peter as he was at the moment, but on the Peter that was to be. Jesus' attitude was like that described by Tennyson where, talking about faith, he says:

> "She spies the summer thro' the winter bud,
> She tastes the fruit before the blossom falls,
> She hears the lark within the songless egg,
> She finds the fountain where they wail'd 'Mirage!'"
> —From "The Ancient Sage"

As a parent sees in an immature child an accomplished and responsible adult, so God sees His children in the perspective of their entire lives. A streetside onlooker may see but one segment of a passing parade, while a person stationed on a high building or riding in a helicopter may see the whole parade. So God looks at us from the vantage point of eternity.

This great truth should make us less prone to judge other people. We should realize how narrow is our spectrum of knowledge regarding our fellow men as compared to God's acquaintance with them. He sees them not as they are, but as they will become.

It should also encourage us to remember that God doesn't look on helplessly as we grope and flounder. Just as our Lord exerted every influence to shape Peter's life and to help him make right decisions, so He works in behalf of His children today. He does not coerce, but He does guide and encourage. As He prayed for Peter, so He prays for us. And His prayers will be answered.

79

TIMES CHANGE

He said unto them, When I sent you without purse, and scrip, and shoes, lacked ye any thing? And they said, Nothing. Then said he unto them, But now, he that hath a purse, let him take it, and likewise his scrip: and he that hath no sword, let him sell his garment, and buy one. Luke 22:35, 36.

In this passage Jesus refers to the time when He sent seventy of His followers "into every city and place whither he himself would come." Those had been days of great promise. When the seventy returned, they rejoiced that "even the devils" were subject to them.

It was in those days of success that Jesus had told His messengers, "Carry neither purse, nor scrip, nor shoes" (Luke 10:4). They needed none of these things because there were enough friendly people to supply their needs. But by the time of the Last Supper times had changed. No longer would they be working in the friendly villages of Galilee, but in the big hostile world. Now they would need money, provisions, and protection; and they were to plan for these needs.

When I was a child two itinerant evangelists came to the community where I lived and held meetings in the local schoolhouse. They belonged to a group that called themselves the "Jesus Way." In their efforts, no doubt sincere, to follow Jesus, they read Luke 10:4 and concluded that they should carry no money or possessions of any kind. They depended entirely on the hospitality of their followers. Unfortunately, they did not read Luke 22:35, 36. They would have found that when conditions changed, Jesus changed His counsel.

There are great fundamental principles, such as those reflected in the Ten Commandments, that never change. There are other things that change with times, customs, culture, and geography. When Paul talked about eating food offered to idols and women talking in church, he was applying the principles of the gospel to local issues in the context of the contemporary culture. When Paul talked about sexual morality, he was talking about basic principles of conduct that do not change.

May God help us to differentiate between that which changes with the times and that which endures.

80

THE MISTAKES OF PETER

The Lord turned, and looked upon Peter. And Peter remembered the word of the Lord, how he had said unto him, Before the cock crow, thou shalt deny me thrice. Luke 22:61, 62.

It seems incredible that Peter could have denied his Lord, that he could curse and swear in order to convince his hearers that he was not a follower of Jesus. His experience is merely a revelation of the weakness of human nature. The pressure was on, his Master was on trial, he had been rebuked for trying to defend Him, all of the followers of Jesus were in danger, and under the impact of fear and frustration he crumpled.

A realization of what he had done brought remorse. It seemed as incredible to him as it does to us, that he could have failed. He did not realize his own frailties. He did not know what he would do under extreme pressure.

Peter's experience has been a source of comfort to all Christians who, like him, have crumpled under the pressures of life. Who has not spoken words he would like to have retrieved? Who has not dissembled to protect his own safety or interest? Who has not tried to escape the responsibilities of discipleship? Who has not slipped back into old patterns of life and thought? And, like Peter, when we feel the Master's gaze, we sorrow because of our faithlessness.

F. W. Robertson, the great preacher of Brighton, England, once said, "Life, like war, is a series of mistakes, and he is not the best Christian nor the best general who makes the fewest false steps. He is the best who wins the most splendid victories by the retrieval of mistakes. Forget mistakes, organize victory out of mistakes."—Quoted in *Christian Herald,* May, 1968, p. 35.

Peter did exactly this. A few weeks later, by the Sea of Galilee, Jesus gave Peter opportunity to reaffirm his commitment. Then we see Peter as the preacher at Pentecost, and as an intrepid leader of the church. Peter was speaking from experience when, in his old age, he said, "But the God of all grace, who hath called us unto his eternal glory by Christ Jesus, after that ye have suffered a while, make you perfect, stablish, strengthen, settle you" (1 Peter 5:10).

81

SIMON CARRIES JESUS' CROSS

And as they led him away, they laid hold upon one Simon, a Cyrenian, coming out of the country, and on him they laid the cross, that he might bear it after Jesus. Luke 23:26.

Clovis G. Chappell records the imaginary testimony of Simon:

"Years ago, as a proselyte, I went from Cyrene to attend the great feast at Jerusalem. . . . To my amazement when I came near Jerusalem, the crowds were headed out of the city, instead of into it. Asking what this meant, I was told that three prisoners were that day to pay the death penalty. . . .

"I elbowed my way through the crowd until I was near enough to have touched the prisoners with my own hand. Two of them were vigorous men, rough, sinewy, and hard as nails. The other, while a fine figure of a man, was evidently suffering from much blood letting. Indeed he was so weakened that even as I looked, his knees buckled and he fell under the weight of his cross.

"Then the ghastly thing happened! A strong hand gripped my shoulder, a short sword flashed in the sun, and a voice of authority thundered at me, 'You there, take up that cross.' . . . Therefore, with a curse on my lips and rage in my heart I shouldered the hated load and fell in beside the man whose burden I had taken.

"This man, so far as I remember, said never a word to me. But the very breath of him somehow cooled the hot fires of my resentment. Even by his silence he seemed to say, 'I am sorry to have involved you in this, but I am not quite up to myself this morning.' Then when we came to the foot of the hill he made as if he would take over. But to my utter amazement I heard myself say, 'Never mind, I will be glad to carry it for you up the hill and all the way.' .

"And carry it I did. I stood by and watched the grim work of crucifixion. I heard him pray for his enemies. I heard him when at last he dropped his tired and tortured body into the arms of eternal Love, praying, 'Father into thy hands I commit my spirit.' By all this he so completely won my heart that I took up his cross of my own choice. From that day to this what was once my shame has been my glory."—*The Cross Before Calvary*, pp. 15, 16.

THE ROAD TO EMMAUS

We trusted that it had been he which should have redeemed Israel: and beside all this, to day is the third day since these things were done. **Luke 24:21.**

The speakers were two dejected, disappointed followers of Jesus. The time was the Sunday following His crucifixion. The place was the road from Jerusalem to a village called Emmaus.

As the two men walked they were "talking and discussing together" (verse 15, R.S.V.). Their subject was the events of the preceding days. The arrest, the trial, the horrible hours of the crucifixion, the burial, were all fresh in their minds.

These two men were confused. They "trusted that it had been he which should have redeemed Israel." Was their faith an illusion? Were their Master's teachings false? Must they go back to their old life and try to forget the wonderful years they had spent with Jesus?

The loving concern of Jesus is shown by the fact that He was there when these two men needed Him. At first He did not identify Himself, but in response to His questions, the two men told their story regarding the Jesus they had known. Jesus resolved their questions by pointing out the passages in the Old Testament that predicted His life, death, and resurrection. At the dinner table in Emmaus He revealed Himself to them; then He "vanished out of their sight." The effectiveness of Jesus' Bible study with them is indicated by their reaction when they discovered His identity: "Did not our heart burn within us, while he talked with us by the way, and while he opened to us the scriptures?" (verse 32).

Filled with joy and enthusiasm, the men returned to Jerusalem much faster than they had gone to Emmaus. They found the eleven and other disciples gathered together, rejoicing in the report of Jesus' appearance to Simon. Then they described their encounter with their Lord.

What a thrilling experience it all was, and what a revelation of the love of Jesus. When two sincere followers needed insight and understanding, He was there to help them. He transformed bitter disappointment into thrilling joy.

83

JESUS ATTENDS A WEDDING

This beginning of miracles did Jesus in Cana of Galilee, and manifested forth his glory; and his disciples believed on him. John 2:11.

The wedding at Cana tells us much about Jesus—much, in fact, that is at variance with the preconceived opinions of many people.

First, it is noteworthy that Jesus was there. Were there not more important things for Him and His disciples to do than go to weddings? The trip to Cana, the wedding itself, and the return trip to other areas of activity may have consumed many days. Was not this a waste of time? Apparently Jesus didn't think so.

Second, it is even more noteworthy that Jesus would exert His ability to work a miracle to maintain the wine supply at a wedding. Did He not come to heal the sick, to cast out devils, to preach the gospel? Was not the shortage of refreshments at a wedding too trivial an item for Him to notice? Apparently not.

Third, many years later, one of the witnesses of this miracle, John the evangelist, referred to it as a manifestation of His glory. Was not this a gross exaggeration? A village wedding, a miracle performed to aid an embarrassed hostess—was this a manifestation of the glory of Jesus? Apparently so.

Fourth, the same reporter recorded that "his disciples believed on him." Some of them had seen Him baptized, had heard the voice of God acknowledging Him as His Son, and had spent hours listening to Him. Did they need an incident like this to cause them to believe? Apparently it helped.

Jesus first unleashed His power to control the processes of nature at a village wedding, to prevent the celebration from grinding to a premature stop. The same Jesus still blesses the ordinary activities of life. He is still interested in the joy and happiness of people. He still intervenes, at times, to smooth the tensions of daily existence. He loves people—all of them—and He is interested in the things that concern them. That is why He came.

We may be eternally grateful that this incident is recorded in the Bible. It is a corrective to the tendency to dehumanize our Lord.

GOD SO LOVED THE WORLD

God so loved the world, that he gave his only begotten Son, that whosoever believeth in him should not perish, but have everlasting life. John 3:16.

Many have been the attempts of men to describe the fathomless love of God for man. All of these attempts fall far short of reality. Probably the most helpful analogy is that of the normal person's love for his children. But after describing this love at its best, we hear our Master say, "If ye then, being evil, know how to give good gifts unto your children, *how much more* shall your Father which is in heaven give good things to them that ask him?" (Matt. 7:11).

"If parents will sacrifice themselves for their little ones, how much more God! If a man will lay down his life for his friends, how much more God! If you will suffer for one whom you love, how much more God! Do you remember how Lacordaire once dramatized this very truth? 'If you would wish to know how the Almighty feels towards us, listen to the beating of your own heart *and add to it infinity.*' " —JAMES S. STEWART, *Heralds of God*, p. 148.

The love of God for man is expressed not only in John 3:16 but in the entire gospel story. The Incarnation was an expression of that love. Jesus' ministry to men was an eloquent attempt to dramatize God's love. The cross was the supreme manifestation of love. The postresurrection appearances, the ministry of the Holy Spirit, Christ's ministry in heaven in behalf of sinners, the second coming of Jesus, life eternal—all these great gospel truths reflect the love of God.

But, says one, if God loves me, why must I suffer, and if God loves the world, why so much pain and sorrow? Part of the answer to this question is found in the words of Paul: "For our light affliction, which is but for a moment, worketh for us a far more exceeding and eternal weight of glory; while we look not at the things which are seen, but at the things which are not seen: for the things which are seen are temporal; but the things which are not seen are eternal" (2 Cor. 4:17, 18).

The love of an eternal God must be evaluated in terms of eternity. His love can be felt now, but it will be understood hereafter.

SPIRITUAL WORSHIP

The hour cometh, and now is, when the true worshippers shall worship the Father in spirit and in truth: for the Father seeketh such to worship him. God is a spirit: and they that worship him must worship him in spirit and in truth. John 4:23, 24.

Jesus is talking to the woman at the well, answering her question as to whether people shall worship God in Jerusalem or Samaria. His answer is a ringing declaration that the important question is not *where* men worship but *how* they worship.

Regarding the worship practices of Jesus' time, Ellen White says:

"Christ saw that something must be done. Numerous ceremonies were enjoined upon the people without the proper instruction as to their import. The worshipers offered their sacrifices without understanding that they were typical of the only perfect Sacrifice. And among them, unrecognized and unhonored, stood the One symbolized by all their service. He had given directions in regard to the offerings. He understood their symbolical value, and He saw that they were now perverted and misunderstood. Spiritual worship was fast disappearing. . . . Christ's work was to establish an altogether different worship." —*The Desire of Ages,* p. 157.

Can it be that modern man has forgotten how to worship God? Just as the people of Jesus' time were pre-eminently concerned with place, so our generation is concerned with togetherness, esthetic satisfaction, and liturgical form. The missing factor in both ages is the acute experience of the presence of a holy God:

"Here with the tinted rays
Of thy Sabbath morning light, comes peace,
Joy lingers, courage is born, and hope sings.
Freed for a while from the fret and care of daily toil,
In the solemn hush of this holy hour I hear God speak,
Steadied and strengthened by this communion sweet,
With lifted head I leave thy templed doors
To dare whatever the day may bring to me,
For I who heard shall heed."

—*Selected*

JESUS HEALS A CRIPPLE

The impotent man answered him, Sir, I have no man, when the water is troubled, to put me into the pool: but while I am coming, another steppeth down before me. Jesus saith unto him, Rise, take up thy bed, and walk. And immediately the man was made whole, and took up his bed, and walked. John 5:7-9.

For thirty-eight years the man had been a cripple at the Pool of Bethesda. Every time ripples appeared on the surface of the water he tried to get there first, but always someone beat him to the water's edge. Great persistence motivated him, persistence born of despair, because he had no other hope.

But one day a new hope dawned in his dark life. A stranger with a personality that radiated confidence asked him to get up, pick up his bedding roll, and walk. This was the blessing for which he had longed for thirty-eight years, but he had always been thwarted. This new hope that entered his life didn't require him to compete with anyone. His response to Jesus' invitation was not dependent on his ability to outrun, outtalk, or outshine any human being. He was on his own, *his* faith could grasp the healing power of the prophet from Galilee, and *he* could be made whole. Nothing like this had ever happened to him before.

This miracle tells us much regarding the way God deals with man. He does not offer salvation to anyone because of who he is, what he can do, or where he happens to be in the line rushing toward the water's edge. God looks past all of these things and sees man's need; and with divine compassion He reaches down to him, *wherever he happens to be,* and supplies that need.

Salvation does not depend on drawing a lucky number, on mental endowment, on physical strength, on accidents of birth. Salvation is the gift of God through Christ. To every person He is saying, "Wilt thou be made whole?" Faith is receiving this blessing. Faith is man's hand, reaching upward to clasp God's hand of grace in order that man may be made whole. Nothing can be more personal, more vitalizing, than the experience of faith in Christ.

BOTH LAWYER AND JUDGE

The Father judgeth no man, but hath committed all judgment unto the Son. John 5:22.

Billy Graham tells the following story:

"When he was a young man, Judge Warren Candler practiced law. One of his clients was charged with murder, and the young lawyer made the utmost effort to clear his client of the charge. There were some extenuating circumstances and the lawyer made the most of them in his plea before the jury. Moreover, there were present in the court the aged father and mother of the man charged with murder; and the young lawyer worked on the sympathies and emotions of the jury by frequent references to the God-fearing parents.

"In due course, the jury retired for deliberation. When they had reached a verdict, they returned to the jury box. Their verdict read: 'We find the defendant not guilty.' The young lawyer, himself a Christian, had a serious talk with his cleared client. He warned him to steer clear of evil ways and to trust God's power to keep him straight.

"Years passed. Again the man was brought into court. Again the charge was murder. The lawyer who had defended him at the first trial was now the judge on the bench. At the conclusion of the trial, the jury rendered its verdict of *'Guilty.'*

"Ordering the condemned man to stand for sentencing, Judge Candler said, 'At your first trial, I was your lawyer, today I am your judge. The verdict of the jury makes it mandatory for me to sentence you to be hanged by the neck until you are dead.' "—*World Aflame,* pp. 244, 245.

Today, Christ is our lawyer. He won that position at the cross. During all of the centuries of His ministry in the heavenly sanctuary, He has looked after our interests, putting into effect every agency that might lead us toward eternal life.

But the Scripture is very clear that the time is coming when He will be our judge, for the Father "hath committed all judgment unto the Son." At that day, the One who has given so much to secure our redemption will utter the verdict that determines our destiny.

QUITTING TOO SOON

You search the scriptures, because you think that in them you have eternal life; and it is they that bear witness to me; yet you refuse to come to me that you may have life. John 5:39, 40, R.S.V.

This passage is not a command to "search the scriptures," but an accusation directed against the Jewish leaders of Jesus' day. In it He pointed out to them that although they studied the Scriptures diligently, they failed to see the real theme of the sacred writings—Jesus. They thought they would receive eternal life from studying the Scriptures, when life was available only in Christ to whom the Scriptures bore witness.

Years ago, a young man started his career as a gold miner. But instead of finding new mines "he began to go through abandoned mines, exploring the veins that were supposed to have been entirely exhausted. He learned that by following the veins further, or by digging deeper, he could often find paying dirt that other miners had overlooked."—W. D. CAVERT, *Remember Now,* p. 48.

So it was with the Jewish students of the Bible in Jesus' day. They thought they had exhausted the mines of truth. They dug no more—they only rearranged the treasures they had already uncovered. But the most valuable truths they had never seen—the truths regarding Jesus, the Saviour of mankind.

And so it may be today. For centuries men have studied the Sacred Word. They have found much that is enlightening, but many of their conclusions have been faulty. Too often, preconceived theories and concepts have shaped the thinking of churchmen and scholars, and have warped their understanding of the Bible. It is our privilege to dig deep in the mine of truth—to go beyond the point where other miners lay down their tools, and to seek treasures not yet seen.

While we are indebted to those who have dug in the past, we must never conclude that the mine is depleted. Let us approach the Word of God with eagerness and anticipation, and let us never quit digging. This is especially important in a time when the Bible is suffering misuse and neglect.

"GO, AND SIN NO MORE"

Jesus said unto her, Neither do I condemn thee: go, and sin no more. John 8:11.

Jesus was sitting in the court of the Temple, teaching a group of people who had gathered about Him. Suddenly there arose a commotion. A group of scribes and Pharisees broke into the group, dragging a very frightened woman. The spokesman, probably a high-ranking Pharisee, spoke: "Master, this woman was taken in adultery, in the very act. Now Moses in the law commanded us, that such should be stoned: but what sayest thou?" If they could only get Jesus to disagree with Moses! If they could only get people to chanting, "Jesus doesn't believe Moses!" This would be the certain way to compromise His influence with a people who were more concerned about Moses than about truth, love, and righteousness.

And their case was airtight! She had been caught in the act. The law said *death*. How could anyone argue? They were saying, in effect, How will Jesus get out of this one? They were aware of His concern for people who were "down," and waited expectantly for His answer.

But He acted as if He didn't hear them. When they continued to question Him, He lifted Himself up, cast at them a look of scorn, and said, "He that is without sin among *you,* let *him* first cast a stone at her." One by one the accusers sneaked away. Conscience had made cowards of them all.

Finally, Jesus addressed the woman: "Hath no man condemned thee? She said, No man, Lord. And Jesus said unto her, Neither do I condemn thee: go, and sin no more."

It is common knowledge that John 8:1-11, the passage containing this story, is not found in many of the ancient manuscripts of the New Testament. Many scholars have concluded that it was not in the original Gospels. There is reason to believe an alternate interpretation— perhaps the story may have been in the original Gospels, but was omitted by copyists who were themselves so legalistic that they could not tolerate the idea of Jesus forgiving an adulteress. The great truth shines forth that Jesus will forgive anybody—yes, *anybody* who will sincerely accept His command, "Go, and sin no more."

THE TESTIMONY OF EXPERIENCE

He answered and said, Whether he be a sinner or no, I know not: one thing I know, that, whereas I was blind, now I see. John 9:25.

The speaker was a young man who had been blind from his birth. Jesus had anointed his eyes and sent him to wash in the pool of Siloam, and he had received his sight.

The neighbors immediately asked three questions: "Is not this he that sat and begged?" "How were thine eyes opened?" and "Where is he?" These three questions represent well the sequence that often takes place in the experience of the converted Christian. First, people are amazed at the change; second, they wonder how the change took place; and third, they seek to find Him who made the change possible.

Then the Pharisees raised questions because this miracle took place on the Sabbath day. They assumed that no one who was "of God" could heal a man on the Sabbath. Then they called the parents, who identified their son, but refused comment on how he was healed because they were afraid of the consequences. Finally, they called the young man who had been healed and said to him, "Give God the praise: we know that this man is a sinner." They were so involved in their prejudices as not to be influenced even by so great a work of love as the healing of this young man.

This must have been very confusing to the man who had never seen before and was now enjoying his introduction to a new life. He had a good answer: "Whereas I was blind, now I see." They reviled him and cast him out of the synagogue, but *he still could see.* Experience was an evidence that no amount of argument could refute. When Jesus returned to the young man and revealed Himself to him as the Son of God, his response was immediate. He believed.

In this incident is a great lesson. When a person has experienced the healing, restoring, saving power of Christ, no amount of argument will convince him that he is mistaken. The greatest witness for Christ in the world is the person for whom the Lord has done something special. The most convincing Christians are those who speak out of personal experience.

91

DO WE DARE BELIEVE?

But ye believe not, because ye are not of my sheep. John 10:26.

People who refuse to believe in Christ present all sorts of intellectual defenses for their disbelief. They may question the historical records of the Gospels. They may quibble about the miracles of the Gospels. They may challenge the divine authorship of the records. But in most cases their disbelief is exactly as Jesus described it—"Ye believe not, because ye are not of my sheep." They don't want to be part of His flock. They don't want to go where He leads. Their unwillingness to acknowledge Him as their Shepherd results in a process of rationalization which, in turn, produces their objections and doubts.

J. B. Phillips expresses this idea very clearly:

"It is worth remembering that behind our ostensible reasons for believing or not believing a thing there are often unconscious reasons which go very deep. There are undoubtedly some who know intuitively how much depends on the historic truth of the Resurrection. Should they once admit it to be true that this earth has been visited by the Creator, then the standards and values of the man who was also God will inevitably challenge and judge their lives. To some minds this must on no account be allowed to happen, and every ingenious argument and every library resource must be employed to avoid the unwelcome conclusion."—*God Our Contemporary,* p. 61.

A truly rational person will dare to believe that for which the evidence is overwhelming, even though the implications of such belief may be disturbing. If belief in Christ demands "love, joy, peace, longsuffering, gentleness, goodness, faith, meekness, temperance," he is willing that Christ lead him into this level of living. If belief in Christ involves the surrender of his own will to the guidance of his Lord, he is willing to make this surrender.

It takes courage to read the story of Christ in the Gospels, and to respond, "I believe." Such a commitment is daring because its implication cannot but revolutionize our lives. We can well take inventory of our acts and attitudes and ask ourselves the question, Can a person who believes in Christ think and act as I do?

92

THE CYNIC

Then took Mary a pound of ointment of spikenard, very costly, and anointed the feet of Jesus, and wiped his feet with her hair: and the house was filled with the odour of the ointment. Then said one of his disciples, Judas Iscariot, Simon's son, which should betray him, Why was not this ointment sold for three hundred pence, and given to the poor?" John 12:3-5.

It was too much for Judas when he witnessed Mary's expression of complete love and commitment. Her beautiful act of worship condemned his duplicity and his self-centeredness. So he did what every other cynic does—he found fault with the person who was better than he.

Dr. Harry Emerson Fosdick says, "Others, like the fox in Aesop's fable, handle the problem of bitterly felt inferiority by calling sour all grapes they cannot reach. The frail youth discounts athletics; the debauchee, really suffering from a sense of guilt, scoffs at the self-controlled as prudes; the failure at school or college, deeply humiliated, scorns intellectuals as 'high-brows'; the girl without charm exaggerates her liability, dresses crudely, adopts rough manners, deliberately looks her worst, professing lofty disdain of charm as a triviality. A major amount of cynicism springs from this course. Watch what people are cynical about, and one can often discover what they lack, and subconsciously, beneath their touchy condescension, deeply wish they had."—*On Being a Real Person,* pp. 62, 63.

Are we allowing cynicism to betray our spiritual poverty? Do we laugh at the person who is very liberal with the church, accusing him of trying to pay his way to heaven? Do we sneer at the person who keeps the Sabbath carefully, accusing him of Pharisaism? Do we make fun of the person who is careful in his conduct, calling him a prude? Do we jeer at the person who is careful what he eats and drinks, calling him a fanatic? In taking these attitudes, perhaps we are labeling ourselves as verily as Judas labeled himself when he found fault with Mary. Cynicism is a disclosure of the weakness of the soul. It is the sick person, trying to convince himself that he would rather be sick than pay the price of health.

JESUS WASHES HIS DISCIPLES' FEET

Jesus knowing that the Father had given all things into his hands, and that he was come from God, and went to God; he riseth from supper, and laid aside his garments; and took a towel, and girded himself. After that he poureth water into a bason, and began to wash the disciples' feet, and to wipe them with the towel wherewith he was girded. John 13:3-5.

A well-known church historian has said, "Though unrecognized as a church sacrament, surely there never was a more impressive one than Jesus' use of the towel at the last meal with His disciples—an act so in keeping with the whole of His life."—SAMUEL ANGUS, *Religious Quests of the Graeco-Roman World*, p. 248. This observation matches a statement made years earlier by Ellen White: "The whole life of Christ had been a life of unselfish service. 'Not to be ministered unto, but to minister,' had been the lesson of His every act. But not yet had the disciples learned the lesson. At this last Passover supper, Jesus repeated His teaching by an illustration that impressed it forever on their minds and hearts."—*The Desire of Ages*, p. 642.

Never in the history of the human race has there been a more arresting scene than that of Jesus washing the feet of His disciples. In this incident was revealed the great truth that salvation involves more than what man does for God—it also includes God stooping, humbling Himself to serve man. It symbolizes the humiliation of Jesus in behalf of mankind. It pictures God's work for man as an act of cleansing—washing away pride, selfishness, and arrogance. These are the sins that we pick up like dust along the paths of life. In the reaction of Peter, this incident portrays the necessity of our acceptance of the grace and love and kindness of God.

What could Jesus have done that would have reflected His godlikeness more perfectly than the simple act of washing His disciples' feet? No sermon could have said so eloquently what Jesus said by an act of love. With sublime artistry and dramatic forcefulness the Master left in the minds of men the picture of Himself, kneeling, towel in hand, before ordinary men.

PETER DEFIES HIS LORD

Peter saith unto him, Thou shalt never wash my feet. Jesus answered him, If I wash thee not, thou hast no part with me. Simon Peter saith unto him, Lord, not my feet only, but also my hands and my head. John 13:8, 9.

Peter meant every word of it when he said with such firmness, "Thou shalt never wash my feet." His sense of fitness was outraged by the idea of Jesus' acting as a servant to him. *He* would have been entirely willing to wash *Jesus'* feet, but the idea of Jesus washing his feet was repugnant to him.

But Jesus had a purpose in confronting Peter in this way. He wanted Peter to realize that his salvation was dependent, not on what he might do for Jesus, but on what Jesus could do for him. The instant Peter saw this truth his defiance melted. He wanted his Master to wash not only his feet but his hands and his head.

From that day to this, professed Christians have repeated Peter's mistake of wanting a do-it-yourself religion. But only a few have repeated Peter's complete reversal in attitude. Only a few have fully recognized that the faith by which men are saved is an acceptance of the cleansing power of divine grace.

How does this work in everyday life? A person becomes a Christian and asks himself, "What can I do to make myself acceptable to God?" He reads the baptismal certificate, and the Bible, looking eagerly for new duties to perform. His zeal is praiseworthy, but eventually he becomes conscious of a lack in his life. He is depending on what he is doing for God rather than on what God can do for him. In his busy earnestness he has failed to meditate and pray. He is so busy working for God that he has no time to let God cleanse him.

When the light finally dawns, and the distraught struggler realizes that God and all His angels are working for him, then, and not until then, fear and uncertainty disappear and peace and security fill the life. Later in life Peter said, "Casting all your care upon him; for he careth for you" (1 Peter 5:6). Peter learned this formula, as we also must, through experience.

95

WHY JESUS WASHED HIS DISCIPLES' FEET

*Ye call me Master and Lord: and ye say well; for so I am.
If I then, your Lord and Master, have washed your feet; ye also
ought to wash one another's feet. For I have given you an example,
that ye should do as I have done to you.* John 13:13-15.

Two great lessons emerge from this passage: First, Jesus was
telling His disciples through all ages that they should be as unselfish and considerate in their attitude toward one another as He
was toward them. Just as He did not insist on what might be considered His prerogatives as their "Master and Lord," so they were
not to be concerned about position and status, but were to serve one
another in love. This is a hard lesson, even for Christians, to learn.

A second lesson of the passage is the significance of Jesus' act
as a symbol of His own humiliation. Of Jesus it is said, "But [he]
made himself of no reputation, and took upon him the form of a
servant, and was made in the likeness of men: and being found in
fashion as a man, he humbled himself, and became obedient unto
death, even the death of the cross" (Phil. 2:7, 8). The incident in
the upper room speaks of this greater humiliation that was part of
the plan of redemption.

In view of the significance of this important incident in the life
of Jesus, some Christian churches have perpetuated the foot-washing
service as a "memorial of His humiliation" (*The Desire of Ages*,
p. 650). This service is infinitely more than an evidence of humility
—it is a *memorial* of the *humiliation* of the Saviour of mankind.
Thus, the service has a profound meaning. It reminds the worshiper
of the grace of God as effectively as do the bread and the wine. At
the same time, it reminds the participant of the bond of fellowship
that ties believers together in Christian love. This service teaches
the perfect way to level barriers between races and classes of men.

The service in itself will never become a meaningless ceremony
to those who remember the humiliation of Jesus and the Christian
principle of the equality of man. It is a graphic reminder of the
greatest event that ever happened in the universe—the act of Jesus
in giving Himself to save the world.

"I HAVE GIVEN YOU AN EXAMPLE"

If I then, your Lord and Master, have washed your feet; ye also ought to wash one another's feet. For I have given you an example, that ye should do as I have done to you. John 13:14, 15.

Dr. Leonard Griffith, former pastor of the City Temple in London, tells the following story:

"Years ago I knew a Christlike man who was the director of a large camp for under-privileged boys. His campers and colleagues affectionately called him 'The Chief.' Everybody loved and respected the Chief, and everybody felt the strength of his Christian influence. He diverted more than one lad from the path of delinquency. Legends grew up about this man after his death, but one of them, that had solid basis in fact, never failed to impress the boys. It seems that in days before the camp enjoyed the comforts of modern plumbing, the Chief used to rise each morning at dawn before anyone else was awake and by himself perform the odious duty of cleaning all the sanitary conveniences. Many times people remonstrated with him and said, 'Why don't you make this a fatigue duty for the boys or at least for some of the maintenance staff? Surely it is not the Chief's work!' He always gave the same reply. 'I do it because I *am* the Chief and because I *choose* to do it. No-one should be *compelled* to perform a task so dirty and disagreeable.'"

Applying this incident to the happening in the upper room, Dr. Griffith continues: "Observing the neglect of the disciples, how simple it would have been for Jesus to say, 'Peter, Andrew, John, is it not your turn to wash the feet tonight?' Even a gentle reminder would have produced immediate results. But Jesus did not believe in coercing men to play the role of a slave. That role has to be chosen, and he, the Chief, chose to fulfil it."—*The Eternal Legacy From the Upper Room,* pp. 41, 42.

"I have given you an example," Jesus said. How well are we following the example, not merely of observing foot washing as an ordinance but of willingly serving our fellow men? How dedicated are we to the welfare of our students, our patients, our clients, our customers, our colleagues, our neighbors?

4

A REVOLUTIONARY COMMANDMENT

A new commandment I give unto you, That ye love one another; as I have loved you, that ye also love one another. John 13:34.

In 1798 the French Revolution was drawing to its close. Thousands of heads had rolled from the guillotine. All authority, including the authority of God, had been defied. Terror had reigned.

In the same year—1798—a different type of revolutionary lived on the shore of Lake Lucerne in Switzerland. Johann Pestalozzi, an educator, assumed the responsibility for eighty orphans left destitute when French troops destroyed their Swiss village. The children were far from an easy assignment. They were covered with vermin, afflicted with sores, undernourished, and ill. Some were brazen and deceitful and devoid of affection. The accepted manner of handling such a motley group would have been to frighten them into submission.

But Pestalozzi had a different idea. He had discovered that the essential principle of education is love, and he proceeded to apply this principle to his eighty ruffians. "I was persuaded," he said, "that my affection would change the state of my children just as quickly as the spring sun would awake to new life the earth that winter had benumbed. And I was not deceiving myself: before the spring sun melted the snow of our mountains my children were hardly to be recognized."—RONALD GROSS (ed.), *The Teacher and the Taught,* p. 65.

After Pestalozzi had spent years of demonstrating the principle of love in the education of children, his countrymen gave him the epitaph "all for others, nothing for himself."

Who was a real "revolutionary"—the hothead of Paris who shouted, "Liberty, Equality, Fraternity," or the quiet teacher of the Alps who whispered, "Love"?

The world in which we live is full of hotheaded revolutionaries. They storm embassies, incite riots, swarm campuses, overturn governments. Some of their causes may be good, but their method is that of hate. Our world needs warmhearted Christians who will reveal the transforming power of love.

VARIETIES OF LOVE

This is my commandment, That ye love one another, as I have loved you. Greater love hath no man than this, that a man lay down his life for his friends. John 15:12, 13.

This passage represents the highest level love can reach. Christians are asked to love one another with the same kind of self-forgetting love that Christ revealed on Calvary. This reminds us that there are different grades of love:

"The love for equals is a human thing—of friend for friend, brother for brother. It is to love what is loving and lovely. The world smiles.

"The love for the less fortunate is a beautiful thing—the love for those who suffer, for those who are poor, the sick, the failures, the unlovely. This is compassion, and it touches the heart of the world.

"The love for the more fortunate is a rare thing—to love those who succeed where we fail, to rejoice without envy with those who rejoice, the love of the poor for the rich, of the black man for the white man. The world is always bewildered by its saints.

"And then there is the love for the enemy—love for the one who does not love you but mocks, threatens, and inflicts pain. The tortured's love for the torturer. This is God's love. It conquers the world."—FREDERICK BUECHNER, *The Magnificent Defeat*, p. 105.

The world can use all the varieties of love listed above, but it is the special privilege of the Christian to reveal the last and greatest variety. This is what Jesus means when He commands, "Love one another, as I have loved you." This is the love Jesus manifested when, on the cross, He prayed for His persecutors. This is the kind of love Moses expressed when he offered to have his name erased from God's book rather than to see his people lost. This was Paul's love: "I could wish that myself were accursed from Christ for my brethren, my kinsmen according to the flesh" (Rom. 9:3).

It is intriguing to speculate what a few statesmen, religious leaders, educators, and businessmen with this type of love might do toward straightening out the affairs of the world.

99

JESUS DEFINES HIS RELATIONSHIP TO HIS FOLLOWERS

Henceforth I call you not servants; for the servant knoweth not what his lord doeth: but I have called you friends; for all things that I have heard of my Father I have made known unto you. John 15:15.

"Not slaves, but friends." The follower of Jesus need not live in cringing fear like a slave. He need not live in ignorance of the plans and purposes of his Master. He need not experience the insecurity that accompanies bondage. For, according to this passage, Christianity is not bondage, it is friendship. Our Lord is our companion, and He reveals to us the wisdom and will of His Father.

This great truth has much to do with the success or failure of our Christian lives. If we live like slaves, cowering before an authority we neither know nor love, we will find little satisfaction in our religious life. But if we commune with our Lord as friends, we will understand the purposes of God and we will have an impelling motivation for our Christian service.

Leslie D. Weatherhead has said, "I cannot be like him by trying to be like him. I can only be like him in the truest sense if, through his endless grace, he gives himself to me. The Christian Gospel offers the 'power to overcome.' Only so is it a gospel—good news—at all. It doesn't say, 'Here is an example; copy it,' for then all the emphasis is on my power to do so, to concentrate, to apply myself to the mighty task. Christianity says, 'Here is a Friend; open your heart to him, for he can do for you and in you and with you something that is now beyond you.'"—*This Is the Victory,* pp. 65, 66.

This is at the center of the Christian doctrine of justification by faith. Christianity becomes more than a set of rules—it is Christ; and the impact of Christianity on our own lives is proportional to our experience with the transforming friendship with Christ. It is not necessary that we live lives of slavish fear when the grand privilege of friendship with Christ may be ours.

"All things that I have heard of my Father I have made known unto you." What a wonderful revelation! Jesus is the go-between who interprets God to His followers.

100

ON BEING A MINORITY

I pray not that thou shouldest take them out of the world, but that thou shouldest keep them from the evil. John 17:15.

In the second century of the Christian era an unknown Christian writer described his fellow believers as follows:

"Christians are not distinguishable from the rest of mankind in land or speech or customs. They inhabit no special cities of their own, nor do they use any different form of speech, nor do they cultivate any out-of-the-way life. . . . But while they live in Greek and barbarian cities as their lot may be cast, and follow local customs in dress and food and life generally, . . . yet they live in their own countries as sojourners only; they take part in everything as citizens and submit to everything as strangers. Every strange land is native to them, and every native land is strange. They marry and have children like everyone else—but they do not expose their children. They have meals in common, but not wives. They are in the flesh, but they do not live after the flesh. They continue on earth, but their citizenship is in heaven. They obey the laws ordained, and by their private lives they overcome the laws. . . . In a word, what the soul is in the body, that is what Christians are in the world."— Epistle to Diognetus, chaps. 5, 6, quoted in T. R. GLOVER, *Conflict of Religions in the Early Roman Empire,* pp. 159, 160.

One sentence of this description seems especially applicable to the twentieth century: "Every strange land is native to them, and every native land is strange." It has often been noticed that Adventist Christians are found almost everywhere in the world. Truly, every strange land is native to us, but the remainder of the statement is also true—"every native land is strange." There is a difference in objectives and in manner of life that is evident in every culture.

As a member of a minority, the Adventist must learn how to be redemptive rather than hostile, distinctive rather than merely different. To be part of the world and yet not influenced by the world's selfishness, violence, impurity, and dishonesty is a worthy accomplishment. Such detached attachment is the foundation of effective witnessing. The second-century Christians set us a good example.

101

"IT IS ACCOMPLISHED"

When Jesus therefore had received the vinegar, he said, It is finished: and he bowed his head, and gave up the ghost. John 19:30.

"Nearly two thousand years of sacred history are contained in that cry from the Cross, 'It is finished!', or in the more accurate translation from the *New English Bible,* 'It is accomplished'. It was a cry of triumph, like the cry of a commando soldier who has smashed the last defence of the enemy and sees the forces of freedom surging through the breach into victory. Though he lies there mortally wounded, he dies peacefully, gasping to his officer, 'Mission accomplished, sir!' That was the meaning of our Lord's cry from the cross—mission accomplished! The purpose of his life fulfilled! The last defence of Satan smashed, and man delivered forever from the tyranny of evil. Christ on Calvary brought to fulfilment the plan of reconciliation which God had been working out ever since man first disobeyed him in the Garden of Eden. On Calvary Christ brought God and man together, paid the terrible price of God's forgiveness and consummated the new covenant between God and man which nothing could annul. 'It is accomplished!' With that triumphant cry the Lord of Glory bowed his head and gave up his spirit. In that sense the Cross represents the finished work of God.

"Yet there is also a sense in which the Cross remains unfinished. We can say that something came to an end on Calvary and that there on that skull-shaped hill outside a city wall a work of God was once and for all accomplished. We can also say, however, that something started on Calvary. For God the Cross represented the end of a drama; for man it represented the beginning."—LEONARD GRIFFITH, *God's Time and Ours,* pp. 88, 89.

Ellen White wrote: "By transgression man was severed from God, the communion between them was broken; but Jesus Christ died upon the cross of Calvary, bearing in His body the sins of the whole world, and the gulf between heaven and earth was bridged by that cross." —In *The SDA Bible Commentary,* on 1 Peter 3:24, p. 941.

A CYNIC IN EDEN

The serpent was more subtil than any beast of the field which the Lord God had made. And he said unto the woman, Yea, hath God said, Ye shall not eat of every tree of the garden? . . . And the serpent said unto the woman, Ye shall not surely die: for God doth know that in the day ye eat thereof, then your eyes shall be opened, and ye shall be as gods, knowing good and evil. Gen. 3:1-5.

The atmosphere of Eden was one of perfect love, trust, and confidence between God and man. Then came the great cynic, whispering into the ear of man, "You're being brainwashed. Eat of the forbidden tree, and you will be as gods, knowing good and evil. Don't be naive. Insist on your rights. Never accept anything on the basis of mere authority."

This has been the message of the great cynic from that day to this. Sin came into the world when man allowed himself to be influenced to distrust God. Sin thrives when cynicism prevails.

When we see someone who is expending great efforts in Christian work we often ask, "I wonder what he's getting out of this." When someone lives very carefully we call him a legalist. When someone seems to be exemplary in character we call him a "square." When someone gives liberally to good causes we accuse him of trying to buy divine and human favor. We are so afraid of being gullible that we look at every good thing with a cynical eye.

"If you want a short-cut to wretchedness, get to the place where you do not believe in anybody. Some people seem to cultivate this disposition as if it were an asset. It is not an asset. It is the worst possible liability. If you want to make a hell for yourself in the here and now, cultivate the habit of seeing a selfish motive back of every seemingly unselfish act."—CLOVIS G. CHAPPELL, *Sermons on Biblical Characters*, p. 122.

It is better to err occasionally on the side of gullibility than on the side of cynicism. To make the mistake of thinking well of an unworthy person is not nearly as serious as to impugn the motives of a good person.

ADAM AND EVE HIDE FROM GOD

They heard the voice of the Lord God walking in the garden in the cool of the day: and Adam and his wife hid themselves from the presence of the Lord God amongst the trees of the garden. Gen. 3:8.

Never before had Adam and Eve been frightened when they heard the approach of God. Why now? They knew that they had disobeyed, and God's coming, which they had previously welcomed, now posed a threat to them.

Phillips Brooks is quoted as saying, "To keep clear of concealment, to keep clear of the need of concealment, to do nothing which he might not do out in the middle of Boston Common at noon-day— I cannot say how more and more that seems to me to be the glory of a young man's life. It is an awful hour when the first necessity of hiding anything comes. . . . Put off that day as long as possible. Put it off forever if you can."—In HARRY EMERSON FOSDICK, *Twelve Tests of Character,* p. 46.

Throughout the centuries many have tried to convince themselves that God is an "absentee landlord" or that He is not interested in the affairs of men or that He is dead. Only when they have disposed of God can they be comfortable in their sins, for the acknowledgment of God implies responsibility, moral rectitude, and final reckoning.

Many are like the small boy who runs away from home only to discover soon that home means security and love, as well as dicipline and responsibility.

In Job 36:26 one of Job's friends exclaims, "Behold, God is great, and we know him not." God *is* great, far greater than we can comprehend. If we don't know Him, might it be because we have hidden from Him as did Adam and Eve? We may be hiding among the trees of secularism—a creed that looks at life as if there were no God. We may be hiding among the trees of indifference, trying to forget the realities of life. We may be hiding among the trees of selfishness, concerned only about our own interests and desires. In any case, God is calling us, as He called Adam and Eve.

TWO BROTHERS WORSHIP GOD

In process of time it came to pass, that Cain brought of the fruit of the ground an offering unto the Lord. And Abel, he also brought of the firstlings of his flock and of the fat thereof. And the Lord had respect unto Abel and to his offering. Gen. 4:3, 4.

The two sons of Adam and Eve came to worship God. It was commendable that neither of these men had forgotten his Creator. It seemed perfectly logical that Cain, the tiller of the soil, should bring of the fruit of the ground; and that Abel, the keeper of sheep, should bring of his flock. Why, then, was God displeased?

In this incident is illustrated a truth about the worship of God that has eternal significance—*worship must have a theological basis.* In other words, worship must not be just what we want to do to honor God, but what God has asked us to do to honor Him.

Throughout the ages men have devised all sorts of ways of worshiping God. Some have bowed down to idols; some have worshiped the heavenly bodies; some have deified animals; some have offered their own children. The story of Cain and Abel teaches us that, however logical and culture-oriented an act of worship appears to be, God is pleased only with the procedures of worship that He Himself has established.

This means that in choosing a day of worship we are to seek to discover God's choice rather than our own; in determining a manner of worship we are to look for our models in the New Testament. Tradition must be tested by a "Thus saith the Lord."

Jesus said that the true worshiper must worship in "spirit and in truth." Cain may have worshiped in spirit—we do not know— but his homage lacked the element of truth. We may worship in truth, but fail to worship in spirit. Apparently Abel sensed both aspects of worship. May we have the grace to do likewise.

When Cain became aware that God was not pleased with his offering, he became very angry, "and his countenance fell." God tried to reason with him, but he seemed unable to react intelligently —he resorted to violence. This, in itself, indicates the shallowness of his worship.

VIOLENCE

God said unto Noah, The end of all flesh is come before me;
for the earth is filled with violence through them; and, behold,
I will destroy them with the earth. Gen. 6:13.

I am writing this section on June 6, 1968, the morning after the shooting of Senator Robert F. Kennedy. A few weeks ago Dr. Martin Luther King was assassinated. All of us remember vividly the shooting of President John F. Kennedy in November, 1963. A news commentator during the past twenty-four hours has pointed out that, since the time of President Lincoln, four presidents have been assassinated, with attempts on the lives of two others. This is a high percentage. In addition to attacks on the lives of public figures, thousands are dying every year at the hands of murderers. As I look out of my office window I can see the American flag flying at half mast. It would not be inappropriate to leave it there permanently.

In the time of Noah, violence was one of the reasons God gave for cutting short the history of that age. The psalmist said, "The Lord trieth the righteous: but the wicked and him that loveth violence his soul hateth" (Ps. 11:5). Regarding his contemporaries, God said to Ezekiel, "They have filled the land with violence" (Eze. 8:17). In his counsel to the soldiers of his day, John the Baptist said, "Do violence to no man" (Luke 3:14).

There are many reasons for this distressing situation, one of which is pointed out by Billy Graham in his book, *World Aflame:* "We have taught during the past few decades that morals are relative, and now we are reaping the harvest."—Page 4. Concerned people are pleading for a solution to the problem of violence. Social scientists are endeavoring to diagnose the problem. Some point to war, some to movies and television, some to social unrest. But few voices are being heard suggesting the *real* solution to the problem—faith in a God who said, "Thou shalt not kill."

Before these words are read, more acts of violence will have taken place. And when these words are read, we will all be nearer that day when it can be said, "Violence shall no more be heard in thy land" (Isa. 60:18).

THE CITY BUILDERS

They said, Go to, let us build us a city and a tower, whose top may reach unto heaven; and let us make us a name, lest we be scattered abroad upon the face of the whole earth. **Gen. 11:4.**

The history of mankind has largely been a history of his cities. While men have a nostalgia for the country and its freedom and fresh air, the real source of power and culture is the city. During recent decades the movement to the city has been dramatic. A large percentage of the people of the world live in cities such as Tokyo, London, New York, Rome, Paris, Chicago, and Los Angeles.

What does the city mean to the church? A study of the New Testament church is a study of the cities of the day. Paul wrote his Epistles to Christians in Rome, Corinth, Ephesus, Thessalonica, and other cities. The seven churches of Revelation were located in seven cities. In other words, New Testament Christianity was largely urban. It began in Jerusalem and jumped from city to city throughout the world of the day.

Most of the readers of this book live in cities and towns. While it is true that the time will come when the cities of the nations will fall, the Christian is now instructed to be a leaven to reflect the love of God in the congested areas where men have largely forgotten Him.

The city church should not be a cell, withdrawn from its environment, interested only in itself. The members of this church should reflect Christ in their places of employment and in their contacts with people. Incidentally, the city church should be where it can be found. Its location, its appearance, and its activities should witness for Christ.

The problems of the city are many. Poverty, crime, and racial tension exist alongside wealth, culture, and education. To some the city means opportunity, to others it means despair. People tend to lose their identity in the city, and what city dweller has entirely escaped the loneliness of the crowd?

The day will come when Babylon and all of its urban successors will fade away, and the New Jerusalem, the city of God, will take its place. In the meantime, may Christians be the "salt" of the cities.

THE MAN WHO STOPPED TOO SOON

Terah took Abram his son, and Lot the son of Haran his son's son, and Sarai his daughter in law, his son Abram's wife; and they went forth with them from Ur of the Chaldees, to go into the land of Canaan; and they came unto Haran, and dwelt there. And the days of Terah were two hundred and five years: and Terah died in Haran. Gen. 11:31, 32.

Terah and his family started for Canaan, but got only halfway to their destination. When they reached Haran, for some reason they settled down until after the death of Terah. Perhaps Haran was a very attractive stopping place, or possibly their resources ran low, or it might have been that they became tired of traveling, or perhaps they were able to rationalize that Haran was actually their destination.

In any case, Terah missed the thrills of seeing the land of promise, because he stopped too soon. It was for his son Abram to complete the adventure begun so many years before.

In this experience is an illustration of what often happens to Christians—they begin well, but stop too soon. The fires of youthful idealism are banked too early. The "first love" of the conversion experience gradually is supplanted by mere routine Christianity. The good seed gives promise of a bountiful harvest, but "the care of this world, and the deceitfulness of riches, choke the word, and he becometh unfruitful" (Matt. 13:22).

"We are like explorers who land on some new continent, and who, on fine days and Saturday afternoons, explore some of the valleys and foothills near the coast, and then build themselves bungalows and settle down on the beach and bathe in the breakers, but who never climb the mighty mountains behind them, where the resources of a continent lie waiting to be explored."—LESLIE D. WEATHERHEAD, *The Transforming Friendship*, p. 52.

How many of us, like Terah, have started for Canaan and stopped in Haran? How many of us have decided that full commitment is too costly, and have settled for something less? Is it not time for us to leave our comfortable stopping places and heed the call that beckons us to explore that which is beyond?

LOT MAKES A BAD DECISION

The Lord said unto Abram, after that Lot was separated from him, Lift up now thine eyes, and look from the place where thou art northward, and southward, and eastward, and westward: for all the land which thou seest, to thee will I give it, and to thy seed for ever. **Gen. 13:14, 15.**

This was not the first time, nor was it the last, that God spoke these words to Abram. A study of the text indicates that God repeated this promise many times, and He seemed always to choose an occasion when the promise was particularly appropriate.

Genesis 13 tells us how Abram and Lot went into partnership in a large cattle business. They were so successful that there was not enough grazing land for their herds. This resulted in tension between the employees of Abram and those of Lot. Each was out to protect the interests of his master.

Someone had to take the initiative to find a solution for the problem. In harmony with his largeness of heart Abram said, "Let there be no strife, I pray thee, between me and thee, and between my herdmen and thy herdmen; for we be brethren. Is not the whole land before thee? separate thyself, I pray thee, from me; if thou wilt take the left hand, then I will go to the right; or if thou depart to the right hand, then I will go to the left" (verses 8 and 9).

Lot was faced with a decision. We are not to conclude that the plain of Jordan with its degenerative cities was his only alternative. But Lot was attracted by the luxury and wealth of the Jordan area and doubtless found various ways to rationalize his choice.

Abram, with his greater wisdom and experience, no doubt recognized the mistake Lot was making. He surely wondered whether he had done the right thing in dealing permissively with the younger man. At this point the familiar voice of God again broke the stillness. Abram's attitude was pleasing to God, and his Friend repeated to him the promise regarding the ultimate destiny of his descendants. With the voice of God echoing in his heart, Abram went to Hebron and "built there an altar unto the Lord" (verse 18). What an object lesson on the results of right and wrong decisions!

"FEAR NOT"

After these things the word of the Lord came unto Abram in a vision, saying, Fear not, Abram: I am thy shield, and thy exceeding great reward. Gen. 15:1.

This is the first occurrence in the Bible of the expression "fear not," a command that is repeated many times.

Abram had just been through a traumatic experience. A battle among the tribal chieftains in the area had resulted in Lot and his family's being taken captive. Although not a man of war, Abram mobilized an army of 318 men, pursued the enemy, and delivered Lot and his family.

Abram evidently had some uneasy moments after this battle was over. What if the defeated kings should retaliate? Could he complete what he started? How about the bloodshed in which he had been involved? All of this was foreign to Abram, and he worried about it.

As in many other stressful situations, God appeared to Abram with the comforting assurance "Be not afraid." As one translation reads, "I am your shield; your reward shall be very great" (R.S.V.). Then, to reinforce this assurance, God repeated to Abram the promise that his posterity would become a great nation.

God has repeated over and over again the same words, "Fear not," to His anxious children. "I will fear no evil: for thou art with me" has been an oft-repeated refrain of the people of God through the ages. "Fear not: for I have redeemed thee. . . ; thou art mine" is one of the most comforting passages of Scripture. "Fear not, little flock" was a part of the message of Jesus. The final book of the Bible tells us, "Fear not; I am the first and the last."

"An English scholar was traveling in India and saw a poor untouchable woman working in a paddy field under a blazing sun. He asked a missionary friend what an illiterate outcast like that could really understand of the Christian faith. And the missionary replied, 'She understands that Christ is stronger than the demons.' "—GERALD H. KENNEDY, *Fresh Every Morning,* p. 155.

Christ has a remedy for fear that is adequate for all. In this age of fear, man needs to listen to the divine command, "Fear not."

ABRAHAM'S FAITH

[Abram] believed in the Lord; and he counted it to him for righteousness. Gen. 15:6.

God had just repeated to Abraham the promise that his posterity would be as numerous as the stars of heaven. This promise seemed incredible, for Abram had no heir. Despite the seeming impossibility that God's promise could be fulfilled, the record says that "he believed the Lord; and he reckoned it to him as righteousness" (R.S.V.).

Many years later, Paul, in his letter to the Romans, reviewed Abraham's experience, endeavoring to show that Abraham was not justified by works. He quoted our text, "Abraham believed God, and it was counted unto him for righteousness" (Rom. 4:3).

Again in the New Testament, James teaches that true faith is accompanied by works. Referring to Abraham's complete dedication to God, he too quotes Genesis 15:6 (James 2:23).

What does this text tell us about Abraham? First, he "believed God." When God told him that a seemingly impossible thing would take place he believed it. When God told him to do a seemingly cruel and destructive thing he believed that, if necessary, "God was able to raise him [Isaac] up, even from the dead" (Heb. 11:19). He accepted God's promise and followed His directions, knowing that all would work out for the best.

This willingness to accept God's word by faith "was counted unto him for righteousness." Abraham was very human, and he made mistakes, but his confidence in God made it possible for God to lead him. He was considered a righteous man. This means that God forgave his sins and helped him perfect a godly life. At all times—even when Abraham wavered—God accepted him as His child.

The parallel between Abraham's faith and ours is made clear in the closing verses of Romans 4. After repeating that Abraham's faith was reckoned to him, Paul says, "But the words, 'it was reckoned to him,' were written not for his sake alone, but for ours also. It will be reckoned to us who believe in him that raised from the dead Jesus our Lord" (R.S.V.).

"CASUALTIES OF IMPATIENCE"

Sarai Abram's wife took Hagar her maid the Egyptian, after Abram had dwelt ten years in the land of Canaan, and gave her to her husband Abram to be his wife. Gen. 16:3.

God had promised Abram that his posterity would be a great nation. This sounded good, but there was one problem—Sarai had no children. After the passing of ten years Abram and Sarai decided to solve the problem by resorting to the common practice of polygamy.

The result of this polygamous arrangement was tragic. If Abram and Sarai had only waited they would have learned that God had a plan beyond their comprehension. The eventual birth of Isaac solved the problem, whereas the union with Hagar only created problems.

How often by our impatience we create problems for ourselves! Dr. Joseph R. Sizoo tells the following story: "I recall very well an experience of the World War. We were at the front on the St. Mihiel sector. The order had come to advance. The artillery behind us was to pour ammunition on the area we were to take. Then, after a period of bombardment, the barrage was to lift and the infantry was to take possession of the territory. Orders were given to the infantry not to advance beyond a certain line, but to wait until the barrage had lifted. But the infantry advanced so rapidly and were so anxious to capture the whole area that they could not wait, and advancing far beyond the agreed position, were shot down by their own artillery. Gradually these casualties began to come back to first aid stations, some on stretchers, some limping. It was a pitiful sight. The enemy had not attacked them. The opposing artillery had not shelled them. They had impatiently advanced and been shot down by their own artillery. In some respects it was one of the most tragic spectacles of the whole war. There they were, the casualties of impatience; they could not wait."—*Not Alone,* pp. 41, 42.

Young people quit school and get a job because they can't wait for financial security. Others marry before they are ready for marriage, and too often increase the divorce statistics. People of all ages precipitate crises over issues that time would solve. Let us not be "casualties of impatience."

112

AN ANCIENT LOVE AFFAIR

Isaac . . . took Rebekah, and she became his wife; and he loved her. **Gen.** 24:67.

"A man consulted a psychiatrist about the best thing to do for his children. He expected to receive advice about their training, their schooling, and the cultural advantages he ought to give them. But the psychiatrist, who was a very wise man, said simply, 'The best thing a father can do for his children is love their mother.' Ah, this is something we forget. The child who lives in a house where love is real is blessed far beyond the child whose father can write him a big check."
—GERALD H. KENNEDY, *Fresh Every Morning,* p. 112.

When two or three airplane accidents occur in close succession, steps are immediately taken to improve air safety standards. When thousands of marriages fail, shouldn't someone get concerned about the wretched problem of broken homes? There is something withering and devastating about divorce. The road from the happy wedding to the divorce court is one of the greatest tragedies that can come in a human life. How can these horrible disasters be prevented?

The experience of Isaac and Rebekah gives a partial answer. First, though their wedding was arranged according to the customs of a different culture, opportunity was granted for the guidance of God. Many young people refuse to give God a chance to lead them. They are afraid He will direct in a way contrary to their wishes.

Second, it is said of Isaac, "He loved her." Apparently his love was the real thing, for it lasted until death separated them. Isaac and Rebekah had their problems. Their twin sons were sometimes a source of concern. The hatred between Jacob and Esau clouded their mother's latter days. But, despite their heartaches, there seems to have been a stability in the home produced by the love Isaac and Rebekah had for each other.

"The family tie is the closest, the most tender and sacred, of any on earth. It was designed to be a blessing to mankind. And it is a blessing wherever the marriage covenant is entered into intelligently, in the fear of God, and with due consideration for its responsibilities."—*The Ministry of Healing,* pp. 356, 357.

THE PRICE OF PEACE

*He removed from thence, and digged another well; and for
that they strove not.* Gen. 26:22.

Isaac is the hero of this story. His servants dug a well in the
valley of Gerar in the southern part of the Philistine country and
found an abundance of good water. Water was precious in that arid
country, and the native herdsmen soon claimed the well.

Then Isaac's servant dug another well, and the neighbors dis-
puted their ownership of that well. Finally, the well diggers sought
a third location and tried again. This time they were allowed to
enjoy the fruits of their labors in peace. Isaac said, "Now the Lord
hath made room for us, and we shall be fruitful in the land" (verse
22, last part).

While the story doesn't go into detail, it seems that Isaac and
his group would rather move than fight. Each of the first two wells
could have been the site of bitter warfare and bloodletting had the
well diggers asserted their rights.

It would be unrealistic to draw from this experience the in-
ference that Christians should never stand up for their rights. There
are times when self-defense is proper. But in many of the experiences of life it would be better to follow the example of Isaac and
his men, and move away from trouble rather than become involved
in conflict.

Paul said, "If it be possible, as much as lieth in you, live peac-
ably with all men" (Rom. 12:18). The person who refuses to fight
generally wins the argument in the long run. God bless the church
member who will never become involved in church squabbles, the
neighbor who is never disagreeable, the player who isn't always
arguing with the umpire, the committee member who avoids friction.

Isaac's attitude would solve many of the problems that beset
churches, homes, businesses, and nations today. Jesus expressed the
same idea in the Sermon on the Mount. "If any man wants to sue
you for your shirt, let him have your coat as well" (Matt. 5:40,
N.E.B.). Some people think nonresistance is impractical, but it has
probably solved more conflicts than all the battles of history.

114

JACOB AND ESAU RECONCILED

Esau said, I have enough, my brother; keep that thou hast unto thyself. And Jacob said, Nay, I pray thee, if now I have found grace in thy sight, then receive my present at my hand: for therefore I have seen thy face, as though I had seen the face of God, and thou wast pleased with me. Take, I pray thee, my blessing that is brought to thee; because God hath dealt graciously with me, and because I have enough. And he urged him, and he took it. Gen. 33:9-11.

This is the beautiful scene of reconciliation between two brothers who had long been enemies. At this touching meeting old hatreds vanished because, for a time at least, each of the brothers was genuinely interested in the welfare of the other. It was selfishness that had torn them apart, and love was now pulling them together. And, incidentally, their fear of each other vanished.

Two brothers lived on neighboring farms. One night the older brother, sitting by his fire with his family around him, said, "My brother must be lonely over there. He has no wife and children. I have so much more than he; I will go out and take some of the sheaves of my field and carry them over to his field."

And over there the other brother thought to himself, My brother must have a hard time of it. I have no wife and children to take care of. He must need much more than I do. I will go and take some of the sheaves of my field and put them on his.

So each added to the other's goods in secret, until one night they met each other with their arms loaded.

What a difference there could be in homes, churches, schools, offices, places of business, and nations if men could catch this idea of mutual concern. Some translations of the Bible render the song of the angels at the birth of Christ as follows: "Glory to God in the highest Heaven! Peace upon earth among men of goodwill" (Luke 2:14, Phillips). A planned effort to add to the happiness of other people will bring happiness both to the giver and the receiver. This is Christian love. This is the way of life that Jesus taught mankind.

AN HOUR OF TERROR

There passed by Midianites merchantmen; and they drew and lifted up Joseph out of the pit, and sold Joseph to the Ishmeelites for twenty pieces of silver: and they brought Joseph into Egypt. Gen. 37:28.

It would be hard to imagine a more terrifying experience than the one here described. Picture a pampered teen-ager who had lived a sheltered life being sold to a caravan of traders. Imagine the fear, the uncertainty, the loneliness of the days and weeks that followed.

There were some things Joseph could not know. He could not foresee the day when he would be a responsible official in the land of his slavery. He could not in his wildest dreams imagine a time when he would be a source of support for his father and his brothers.

"A weaver stands before his loom. Before him there are many shuttles. Each shuttle holds a tinted thread. One is orange, another is blue, this one is violet, that one is gray and another is black. It is grossly unfair to judge the purpose of the weaver by one thrust of the shuttle with the black or the gray. Wait until all the shuttles have tangled their threads into a perfect tapestry of beautiful design. God is at the loom. Before Him are many shuttles with many tinted threads of the days of life. Some days are brilliant like crimson; some are gay like the violet; some are hopeful with blue; some are gray and black. Do not judge the weaver until He has emptied each shuttle of its last stray thread and woven them into the tapestry of a triumphant life. Give Him time."—JOSEPH R. SIZOO, *Way of Faith,* pp. 19, 20.

Out of darkness, discouragement, misfortune, and despair have emerged some of the richest lives. Think of Helen Keller and her struggle with blindness and deafness. Think of Robert Louis Stevenson and his battle with tuberculosis. If any reader of these lines is facing apparent defeat, and is wondering whether God has a plan for his life, let him remember the terrified teen-ager following a camel train to the land of his slavery. And let him never forget how God was able to bring good out of evil. Give God time. Out of our hours of terror may come the richest experiences of life.

JOSEPH'S BROTHERS SEARCH THEIR CONSCIENCES

They said one to another, We are verily guilty concerning our brother, in that we saw the anguish of his soul, when he besought us, and we would not hear; therefore is this distress come upon us. Gen. 42:21.

Many years earlier, ten ruthless and wicked young men sold their younger brother to a wandering group of traders. In order to cover up their cruel act, they deceived their father into believing that he had met with an accident.

It is not hard to imagine the self-hatred and remorse that had gripped these men through the years. No doubt they often dreamed of that day when they had rejected their brother's plea for mercy. To sell a teen-age boy into slavery was a terrible crime, and the guilty brothers realized this fact more and more as they grew older.

Whenever misfortune came, they were tempted to feel that, at last, Providence was punishing them. Such was the case when they made the admission recorded in our text for today. They were in the grip of a famine and had gone to Egypt for supplies, but the officer who distributed the grain demanded that they bring their younger brother. This request stirred up memories of their crime of many years before, memories that were far from pleasant.

Never could these guilty brothers find happiness until their guilt was discovered and some sort of redress was made for their cruelty. Yet, not one of them dared admit what he had done. They doubtless tried to rationalize their deed, but the passing of many years could not erase it from their minds.

There is no tyrant so cruel as an accusing conscience. There is no escape from it except making the wrong right. Sometimes, as in the case of Joseph's brothers, circumstances bring the sin to light. In other cases men carry their guilt to their graves. The Christian gospel has a wonderful provision for guilty people—forgiveness, offered free to those who ask for it in faith. This forgiveness is not a lack of concern for sin. It is a type of soul surgery that results in changed lives. The surgery may be painful, but there can be no spiritual health until the dark secrets of the past are forgiven.

117

JOSEPH REASSURES HIS BROTHERS

Joseph said unto his brethren, Come near to me, I pray you. And they came near. And he said, I am Joseph your brother, whom ye sold into Egypt. Now therefore be not grieved, nor angry with yourselves, that ye sold me hither: for God did send me before you to preserve life. Gen. 45:4, 5.

Joseph's forebearance and insight have their modern counterpart in a story attributed to a Presbyterian minister, Frederick A. Roblee:

"Some years ago during an outbreak of anti-Semitism on the campus of one of the universities of New York City, a certain Gentile student attacked a certain Jewish student with such violence that he feared he had killed him. In panic, he fled and, eluding detection, made his way to a distant part of the country. There, after some years, he prospered and became an official of a utilities company. A serious problem arose and his company sent for a specialist of a big Eastern utility concern. To his horror, when the specialist from the East arrived, who should it be but this Jew . . . !

"Now, bent and crippled for life as he was, the Jew sensed the situation at once. Quietly, he said: 'I know some of the things that must be going through your mind. Let me say a word or two, and then we'll just mark it down as a closed incident. I spent two years in a hospital. That gave me a lot of time to think things through. It made me more than ever determined to make good—not only for myself, but also for you and others like you, who, for some reason or another, do not believe that Jews are entitled to the advantages and opportunities of our American system. . . . My deformity has been a driving force, an incentive, and not an unsurmountable handicap. I bear no ill will toward you. On the contrary, I intend to throw our whole resources behind your organization and make it possible for you to undertake a large expansion here.'"—*Source Unknown.*

The stories of Joseph and this modern Jew teach us several things: first, misfortune need not bar the way to success; second, the wheel of life often makes a complete turn, forcing us to face our sins; and finally, one of the greatest attainments a great man can reach is the willingness to forgive his worst enemies.

JOSEPH SEES GOD BEHIND THE SHADOWS

As for you, ye thought evil against me: but God meant it unto good. Gen. 50:20.

It is hard to imagine a greater wrong than that which Joseph had suffered at the hands of his brothers. He had been threatened with death, was imprisoned in a pit, and sold as a slave. He had been taken to a far country and unjustly imprisoned. Finally, however, through the grace of God and his own excellence, he had achieved a position of trust.

Joseph could have said to his brothers, "It matters not that I have achieved success in Egypt. You were cruel and wicked in your treatment of me, and I can never forgive you. Now is my opportunity to treat you as you deserve." But Joseph was willing to forgive because his appreciation of the providence of God was greater than his resentment of the wickedness of man.

Herein is a principle of great value. All through life we are constantly called upon to suffer as the result of man's inhumanity to man. To a greater or less degree, every person feels the sting of neglect, cruelty, misunderstanding, envy, jealousy, lack of concern. These experiences become especially painful when they involve those who should love us and protect us.

In many cases these bitter experiences breed lasting resentment that robs the sufferer of his peace and happiness. Sometimes people who are in the last years of their lives cannot forget the injustices of childhood. Sometimes those who have been cheated—perhaps out of an inheritance—can never be happy again, because they continually brood over their loss. Sometimes people boil inwardly for endless years over a lost job, a lost friendship, or a quarrel.

Joseph teaches us a better way to meet these inevitable conflicts. His prescription is to see in these unpleasant things the working of the hand of God. It was a long time before Joseph could see any good resulting from his suffering, but eventually the mystery was made clear. In many instances the hand of God may not be seen in this life, but eternity will demonstrate that God was at work even though His activity was never discerned.

119

MOSES BEGINS A NEW CAREER

Come now therefore, and I will send thee unto Pharaoh, that thou mayest bring forth my people the children of Israel out of Egypt. Ex. 3:10.

Picture yourself in Moses' place. Forty years earlier he had escaped Egypt as a criminal, wanted for murder. For four long decades he had been a shepherd in Midian—not a very exciting occupation. A failure at eighty, his prospects for the future amounted to a few more years herding sheep—then even greater oblivion.

His mind often went back to more interesting days—his early life in the palace, his young manhood in the Egyptian culture. But now—no hope; and for the future—no hope.

All this was changed the day he saw the burning bush. He received a challenging commission, with the promise of divine aid. Humbly he accepted the call, left his sheep, and set out for Egypt over that trail he had traversed forty years earlier. His return was not easy, but with God's help he accomplished his mission.

The next time he visited the area where he had been a shepherd, he was the leader of Israel's exodus from Egypt. The God who had talked to him from the bush addressed the entire multitude from the top of Sinai. In place of the sheepherder's simple camp, there was the encampment of Israel, with its pillar of cloud and fire. For forty years this man of God carried the burden of the leadership of Israel, a most demanding assignment.

What does Moses' experience teach us? First, that God's ways are inscrutable. No one could have planned a life like that of Moses. But when the time came, God had a man to do what needed to be done.

Second, that God does not forget His people. Humanly speaking, the lot of Israel seemed hopeless, but God had a plan for them.

Third, that God does not free His servants from anxieties and obstacles. The hardest period of Moses' life was the last forty years, and his career ended in a great disappointment.

But it was he who appeared on the Mount of Transfiguration with our Lord!

THE PEOPLE BELIEVED AND WORSHIPED

The people believed: and when they heard that the Lord had visited the children of Israel, and that he had looked upon their affliction, then they bowed their heads and worshipped. Ex. 4:31.

Moses and Aaron had arrived with good news for Israel—God was about to deliver them from slavery. The two brothers told the story of God's revelation to them and produced some convincing signs. As a result, "the people believed." They were convinced that God had commissioned Moses and Aaron to deliver them.

The people did something more than simply believe—"they bowed their heads and worshipped." Belief brought gratitude and appreciation, which they expressed by words of praise.

There is much concern in church circles regarding worship. Many books have been written on the subject, and many forms have been devised in an effort to structure the worship of Christians. Many definitions of worship have been suggested. Some time ago I was in a small group that was discussing the question of worship with a professor of a leading university, himself a recognized authority in the field of Christian worship. He stated the conviction that two of the main problems in maintaining a high level of worship in our time are (1) the lack of family worship in the home, and (2) the lack of confidence in the Bible. This man was saying that faith must precede real worship.

On another occasion I heard John R. W. Stott, pastor of All Souls Church, Langham Place, London, state in a sermon that a person cannot really worship who has not known what it means to be redeemed. Again, faith is presented as a prerequisite of worship.

Sometimes we wonder why decorum is poor in church services, why "worshipers" seem to do everything but worship. Can it be that we, like Israel, must believe before we can worship? Can it be that the lack of a living, radiant, saving faith is the reason for our clumsiness in the presence of God?

When people get a vision of the grace of God and the love of Christ, they cannot but worship. Without this vision, worship is empty form. Christian experience is the only foundation for it.

121

LET MY PEOPLE GO

Moses and Aaron came in unto Pharaoh, and said unto him, Thus saith the Lord God of the Hebrews, How long wilt thou refuse to humble thyself before me? let my people go, that they may serve me. Ex. 10:3.

Over and over again Moses and Aaron appeared before Pharaoh with the same request, "Let my people go." Time and again the request was denied, but God kept increasing the pressure until His people were free. From the familiar experience of nearly thirty-five hundred years ago may be drawn a lesson that has lost none of its meaning—*God does not want His people in slavery.*

A few hundred years later Israel went into captivity again. Although the Babylonian captivity was the result of Israel's own mistakes, God finally found men who made it possible for those who wished to return to Jerusalem and freedom to do so.

During the centuries that followed the return from Babylonian exile the Jews became involved in spiritual bondage to a legalistic system of religion. Their lives were controlled by numerous regulations of human origin, and religious life became a burden. Again, God acted to free His people through the gospel of Jesus Christ. Speaking of this deliverance, Paul said, "Stand fast therefore in the liberty wherewith Christ hath made us free, and be not entangled again with the yoke of bondage" (Gal. 5:1).

There is yet another freedom that God desires: "But now being made free from sin, and become servants to God, ye have your fruit unto holiness, and the end everlasting life" (Rom. 6:22). This is the greatest freedom of all.

In the struggle against sin it is heartening to know that God wants us to be free. In fact, He desired our freedom so much that He gave His only Son to obtain that freedom. This is the very heart of the gospel.

Freedom from oppression, freedom from dehumanizing tradition, freedom from sin—these are the three freedoms God desires for us. To all the forces that would enslave man, God is saying, "Let my people go."

READY TO GO

Thus shall ye eat it; with your loins girded, your shoes on your feet, and your staff in your hand; and ye shall eat it in haste: it is the Lord's passover. Ex. 12:11.

Israel was preparing for their escape from Egypt. The lamb had been killed, the blood had been sprinkled on the doorposts, the Passover meal had been eaten, that which remained had been burned.

And here were the people—prepared to leave on a moment's notice. How glad they were to forsake their slave huts, their taskmasters, and the hardships of a life of slavery. How thrilled they were with the prospect of freedom, of adventure, and ultimately of a country of their own.

Regarding another and greater crisis in the world's history, Jesus says, "Be ye also ready." Readiness has important implications.

Being ready to go when the curtain is finally drawn will mean a complete severance of ties with this world. A ship cannot leave the dock until the ropes are all loosed. There is an old story of two men who rowed across a lake from their home to the nearest town, got drunk, and finally in the small hours of the morning, returned to their boat to row home. After hours of unsteady rowing, returning daylight and sobriety revealed that they had forgotten to untie the boat. All our ties with the past will have to be broken. There must be no looking back.

Being ready to go at the last day will also involve complete confidence in the One who is arranging for our exodus to the land of promise. Just as the Israelites had to have implicit trust in Moses and Aaron, risking their entire future in their hands, so the Christian must dedicate himself entirely to his Leader, Jesus Christ. There is no other way to life and freedom.

Finally, being ready to go when the Lord comes involves a deep desire for that which the Lord offers. Deliverance will be for those who "love his appearing." That love will not be generated in a moment, but will result from years of acquaintance with the Master.

Regarding that day, Jesus says, "Hold your heads high, for you will soon be free" (Luke 21:28, Phillips).

BEWARE OF SHORT CUTS!

It came to pass, when Pharaoh had let the people go, that God led them not through the way of the land of the Philistines, although that was near; for God said, Lest peradventure the people repent when they see war, and they return to Egypt: but God led the people about, through the way of the wilderness of the Red Sea. Ex. 13:17, 18.

"I can tell you about a short cut that will save you many miles." Did you ever hear these words as a response to your request for directions? And did you ever discover that the so-called short cut turned out to be longer, slower, and rougher than the main road?

Yes, there was a short cut to Canaan; but God saw that Israel was not ready to meet the dangers along the way. With good fortune they might have reached their destination in a few weeks. On the other hand, they might have become so frightened they would have returned to Egypt and bondage. Also, God recognized that Israel needed to mature before they were ready for nationhood. The experiences of the wilderness were intended to transform them from a nation of slaves to a responsible people.

Young people often look for short cuts. They say, "Why go to school for years and years when I can get a good job, get married, and avoid all this drudgery?" Many have taken this short cut, only to find themselves, in time, on a dead-end street.

Students try short cuts. "Why study so hard when I can bluff a little and cheat a little and get by!" Short cuts can prove disastrous.

Workers try short cuts. "Why be so particular about the material I put in this house, or the way I plan this classroom lecture, or the examination I give this aging patient, or the repair job I do on this motor?" Later in life the "short cutters" wonder why others are succeeding while they are failing. They blame politics, bad luck, bad breaks—everything but the real reason.

Christians try short cuts. "Why be so careful about my devotional life and my conduct? Surely the Lord isn't that particular!"

God doesn't seem to know about the short cuts. He generally takes us by the longest route. But if we follow on, we will arrive!

THE COMPLAINERS

They said unto Moses, Because there were no graves in Egypt, hast thou taken us away to die in the wilderness? wherefore hast thou dealt thus with us, to carry us forth out of Egypt? Is not this the word that we did tell thee in Egypt, saying, Let us alone, that we may serve the Egyptians? For it had been better for us to serve the Egyptians, than that we should die in the wilderness. Ex. 14:11, 12.

The first crisis at the Red Sea brought the first wave of complaints, and every subsequent crisis brought renewed complaints. It mattered not what the problem was—Egyptians, lack of water, lack of food, delay—the people always heaped their blame on their two best friends, God and Moses.

What is the better way to meet the crises of life? Robert Louis Stevenson—who encountered plenty of problems in his own experience—is quoted as saying, "Quiet minds cannot be perplexed or frightened, but go on in fortune or misfortune at their own private pace like the ticking of a clock during a thunderstorm." I think of the antique clock in my childhood home. For nearly forty years that clock rested on the same shelf, ticking away the hours, the days, and the years. All it demanded was to be wound once a week. There were two world wars and a depression during those forty years, but the clock never changed its pace.

Every pastor knows what I am talking about. There are people in his congregation who are always steady, no matter what befalls them. In prosperity or adversity, in sickness or in health, in success or failure, these people never waver. Their faith holds, their love continues, their hope burns bright. There are other people in many churches who are like those in Moses' congregation. Continually they complain. They are at odds with their neighbors, with their fellow church members, with their pastor. They are usually unhappy and often in a state of rebellion.

It has been said, "Mishaps are like knives, which either cut us or serve us, depending on whether we grasp them by the blade or by the handle." Have we learned how to face life?

WHEN THINGS SEEM HOPELESS

The Lord shall fight for you, and ye shall hold your peace.
Ex. 14:14.

Israel was encamped on the shore of the Red Sea. The army of Pharaoh was behind them, and the waters were in front of them. They were trapped. Their hopes for a better life were about to be dashed to pieces. Waves of paralyzing fear swept over the people, and a cry of anguish arose to God.

"And Moses said unto the people, Fear ye not, stand still, and see the salvation of the Lord, which he will shew to you to day" (verse 13). One can feel the struggle of fear against faith.

One of the great lessons taught in Scripture is that God often permits people to get into dangerous and difficult situations, then comes to their rescue. Obviously, God could have prevented the Egyptian armies from mobilizing. He could have struck them with a plague that would have stopped them far from the Red Sea. But He didn't choose to accomplish His purpose in this way. He permitted events to develop until the situation seemed hopeless, then He intervened.

Moses had grasped this idea. His faith overcame his fear, and he sent the word throughout the camp, "The Lord will fight for you, and you have only to be still" (R.S.V.). The way God delivered Israel is a matter of record. The people were commanded to go forward, and the sea parted before them.

The crises that frighten men and women today are different but no less real. One person may face financial loss; another, academic disgrace; another, the shattering of a love relationship; another, disabling illness; another, professional failure. These threats are as frightening as the Red Sea, the armies of Pharaoh, a lion's den, or a cross. To all who face these problems comes a Voice from beyond—"The Lord will fight for you." Millions have heard that Voice and, like Israel, have gone forward, and the sea has parted before them.

"You have only to be still." Patient trust is the *attitude* that can prepare the way for a solution to man's dilemmas. "Go forward" is the *procedure* that initiates the solution.

MOSES PRAISES GOD

The Lord is my strength and song, and he is become my salvation: he is my God, and I will prepare him an habitation; my father's God, and I will exalt him. Ex. 15:2.

Israel is now on the safe side of the Red Sea. The threat to their security is gone, and Moses is commemorating the great deliverance in song. In this song he testifies to what God means to him personally. The Lord, he says, is *my* strength, *my* song, *my* salvation, *my* God. Moses was able to make these assertions because of a long succession of personal experiences that had brought God very close to him.

The remainder of the text introduces a fascinating idea. After speaking so positively about *his* God, Moses adds, "My father's God." He recognized the object of his worship as the same God his father had served before him.

Someone has truthfully said, "God has no grandchildren." Religious experience cannot be inherited or reflected. In his book *World Christianity,* Dr. Henry P. Van Dusen mentions the familiar observation that "a great financial fortune in America may be expected to last about four generations. It is accumulated by the first; it is enjoyed by the second; it is dissipated by the third; it is gone for the fourth."

Dr. Van Dusen points out that a religious movement begins with a faith that is "a living, vibrant, all-pervading, all-controlling inner reality, holding unchallenged sovereignty over the purposes and loyalties and conduct of life." The next generation accepts their fathers' faith as an "inherited treasure," "gently removed from the controlling center of life." The third generation removes religious concerns still further from the center until they become "one among the incidental concerns of life." And, finally, the next generation forsakes God as unnecessary and "irrelevant." (Page 246.)

The process of disintegration, while all too common, is neither normative nor unavoidable. Like Moses, those who come from God-fearing lineage may have an experience of their own and may recognize God as their own, as well as their father's, God.

127

QUALITIES OF LEADERSHIP

Moreover thou shalt provide out of all the people able men, such as fear God, men of truth, hating covetousness; and place such over them, to be rulers of thousands, and rulers of hundreds, rulers of fifties, and rulers of tens. Ex. 18:21.

This instruction has an ageless application to church leaders— elders, deacons, Sabbath school teachers, lay activities leaders, and all the rest. It lists four qualifications for all who would aspire to positions in the church of God.

First, they must be "able men." No amount of sincerity will take the place of ability to do the thing that needs to be done. Ability, whether native or cultivated, is essential to successful leadership. This means that elders should learn how to read their Bibles aloud, to pray in public, to lead a worship service, to give good counsel on a church board. Deacons should be able to manage the business affairs of the church they serve. And all other officers should seek to be equal to their tasks.

Second, they must "fear God." Ability without dedication can be a curse. To fear God means to love, worship, and obey Him. It means to accept God as the center of the life.

Third, leaders must be "men of truth." The R.S.V. says, "men who are trustworthy." This means that the leader can be trusted. He will fulfill his promises and pay his obligations. He will meet his appointments and perform his work. No one ever has to check up on him to see that he is doing his duty. He takes responsibility, even though to do so sometimes means personal sacrifice. People like this were in demand in Moses' day, and they are still needed.

The fourth qualification, "hating covetousness" is rendered in R.S.V., "who hate a bribe." They cannot be bought. They will do what they believe is right, regardless of pressures. They are fair in their judgments.

These characteristics are not only necessary for rulers of thousands—they are also needed for rulers of tens. No church is so small that these requirements may be waived. No church is so large that violations of this code of leadership can be overlooked.

MOSES PLEADS FOR HIS PEOPLE

Moses returned unto the Lord, and said, Oh, this people have sinned a great sin, and have made them gods of gold. Yet now, if thou wilt forgive their sin—; and if not, blot me, I pray thee, out of thy book which thou hast written. Ex. 32:31, 32.

Here is one of the greatest examples in history of dedicated leadership. Israel had been difficult. From the Red Sea to Sinai they had blamed Moses for everything that had gone wrong. There had been no appreciation for his leadership. Now the congregation had let him down completely. The people who had heard the voice of God saying, "Thou shalt not make unto thee any graven image," had worshiped a calf, in Egyptian style.

But Moses had grown to love these rebellious people. They were his great concern, and he could not abandon them to the results of their waywardness. He was so closely identified with them that he was willing to share their punishment.

Such leadership is scarce. Dr. George Buttrick has told the story thus: "There are businessmen who see only things—sales-resistance, charts, profits; there are other businessmen who see faces—the faces of those who work for them, and the faces of those who have no work. There are statesmen who see only things—battleships, voting-booths, newspaper-headlines; and there are other statesmen who see faces—faces of the poor, faces of little children, and myriad faces slain in war. There are would-be preachers who see only things—church buildings, card-indices, year-book figures; and there are other preachers, ordained by a tenderness beyond the hand of man, who see faces—faces wistful and sin-scarred, lonely and brave. Jesus saw nothing on earth but faces; nothing in heaven but faces."—*Jesus Came Preaching,* p. 120.

Moses saw faces as he visualized his rebellious people. He saw men and women who had known nothing but the brutal lash of the taskmaster. He saw little children whose lives had been impoverished by poverty and slavery. His heart went out to these people, and he loved them despite their murmuring and their waywardness.

All who deal with people, take notice.

MOSES STRIKES THE ROCK

Moses and Aaron gathered the congregation together before the rock, and he said unto them, Hear now, ye rebels; must we fetch you water out of this rock? And Moses lifted up his hand, and with his rod he smote the rock twice: and the water came out abundantly, and the congregation drank, and their beasts also. Num. 20:10, 11.

For years Moses had been a paragon of patience. People had murmured, accused him falsely, rebelled against him, reviled him, but he always kept cool. I can imagine the skeptics in the crowd—and there always are such—saying about him, "You just wait. Some-day the old man will blow his top." And he did. Moses was a wonderful man, but he was human. He had his boiling point.

We may ask, Why was God so severe with Moses when he had served Him so well for so long? Could not God overlook Moses' action in a moment of impatience? God did forgive Moses and gave him a special entrance into heaven, but when Moses lost his temper he lost his influence.

Leadership carries a high price tag. Other people could reveal their impatience every day, but not Moses. The people expected more of him than they expected of themselves. Even though it was their rebelliousness that had provoked him, they were not mature enough to take that fact into account. They might justify their own sins, but never the smallest mistake in their leader.

The ancient Greeks recognized a certain quality of leadership, which they termed *ethos*. The word describes not what a man does, but what a man is. A minister, for example, is not only judged by his sermons and his skill as a leader but also by the image his parishioners have in their minds as to what a minister should be. This standard is usually higher than they hold for themselves.

Fortunately, God sees the heart, and He is more tolerant than people. But we live in a world of people, and our influence depends, not on what we are, but on what they think we are.

Yes, the price of leadership and influence is high—sometimes unreasonably high—but true leaders are willing to pay that price.

"HOW TO SIN AND BE HAPPY"

Balaam said unto the angel of the Lord, I have sinned; for I knew not that thou stoodest in the way against me: now therefore, if it displease thee, I will get me back again. Num. 22:34.

Balaam was playing a game with God. He was anxious to reap profit from serving Balak, yet he wanted to continue as a prophet of God. So he went as far as he dared in disobedience to God under the pretense that he was submitting to the guidance of God. Fortunately, God did not allow His prophet to go past the point of no return.

In his book *It Will Be Daybreak Soon* Archibald Rutledge tells of meeting old Anthony Lee, a Negro sage of repute, coming down the road one morning. A new preacher had come to town, and all the young people, or most of them, were flocking to hear his sermons. Rutledge asked Anthony what he thought of the new preacher.

Anthony replied, "Those young people who are going to hear him don't want religion. What they want is some one who can tell them *how to sin and be happy.*"—Page 93.

"How to sin and be happy." This was exactly what Balaam was trying to do. Balak had promised to give him anything he wanted if he would only pronounce a curse on Israel. Balaam desired the possessions and honor that Balak promised him. This overwhelming desire came in conflict with his loyalty to God. As a prophet, he could not easily wave aside the claims of God; but as a man he saw the fulfillment of his dreams in the promises of Balak. After several miserable days, the prophet learned that he could not sin and be happy.

Many are going through Balaam's experience. The world says to them, "Disregard God, and you may have riches and honor." The Lord says, "Follow me." Frequently they try, like Balaam, to do both. They attempt to rationalize un-Christian behavior, and to avoid taking up the cross. They want to serve Christ, but they don't want to pay the price.

131

THE UNWILLING PROPHET

Balaam said unto Balak, Lo, I am come unto thee: have I now any power at all to say any thing? the word that God putteth in my mouth, that shall I speak. Num. 22:38.

Balak, the king of Moab, was concerned about the large number of Israelites skirting his country on their way to Canaan. He felt his security would be strengthened if he could get a prophet to pronounce a curse upon the newcomers. He sent his representatives to Balaam, offering him a large fee if he would take the assignment. Balaam inquired of God and was told to refuse.

Balak would not take No for an answer. He sent more influential officers with a larger fee. Instead of saying No, Balaam inquired of God again, and God gave permission—with the understanding that Balaam speak only the word of God.

Balaam should have recognized how untenable his position was and should have refused to go. But he went. He had transportation problems on the way, but with a persistence worthy of a better cause, he kept on going. Having arrived, he found himself in a most embarrassing situation. After all the offerings had been offered and the preliminaries had been completed, Balaam heard his own voice blessing Israel in the presence of Balak and his princes. If there ever was a man who wished he had stayed home, it must have been Balaam, as line after line of praise for Israel flowed from his lips.

Balaam's experience is a classic example of the tension between duty and desire. Balaam knew full well that he should not respond to Balak's invitation, but he wanted a house in a better part of town, a new method of transportation, and his wife wanted some new clothes. Perhaps, somehow, he could serve God and collect the fee, also.

Balaam's mistake is being repeated every day. It is repeated by preachers who stifle their convictions in order to secure advancement, by politicians who cast their votes with the next election in mind, by businessmen who give liberally to charity to soothe uneasy consciences. When desire and duty clash, duty must win!

REWARD WITHOUT EFFORT

Moses said unto the children of Gad and to the children of Reuben, Shall your brethren go to war, and shall ye sit here? Num. 32:6.

The advancing Israelites were approaching Canaan from the east. The real test of their strength would come when they crossed the Jordan and challenged the inhabitants of the land. Before reaching the Jordan, the leaders of the tribes of Gad and Reuben recognized that the country east of the Jordan was well suited for their cattle, and asked that they might have their inheritance in that area.

Our text was Moses' initial response to this request. He recognized that there would be many battles beyond the Jordan, and it was not fair to excuse Gad and Reuben from the struggle.

The solution was forthcoming. Gad and Reuben suggested that their men first establish their families and their cattle east of Jordan, and then accompany their brethren in the conquest of Canaan. They said, "We will not return unto our houses, until the children of Israel have inherited every man his inheritance."

Years later, the conquest complete, Joshua called the Reubenites and the Gadites together, commended them for their faithfulness, and said, "Now return ye, and get you unto your tents, and unto the land of your possession, which Moses the servant of the Lord gave you on the other side Jordan" (Joshua 22:4).

This is a story of responsibility and honor. Too many people try to get the rewards of life without effort. Young people sometimes avoid the rigors of higher education, but desire the rewards of the educated. Young men in professions and business try to skip the rounds of the ladder and reach the top in as little time and with as little effort as possible. They cash in on the diligence and self-sacrifice of others, with minimum effort on their own part.

The men of Gad and Reuben, fighting manfully alongside their brethren to provide security for *all,* are an example for people everywhere. Through long months of loneliness and danger they did their part; then they returned to their homes with a sense of "mission accomplished." May God bless their memory!

LEST THOU FORGET

Take heed to thyself, and keep thy soul diligently, lest thou forget the things which thine eyes have seen, and lest they depart from thy heart all the days of thy life. Deut. 4:9.

In one of his farewell speeches to Israel, Moses warned his people against the dangers of prosperity in the land of Canaan. He was anxious that they never forget the One who was responsible for their blessings.

"When Queen Victoria celebrated the jubilee of her coronation there were brought to London in pomp and power the soldiers of her far-flung Empire. The city was emblazoned with flags and pennants announcing the triumph of imperialism. The ships of Great Britain were riding at anchor in the Thames in great display. Through the streets of London there tramped in unending procession these symbols of might from every portion of the Empire. Editors were writing editorials on the prowess of the day. Poets were vying with one another in boasting of the achievement of England. Every Britisher in the Empire took part in the jubilee. Kipling alone remained silent; not one word came from his pen. The editor of one of the London papers called to the attention of Kipling that while everyone was contributing to the glory of that day, he alone remained silent. The editor asked him to write a poem for the occasion. When Kipling received the communication he withdrew from the tumult, and after two days sent his contribution to the London press. 'The Recessional' shocked England."—JOSEPH R. SIZOO, *Way of Faith,* p. 43.

The first stanza of Kipling's "Recessional" speaks to our situation as Christians in a world that is forgetting God:

> "God of our fathers, known of old—
> Lord of our far-flung battle line—
> Beneath whose awful hand we hold
> Dominion over palm and pine—
> Lord God of hosts, be with us yet,
> Lest we forget—lest we forget!"

THE HAZARDS OF PROSPERITY

When the Lord thy God shall have brought thee into the land which he sware unto thy fathers, to Abraham, to Isaac, and to Jacob, to give thee great and goodly cities, which thou buildest not, and houses full of all good things, which thou filledst not, and wells digged, which thou diggedst not, vineyards and olive trees, which thou plantedst not; when thou shall have eaten and be full; then beware lest thou forget the Lord, which brought thee forth out of the land of Egypt, from the house of bondage. Deut. 6:10-12.

"According to a fable said to have come from Denmark, a spider once slid down a single filament of web from the lofty rafters of a barn and established himself upon a lower level. There he spread his web, caught flies, grew sleek and prospered. One day, wandering about his premises, he saw the thread that stretched up into the unseen above him. 'What is that for?' he said, and snapped it— and all his web collapsed."—HARRY EMERSON FOSDICK, *Twelve Tests of Character*, p. 63.

How accurate a parable of life! Men long for the good things life offers. They work and plan, and with the blessing of God they achieve a certain degree of affluence and influence. Instead of humbly thanking God for these blessings, they take all of the credit for themselves and forget God entirely.

They are like the boy who was working on a steep roof, lost his footing, and began to slide. Frantically he began to pray for help. His trousers caught on a protruding nail, checking his fall, and he succeeded in getting on his feet. Then he said, "Never mind, Lord, I don't need You now."

Forgetting God in prosperity, remembering Him in adversity— this is an age-old pattern. Would it not be well for every Christian to re-examine his attitude toward God?

Can we stand prosperity? Can we survive success? Must God allow us to prove our own inadequacy before we will recognize His claims on our life? Paul said, "I know how to be abased, and I know how to abound." Have we reached this level of maturity?

135

CHOOSE LIFE

I call heaven and earth to record this day against you, that I have set before you life and death, blessing and cursing: therefore choose life, that both thou and thy seed may live: that thou mayest love the Lord thy God, and that thou mayest obey his voice, and that thou mayest cleave unto him: for he is thy life, and the length of thy days. Deut. 30:19, 20.

Moses is giving his farewell address to Israel. As a dedicated leader, he is concerned for the future of the people to whom he has given his life. He outlines for them the attitudes and actions that lead to life, and the way that leads to death, and then says, "Choose life." He makes clear what he means: "Love the Lord thy God," he says; "obey his voice"; "cleave unto him: *for he is thy life.*"

For the person who does not choose God, life takes on limited significance. Many centuries ago an Englishman named Bede compared life to a sparrow flying swiftly into a banquet hall, and immediately flying out again. Another writer compared life to a narrow vale between the mountain peaks of two eternities. To millions, all there is to life is a series of stimuli and responses on the part of an animate organism. When the brief interlude is over the sparrow flies out into the unknown and is soon forgotten.

But life is more than this—much more. Life includes the divine purpose for the individual. God sees in each person what he can become and endeavors to influence His creatures toward the fulfillment of their greatest possibilities. Real life is more than responding to the stimuli of environment—it is responding to the love of a gracious God who guides us toward satisfying achievements.

And life is yet more. Jesus said, "I am the resurrection, and the life." The grave is not the end. God will create anew every person who can be trusted to inhabit a sinless universe.

"And the years of eternity, as they roll, will bring richer and still more glorious revelations of God and of Christ. As knowledge is progressive, so will love, reverence, and happiness increase. The more men learn of God, the greater will be their admiration of His character."—*The Great Controversy*, p. 678.

CALEB REFUSES TO RETIRE

Give me this mountain, whereof the Lord spake in that day;
for thou heardest in that day how the Anakims were there, and
that the cities were great and fenced: if so be the Lord will be
with me, then I shall be able to drive them out, as the Lord said.
Joshua 14:12.

Caleb was eighty-five years old. In modern terms he had been eligible for full Social Security for twenty years. But, rather than retire, he requests as his inheritance an unconquered, giant-infested mountain—"if so be the Lord will be with me, then I shall be able to drive them out, as the Lord said."

What was the background of this remarkable man? Forty-five years earlier he had been a member of the reconnaissance squad sent by Moses from Kadesh-Barnea to bring a report on the land of Canaan. The majority reported that it was a wonderful country, but unconquerable. A minority of two dissented. Caleb and Joshua agreed that it really was a wonderful country, and "Caleb quieted the people before Moses, and said, 'Let us go up at once, and occupy it; for we are well able to overcome it'" (Num. 13:30, R.S.V.).

The people refused to accept the minority report, and the invasion that might, under God, have been successful was delayed many years. But of Caleb, God said, "Because he has a different spirit and has followed me fully, I will bring [him] into the land into which he went, and his descendants shall possess it" (chap. 14: 24, R.S.V.).

Having been voted down by an overwhelming majority, Caleb might have grown petulant and resentful. Instead, he continued on with his faithless and cowardly colleagues for more than four decades, knowing all the while that Israel might have been in Canaan rather than in the desert.

This man with a "different spirit" finally accomplished his objective. The sons of the giants he had seen forty-five years before were conquered. The old veteran finally proved that it could be done.

God needs people like Caleb today, people with a "different spirit" who will not be frightened by the giants that infest the land.

THE PERILS OF MISUNDERSTANDING

When they came unto the borders of Jordan, that are in the land of Canaan, the children of Reuben and the children of Gad and the half tribe of Manasseh built there an altar by Jordan, a great altar to see to. . . . And when the children of Israel heard of it, the whole congregation of the children of Israel gathered themselves together at Shiloh, to go up to war against them. Joshua 22:10-12.

The men of Reuben and Gad had performed valiantly during the conquest of Canaan. Now, with the half-tribe of Manasseh, they were ready to return to their inheritance across the Jordan.

And then it happened! Word spread that the tribes beyond Jordan had built a very imposing and impressive altar on their side of the river. All kinds of rumors spread. "They are rebels," cried the crowd. "There can be only one altar, and that is the altar at the Lord's tabernacle." "They are heretics," cried others. "Burnt offerings and sacrifices are forbidden anywhere but at the tabernacle."

Fortunately, the leaders of Israel were wise enough to investigate the charges before taking action. Phinehas, the son of Eleazer the priest, and ten princes were sent as an investigating committee. Obviously they were biased against the trans-Jordan tribes and their new altar. Very bluntly they said, "Rebel not against the Lord, nor rebel against us, in building you an altar beside the altar of the Lord our God" (verse 19).

Then the truth came out. The accused tribes had *not* built the altar for burnt offering or sacrifice. They had built the altar as a monument to remind their children what the altar of God was like. There was not the slightest intention of rebellion or heresy in their action. The memorial was to be a reminder that they were one with their brethren in loyalty to God.

Fortunately, Phinehas and his committee were convinced. Israel was convinced. The armies went home. The altar remained as a "witness between us that the Lord is God."

Would that all regrettable misunderstandings were so amicably settled! Not all that so appears is rebellion and heresy.

JOSHUA'S LAST SPEECH

Fear the Lord, and serve him in sincerity and in truth: and put away the gods which your fathers served on the other side of the flood, and in Egypt; and serve ye the Lord. And if it seem evil unto you to serve the Lord, choose you this day whom ye will serve; . . . but as for me and my house, we will serve the Lord. Joshua 24:14, 15.

Joshua was 110 years old. As a retiring leader he might be compared to General Washington at the end of his illustrious career, or to Winston Churchill in his later years. Joshua had led his country with courage and imagination in their conquest of the Promised Land, but now it was time for taps.

His final speech, recorded in Joshua 24, was addressed to the leaders of Israel assembled at Shechem. He did not recount his own accomplishments, but began by saying, "Thus saith the Lord God of Israel . . ." then he proceeded to recall what God had done for Israel. He asked for no monument in his own honor, but dedicated a stone in Shechem as a reminder of Israel's covenant with God. His concern was not that he be remembered, but that God be remembered. "Fear the Lord, and serve him in sincerity and in truth," he counseled them. "As for me and my house, we will serve the Lord," he resolved.

Joshua's influence was lasting. "Israel served the Lord all the days of Joshua, and all the days of the elders that overlived Joshua, and which had known all the works of the Lord, that he had done for Israel" (verse 31).

How many leaders of men have been so completely overshadowed by their God? It was customary in ancient times for a new king to erase the name and exploits of his predecessor from the monuments, lest they detract from his own glory. Joshua's only concern was for God's glory. This self-effacing dedication is Joshua's greatest claim to fame.

"To serve God and enjoy Him forever" was the goal of the devoted Calvinist in Reformation times. Our self-centered generation needs to rediscover this philosophy. May we learn to know, to love, and to serve our God as wholeheartedly as did Joshua!

139

THE TOWN THAT FAILED TO DO ITS PART

Curse ye Meroz, said the angel of the Lord, curse ye bitterly the inhabitants thereof; because they came not to the help of the Lord, to the help of the Lord against the mighty. Judges 5:23.

Deborah and Barak had delivered Israel from the armies of Canaan under Sisera. In celebration, they sang the song recorded in Judges 5. One theme of the song was appreciation for the cooperation of the people. Verse 2 says, "Praise ye the Lord for the avenging of Israel, when the people willingly offered themselves." In verse 9, Deborah says, "My heart is toward the governors of Israel, that offered themselves willingly among the people." In recounting the exploits of various tribes, verse 18 says, "Zebulun and Naphtali were a people that jeoparded their lives unto the death."

But there was one exception to the general spirit of cooperation. A now-unknown town by the name of Meroz is cursed by the angel of the Lord because, while the rest of the folks were doing their part, the Merozites refused to become involved. They may have been afraid, they may have been preoccupied, they may have been unconcerned. But when the call came for help, they weren't there.

Where are we when calls come to support the work of God? Where are we when it becomes necessary to defend the Word of God? Where are we when the people of God need help? Do we stand up to be counted when our fellow men are threatened and oppressed? Do we take a firm position against dishonesty and corruption even though we may suffer for so doing? Do we seize our opportunities to witness for our God?

"But," we say, "the Lord doesn't need my help." Probably the Merozites thought they were too small and insignificant to help in the battle against Sisera. "Our tiny resources won't make any difference," they may have said. While, theoretically, the Lord may not *need* our help, He often *asks* for it. We need to give it. Often the "help" of a small boy is more hindrance than it is help.

God's "Help Wanted" sign is always out—and a curse rests on those who ignore it. Great blessings are being missed by those who fail to respond when God calls them.

GIDEON CALLED TO SAVE ISRAEL

The Lord looked upon him, and said, Go in this thy might, and thou shalt save Israel from the hand of the Midianites: have not I sent thee? And he said unto him, Oh my Lord, wherewith shall I save Israel? behold, my family is poor in Manasseh, and I am the least in my father's house. And the Lord said unto him, Surely I will be with thee, and thou shalt smite the Midianites as one man. Judges 6:14-16.

Manasseh was not an important tribe, Gideon's family background was humble, and Gideon himself was unknown. Israel had been looking for years for a deliverer, but never once had they looked Gideon's way. All at once this obscure man was rocketed into a place of leadership, and he delivered Israel from their enemies.

How often this has happened in the history of man. Who would have recognized in the indifferent student at Eton the future Winston Churchill, deliverer of England? Or who would have guessed that the rail splitter in Illinois would become the great Abraham Lincoln? Who would have seen Daniel in the captive boy, or Jesus in the carpenter's son? No generation knows where to look for its heroes. Almost invariably they come from unexpected sources.

These examples can be a source of encouragement to young people. Success is not dependent on being born into an influential family, or on wealth. God often chooses His men from unlikely places.

Years ago, the challenge came to Adventist young people:

"Are you ambitious for education that you may have a name and position in the world? Have you thoughts that you dare not express, that you may one day stand upon the summit of intellectual greatness; that you may sit in deliberative and legislative councils, and help enact laws for the nation? There is nothing wrong in these aspirations. You may every one of you make your mark. You should be content with no mean attainments. Aim high, and spare no pains to reach the standard."—*Messages to Young People,* p. 36.

It is still possible for a young person to surmount handicaps and achieve success. God still calls Gideons from threshing floors to positions of leadership. Youth's dreams need not be in vain.

JOTHAM'S PARABLE

The trees went forth on a time to anoint a king over them;
and they said to the olive tree, Reign thou over us. But the olive
tree said unto them, Should I leave my fatness, wherewith by me
they honour God and man, and go to be promoted over the trees?
Judges 9:8, 9.

Abimilech, son of Gideon, slew his seventy brothers in order that
he might become king of Shechem. The youngest brother, Jotham,
hid from the slaughter. He went to Shechem and delivered an address
to the populace in defense of his slain family, and in defiance of his
unscrupulous brother. In this speech he told an interesting and picturesque allegory. The olive tree, the fig tree, and the vine were all
offered kingship over the trees, but refused because they would have
to sacrifice their role as benefactors of mankind. But the bramble,
bent on distinction and destruction, accepted the kingship.

Jotham was not thinking of our generation when he gave this
parable, but he touched a sensitive nerve in today's world. How many,
like the trees in the parable, are so bent on serving and blessing mankind that they would refuse a great honor that might stand in the way
of their service? Is it not more common to find people who, like the
thorny bramble, are intent on overshadowing others and are willing
to destroy others for their own advantage?

Jesus had something to say on this point. The mother of James
and John had requested places of honor for her sons in Christ's kingdom. The other ten disciples were indignant, but Jesus said, "Ye
know that the princes of the Gentiles exercise dominion over them,
and they that are great exercise authority upon them. But it shall not
be so among you: but whosoever will be great among you, let him be
your minister; and whosoever will be chief among you, let him be
your servant" (Matt. 20:25-27).

Jesus was like the olive tree, the fig tree, the vine of Jotham's
parable—eager to serve. The disciples were still a bit like the bramble
—eager to rule. In our own lives we often find ourselves pulled both
ways. There is one instinct for unselfish service, and another for power.
Our closeness to Christ will help determine which force wins.

SAMSON JOINS THE NOW GENERATION

Samson said unto his father, Get her for me; for she pleaseth me well. Judges 14:3.

No young man ever had a better chance to succeed than Samson. He was from a good family, God had a specific plan for his life, and he had been brought up in the atmosphere of love and prayer. He had great personal charm, unusual physical strength, and distinctive leadership ability.

But this promising young man did not have the patience to allow God or his parents to guide him in his personal affairs. He saw a woman in the Philistine country and he wanted her—now. His parents tried to reason with him. They reminded him of all the fine girls in Israel, but he remained unconvinced. They warned him of the dangers of marrying a wife from among the enemies of Israel, but he knew better. He had no rational arguments for his course of action; he merely said, "She pleaseth me well."

Thousands of young people in our contemporary world are following the example of Samson. They call themselves the "now generation." "You waited," sniffed a representative of this philosophy. "We won't." The idea of slaving and saving for future success is not acceptable to them. The traditional Christian morality that defers sexual experience until marriage is out. Life's humdrum must be erased by drugs. Questions of right and wrong must not interfere with personal preference. Samson would have been right at home on Haight and Ashbury streets—long hair and all! He would have been a leader in the revolt against the establishment, and no qualms of conscience would have kept him from doing anything that pleased him well. He would have hooted at the middle-class morality of his parents and his church, and sought complete emancipation from both.

Samson and his modern counterparts refuse to accept responsibility. They want "kicks" *now,* and they are unconcerned about the results of their actions. They are unwilling to shoulder the burdens of life—they are only interested in the rewards. Samson's failure is a warning to the now generation that there is a future when each person must reap the results of today's folly.

SAMSON WASTES HIS STRENGTH

Samson called unto the Lord, and said, O Lord God, remember me, I pray thee, and strengthen me, I pray thee, only this once, O God, that I may be at once avenged of the Philistines for my two eyes. Judges 16:28.

A large earth-moving machine, obviously capable of moving mountains, was lumbering down a country road. Fastened behind the giant machine was a little boy's coaster wagon, and in it were two bricks. Someone with a sense of humor had conceived how ridiculous it would look to see an earth mover pulling a child's wagon.

Is it not equally ridiculous to see capable people wasting their lives doing petty, useless, perhaps even harmful things—pulling loads far below their possibilities? There are millions of underachievers in the world.

Samson was a striking example of this type of futility. He had physical strength, mental ability, personality, charm, and position. What did he do with all of these advantages? He tore a threatening lion to shreds. He propounded a silly riddle at a Philistine wedding feast, and killed thirty men to pay his gambling debts. He fitted three hundred foxes with incendiary equipment, and turned them loose on the Philistine farms. He went on a homicidal rampage with a donkey's jawbone as his weapon, slaughtering a thousand men. He carried away the gates of a city. He attracted women of questionable character. Finally he pulled a building down on himself and his enemies.

Think what a great judge Samson might have been if he had used his phenomenal strength and ability in really worth-while undertakings. Think of the stature he might have given to Israel. Instead of the contempt of his enemies, he could have gained their respect. Instead of meeting an inglorious death as a blinded prisoner, he could have lived to provide strong and wise leadership for his country. Instead of a self-willed, self-centered, immature failure, he might have been a man of grace and distinction.

His glaring weakness was his inclination to waste his strength on the harmful and inconsequential. He went through life like an earth mover pulling a coaster wagon! Are we pulling coaster wagons?

GREAT LOYALTY

*Ruth said, Intreat me not to leave thee, or to return from
following after thee: for whither thou goest, I will go; and where
thou lodgest, I will lodge: thy people shall be my people, and
thy God my God: where thou diest, will I die, and there will I
be buried: the Lord do so to me, and more also, if ought but death
part thee and me.* Ruth 1:16, 17.

"'If Ruth came back,' I once heard Dr. Fosdick say, 'we should
put her sickle in a museum, for we have vast machines which storm
across the prairie and do the work of a thousand men; but Ruth in her
loyalty to her mother-in-law would put us to shame. We have improved on Ruth's sickle, but have we improved on Ruth?'"—LESLIE D.
WEATHERHEAD, *This Is the Victory*, p. 38.

It would be hard to imagine a more beautiful example of loyalty
than Ruth. In the first place, Naomi was not her mother but her
mother-in-law, and Ruth's husband was dead. Seldom does the tie of
loyalty remain strong in a situation like this. Second, her mother-in-
law was of a different nation and a different faith. This meant that
Ruth's loyalty demanded changes in her own life.

It may be appropriate to ask the question as to whether, in our
praise of Ruth, we have neglected Naomi. Surely she must have been
a wonderful person to have deserved and received Ruth's loyalty. She
must have represented her faith and her nation well to have convinced her daughter-in-law to make such a radical change in her life.
Naomi must have reacted nobly to her bereavement to be such a comfort to her daughter-in-law in her sorrow. Perhaps we should give
Naomi a higher place among "the great cloud of witnesses" of the
Old Testament! She was more than merely a mother-in-law.

Little did Ruth know that her decision would result in her becoming
the great-grandmother of King David. Loyalty is not always as obviously rewarded, but it does have built-in compensations. To be loyal
to a great person or a great cause is really to live. The story of Ruth
sparkles like a jewel amid the sordid records of man's selfishness and
baseness. This simple narrative restores our confidence in the real
values of life.

A GREAT SACRIFICE

For this child I prayed; and the Lord hath given me my peti-
tion which I asked of him: therefore also I have lent him to the
Lord; as long as he liveth he shall be lent to the Lord. 1 Sam.
1:27, 28.

There is an abundance of human interest in this touching story.
Hannah had suffered for years from the results of the practice of
polygamy. Her husband Elkanah's other wife had children, but she
herself did not. In the culture of that time, this was a disgrace. In her
heartache and desperation Hannah promised God that if she might
have a son she would devote him, for life, to the service of the Lord.
Her request was granted, and her baby was named Samuel.

Hannah may have wavered at times when she thought of fulfilling
her pledge. How could she give up this precious child? Possibly she
heard that there was corruption in the high priest's household. But if
she knew, her thoughts are not found in the record. When the proper
time came, she said with brave forthrightness, "For this child I prayed;
and the Lord hath given me my petition which I asked of him; therefore also I have lent him to the Lord."

Are we as faithful in fulfilling our promises to God? Perhaps in
some time of danger or adversity we promised God that if He would
remember us, we would remember Him. When things got better, did
we remember our promise? Or, perhaps, at a time of spiritual revival we promised our lives to God in Christian service. Have we
found ways to rationalize deviation from those solemn promises?
Never was a promise harder to keep than that of Hannah. How her
heart must have ached when she left Eli's house with empty arms,
knowing that she would not see her child for many months, and then
only for a brief visit.

Think what her loyalty meant to the world. Her boy grew up to
be a man of integrity—a man who did more than any other to stem
the tide of apostasy in his day. It seemed that Hannah's honesty and
dedication were passed along to her son. Whether Hannah lived to
see the great work of her son, we do not know; but the world was a
better place because of her deep sense of devotion.

"WE DON'T WANT TO BE DIFFERENT"

*Nevertheless the people refused to obey the voice of Samuel;
and they said, Nay; but we will have a king over us; that we may
be like all the nations; and that our king may judge us, and go
out before us, and fight our battles. 1 Sam. 8:19, 20.*

For many years, Samuel had given wise and competent leadership to Israel. He had carried on his work in a simple way, without the extravagant and pompous procedures of royalty. His success was the result of close fellowship with God, wisdom, and love for his people.

The glimpses of Samuel in the Scriptures depict an honest and conscientious leader. As a boy, commissioned with a message for Eli, he behaved admirably. When Israel was under the rule of the Philistines, Samuel told his people that God would deliver them if they would "return unto the Lord" with all their hearts, "put away the strange gods," and prepare their "hearts unto the Lord and serve him only" (1 Sam. 7:3). Then we see Samuel praying earnestly for Israel's deliverance, "and the Lord heard him" (verse 9), and Israel had peace during Samuel's long administration.

When Samuel grew old the elders of Israel got together and decided it was time for a change, not only of leaders but of form of government. They were tired of the simple, spiritual leadership of Samuel, successful as it had been. They wanted something more glamourous and exciting. They knew about the kings of surrounding nations, and said, "We don't want to be different. Appoint a king to judge us like all the other nations."

The elders of Israel failed to see how much more simple, effective, and safe was the direct rule of God through a judge and prophet. They overlooked the taxes they would have to pay in order to support a royal court like those of other nations. They never had it so good as when Samuel was judge, yet they were not content.

Could it be that God is trying to say something to us through Israel's experience? Could we profit by being more sensitive to the simple, direct guidance of God in our personal affairs and in the affairs of the church? Are we missing something because we don't want to be different?

A MAN OF INTEGRITY

Behold, here I am: witness against me before the Lord, and before his anointed: whose ox have I taken? or whose ass have I taken? or whom have I defrauded? whom have I oppressed? or of whose hand have I received any bribe to blind mine eyes therewith? and I will restore it you. And they said, Thou hast not defrauded us, nor oppressed us, neither hast thou taken ought of any man's hand. 1 Sam. 12:3, 4.

It is a wonderful thing when a man devotes a lifetime to public service and no one can challenge his integrity.

The name of Abraham Lincoln has become synonomous with honesty. When Lincoln was running for a seat in the Illinois State Legislature, an opponent endeavored to block his chances for success. It is said that Lincoln replied as follows:

"I am not so young in years as I am in the tricks of the politicians, but live long or die early, I would rather die than change my views and by that change obtain office. You may burn my body and scatter the ashes to the four winds of heaven; you may drag my soul down into the pit; but you will never get me to support what I believe to be wrong."

Lincoln was defeated for office on several occasions, but he maintained his integrity.

In contrast to some other religions of the world, Christianity demands honesty of its adherents. The Old Testament prophets were insistent on this point. Jesus upheld strict principles of personal integrity. Nearly all of Paul's Epistles end with a section on the Christian way of life, and one of his basic propositions is "provide things honest in the sight of all men."

In a day when cheating begins in school and marks men's business and social conduct all through life, it is refreshing to find Christians who, like Samuel, can look their world in the eye with nothing to hide and with no fear of scandal.

Often we talk in our evangelism about "looking for the honest in heart." The gospel is supposed to *make* people honest. Honesty will be one of the tests applied to every person in the day of judgment.

148

THE SECOND CHANCE

Samuel said unto the people, Fear not: ye have done all this wickedness: yet turn not aside from following the Lord, but serve the Lord with all your heart.... For the Lord will not forsake his people for his great name's sake: because it hath pleased the Lord to make you his people. 1 Sam. 12:20-22.

Samuel was unambiguous in reminding Israel that they had done wrong in asking for a king. Furthermore, they had rejected the Lord as their king, and he had punctuated his rebuke by calling forth a great storm of thunder and rain in their presence.

The people were frightened, and asked that Samuel pray for them, which he promised he would never cease to do. But the fascinating part of the incident was Samuel's encouragement of the people despite their apostasy.

One of the characteristics of God stressed in the Old Testament is this quality of being "long-suffering," "not willing that any should perish." His people might sin, and He might find it necessary to punish them, but when they were ready to repent He was ready to forgive. Samuel reminded Israel, however, that God's forbearance was not without limit. Later in this chapter Samuel says, "But if ye shall still do wickedly, ye shall be consumed, both ye and your king."

Herein is eternal truth. God is *still* gracious and forgiving. He is often more willing to forgive us than we are to forgive one another. Patiently He calls after His children, endeavoring to persuade them to accept His grace and commit their lives to Him. "There's a wideness in God's mercy, Like the wideness of the sea."

But the time is coming when God will put an end to sin and sinners. There is no other conceivable outcome. His principle of free choice keeps Him from forcing men to serve Him. But His divine love makes incredible an eternity of sin with no end. So the day of final reckoning will come when love has finished its work, and rebellion will disappear from the universe.

This is the goal toward which the whole creation moves. Happy are those who are not presumptuous in their reaction to God's love. "Behold therefore the goodness and severity of God" (Rom. 11:22).

WHEN SAUL WAS HUMBLE

Samuel said, When thou wast little in thine own sight, wast thou not made the head of the tribes of Israel, and the Lord anointed thee king over Israel? 1 Sam. 15:17.

A certain man was asked to pronounce the invocation at a gathering of sophisticated people. He prayed thus: "Lord, justify if You can the high opinion we have of ourselves."

The trouble is, He can't! He can use people who are little in their own sight, but when they lose their humility they are no longer of much value to Him.

There is a fable about an ancient saint who had lived an exemplary life. An angel appeared to him one day and offered him the gift of miracles. He declined, fearing that he might lose his humility. He was offered the power to convert men, but again he declined, explaining that conversion was the work of the Holy Spirit. He was offered the status of being a model of goodness, but again he felt unworthy. Finally, the angel asked the saint to name any blessing he might desire. His answer was, "That I might have His grace so that I might do good to men without knowing it."

This is the opposite of the religious pride that has ruined the usefulness of thousands of people. The real Christian walks *humbly* with his God. He is never guilty of a "holier than thou" attitude, yet he has self-respect. He is not trying to be humble, but humility is a by-product of his commitment, his reverence, and his love.

It is noteworthy that the greatest people are often the most humble. Really superior people do not have to put on airs to convince others of their greatness. Such people also are keenly aware of their limitations. God can use people like these, just as He could use Saul in his humbler days.

An inordinate desire for recognition is often a sign of insecurity. Someone has said, "There is no limit to what a person can accomplish if he does not care who gets the credit for it." One of Saul's great problems was his hostility to David, who was gaining greater recognition than he. Humility glorifies. Arrogance destroys.

GOD CHOOSES A KING

[Samuel] looked on Eliab, and said, Surely the Lord's anointed is before him. But the Lord said unto Samuel, Look not on his countenance, or on the height of his stature; because I have refused him: for the Lord seeth not as man seeth; for man looketh on the outward appearance, but the Lord looketh on the heart. 1 Sam. 16:6, 7.

Eliab was the first of the sons of Jesse to pass before Samuel as a candidate for the throne of Israel. He apparently looked the part of a king—probably he was tall, mature, dignified, and handsome. But God revealed to Samuel that Eliab was not the man. One after another of Eliab's brothers joined the procession, with the same result.

But there was one left—the "kid brother" looking after the sheep. No one would have imagined that this handsome young harpist contained the stuff of which kings are made. But such was the case.

In evaluating people we are limited to those characteristics which we can observe—good looks, bearing, personality, leadership, competence. There is one very important area that we cannot investigate— what is going on in the person's mind. Persons who appear brave may be cowardly. Persons who seem pure may be corrupt. Men who seem to have faith may be doubters. Those who give every evidence of being men of good will may lack integrity. God looks behind the drawn curtain of the human mind and sees what is taking place backstage.

This is why the guidance of God is so necessary in the enterprises of the church. Boards, nominating committees, administrators, would often choose Eliab and never even hear about David—unless the Spirit of God controls them to the extent that He controlled Samuel. This guidance can come only through dedication and prayer.

"The Lord looketh on the heart." This is both reassuring and threatening, depending upon what He sees. This is why there will be no errors in the final judgment, but there will be many surprises. Good deeds may be done for bad reasons. Wrong actions may not always represent the deeper motives of the person who committed them. How thankful we may be that "the Lord seeth not as man seeth."

"IN THE NAME OF THE LORD"

Said David to the Philistine, Thou comest to me with a sword, and with a spear, and with a shield: but I come to thee in the name of the Lord of hosts, the God of the armies of Israel, whom thou hast defied. 1 Sam. 17:45.

"Through nineteen centuries the Church has been David against the Goliath of the world. People seldom take it very seriously, and so far as its strength is concerned, they are likely to ask Stalin's question about the Pope's strength: 'How many battalions does he have?' Yet Hitler was not the first dictator and in all probability will not be the last to be surprised by the strength of the Church which has seemed so weak. For when the crisis comes, there has been an unseen spiritual power possessed by the church which has brought down tyranny. As James Russell Lowell put it in 'The Present Crisis,' if right is on the scaffold and wrong is on the throne, still it is the scaffold that sways the future. We believe that God stands in the shadows keeping watch."—GERALD H. KENNEDY, *Fresh Every Morning,* pp. 62, 63.

This contrast is especially true in our contemporary era, which has often been spoken of as the post-Christian age. Forces of materialism seem overwhelming. The younger generation is, by and large, growing up with little knowledge of God and less commitment to Him.

A very ordinary noncombatant medic saved seventy-five men, won the Congressional Medal of Honor, and has become a legend of World War II. Desmond Doss was like David fighting Goliath; and, like David, he came forth a hero because he faced his crisis "in the name of the Lord."

In the future more and more Goliaths will saunter forth to challenge the Christian's God. More and more seemingly impossible obstacles will be placed in the way of the proclamation of the Christian gospel. The contrast between the power of the church and the power of the world will grow greater and greater. The security of the cause of Christ will rest with weak, ordinary people who speak and act "in the name of the Lord."

DAVID SPARES SAUL'S LIFE

David said to Saul, Wherefore hearest thou men's words, saying, Behold, David seeketh thy hurt? Behold, this day thine eyes have seen how that the Lord had delivered thee to day into mine hand in the cave: and some bade me kill thee: but mine eye spared thee; and I said, I will not put forth mine hand against my lord; for he is the Lord's anointed. 1 Sam. 24:9, 10.

Saul, with an army of three thousand men, was combing the countryside to find David. Saul entered a cave where David and his men were hiding, giving David ample opportunity to take the life of his enemy. David refused, using the opportunity to try to persuade Saul that he was not wishing to harm him. Along with his faults, David possessed in a remarkable degree the grace of magnanimity.

While on a political campaign, President William McKinley was followed by an energetic young reporter from an opposition newspaper. "The young man was on the job and did his work of misrepresentation and vilification with dispatch. McKinley went from place to place in a closed carriage, while the reporter sat with the driver on the outside. Noticing that the reporter was ill-clad and was suffering from cold, McKinley stopped the carriage, stepped out, and said to the young reporter, 'Come down from there, young man.' The reporter thought that the hour of vengeance had come. He came down, and McKinley offered him his coat and invited him to ride inside the carriage.

"The reporter hesitated, 'But you must not know who I am. I have been whipping you to pieces during this whole campaign.'

" 'I know,' replied McKinley, 'but put on this overcoat and get inside so you can do a better job.' "—A. L. BIETZ, *The "Know-how" of Christian Living*, p. 150.

Only people with large hearts, people who are themselves secure, can react in this way to opposition. In our modern highly competitive society we too often see people trying to destroy the influence of those who disagree with them. The Christian is commanded to love his enemies. How well do we reach this ideal?

THE ROAD TO TRAGEDY

Saul died, and his three sons, and his armourbearer, and all his men, that same day together. 1 Sam. 31:6.

This was a tragic end to what might have been a great career. Saul was a man of ability, personality, strength, and leadership. He was anointed by God as leader of His people. He had a dedicated prophet to give him counsel, and a loyal people to give him support. No one ever had greater opportunity to lead a useful life.

But Saul was not sensitive to the guidance of God. When he was specifically instructed to follow a certain course of action, he followed his own judgment in place of God's directions.

Saul also allowed himself to become obsessed with jealousy, and he wasted his own energies and the resources of his kingdom trying to take the life of David, who had done him no wrong.

Finally, in desperation, Saul sought counsel from a witch, and was told that the morrow would be the last day of his troubled life.

Saul's life reminds us of the story of the motorist who saw a large sign on the highway, "Road Under Construction, Detour." The road looked passable to him as far as he could see, so he disregarded the sign. For miles he traveled at high speed, congratulating himself that he had not detoured. Then he saw another sign, "Travel This Road at Your Own Risk." He continued on, though more slowly. But the road grew worse and worse. Finally, after the sun had set, the road ended in a gravel pit. Looking about him in despair, the motorist saw another signboard among the rocks. Climbing out of his car and lighting a match, he read this infuriating message, "Now don't you wish you had detoured?"

Saul doubtless spent the last troubled night of his life wishing he had followed the signs; but it was too late. He could neither back up nor turn around. The next day found him, a pitiful figure, impaled on his own sword.

The commandments of God are signboards along life's highway, warning of dangers and detours. They are not intended to condemn, but to protect. Those who repudiate them, as did Saul, cannot escape the consequences!

UZZAH TRIES TO HELP GOD

When they came to Nachon's threshingfloor, Uzzah put forth his hand to the ark of God, and took hold of it; for the oxen shook it. And the anger of the Lord was kindled against Uzzah; and God smote him there for his error; and there he died by the ark of God. 2 Sam. 6:6, 7.

It is not easy to understand why God dealt so harshly with a person who seemed to be doing his duty. David, like ourselves, looked on the incident with astonishment and alarm. According to the record, "David was afraid of the Lord that day" (verse 9).

A study of the incident, however, indicates that David and his people were in error in transporting the ark on a cart. According to the directions given Israel, it should have been carried on the shoulders of certain specified men. Uzzah was entirely out of place in his relationship to the ark. "Transgression of God's law had lessened his sense of its sacredness, and with unconfessed sins upon him he had, in face of the divine prohibition, presumed to touch the symbol of God's presence."—*Patriarchs and Prophets,* p. 706.

What does this tragic incident say to us? Bishop Kennedy has used it as the text for a sermon entitled, "Dealing With the Eternal." He says, "To me this story is saying that there are some things which are not to be manipulated or interfered with by human beings."—GERALD H. KENNEDY, *Fresh Every Morning,* p. 2. One of these sacred things, Kennedy points out, is morality. He says, "I believe in the moral law. I believe that God has established this law as unchangeable and as unmanipulatable as the law of gravity. I believe that the only choice we have is to discover what the law is and live by it or to ignore it and die by it."—Page 3. Uzzah's fate is a symbol of the final outcome of disregard for divine instruction.

Another lesson from this incident is the futility of trying to come to the rescue of God. John Newton wrote, "If you think you see the Ark of the Lord falling, you can be quite sure that it is due to a swimming in your own head." If His ark seems to be falling, we had better let Him solve the problem.

THE MAN WHO WANTED TO RUN

Ahimaaz the son of Zadok said again to Joab, "Come what may, let me also run after the Cushite." And Joab said, "Why will you run, my son, seeing that you will have no reward for the tidings?" "Come what may," he said, "I will run." So he said to him, "Run." Then Ahimaaz ran by the way of the plain, and outran the Cushite. 2 Sam. 18:22, 23, R.S.V.

Joab and his men had killed David's disloyal son Absalom in battle. Ahimaaz, a fast runner, begged Joab to let him carry the message to David. Joab knew that the news would be crushing to David, even though it meant victory, and he preferred that a man known as "the Cushite" should be the one to break the news.

But Ahimaaz insisted on running, so Joab finally said, "Run." And he was a fast runner. He soon passed the Cushite, and in time David's watchman recognized him. David's hopes rose, and he said, "He is a good man, and comes with good tidings." He did have good tidings—victory had come—but David's concern was, "Is it well with the young man Absalom?" Ahimaaz could not bring himself to answer this question. He stalled by saying, "I saw a great tumult, but I do not know what it was."

The world is full of people like Ahimaaz who want assignments of importance in life, but who are unwilling to meet the responsibilities involved. They can run—they can even outrun others—but under a crucial test, they cannot face reality.

They are like the hound described by one writer. "He would come up behind a fox, put on an extra burst of speed, and run right on past him. . . . The fox suddenly discovered he was chasing the hound and couldn't keep up with him."—GERALD H. KENNEDY, *Fresh Every Morning*, p. 85. The hound didn't seem to sense that running was not an end in itself. He put forth a great deal of energy, but failed to accomplish an objective.

According to the Old Testament story, the Cushite came in second in the race, but when he was asked about Absalom he had a tactful but clear answer. After all, wasn't his message more important than his miles per hour?

156

SHIMEI WELCOMES DAVID

Shimei the son of Gera fell down before the king, as he was come over Jordan; and said unto the king, Let not my lord impute iniquity unto me, neither do thou remember that which thy servant did perversely the day that my lord the king went out of Jerusalem, that the king should take it to his heart. For thy servant doth know that I have sinned: therefore, behold, I am come the first this day of all the house of Joseph to go down to meet my lord the king. 2 Sam. 19:18-20.

This sounds like sincere repentance—but was it? Let us look into the background of Shimei.

As a result of Absalom's rebellion, David was forced to flee the country. David and his men were on their way to safety, Shimei "went along the hill's side over against him, and cursed as he went, and threw stones at him, and cast dust" (2 Sam. 16:13). Previous to this time, Shimei had seemed to be a loyal subject, but in the hour of David's humiliation he revealed his real attitude. He was determined to be on the winning side.

After David's victory over Absalom, he returned to his kingdom in triumph; and who was the first to meet him when he came to the Jordan River? Shimei! It was at this point that he repented with such apparent sincerity that David allowed him to live, but he could no longer trust him. Before his death he warned his son, Solomon, to keep an eye on Shimei. Solomon responded by ordering Shimei never to leave Jerusalem. Despite solemn promises to conform, Shimei sneaked away one day in search of two of his servants who had run away. On his return, Solomon's executioners were awaiting him.

Shimei is an example of the many persons who always want to be on the winning side. Such people always have a moistened finger in the air, trying to determine which way the wind is blowing. Their decisions are based, not on convictions, but on political advantage. Like Shimei, they can never be trusted.

On the contrary, how encouraging it is to find people—and there are many such—who are genuinely sincere and honest. Both the world and the church need such people.

157

DAVID REPENTS AFTER NUMBERING ISRAEL

David's heart smote him after that he had numbered the people. And David said unto the Lord, I have sinned greatly in that I have done: and now, I beseech thee, O Lord, take away the iniquity of thy servant; for I have done very foolishly. 2 Sam. 24:10.

For nine months and seven days the census taker had been at work. Against the advice of his counselors, and contrary to the will of God, David had "numbered the people." "With a view to extending his conquests among foreign nations, David determined to increase his army by requiring military service from all who were of proper age. To effect this, it became necessary to take a census of the population. It was pride and ambition that prompted this action of the king."— *Patriarchs and Prophets*, p. 747.

Finally, David's conscience gripped, and he confessed his mistake to God. In his confession he said, "O Lord, take the iniquity of thy servant." The Lord did exactly what David requested, but not without suffering. The plague that followed brought great sorrow to the heart of the king.

When a penitent sinner asks God to take away sin he is not asking for erasure, but for surgery. It would be simple if God could eradicate sin like we erase words from a blackboard, but it cannot be done that way. Too much is involved. When God removes sin, He works through experiences that may burn and tear and scar. He doesn't do it this way because He is vindictive or sadistic, but because He recognizes that sin, like a deep-seated cancer, can be removed only at the cost of suffering. If guilt could be taken away by good resolutions, by the payment of money, or by visiting a confessional booth, man would lose sight of the seriousness of sin.

We often quote 1 John 1:9: "If we confess our sins, he is faithful and just to forgive us our sins." This sounds easy, but we must not forget the remainder of the text, "and to cleanse us from all unrighteousness." When we ask for forgiveness, we also ask to be cleansed, and cleansing isn't easy. It may require deep and painful surgery, but that surgery is done by a kind and skillful Hand.

SOLOMON'S PRAYER FOR UNDERSTANDING

Give therefore thy servant an understanding heart to judge thy people, that I may discern between good and bad: for who is able to judge this thy so great a people? 1 Kings 3:9.

In his prayer when he became king of Israel Solomon asked, literally, for a "hearing" heart, that he might make right decisions. This is a fitting petition for every Christian.

"John Wesley tells us of a man against whom year after year his choler rose. He thought of him contemptuously as covetous. One day when he gave to one of Wesley's favorite philanthropies a gift that seemed too small, Wesley's indignation burst all bounds, and he raked him fore and aft with scathing condemnation. Wesley tells us in his diary that the man quietly said: 'I know a man who at the week's beginning goes to the market and buys a penny's worth of parsnips and takes them home to boil in water, and all that week he has the parsnips for his meat and the water for his drink; and meat and drink alike cost him a penny a week.' 'Who is the man?' said Wesley. 'I am,' was the reply. And Wesley adds, 'This he constantly did, although he then had two hundred pounds a year, that he might pay the debts he had contracted before he knew God. And this was the man that I had thought to be covetous.' We cannot be just to anyone whom we do not understand."—HARRY EMERSON FOSDICK, *The Meaning of Service,* p. 101.

No, we cannot be just unless we understand. Everyone who deals with people—the teacher, the minister, the judge, the social worker, the physician—must remember this maxim.

It takes time and thought to understand. It is far easier to jump to conclusions, to make quick judgments. "How often serious difficulties arise from a simple misunderstanding, even among those who are actuated by the worthiest motives; and without the exercise of courtesy and forbearance, what serious and even fatal results may follow."— *Patriarchs and Prophets,* p. 519.

The crowded, complicated life of the twentieth century makes understanding more important than ever before. Man lives so close to his neighbor. May God give us understanding hearts!

QUITTING TOO SOON

He came thither unto a cave, and lodged there; and, behold, the word of the Lord came to him, and he said unto him, What doest thou here, Elijah? And he said, I have been very jealous for the Lord God of hosts: for the children of Israel have forsaken thy covenant, thrown down thine altars, and slain thy prophets with the sword; and I, even I only, am left; and they seek my life, to take it away. 1 Kings 19:9, 10.

The greatest experiences of Elijah's life were yet ahead of him, but he wasn't aware of it. He could not foresee his great contribution in re-establishing the schools of the prophets, nor could he anticipate his influence on the kings of Syria or on his successor, Elisha. He did not yet know about the seven thousand faithful souls who had remained true to God. He was ready to quit as he stood at the door of a great future.

Dr. Peale tells of a man who staked a gold claim in the far West. "The claim was in a lonely spot in the mountains. When [the man] started to dig for gold, he found evidence that much work had been done on the claim a long while before. Farthest in, in the excavation, he found an old rusted pick, its handle rotted off but its point sticking firmly in the rocky soil. He threw the pick aside and went to work and to his amazement, just a few feet beyond where he had found it, he came upon a rich vein of gold. He could not escape thinking about the tragedy of the old pick, and some time later he heard the story.

"A prospector had learned of the probability of a rich strike in this locality, had staked out his claim and had gone to work. Day after day, until his back ached unbearably, he worked with his pick, but never a glimpse of gold did he see. Gradually, the acid of discouragement crept through his system, eating away his resolution. His courage slowly ebbed, and one day in desperation, and with a sense of complete futility, he drove his pick hard into the rocky earth, gathered up his belongings, and went away."—NORMAN VINCENT PEALE and SMILEY BLANTON, *Faith Is the Answer,* 1940 ed., p. 83.

Are we guilty of giving up, just on the verge of victory? Do we become tired of the struggle when the going is hard? Remember that Elijah's most productive years followed his greatest discouragement.

LITTLE MISTAKE—GREAT MISFORTUNE

Satan stood up against Israel, and provoked David to number Israel. 1 Chron. 21:1.

Satan has subtle methods. He didn't provoke David to do something illegal, immoral, or cruel, but something that seemed harmless, even wise. Why shouldn't David take a census if he wished to do so? To this day we do not know all the reasons why God disapproved of David's action. Obviously he was stirring resentment among the people by arousing their fear of military conscription; clearly he was failing to give proper recognition to the power of God as against the might of armies. Whatever the reasons may have been, the results of a seemingly harmless but forbidden act were tragic in the extreme.

"Readers of the life of Grenfell of Labrador will remember that his admirers saved up to give him a motor boat so that his fine service to the people living in the islands off the coast might be facilitated. Soon after the boat arrived, Dr. Grenfell received an urgent summons in the night. It was dark and foggy, but since he had his good motor boat and its compass, he started happily enough. To make a thrilling story very short, long after the time had elapsed when by all reckoning he should have reached the island he sought, his men saw looming up in front of his boat a dangerous rock which they knew was miles down the coast and quite in the wrong direction. After the harassing night— in which a mother lost her life—examination was made, and inquiries were set on foot; and at last it was found that a young lad who had been entrusted in Liverpool with the task of fastening the compass to its wooden base had lost one of the brass screws and used a steel one. The compass apparently was not tested after fixing, and the lack of one brass screw cost a life, and nearly cost the life of one of the finest men in our time."—LESLIE D. WEATHERHEAD, *The Significance of Silence,* p. 150.

"Little" mistakes, trifling errors, small oversights, minor lapses of judgment may have far-reaching and grievous results. Satan is still provoking God's children to do things that seem harmless but which God has forbidden. May God help us to be careful! Much may depend on our faithfulness in little things.

HAMAN HONORS MORDECAI

Then took Haman the apparel and the horse, and arrayed Mordecai, and brought him on horseback through the streets of the city, and proclaimed before him, Thus shall it be done unto the man whom the king delighteth to honour. Esther 6:11.

Never in the long history of mankind was there a more unhappy man than Haman. The honor he had desired and suggested, supposing it would be his own, was being conferred, instead, upon his bitterest enemy. And Haman himself was forced to be the master of ceremonies! It is hard to imagine the hatred that marked his face and stirred his soul as he shouted, "Thus shall it be done unto the man whom the king delighteth to honour."

Haman may be considered as a type of the selfish, grasping man of the world, determined to secure success and recognition at any price. He had been promoted, and expected everyone to recognize him. When Mordecai, for reason of conscience, failed to bow low whenever Haman passed, Haman was incensed. He not only sought to punish Mordecai, but Mordecai's people as well. To accomplish his end he would stoop to anything.

Mordecai was a different type of person. Humble and dedicated, he served well both his God and his king. With prophetic insight he challenged his foster daughter, "Who knoweth whether thou art come to the kingdom for such a time as this?" He met life's problems with coolness and insight.

This was not the only time in history when, figuratively speaking, a man was hanged on gallows he had built for another. How often the person who is ruthless finally eats the bitter fruit of his ruthlessness. How often a man who is utterly selfish in life is utterly desolate in death.

No, it doesn't *always* work this way in this world. Sometimes the Hamans hang the Mordecais and destroy their people, but by no means is this always the case. God still stands behind the shadow, keeping watch over His own. And ultimately, if not immediately, the Mordecais receive their deserved rewards.

162

NEHEMIAH REBUILDS JERUSALEM

I told them of the hand of my God which was good upon me; as also the king's words that he had spoken unto me. And they said, Let us rise up and build. So they strengthened their hands for this good work. Neh. 2:18.

Nehemiah held a lucrative, easy, secure job as cupbearer for the Persian king. Probably he had never had it so good. But one day duty called. His brother from Jerusalem visited him and told him how the walls were broken down and the gates burned with fire. As the result of this visit, Nehemiah asked for the job of rebuilding his city.

What if he should fail? Perhaps finances would not be adequate. Perhaps the people would not cooperate. Perhaps opposing armies would overcome them. All of these dangers were real. What assurance of success did Nehemiah have in so difficult an undertaking?

Picture the workers on the walls—half with trowels, the other half with swords. "So neither I, nor my brethren, nor my servants, nor the men of the guard which followed me, none of us put off our clothes, saving that everyone put them off for washing." It was easier—far easier—to be a cupbearer!

Nehemiah's venture was expensive. For twelve years he labored without pay. One hundred and fifty Jews and rulers, besides visiting dignitaries, ate at his table. In addition, he made a large donation to the project. It was much cheaper to be a cupbearer!

And his job was politically crushing. He had to oppose people, and they didn't like it. He had to cancel foreign alliances and prohibit mixed marriages—both unpopular measures. Cupbearing made fewer enemies!

Why did Nehemiah take such risks? "I told them of the hand of *my* God." Repeatedly he speaks of God as *"my* God." There was an intimate friendship between Nehemiah and his God. The farther men drift from God, the less willing they are to risk anything for Him, but the closer they come to God, the less important are the values of this world. The program of the church is carried on the backs of the people who are dedicated to God. Careless Christians do not make Nehemiahs!

163

A FATHER PRAYS FOR HIS CHILDREN

And it was so, when the days of their feasting were gone about, that Job sent and sanctified them, and rose up early in the morning, and offered burnt offerings according to the number of them all: for Job said, It may be that my sons have sinned, and cursed God in their hearts. Thus did Job continually. Job 1:5.

Job's seven sons and three daughters were "living it up." Their father was prosperous, and they apparently shared in the family wealth. The sons took turns putting on big parties for the clan, and included their sisters. They were living lives of carefree luxury.

Job was a man of great spiritual sensitivity. He was "perfect and upright, and one that feared God, and eschewed evil." To him the hilarious celebrations of his children were fraught with danger. He feared that they might lose their respect for God.

What did he do? After their party season was over, he held a religious service. After the manner of his time, he offered burnt offerings for each of these children, calling upon God to make them all that they ought to be. This he did, not just once but "continually."

Job was not the only father who has been concerned about his children. From the vantage point of experience, fathers can detect dangers in activities that appear harmless and pleasant to their children. They can also detect the superficiality that goes with immaturity. As Job took his ten children before God in the context of worship, so every parent may seek God's guidance and protection for his children.

The facts were that God loved Job's children more than Job did. Job's prayers in their behalf were not desperate gestures of a father in panic. They represented a recognition on Job's part that God could do for his sons and daughters what he could not, so he committed them to the care and guidance of a heavenly Father.

There is an interesting footnote to this experience. Job feared that pleasure and prosperity might cause his sons to curse God. Soon Job was being goaded by affliction to do the very same thing, and the mother of his sons encouraged him to yield. But the man who had prayed for the spiritual stability of his sons, himself stood firm.

"EVERY MAN HAS HIS PRICE"

Satan answered the Lord, and said, Doth Job fear God for nought? Hast not thou made an hedge about him, and about his house, and about all that he hath on every side? thou hast blessed the work of his hands, and his substance is increased in the land. But put forth thine hand now, and touch all that he hath, and he will curse thee to thy face. Job 1:9-11.

The powers of evil try in two ways to destroy man—either they work through wealth, power, and position to influence him to compromise and forget God, or they engulf him with suffering, misfortune, and discouragement in an endeavor to break his faith and morale. It seems that the average man can endure only so much prosperity or so much adversity without buckling under the strain.

Job had stood the test of prosperity, and remained "perfect and upright, and one that feared God, and eschewed evil" (Job 1:1). Now he was to be subjected to the test of adversity. The devil was saying to God with a sneer, "Every man has his price. Job will fold under adversity." God was about to demonstrate to the world that there are men who can be destroyed neither by prosperity nor adversity.

"You have met the man who says that every fellow has his price. But whenever you hear a man say that you know that there is at least one man who does have his price, and that is the man who is making the statement. You can compromise till you come to persuade yourself that compromise is the law of life. You can play with honesty till you come to believe in the dishonesty of the whole world."—CLOVIS G. CHAPPELL, *Sermons on Biblical Characters,* p. 87.

No, there are men like Job who do not have a price; but, don't forget it, their steadfastness has its own price. It wasn't easy for Job to keep his faith, neither is it easy to accept what life sometimes hands out today. All honor to the person who has the fortitude not to fold when life gets hard!

We ourselves may not know whether we have a price until the test comes. Trying experiences may be God's means of enabling us to know ourselves and to develop uncompromising integrity.

DRY RIVERS

My brethren have dealt deceitfully as a brook, and as the stream of brooks they pass away; which are blackish by reason of the ice, and wherein the snow is hid: what time they wax warm, they vanish: when it is hot, they are consumed out of their place. Job 6:15-17.

Anyone who lives in an arid or semi-arid country is acquainted with dry rivers. The rock-strewn riverbed is marked by only a brackish puddle here and there until a heavy rain comes, then it becomes a raging torrent.

Job compares his three friends to this kind of river. "My brethren," he says, "are treacherous as a torrent-bed, as freshets that pass away. . . . In time of heat they disappear; when it is hot, they vanish from their place" (R.S.V.). Then Job describes how travelers look to the river for water and are disappointed. "Such you have now become to me" (verse 21, R.S.V.), he tells his friends.

Some Christians might be compared to dry rivers. They disappoint when they are really needed. The world looks to them, expecting to find absolute honesty, untainted purity, Christian kindness, high standards of personal conduct, and a message of hope. Instead, they find only a mocking, dry riverbed, with no water to quench their thirst. Like all dry rivers, the Christian in question probably started well. The Mississippi River and the Los Angeles River are probably quite similar at their sources. One grows to a mighty river, the other disappears ignobly in an ugly bed of hot sand and hard cement. Likewise, how many Christians start well, only to stop too soon.

There is another respect in which some Christians resemble dry rivers—at times they overflow their banks. Occasionally an empty life becomes obsessed with fanatical zeal and rages for a while like a swollen torrent. Eventually the flood subsides and the life is as empty as before, with only the marks of destruction remaining. God is looking for lives that resemble real rivers, beautiful to look upon, bringing blessing to all, but keeping within their banks. These lives are like rivers that neither disappoint nor destroy.

WISDOM AND UNDERSTANDING

Behold, the fear of the Lord, that is wisdom; and to depart from evil is understanding. Job 28:28.

The context of this passage—the twenty-eighth chapter of Job—is most interesting. The first eleven verses of the chapter describe ancient mining operations. The miners

". . . open shafts in a valley away from where men live;
    they are forgotten by travelers,
    they hang afar from men,
    they swing to and fro" . . .
"Man puts his hand to the flinty rock,
    and overturns mountains by the roots.
He cuts out channels in the rocks,
    and his eye sees every precious thing.
He binds up the streams so that they do not trickle
    and the thing that is hid he brings forth to light"
                     (verses 4, 9-11, R.S.V.).

These were exciting accomplishments in ancient days. "But," Job asks, "where shall wisdom be found?" and his answer is that it cannot be purchased by any treasures extracted from the earth. It is not to be found in nature nor in the accomplishments of men. Its worth outweighs all material values.

Then Job repeats the question, "Whence then comes wisdom?" The answer comes clear and strong:

"God understands the way to it
    and he knows its place."

Wisdom is to be found in God, not in the works of man. The implications of this truth are found in our text:

"Behold the fear of the Lord, that is wisdom; and to depart from evil is understanding."

Recognition of God, submission, humility, reverence, respect, adoration, faith—these constitute wisdom beyond the most striking exploits of man. Right living, honesty, integrity, dependability—these constitute understanding surpassing the philosophy of man.

167

THE FORGOTTEN GOD

Behold, God is great, and we know him not. Job 36:26.

Never in the history of mankind was there so much evidence of the greatness of God as now. Every new discovery of science, properly understood, enhances the power and wisdom of the Creator. From the discovery of the power of the atom to the unfolding revelations of the vastness of the universe, all knowledge tells the story of a magnificent Mind.

But man reacts strangely to these revelations of the greatness of God. The more he learns of the mysteries of the universe, the more self-sufficient he feels, and the less regard he pays to God. He seems to worship his own ability to learn instead of the One who created his mind and provided the data to which his mind reacts.

Suppose a boy were to be shown a large aircraft—let us say a Boeing 707—and suppose he should react with awe and respect for the designer of the craft. Then suppose, when the boy grows up, he should learn the science of aircraft design. Would you expect him to say, "Now that I understand the construction of a Boeing 707, I no longer respect its designer"? Should not understanding increase rather than diminish the regard for the mind behind the accomplishment? Do we worship ourselves for our God-given ability to understand a bit of what God has created?

Our text says, "Behold, God is great, and we know him not." A renowned scientist recently asserted that he no longer needed the hypothesis of God. Many people, content with their gadgets and their security for the future, live as though God did not exist.

We may know Him, "whom to know is life eternal." We may learn of Him through His works, through His Word, and through His Son. We may come close to Him as we contemplate and pray. We may partake of His Spirit as we cooperate with Him in ministry for His other children. If we look we will see His footprints everywhere; if we listen we will hear His still, small voice.

Our God has said, "I will never leave thee, nor forsake thee" (Heb. 13:5). This should rebuke our forgetfulness and neglect. Let us give God His proper place in our lives.

JOB FINDS HELP IN GOD

I have heard of thee by the hearing of the ear: but now mine eye seeth thee. Job 42:5.

"From the depths of discouragement and despondency Job rose to the heights of implicit trust in the mercy and the saving power of God."—*Prophets and Kings,* p. 163. Through what succession of experiences did Job make this transition? If we can discover how he recovered from tragedy and discouragement, we will find help in our experiences.

Without warning Job lost his belongings, his health, and his sons and daughters. His wife advised him to "curse God, and die." His friends, in harmony with the philosophy of their day, thought he must be a great sinner. He had no hint of the backstage dialog between God and Satan, which would have explained his misfortunes.

At first Job was so bitter over his misfortunes that he cursed the day of his birth. Finally, a ray of light began to shine through the darkness. He said, "Even now, behold, my witness is in heaven, and he that vouches for me is on high" (Job 16:19, R.S.V.). He was still confused and discouraged, but he began to look hopefully to God to vindicate him.

Then his trust in God grew. He said, "For I know that my Redeemer lives, and at last he will stand upon the earth" (chap. 19:25, R.S.V.). Hope began to appear in his life.

At last he developed insight. Although he did not yet know of Satan's specific designs against him, Job said, "But he knoweth the way that I take: when he hath tried me, I shall come forth as gold" (chap. 23:10). He had progressed far from the day when he cursed the day of his birth.

God soon revealed Himself to Job and gradually removed his questioning and despair. "Now mine eye seeth thee," he said.

His entire experience reveals to the Christian that there is a ladder to triumph from the depths of despair. No matter how hopeless and tangled life becomes, there is a God who provides hope in the dark hours, and eventual solutions to life's problems. But these solutions do not come in a moment. Remember the patience of Job.

169

"BE STILL"

Commune with your own heart upon your bed, and be still.
Ps. 4:4.

A newspaper editor once made the observation, "What we need most is a renaissance of the ability to sit still." This comment reflects the restlessness of our generation.

Relaxation is essential to maximum achievement. The human organism is geared to a pendulumlike swing between work and rest, tension and release, excitement and tranquillity. Ideally, we enjoy work, tension, and excitement if it is properly punctuated by rest, release, and tranquillity. Modern life cheats the rhythm of nature by introducing continual work, continual tension, continual excitement, and this results in physical and emotional illness.

There was a time when, after a hard day's work, the family spent the evening at home playing games, visiting, or reading. Now the family is scattered in as many directions as there are available automobiles, and those left at home are probably watching television. Few of the usual activities are relaxing and recreative.

This principle of relaxation has spiritual implications. Many people with little religious experience hear God's call, but are too busy to do anything about it. They are too busy to read their Bibles, too busy to pray, too busy to worship, too busy to witness. Their lives are a mad rush of work, social life, family activity. Now and then, possibly during a spell of illness, they suffer pangs of remorse because they haven't taken time to think about God. But when health returns they are back at the same old "rat race."

Often their problems result from poor planning. Most of us will not find time to meditate and pray and read the Bible unless we set apart a portion of our day for that activity. The quiet hour, or half hour, or even quarter hour, when we shut out the world and its hubbub and open the avenues to the soul for God, can prove to be the most significant time in our lives. Strength may be drawn from outside ourselves that will prepare us for the experiences and decisions of life. God speaks with a "still, small voice." How much we miss when we fail to "be still."

THE GOD WHO IS ALWAYS THERE

The heavens declare the glory of God; and the firmament sheweth his handywork. Ps. 19:1.

In his *Fifth Avenue Sermons* Dr. John Sutherland Bonnell tells the story of a walk he took with a young Highlander through a beautiful glen on the Isle of Skye:

"In that hour I experienced the emotions that sweep over a Highlander in his native haunts. The silence of that weird place was broken only by the murmur of a distant stream which, clear as crystal, flowed down the mountainside. There came to my mind the words of Coleridge:

> So lovely 'twas, that God himself
> scarce seemèd there to be.

"I found myself wondering whether anybody else had ever penetrated into that mysterious Glen, when suddenly I caught sight of a boulder, one side of which was worn smooth by the wind and rain. On that surface, a geometrical figure had been drawn. Someone had amused himself by working out a problem in Euclid. . . .

"So has it been in the history of scientific progress. Wherever man has turned his telescope upon the starry heavens, no matter how deep he has penetrated into the vast solitudes, everywhere he sees the work of Mind, and he knows that Somebody has been there before him." —Pages 205, 206.

When the psalmist looked at the heavens he recognized that "Somebody had been there before him." When we look at the same heavens through the largest telescope, we should be all the more convinced of the infinite knowledge of God.

We do not have to peer into the heavens to sense the greatness of God. The microscope as well as the telescope tells us of a Creator. Plants, animals, and man witness to His creative power. And these things not only tell us that there *is* a God, they give us a glimpse of what our God is like. "The heavens declare the glory of God"—His character, His dependability, His power, His greatness. So much of life is temporary and misleading that it does our souls good to look up into the heavens and consider Him who is changeless and eternal.

DELIVERANCE FROM FEAR

I sought the Lord, and he heard me, and delivered me from all my fears. Ps. 34:4.

"There is a legend of a peasant who, driving into a city in Europe, was hailed by an aged woman who asked him to take her up and drive her into the town with him. Looking at her as they drove along, the peasant became alarmed and asked who she was. She told him that she was the plague, cholera. The peasant then ordered her out of his cart, but she assured him that in the city she would kill only ten persons. As proof of her pledge she handed him a dagger and told him that if she slew more than ten, he was to take the dagger and slay her. After they reached the city, more than a hundred perished with the plague. The angry peasant, meeting the woman on the street, drew his dagger and was about to slay her. But she lifted her hand and told him that she had kept her word. 'I killed only ten. Fear killed the rest.'"
—CLARENCE E. MACARTNEY, *You Can Conquer,* pp. 10, 11.

Fear continues to take its heavy toll. Physicians tell us that a large percentage of the illnesses of man are not organic, but are triggered by fear. People fear failure, they fear loss of love, they fear other people, they fear the future, they fear death. What is the remedy? The psalmist tells us: "I sought the Lord." This suggests prayer, meditation, study. It suggests seeking to learn about God. It suggests concern about the things of God. The results? The psalmist does not say that he was delivered from pain, misfortune, or the prospect of death. He does suggest that he was delivered from the fear of these things. In the twenty-third psalm we read: "Yea, though I walk through the valley of the shadow of death, I will fear no evil." We are not assured of deliverance from the "valley of the shadow," but from fear.

It would be the height of folly to suggest that there is no reason for fear in the present world. Danger lurks everywhere, but the Christian rests secure in his confidence in the eternal purpose of God. He believes in the love of God and the eventual triumph of right. Thus fear melts away in the context of knowledge and faith.

A CURE FOR ANXIETY

Why art thou cast down, O my soul? and why art thou disquieted in me? hope thou in God. Ps. 42:5.

The psalmist is addressing himself. The problems and disappointments of life have been crushing him, yet he recognizes the providence of God. But why be so discouraged when he can depend on God?

The English literary genius, William Cowper, is an extreme example of a person who suffered such anxiety: "He had received an appointment to a clerkship in the House of Lords, but as soon as he received the appointment he began to conjure up visions of the terrors of an examination, and of hostility to him in the office where he had to study the *Journal,* until his mind was deranged. First he tried to take his life with laudanum; then he resolved to fly to France, change his religion, and bury himself in a monastery; then he turned again to self-destruction, and, taking a coach, ordered the coachman to drive him to the Thames, intending to throw himself into the river. But once again he drew back. On the night before the day appointed for the examination before the Lords, he lay for some time with the point of his penknife pressed against his heart, but could not bring himself to drive the knife home. Then he tried to hang himself, but the rope by which he was suspended broke."—CLARENCE E. MACARTNEY, *You Can Conquer,* p. 87. This was the man who wrote:

"God moves in a mysterious way
　　His wonders to perform;
　He plants His footsteps in the sea,
　　And rides upon the storm.

"Ye fearful saints, fresh courage take;
　　The clouds ye so much dread
　Are big with mercy, and shall break
　　In blessings on your head.

"Judge not the Lord by feeble sense,
　　But trust Him for His grace;
　Behind a frowning providence
　　He hides a smiling face."

HALF AND HALF MEN

I hate vain thoughts: but thy law do I love. **Ps. 119:113.**

The Authorized Version rendering of this text does not do it justice. The Revised Standard Version reads, "I hate double-minded men," and Moffatt puts it even more strikingly: "I hate men who are half and half."

The term "half and half" says something to us. We think of a dairy product that is neither milk nor cream, or we may think of a brand of gasoline that is neither high octane nor low. "Half and half" tells us of a product that is neither weak nor powerful, neither inferior nor superior.

Many people have decided—often without thought—that this middle ground is the safest. If they are zealous and highly committed, they will be considered fanatical; if they are listless and uncommitted, they will not be taken seriously. So they decide to appear to be good without being too good, to be busy without being too busy, and to be religious without being too religious.

A great preacher once made the following comment on this text: "During the War had a man strolled into a recruiting office and explained that owing to his business and its claim on him, he couldn't afford much time, but that he didn't want to be quite out of it, and would like to do something, and with that offered (what many people think is quite enough for God) a quarter of an hour in the morning, and a like period in the evening, always provided, of course, he was not too rushed, the sergeant would have turned upon him with strange and bloodcurdling oaths. 'We are at war,' he would have growled, 'and your wretched business is of no importance. The Army claims, not something you think you can spare, but you; all that you have, all that you are, all that you hope to be. If you are not willing to give us that, then out of this!' So Christ claims you, to work for Him, live for Him, die for Him, the whole of you. To offer to go shares with Him, to grant Him some place in your life is to insult Him."—ARTHUR J. GOSSIP, *The Hero in Thy Soul,* pp. 181, 182.

"I hate men who are half and half," the Lord says—lukewarm men, uncommitted men, hesitant men. Are we wholly dedicated to Him?

"STRENGTH IN MY SOUL"

In the day when I cried thou answeredst me, and strength-enedst me with strength in my soul. Ps. 138:3.

How often in life we meet disappointments and bereavements. Cherished hopes may not come true. Our friends, even our loved ones, may let us down. Health may desert us or accident may incapacitate us or a loved one's death may bereave us.

Harry Emerson Fosdick tells the story of a woman who found strength to endure:

"I was living at Sandy Hook when I met Jacob Walker. He kept the Sandy Hook lighthouse. He took me to that lighthouse as his bride. . . .

"After a few years my husband was transferred to Robbins Reef. The day we came here I said, 'I won't stay. The sight of water which-ever way I look makes me lonesome and blue.' I refused to unpack my trunks and boxes at first. I unpacked them a little at a time. After a while they were all unpacked and I stayed on. . . .

"My husband caught a heavy cold while tending the light. It turned into pneumonia. It was necessary to take him to the Smith Infirmary on Staten Island, where he could have better care than I could give him in the lighthouse.

"I could not leave the light to be with him. He understood. One night, while I sat up there tending the light, I saw a boat coming. Something told me what news it was bringing me. I expected the words that came up to me from the darkness.

" 'We are sorry, Mrs. Walker, but your husband's worse.'

" 'He is dead,' I said.

"We buried him in the cemetery on the hill. Every morning when the sun comes up I stand at the port-hole and look in the direction of his grave. . . . But there always seems to come a message from that grave. It is what I heard Jacob say more often than anything else in his life. Just three words, 'Mind the light.' "—*Twelve Tests of Character,* pp. 206, 207.

Mrs. Walker, still keeping the light, was seventy years old when interviewed, and her husband had been dead for thirty-two years.

175

GOD WITH US

*Whither shall I go from thy spirit? or whither shall I flee
from thy presence? If I ascend up into heaven, thou art there:
if I make my bed in hell, behold, thou art there.* Ps. 139:7, 8.

A little girl was once heard to say, "God, I wish you wouldn't
follow me around all the time." Do we resent or welcome the inescap-
able proximity of God?

The person who has committed his life to selfishness and sin feels
like this little girl. Such a person wishes that somehow, somewhere,
he might get away from God's presence, but he can't. If a person is
dishonest, there is One looking over his shoulder as he endorses the
checks that represent ill-gotten gains. If a person is immoral, there is
One standing at the door of any den of vice he may visit. If a person
is deceitful, there is a Recorder of every misleading word and hypocriti-
cal act. If a person's heart is filled with hatred, there is One by his
side who knows every thought.

No amount of wishing will persuade God to go away. We can't
elude Him, avoid Him, or fool Him. Our lives are an open book before
Him.

But there is a bright side to this fact of life. God not only follows
people on their way to hell, He is also near those who are on their way
to heaven. Every unsung act of kindness has a witness, every temptation
resisted brings happiness to Him, every noble thought is recorded,
and He rejoices as we grow in spiritual stature.

The psalmist continues, "If I take the wings of the morning, and
dwell in the uttermost parts of the sea; even there shall thy hand lead
me, and thy right hand shall hold me. If I say, Surely the darkness
shall cover me; even the night shall be light about me" (verses 9-11).

There is a tradition at Princeton that Aaron Burr once attended
some revival meetings. One night he shut himself in his room, announcing that he was going to decide for or against God. According to the
story, late at night the students living near him heard him throw open
the shutters and shout, "Good-by, God."

John Wesley on his deathbed said, "The best of all is, God is with
us." Whether we resent or welcome God's presence depends on us.

COMPREHENSIVE COUNSEL

Keep thy heart with all diligence; for out of it are the issues of life. Put away from thee a froward mouth, and perverse lips put far from thee. Let thine eyes look right on, and let thine eyelids look straight before thee. Ponder the path of thy feet, and let all thy ways be established. Prov. 4:23-26.

The author of this passage knew how to pack a lot of wisdom into a few words. First, he concerns himself about the mind. Police it, protect it, develop it, discipline it, he implies, "for from it flow the springs of life" (R.S.V.). The mind is like a vacant lot—untended, it grows up to unsightly weeds; cultivated, it may be the site of a beautiful home or a lovely park or an imposing business building. "The cultivated mind is the measure of the man," says Ellen G. White (*Counsels to Parents and Teachers,* p. 475).

But the mind works through other organs of the body in the development of a complete personality. "Put away from you crooked speech, and put devious talk far from you" (R.S.V.). "Out of the abundance of the heart the mouth speaketh" (Matt. 12:34). Words are symbols of the thoughts that originate in the mind. "If any man offend not in word, the same is a perfect man, and able also to bridle the whole body" (James 3:2). How well we know that "the tongue is a fire, a world of iniquity" (verse 6).

And then there are the eyes. "Let your eyes look directly forward, and your gaze be straight before you" (R.S.V.). There are many diversions that cause us to look to the right or to the left. And often we change our course in the direction of that which attracts our interest. Thus worthy objectives are missed because of wandering eyes.

And finally, "Take heed to the path of your feet, then all your ways will be sure" (R.S.V.) Watch where you are going! Don't just wander through life. Go somewhere.

Our minds, our mouths, our eyes, our feet—all need to be directed and disciplined by an overmastering loyalty and that loyalty must be directed Godward. Man is a unit and there should be consistency in his words, thoughts, interests, and actions. The life that centers in Christ has a unifying principle that will control thought and conduct.

SEVEN ABOMINATIONS

These six things doth the Lord hate: yea, seven are an abomination unto him: a proud look, a lying tongue, and hands that shed innocent blood, an heart that deviseth wicked imaginations, feet that be swift in running to mischief, a false witness that speaketh lies, and he that soweth discord among brethren. Prov. 6:16-19.

We are often reminded to dwell on the positive, not the negative. This is generally true, but we must not forget that the Ten Commandments were cast in negative form. Sometimes No is more effective than Yes. Our passage is an illustration of the power of the negative. God's displeasure with these seven sins is not mild, He *hates* them.

"A proud look" implies a feeling of superiority over one's fellow man, and an attitude of complacency regarding oneself. "Haughty eyes," the Revised Standard Version translates it. To God, how distasteful is man's lack of humility!

"A lying tongue" is an affront to the God of truth. Dishonesty is one of the cardinal sins. Outside the New Jerusalem will be "whosoever loveth and maketh a lie" (Rev. 22:15).

"Hands that shed innocent blood" may not always be those of actual murderers, but who take advantage of those who are weaker than themselves. The prophets of God constantly warn against this vice.

"A heart that devises wicked plans" (R.S.V.) reminds of the cunning, designing person who plans, with malice aforethought, courses of action that are impure, dishonest, and destructive. He does not blunder into sin—his wrongdoing is premeditated.

"Feet that make haste to run to evil" (R.S.V.) pictures the person who can't wait until he becomes involved in something questionable. If there is half a chance to do wrong, he will find it.

"A false witness that speaketh lies" is particularly reprehensible because he is doing untold harm to someone by his perjury.

"He that soweth discord among brethren" is the talebearer, the whisperer, the conveyer of gossip. He separates friends with fiendish delight. When he is around, peace turns to hostility.

However respectable these sins may appear on the outside, they are an abomination to God.

THE LIBERAL GIVER

There is that scattereth, and yet increaseth; and there is that withholdeth more than is meet, but it tendeth to poverty. The liberal soul shall be made fat: and he that watereth shall be watered also himself. Prov. 11:24, 25.

The quaint English of the King James Version does not make the point of this passage quite as clear as the more modern reading of the R.S.V.: "One man gives freely, yet grows all the richer; another withholds what he should give, and only suffers want."

There is something inspiring about the person who is sensitive to human need and willing to give sacrificially to meet that need. In his biography Booker T. Washington tells of an old, crippled, poorly clad Negro woman who came to him one day and said, "Mr. Washin'ton, God knows I spent de bes' days of my life in slavery. God knows I's ignorant an' poor; but I knows what you an' Miss Davidson is tryin' to do. I knows you is tryin' to make better men an' better women for de coloured race. I ain't got no money, but I wants you to take dese six eggs, what I's been savin' up, an' I wants you to put dese six eggs into de eddication of dese boys an' gals." Says Mr. Washington, "Since the work at Tuskegee started, it has been my privilege to receive many gifts for the benefit of the institution, but never any, I think, that touched me so deeply as this one."—*Up From Slavery* (Dial Press, 1901), p. 132.

Stories like this remind us of the poor widow whom Jesus commended for placing her very small offering in the treasury. We must remember, however, that all sacrificial gifts are not made by the very poor. The Bible also commends Barnabas who, "having land, sold it, and brought the money, and laid it at the apostles' feet" (Acts 4:37). The very poor may provide us examples of giving, but it is the generosity of the more prosperous that meets the material needs of man and of the church.

It is worthy of notice that in many cases people who give liberally are well-organized, self-disciplined people who never seem to want for necessary funds. On the other hand, people who never have anything to give are often disorganized and poorly disciplined.

179

A GOOD WORD

Heaviness in the heart of man maketh it stoop: but a good word maketh it glad. Prov. 12:25.

Anxiety is not a new problem in human experience. Heaviness weighed down the hearts of men three thousand years ago! Jesus recognized the problem in His day when He said, "Be not anxious." Should we be surprised if a thick cloud of anxiety sometimes envelops our own lives?

The ancient maker of proverbs not only recognized the age-old problem of a heavy heart but he also knew the answer—"A good word maketh it glad." We must not expect that the anxious person will always find his solution without help. He needs "a good word" from someone else. It may be a cheery "Good morning." It may be a deserved compliment, it may be encouragement to carry on, it may be a reminder of the kindness of God.

Suppose a friend comes to us with his anxieties, seeking relief. How can we speak the "good word" that will cause the sun to come out from behind the clouds? First, we can be good listeners. Often the discouraged person needs to share his problems. He is not helped so much by the multitude of words spoken by his counselor, but by their quality. Second, we must not be shocked at the disclosure of doubts, fears, and sins. If we appear shaken, the chance to speak the appropriate "good word" may not be ours. Third, we must not rebuke the person who is confiding in us. "You have certainly made a mess of your life" is not the "good word" that will help restore him. He already knows that.

Finally, after we have tried to be of help—perhaps in a faltering way—we must never betray his confidence. "This is the hardest 'don't' to observe, and frankly, very few people can do it. Perhaps they tell their wives or they tell another person, prefacing the revelation with, 'Now I know you won't tell anyone but . . .' or, 'I am telling you in greatest confidence, but . . .' , and frequently the hearer proceeds to spread the story with the same preliminaries."—LESLIE D. WEATHERHEAD, *Prescription for Anxiety*, p. 68.

Let us become experts at speaking the "good word" that lifts burdens from heavy hearts.

YOU ARE WHAT YOU THINK

As he thinketh in his heart, so is he. Prov. 23:7.

"You are not what you think you are, but what you think, you are." This is another way of expressing the principle that the wise man taught when he said, "As he thinketh in his heart, so is he." Your actions may not be you. Expediency may lead you to behave in a way that does not accurately represent your real character. Your words may not be you. A wide gap may exist between what you say and what you are. Your reputation may not be you. People may think you better than you really are. *Your thoughts are you!*

William James is quoted as saying: "Think of evil and, down among the nerve cells and fibers the molecules are registering it, storing it up against us when the next temptation comes." The problem of evil thinking must be met realistically by every person. Strong drives within and prevalent enticements without present the mind with a constant temptation to operate on the sensual level. Conduct is generally restrained by an ethical code, by the desire for approval of the group, or by religious considerations. Often these deterrents to evildoing confine themselves to the overt act and leave the realm of thought ungoverned. Jesus recognized this principle in the Sermon on the Mount. First, He reminded His hearers that the pure in heart would see God. Then He pointed out that hatred and murder, lust and adultery, are violations of the same law. Jesus probed into the realm of thought and made it clear that no person could enter the kingdom whose mind was not converted as well as his actions.

Many a person is frustrated because he is ashamed of his thoughts. He recognizes that although his outward actions are acceptable to society, his inward self is not acceptable to God. The Scriptures tell of a gospel that is adequate to bring into captivity every thought (2 Cor. 10:5). The Christian transformation of character includes "the renewing of your mind" (Rom. 12:2). There is power in Christ, not only to make conduct proper, but also to make minds pure.

The Bible tells us that "the thoughts of the wicked are an abomination to the Lord" (Prov. 15:26). The converse is also true—the thoughts of the righteous are His delight.

181

AGUR'S PRAYER

Two things have I required of thee; deny me them not before I die: Remove far from me vanity and lies: give me neither poverty nor riches; feed me with food convenient for me: lest I be full, and deny thee, and say, Who is the Lord? or lest I be poor, and steal, and take the name of my God in vain. Prov. 30:7-9.

This gem is part of a prophecy by an unknown writer, Agur the son of Jakeh. Whoever Agur may have been, it is obvious that he had an uncanny understanding of human nature. He saw the dangers both of poverty and of riches. He had heard rich men in their self-sufficiency deny God. He had also heard poor men in their despair curse God. So he asked God to give him enough to keep him above despair but not so much that he would forget the Giver.

In this prayer may be seen a reflection of the world in which we live. A large percentage of the world's population live in or near despair. They are always hungry, with little or no hope for a better future. It is hard for these multitudes to grasp the concept of a loving heavenly Father.

Other millions live in luxury, enjoying all the comforts that modern technology has made possible. These people feel no need of God. Their kingdom is of this world. Practically everything they want is available for a price, and they have the price.

It is noteworthy that both extremes—the hopelessly poor and the extremely wealthy—have a strong tendency to forget God. There are exceptions, of course, to this rule, but not many. Devout worshipers of God often fall between the two extremes of want and affluence.

But God should not be merely a middle-class Deity. His compassion embraces both the needy multitudes and the wealthy. His gospel is not limited to any one stratum of humanity. The message of the church should be beamed to all men on all levels of life. The gospel unites master and slave, rich and poor, educated and uneducated. The gospel, rightly understood, breaks down walls of caste, race, and economic difference. It is the "power of God unto salvation to *every one* that believeth." The love of God embraces all men.

THE GOOD OLD DAYS

Say not thou, What is the cause that the former days were better than these? for thou dost not enquire wisely concerning this. Eccl. 7:10.

There are those who live in a state of perpetual nostalgia, longing for the "good old days." Back there, they say, life was less complicated, people were more dedicated, people lived more exemplary lives. The past, according to these people, was the day of opportunity.

We who are teachers and parents hear this cry often. We read of student riots and youthful crime, and we hear it said, "It wasn't that way when I was young." But a look at history reminds us that the basic problems of mankind, young and old, have been quite the same in every age.

Twenty-five centuries ago Socrates is reported as having said:

"Our youth now love luxury. They have bad manners, contempt for authority. They show disrespect for elders and love chatter in place of exercise. Children are now tyrants, not the servants of their households. They contradict their parents, chatter before company, gobble up their food, and tyrannize their teachers."

It is human nature to forget the unpleasant things in the past and remember that which was pleasant. We forget the low income, and remember the low cost of living. We forget the long summer days in the fields, and remember the long winter evenings by the fireplace. We forget the insecurities and inconveniences of past generations, and remember the low taxes. We forget the infidels we once knew, and remember the saints. We forget the riots and revolutions of history, and react in panic to the happenings of today.

In many respects it is fortunate that the passing of time clothes the past with an aura of beauty. But in our reflective moments we must be realistic. The past had its sordidness, its sin, its suffering. So does the present. The past had its opportunities, its satisfactions, its joys. So does the present. The God whom we serve is the God of the past, the present, and the future. Our age is one of the most fascinating periods in all history. Let us learn from the past, live in the present, and look toward the future. The best day of all is today.

DON'T GIVE UP

Whatsoever thy hand findeth to do, do it with thy might.
Eccl. 9:10.

A generation ago there was a famous preacher by the name of
S. Parkes Cadman. In the early days of radio he preached to more than
5 million people every Sunday. One of the most astonishing things
about this man was that he went to work in a coal mine in England
when he was eleven years old, and for ten years worked underground
eight hours each day to help support his younger brothers and sisters.

"It didn't look then as if he were ever going to get an education.
Yet he became one of the most widely read men in America. He once
told me that he had a fair knowledge of every branch of English literature. When he was working as a 'pony boy', down in the coal mines,
he always had to wait a minute or two each time his car was unloaded;
and while he waited, he dived into his pocket and pulled out a book. It
was so dark down there in the mines that you couldn't see your hand
before you; and he had to read by the light of a dim, old lantern; and
he seldom had more than 120 seconds at a time in which he could read.
Yet he always carried a book. He told me that he would rather have
gone without lunch than to have gone without his books.

"He knew there was only one way to get out of that coal mine,
and that was to read himself out of it. So during the ten years that he
worked as a coal miner, he read every book he could beg or borrow in
the neighbouring village—more than a thousand volumes. No wonder
that boy got ahead. You couldn't have stopped him with anything less
potent than a shot gun. Ten years after he started in the coal mine,
he had educated himself sufficiently to pass his college examinations
with honours and to win a scholarship at Richmond College."—DALE
CARNEGIE, *Little Known Facts About Well Known People* (1947 ed.),
pp. 69, 70.

I can hear someone say, "That might have happened in the nineteenth century but it couldn't happen today. 'Rags to Riches' stories
are a thing of the past." It is true that we live in a different world, where
individualism finds it harder to survive, but it is also true that there are
still men who start at the bottom and succeed despite all obstacles.

THE REAL UPPER CLASS

There was a little city, and few men within it; and there came a great king against it, and besieged it, and built bulwarks against it: now there was found in it a poor wise man, and he by his wisdom delivered the city; yet no man remembered that same poor man. Then said I, Wisdom is better than strength: nevertheless the poor man's wisdom is despised, and his words are not heard. Eccl. 9:14-16.

This is a mixed-up world. People are categorized, not by what they are but by what they have. In 1959 Vance Packard published his well-known book, *Status Seekers.* In this book he described the stratification of American society into five classes, (1) The Real Upper Class, (2) The Semi-Upper Class, (3) The Limited-Success Class, (4) The Working Class, and (5) The Real Lower Class.

Regarding the "real upper class," Packard quotes an informant who describes what it takes to stay on that level. "First, I'd say money is the most important. In fact nobody's in this class if he doesn't have money; but it just isn't money alone. You've got to have the right family connections, and you have got to behave yourself or you get popped out. And if you lose your money, you're dropped. If you don't have money, you're just out."—Page 40.

Solomon recognized this point of view in his day. Here, in our text, was a man who was known to be wise, and who revealed his worth by saving his city in time of siege. The rich and poor alike owed their lives to him, but he couldn't make the social register because he was poor. In a class-conscious society he was soon forgotten.

There is one place where Mr. Packard's five stratifications should not apply, and that is in the church. Jesus taught a gospel of equality before God. He stressed service as the mark of superiority. He preached His gospel to the rich and poor alike, and He expected them to live together in the church as brothers.

In the church, recognition should be determined by a man's worth as a person, not by his bank account. Position, education, and power should fade into the background, and all should stand equal at the foot of the cross. Unfortunately, it doesn't always work this way.

SLAVES ON HORSEBACK

I have seen servants upon horses, and princes walking as servants upon the earth. Eccl. 10:7.

Never judge a man by outward appearances.

Several years ago I went to a famous Washington, D.C., church to hear a world-renowned preacher. When the time arrived for the service to begin, two men took their places behind the pulpit. One had all the marks of a professional man—dignity, bearing, immaculate dress, good grooming. The other man was far from handsome, somewhat ungainly in his bearing, and less than professional in appearance. I had never seen the renowned preacher, so I immediately assumed that the more impressive man was he. Imagine my surprise when the man who didn't look like a minister turned out to be the famous preacher! It is not safe to judge by external appearance.

Dishonest confidence men who wish to prey upon the gullibility of the innocent and uninformed often are meticulous in assuming all of the outward appearances of respectability. In this way they establish an ethos to which they are not entitled and succeed in persuading the unwary. Many people have learned to their sorrow that it does not pay to depend on outward appearance.

Early in the school year in a medical school, the head of the anatomy department was watching the students perform their tasks in the laboratory. He was dressed in casual clothes and was assuming no airs of status. A new student, thinking him to be a janitor, asked him to clean up the floor. The brilliant anatomist complied without a word. He was the type of person the author of Ecclesiastes was describing when he said he had seen "princes walking as servants upon the earth."

Often men of great stature and accomplishments are extremely unconcerned about status and appearance. A few years ago a columnist in a Western newspaper, describing a prominent figure, stated: "He is so successful that he no longer needs to drive a Cadillac." How often status symbols are marks of insecurity rather than indications of success.

DON'T WAIT—WALK

He that observeth the wind shall not sow; and he that regardeth the clouds shall not reap. Eccl 11:4.

There is seldom a convenient time for doing the things that we ought to do.

If we wait until we have time to visit a shut-in friend, the visit may never be made.

If we wait until we can afford to give a substantial gift to missions, the gift may never be given.

If we wait until we feel like apologizing for the angry words we spoke to a loved one or a friend, the apology may never be offered.

If we wait until it is easy to do the devotional reading that we know we should do, the reading may be indefinitely postponed.

If we wait until it seems the natural thing to witness for Christ to a friend or associate, the witness may never be given.

If we wait until we have an overwhelming urge to do missionary work, the urge may never come.

Some cities have pedestrian crossing signs on which the words *wait* and *walk* are illuminated alternately to direct foot traffic. While it is dangerous to walk when the sign says wait, no pedestrian ever reaches his destination who waits when he ought to walk.

So it is with life. It is true that we must not act impulsively. It is proper to wait for the right time to do the things we ought to do, but we must not always wait for the wind to be favorable—we must sow anyhow. Neither should we be too concerned about the clouds when there is reaping to be done. We must be cautious, but not overcautious; careful, but not fearful.

The world is full of timid Christians. The time has come for followers of Christ to seize the initiative, and *do* the things they ought to do with dispatch and courage. While we must prepare to serve God, ultimately we must *do* that for which we have been preparing. While God honors our good intentions, we must act upon these intentions or they will be futile. Dynamic Christian living implies eagerness, daring, action. To stand still is to become a target for the enemy.

187

ISAIAH'S SOCIAL GOSPEL

Wash you, make you clean; put away the evil of your doings from before mine eyes; cease to do evil; learn to do well; seek judgment, relieve the oppressed, judge the fatherless, plead for the widow. Isa. 1:16, 17.

Regarding Isaiah's time Ellen White says: "The outlook was particularly discouraging as regards the social conditions of the people. In their desire for gain, men were adding house to house and field to field. Justice was perverted; and no pity was shown the poor. . . . Even the magistrates, whose duty it was to protect the helpless, turned a deaf ear to the cries of the poor and needy, the widows and the fatherless."—*Prophets and Kings,* p. 306.

And yet these same people were very religious! They brought their multitude of sacrifices to God; they frequented the places of worship; they observed feasts and fasts; they made many prayers. Yet all about them men and women were suffering and these avid religionists were not only unconcerned but were often responsible for their suffering. It is hard for us to understand why people who were so conscientious could be so callous toward their neighbors.

We must not assume, however, that this problem was limited to the time of Isaiah. There are still very religious people who have never heeded the Master's command, "Thou shalt love thy neighbour as thyself."

What about the professed Christian employer who keeps back "the hire of the labourers"? And what about the employee who does not give his employer a fair day's work?

What about the Christian who feels no concern whatsoever for the welfare of his fellow church members or his fellow citizens? Can a person be a Christian and contribute nothing to the needs of humanity?

What about the Christian who feels that his duty is done when he attends the church of his choice and lives a fairly decent life? A follower of Jesus will feel some of the pain of human suffering and injustice and will do what he can to show his concern. The spirit of Christ is the spirit of compassion.

REASON AND GRACE

Come now, and let us reason together, saith the Lord: though your sins be as scarlet, they shall be white as snow; though they be red like crimson, they shall be as wool. Isa. 1:18.

The first part of this verse talks about reason, the last part about grace. George Adam Smith may have been correct when he translated the first statement, "Come now and let us bring our reasoning to an end."

God invites us to exercise the power of reason. He wants us to think as clearly and logically about spiritual truth as about secular knowledge. God does not ask us to check our minds at the door when we go to church. In fact, the only way we can know anything about God is through our minds.

But Christian faith is not limited by the logical structures created by the human mind. When God promised to forgive the most heinous sins He did not attempt to defend His action by logic—He was operating in the realm of grace. He brushed aside the judicial factors of guilt and punishment, and declared that the most guilty sinner would be as white as snow or as wool.

It must not be overlooked, however, that although God washes people white He does not whitewash them. The grace of God is only for people who are willing to receive it and who will obey its demands. The very next verses in the chapter read, "If ye be willing and obedient, ye shall eat the good of the land: but if ye refuse and rebel, ye shall be devoured with the sword." Grace is abundant, it is free, it is bestowed generously; but the recipients must be willing to accept it.

There is a parable about a post office in heaven. According to the story, there are millions of packages there, loaded with gifts and properly addressed but *unclaimed*. The beneficence of God is beyond our wildest imagining. In a sense, our God is a "compulsive giver." Yet we possess very few of His gifts. "If any of you lack wisdom [or any other good thing], let him ask of God, that giveth to all men liberally, and upbraideth not; and it shall be given him" (James 1:5). His most valuable gift is the forgiveness of sin and deliverance from its power.

RELIGION AND MORALS

Many people shall go and say, Come ye, and let us go up to the mountain of the Lord, to the house of the God of Jacob; and he will teach us of his ways, and we will walk in his paths. Isa. 2:3.

"That is to say, a profound revival of spiritual religion will be accompanied by *loftier and more exacting moral standards.* He will teach and we will walk. Morals always grow lax when piety gets cool. When religion becomes a mere conventionality, morality always loses its awful sanctions. Wipe out God and your moral standards will surely fall. If I neglect the temperature of my greenhouse, or if I play fast and loose with it, my tender plants will assuredly droop. And if I neglect my spiritual temperature, which is the climate of my soul, my moral and spiritual flowers will be smitten and pinched. We cannot lower our spirituality and yet have our morality keep its winsome bloom. Let me ask you,—Have you ever known anyone grow loose and careless in their religion, and at the same time become correspondingly nobler and purer, and more scrupulously faithful in their daily life? Have you ever known anyone drop Christ and then become more like Him? . . . When the spirit deteriorates the moral life becomes diseased.

"On the other hand, let there be an enrichment in vital godliness and our conduct will begin to shine like burnished gold."—J. H. JOWETT, *The Whole Armour of God,* pp. 243, 244.

Many people deplore the moral state of our society but overlook the only lasting remedy for it. When modern man listens to God and lets Him teach us His ways, then, and only then, will high standards of moral conduct be restored. True, there are noble pagans who live exemplary lives without God, but they are exceptions to the rule. It is also true that there are professed Christians with low moral standards, but they also are exceptions.

The Christian religion is the most successful factor in the world's history in taming the beast in man. When a man accepts Christ as his Lord, a tremendous motivation for purity, honesty, and goodness comes into his life. If he is sincere he will be transformed by the power of the gospel.

190

ISAIAH WORSHIPS GOD

Then said I, Woe is me! for I am undone; because I am a man of unclean lips, and I dwell in the midst of a people of unclean lips: for mine eyes have seen the King, the Lord of hosts. Isa. 6:5.

"Mine eyes have seen the King." What an experience! The young prophet was granted a glimpse of the Ruler of the universe. He saw His celestial attendants, and he heard their songs of praise. This was the great moment in Isaiah's life.

His reaction to this glorious vision was not ecstasy, but humility. "Woe is me," he said, as he contrasted his own inadequacy and that of his people with the perfection of God. The One on the throne responded to Isaiah's confession by sending one of the beings above His throne to touch his lips and declare his sins forgiven. "Whom shall I send, and who will go for us?" the Lord asked. Immediately came the prophet's response, "Here am I; send me." The Lord responded, "Go, and tell this people."

The experience of Isaiah should be a pattern for every Christian who enters a place of worship. The worshiper should be aware of the presence of God. Helps to this end are intelligent, worshipful prayers; effective reading of the Scriptures; reverent preaching of the Word. There can be no worship until pastor and people see the Lord.

Somewhere in every service should be an acknowledgment of sin. Ministers and people should feel and confess their need of God, and a genuine sense of need will be followed by the assurance of sins forgiven. People may come to church burdened, frightened, discouraged, and remorseful, but they should never go away feeling thus. True worship will bring courage and strength.

No service should close without dedication. The worshiper should leave the house of God willing to go where his Lord wants him to go and do what his Lord wants him to do. Thus worship will have its effect on daily life.

God grant that every Sabbath worship hour may bring this type of experience to every Christian.

HEZEKIAH ENTERTAINS VISITORS

Then said he, What have they seen in thine house? And Hezekiah answered, All that is in mine house have they seen: there is nothing among my treasures that I have not shewed them. Isa. 39:4.

The king of Babylon sent a good-will mission to Hezekiah, king of Judah. Hezekiah was flattered, and arranged a tour for his guests during which he showed them "the house of his precious things, the silver, and the gold, and the spices, and the precious ointment, and all the house of his armour, and all that was found in his treasures: there was nothing in his house, nor in all his dominion, that Hezekiah shewed them not."

Soon after, Isaiah called on the king and inquired about the visitors. He asked Hezekiah the searching question, "What have they seen in thine house?" Still unaware that he had betrayed his nation, Hezekiah told Isaiah how he had showed them everything. At that point Isaiah revealed the coming siege and captivity of Judah.

What *should* Hezekiah have shown his visitors? The heritage of faith in Jehovah was Israel's unique possession. Their real strength lay, not in their treasures, but in their sacred books, their worship, their religious concepts. If Hezekiah had explained these things to his visitors they might have been led to respect the source of Israel's strength, rather than to covet her treasures.

What witness do we as Christians give to the world? What do non-Christians see in our house? Do we boast of our schools, hospitals, churches, and missions, or do we reveal the source of our power— our faith in Jesus Christ and our hope that He is coming again? Does the world see what we have or what we are? The Christian has treasures that are unique and that are of inestimable worth. Let us display these spiritual treasures.

Hezekiah was a good king, but pride caused him to make a fatal mistake. All of Judah's material wealth was carried to Babylon—all of ours will be destroyed in the final conflagration. Only the spiritual values will survive, and they alone must distinguish us from the world. Our effectiveness is proportional to our faith.

ISAIAH REVEALS GOD'S FREE GRACE

Ho, every one that thirsteth, come ye to the waters, and he that hath no money; come ye, buy, and eat; yea, come, buy wine and milk without money and without price. Isa. 55:1.

"In oriental cities, where water is often scarce, water carriers go through the streets selling water at so much per drink. And their cry is this: 'The gift of God, who will buy? Who will buy?' And sometimes a man will buy the whole supply, and then allow the water carrier to give it away. And as he goes back down the street, he no longer says, 'The gift of God, who will buy?' but 'The gift of God, who will take? The gift of God, who will take?' "—CLOVIS G. CHAPPELL, *Sermons on Biblical Characters*, p. 80.

This is the very central idea of the gospel. In one brief paragraph in the fifth chapter of Romans, the righteousness of Christ is mentioned five times as "the free gift" (verses 15-17, R.S.V.). Time and again Paul emphasizes that salvation comes to man, not in payment for his works, not by virtue of his national origin, not because he keeps the law, but as a *gift*. Salvation is "without money and without price." It is the gift of God bestowed on everyone who will accept it.

The act of accepting this free gift is *faith*. How easy it all sounds, but how hard it is to experience! Salvation by works has been called the "fatal tendency of the human heart." The idea of the gospel as an offer, not a demand, is an essential principle of the Christian faith. If the gospel were a demand, the saved would parade all over heaven showing their medals. Salvation cannot be deserved, it cannot be earned, it can only be accepted as a free gift from God.

Faith is the receptive factor of the soul. Dedication, good works, Christian character, are the results of exercising faith. Having accepted this free gift, we have a new incentive to worship and serve the great Giver.

Justification by faith is "the work of God in . . . doing for man that which it is not in his power to do for himself" (*Testimonies to Ministers*, p. 456). Let us respond to God's efforts in our behalf. May we rejoice that the experience of being right with God is free to everyone.

"FOR A LIMITED TIME ONLY"

Seek ye the Lord while he may be found, call ye upon him while he is near. Isa. 55:6.

"One of the old Saxon kings set out with an army to put down a rebellion in a distant province of his kingdom. When the insurrection had been quelled and the army of the rebels defeated, the king placed a candle over the archway of his castle where he had his headquarters and, lighting the candle, announced through a herald to all those who had been in rebellion against him that all who surrendered and took the oath of loyalty while the candle was burning would be spared. The king offered them his clemency and mercy, but the offer was limited to the life of that candle."—CLARENCE EDWARD MACARTNEY, *The Greatest Texts of the Bible,* p. 34.

How true to life is this ancient tale. Most of the opportunities of life are like department store ads—"for a limited time only." The chance to gain education beckons and is gone. Those who fail to heed often look in vain for the opportunity to return. Financial success appears in the sky like a comet and vanishes away, and for a lifetime we repeat, "If we had only known!"

But is it correct to conclude that the Lord makes His offer of salvation "for a limited time only"? Our text seems to imply this. What does it mean? Is not the Lord always near? Can He not be found at all times? It is possible to discover that we are far from God, not because He has departed from us but because we have departed from Him. One place to find God is in His Word, but we may neglect it until it loses its appeal to us. Another place to find God is in prayer; but if we cease praying for a long time, it may be hard to begin again. Conscience leads us to God, but if we ignore it or wrongly educate it, it can also lead us away from God.

Sometimes God comes near in a service of worship or an evangelistic meeting, or in some great experience of life. We may call upon Him or we may walk away. The candle burns but a little while, and it may not be lighted again for years. Now is the time to respond. "Let the wicked forsake his way, and the unrighteous man his thoughts: and let him return unto the Lord."

SKILLFUL SINNERS—BUNGLING SAINTS

They are wise to do evil, but to do good they have no knowledge. Jer. 4:22.

Another version translates this text, "They are skilled in doing evil, but how to do good they know not" (R.S.V.). How true this statement is, in every age. A tremendous expenditure of human skill is wasted on things that are destructive, but it is hard to command the necessary resources to accomplish that which is good.

If all of the billions under the control of the underworld could be spent for human betterment, how easily the problems of poverty could be solved.

If the money spent for things that destroy health—liquor, tobacco, drugs—could be diverted to products and activities that promote health, what blessings would result.

If the vast fortunes made and spent in Hollywood could be channeled into the processes of education, what strides could be made in raising the intellectual level of our population. And if the tremendous skill developed in Hollywood for the purpose of mere entertainment —much of it of questionable quality—could be applied to more serious pursuits, how greatly the level of culture could be raised.

The world is filled with skillful sinners—clever crooks, astute gamblers, adroit manipulators, big-time operators of all types, whose goals in life are to debase and injure their fellow men for their own profit. These people apply themselves assiduously to the task of doing their nefarious work effectively. They spare no efforts to reach their objectives.

There are also—it is sad to say—many presumably good people who wouldn't think of doing anything base or criminal, who fail to become skillful in doing constructive and worth-while things. They worship mediocrity. Among them are the poor teachers, preachers, lawyers, doctors, nurses, businessmen, et cetera, who might be effective in their fields if they were willing to put as much skill into their jobs as do some of their contemporaries who are engaged in wrong and harmful pursuits. Let us not be satisfied to do good poorly, while others are doing wrong skillfully.

"HE MADE IT AGAIN"

The vessel that he made of clay was marred in the hand of the potter; so he made it again another vessel, as seemed good to the potter to make it. Jer. 18:4.

Nearly everyone has watched a potter at work at his wheel. Out of a piece of unpromising clay he deftly shapes an object of utility and beauty. But even the best potter does not always succeed. The consistency of the clay may not be correct, or a foreign object may be present—whatever the cause, the vessel may be "spoiled" on the potter's wheel.

Our Scripture passage might have pictured the potter as throwing the clay away in disgust, but such was not the case. He "reworked it into another vessel" (R.S.V.), and thus was realized his dream.

What an expressive parable of life! How often the heavenly Potter is unable to make of us what He would like us to be. The fault is not with the Potter, but with the quality of the clay. Despite the resistance of the material, the Potter patiently tries again and again until He succeeds in shaping something of which He can be proud.

As a young Pharisee, Saul was about as stubborn clay as could be found. He was arrogant, cruel, uncompromising, and fully dedicated to his destructive objectives. It took drastic action on the part of God to reshape his life. Christ's appearance to him on his way to Damascus did it. The badly shaped vessel was remade and became a thing of beauty.

Not every life is reshaped as dramatically as was Paul's, but the Potter remains at the wheel. Of thousands of lives it can be truthfully said, "He made it again." Thousands of Christians witness to the work of God in changing their lives. Thousands more who have grown up in the Christian faith recognize the providence of God in keeping them from the pitfalls of sin.

When, in eternity, the redeemed of God from all ages will have been gathered together, they will be a tremendous display of the work of the Master Potter. Characters will be there, made beautiful by the transforming touch of God. Every one of us may be in that group if we will let God make us again.

GOD CONTROLS EZEKIEL'S LIFE

The hand of the Lord was there upon me; and he said unto me, Arise, go forth into the plain, and I will there talk with thee. Then I arose, and went forth into the plain: and, behold, the glory of the Lord stood there, as the glory which I saw by the river of Chebar: and I fell on my face. Then the spirit entered into me, and set me upon my feet. Eze. 3:22-24.

In a picturesque way Ezekiel reveals his responsiveness to the guidance and influence of God. First of all, the hand of the Lord rested upon him and the Lord bade him go forth to the plain. "Then I arose, and went forth into the plain." Then the glory of the Lord appeared, "and I fell on my face," he says. Finally the Spirit entered into him and set him upon his feet. We may not understand how God's "hand," His voice, His "glory," and His "spirit" were manifested to Ezekiel, but there can be no question about the genuineness and spontaneity of Ezekiel's response.

Every life has its times when important decisions must be made. Perhaps a young person is deciding on his career or on his life partner. Perhaps choices are being made regarding the selection of a home or a school. Perhaps religious decisions regarding deep loyalties and faith in God are the issues. In any case, happy is the person who can sense the presence of God in the decision-making process. There may be no Urim and Thummim, as on the high priest's breastplate, there may be no fleece, as in the experience of Gideon, but in subtle ways the Lord still directs in the decisions of His children, if they let Him. God's guidance may be sensed in the circumstances that surround our lives. His voice may be heard in the counsel of friends and loved ones. His presence may become real to us as we pray and study His Word. His directing hand may be felt in the hour of worship.

"When you swerve to right or left, you hear a Voice behind you whispering, 'This is the way, walk here'" (Isa. 30:21, Moffatt). Like the radio beam that directs an airplane through the foggy night to the airfield, so the whispers of God keep us going in the right direction. Such guidance adds great security to life.

TWO LEVELS OF LIVING

Then said he unto me, Son of man, hast thou seen what the ancients of the house of Israel do in the dark, every man in the chambers of his imagery? for they say, The Lord seeth us not; the Lord hath forsaken the earth. Eze. 8:12.

Ezekiel was carried in vision to the court of the Temple in Jerusalem, where his attention was directed to a hole in the wall. He was ordered to dig, and in doing so discovered a door. Opening the door, he entered a room whose walls were decorated with all sorts of abominable and idolatrous pictures. In the room were seventy of the leading men of Israel, burning incense to these pictures.

As the prophet stood in shocked silence, his divine guide said to him, "Son of man, have you seen what the elders of the house of Israel are doing in the dark, every man in his room of pictures? For they say, 'The Lord does not see us, the Lord has forsaken the land'" (R.S.V.).

Some people live on two levels. Above the surface they are respectable, correct, God-fearing church members and exemplary citizens. Below the surface they live in a world of vanity, idolatry, and impurity. In the daylight, like Ezekiel's priests, they worship God in the temple; in the dark, they worship the images that decorate the walls of their own undisciplined minds.

This duplicity may never be detected. A person may go to his grave with a reputation for sanctity and correctness of behavior, but the judgment day will reveal where his mind actually lived and what he really worshiped.

> "I have a house inside of me;
> A house that people seldom see;
> It has a door through which none pass
> And windows, but they're not of glass.
> 'Where do you live?' ask folks I meet,
> And then I say, 'On such a street.'
> But still I know what's really me
> Lives in a house folks never see."
> —*Author Unknown.*

198

TEEN-AGERS IN BABYLON

The king spake unto Ashpenaz the master of his eunuchs, that he should bring certain of the children of Israel, and of the king's seed, and of the princes; children in whom was no blemish, but well favoured, and skilful in all wisdom, and cunning in knowledge, and understanding science, and such as had ability in them to stand in the king's palace, and whom they might teach the learning and the tongue of the Chaldeans. Dan. 1:3, 4.

A superficial reading of this text might give the impression that the young Hebrews brought to Babylon were the pleased recipients of something comparable to a Fullbright scholarship. It seems most doubtful that these young men were thrilled with the opportunity.

First of all, the boys were doubtless teen-agers. They had been brought up to fear Babylon, and they were going to that formidable city as prisoners. Their security had been destroyed as their country was ravaged by its conquerors. They were torn from their families and friends and from all that was familiar and dear to them. No doubt they were as frightened a group of boys as could be imagined.

The inspiring lesson of this incident is the way in which these youth reacted to a difficult and frustrating situation. They might have decided that they had no alternative but to conform. This would have been easy, and the temptation to do so was no doubt great. They might, in their inexperience, have blundered in relating to their superiors, and lost the confidence of those in whose hands their fate rested. The result could have been tragic.

But the boys kept cool under pressure. They demonstrated their ability, their dedication, their good sense. They had received a good education in their earlier years—and now had an opportunity to apply what they had learned, under unusual circumstances.

Modern Christian youth meet similar situations in the army, in universities, in business, and in society in general. Like the teen-agers in Babylon, they can hold their own if they are wise and dedicated, for the same God still lives who helped those young men meet their crises. In the providence of God, they had invested their time and talents well *before* the test came.

DANIEL MEETS A TEST

Daniel purposed in his heart that he would not defile himself with the portion of the king's meat, nor with the wine which he drank. Dan. 1:8.

There are times in the life of many a man when,

> ". . . God stoops o'er his head,
> Satan looks up beneath his feet—both tug."

Such a time it was in the life of Daniel. He had been uprooted from his Judean home and transplanted into a foreign land. Because of his high intelligence and great promise he was selected, among others, to be trained for service in the court of his captors.

Then came the test. The manner of life prescribed by the king included eating and drinking things Daniel had always been taught to let alone. Some of the items of food were contrary to the Levitical code, others may have been associated with idol worship. In any case, they were abhorrent to a sincere Jew.

What should he do? Forget his scruples and say, "When in Babylon do as the Babylonians do"? Or should he be rebellious and defiant? Daniel chose neither course. He appealed to the sense of fairness of those responsible for him. He asked for ten days to prove that he and his friends could not only live but prosper without eating the gourmet diet of the king's palace. Daniel not only preserved his integrity, he also proved his ability to act with diplomacy and grace in a sensitive situation.

Of the great Christian statesman William Wilberforce it was said, "He could refuse to conform without seeming to condemn—a rare gift."—R. COUPLAND, *Wilberforce,* p. 248. All through his dramatic career Daniel revealed that same gift. Whether under Nebuchadnezzar or Belshazzar or Darius, Daniel maintained communication and respect; never once did he sacrifice principle.

Christians in today's world do not witness by retreating to an isolated mountaintop or by surrendering to a secular culture. The best witness is like that of Daniel—tactful, dedicated living. Now as then, this type of witness requires wisdom and grace.

"NOT FOR ME BUT FOR YOU"

As for me, not because of any wisdom that I have more than all the living has this mystery been revealed to me, but in order that the interpretation may be made known to the king, and that you may know the thoughts of your mind. Dan. 2:30, R.S.V.

In a remarkable manner this text reveals the spirit of Daniel. He had been singled out from the wise men of Babylon to interpret the king's dream. He knew the dream and the interpretation because God had revealed it to him. This might have been his great opportunity to promote his own interests before the king. Rather than do so, however, he disclaimed any wisdom above other people and declared that the mystery had been revealed for the sake of the king.

Daniel had already requested that the wise men of Babylon *not* be destroyed. It would have been easy for him to let the ax fall on the impostors, and save himself. It would have been human for him to hope that he might be advanced over all the wise men of the realm, but his concern was the proclamation of the message God had given him, not personal glory.

Every organization is cursed with climbers—people who are determined to get to the top at any cost. They scheme, they pull wires, they misrepresent their fellow workers, they are insincere. They use other people for their own advantage. Sometimes these people actually reach the top, often by climbing over the bodies and souls of people better than themselves. Sometimes, too, they fall from their ill-gotten positions, though not always. "The kingdom of Satan is a kingdom of force; every individual regards every other as an obstacle in the way of his own advancement, or a steppingstone on which he himself may climb to a higher place."—*The Desire of Ages,* p. 436.

How refreshing it is to find people like Daniel who believe that God's blessings are poured out on them, not to enhance their own prestige, but to enlighten and bless others. This is the true spirit of the Christian faith. "I receive that I may give" is the motto of the truly dedicated servant of God. Daniel's spirit of humility was as much an evidence of his dedication as was his prophetic gift.

201

DANIEL REFUSES TO COMPROMISE

When Daniel knew that the writing was signed, he went into his house; and his windows being open in his chamber toward Jerusalem, he kneeled upon his knees three times a day, and prayed, and gave thanks before his God, as he did aforetime. Dan. 6:10.

Daniel might easily have rationalized that it would be better to pray quietly and unnoticed until the excitement died down. No doubt he felt the gaze of onlookers as he "prayed, and gave thanks before his God" during those tense days. And, as he no doubt feared, his courage took him straight to the lions' den. Suppose he had weakened!

It is impossible to estimate the influence of Daniel's faithfulness on those who observed him. Surely his willingness to risk his life for his faith must have made a lasting impression.

Charles Reynolds Brown tells the following story: "One night at the college where I studied a senior was crossing the yard. It was late and he had spent his evening in a wretched debauch. . . . As he crossed the campus he looked up and saw the oldest and best beloved member of the faculty sitting at his desk busily writing under the glow of an evening lamp. The young fellow knew that the old man was at work upon something which he believed would be useful to the world. And the contrast between that picture and the way he had spent his own evening smote him to the heart. Then and there he turned over a new, clean leaf and began to write upon it the record of a decent life. The old professor was not sitting there to be looked ,at; he knew nothing about that young chap out there in the dark; he had been so absorbed in his work that he had forgotten to pull down the shades. It was the simple unconsciousness of his useful action, as it was the simple unconsciousness of his useful life, which made him a power for good on that campus."—*Yale Talks,* p. 91.

Two men by two windows—one, a prophet of long ago; the other a professor of more modern times—exerted a telling influence on passers-by. Whether we like it or not, much of our life is spent in front of "windows" with people looking in to see how we live. May the onlookers be challenged, inspired, and transformed by what they see!

HOSEA TAKES BACK A WAYWARD WIFE

I bought her to me for fifteen pieces of silver, and for an homer of barley, and an half homer of barley. Hosea 3:2.

Who was this woman Hosea bought for fifteen pieces of silver and a few bags of barley? It was his own wife, mother of his daughter and two sons. When Hosea married Gomer he knew she hadn't been an exemplary young woman, but he doubtless thought she would settle down. The children came, and it seemed that Hosea's hopes were justified; but, as in many such instances, the old problems reappeared and Gomer left her family for the life of a harlot.

She might be called the prodigal daughter of the Old Testament. Her degradation was so complete that she eventually became a slave. She might have spent the rest of her days in slavery, but along came the husband whose love she had spurned, and bought back the one who was once his own.

This story teaches two great lessons, the first of which is the persistence of real love. Hosea might have been thoroughly justified in saying, "I can't love *her* anymore after what she has done to me." He might have let Gomer continue in the slavery she had brought upon herself. But he could never quite forget the tenderness of their early association; and the vows he had taken to love and cherish her he could not forget. Wherever her waywardness took her, his love followed.

The other lesson—the real point of the story—is the persistence of divine love. God uses the experience of Hosea and Gomer as an analogy to reveal His attitude toward Israel, and thus to His wayward people in all ages. Their unfaithfulness is as pronounced as that of Gomer, and His love is as lasting as that of Hosea. This love is so great that He is willing to buy back—to redeem—His wayward people. This is the central idea of the gospel.

Henry Drummond once wrote a book about love entitled, *The Greatest Thing in the World.* Truly there is nothing greater than the love that prompted Hosea to buy Gomer back and that prompted Jesus to give His life for you and me. That love was much more than mere sentiment; it cost something. No love worthy of the name is cheap.

JONAH MOURNS HIS SUCCESS

Then said the Lord, Thou hast had pity on the gourd, for the which thou hast not laboured, neither madest it grow; which came up in a night, and perished in a night: and should not I spare Nineveh, that great city? Jonah 4:10, 11.

Seldom has any man lived through a series of more emotionally charged experiences than Jonah. When he was called to warn Nineveh, it was as if a modern evangelist should be called to hold meetings in Peking! When he tried to evade his appointed mission God brought him back to his duty in a most dramatic way. And, most overwhelming of all, when he delivered his message to Nineveh its inhabitants, from the king on down, repented.

Finally, we see an exhausted, mixed-up prophet sitting on the east side of the city, angry because his dire prediction had not been fulfilled, upset because his shade tree had withered, discouraged because the sun was hot.

Into this chaos of emotional confusion moves the Lord. "Do you think it's right," He said in effect, "for you to be so concerned about a shade tree and so unconcerned about sixty thousand people? You should be so happy about the conversion of these people as to forget your own comfort." The last we see of Jonah he is still unhappy, not over failure, but success.

A few centuries later, another Man stood on the east side of another city. He, too, was emotionally moved. The tears were streaming down His face as He said in choked utterances of grief, "O Jerusalem, Jerusalem, thou that killest the prophets, and stonest them which are sent unto thee, how often would I have gathered thy children together, even as a hen gathereth her chickens under her wings, and ye would not!" (Matt. 23:37).

Are we moved by emotions of prejudice, self-love, and hurt pride as was Jonah? Or do we have the spirit of compassion that characterized Jesus? Are we sensitive to human suffering, or to our own desire for recognition and status? In our search for a shady spot, are we forgetting the needs of humanity?

MICAH SUMMARIZES REAL RELIGION

He hath shewed thee, O man, what is good; and what doth the Lord require of thee, but to do justly, and to love mercy, and to walk humbly with thy God? Micah 6:8.

In these familiar words Micah endeavored to show the futility of religious observances on the part of people who loved neither God nor their fellow men. To use his own hyperbole, he had seen "thousands of rams" and "ten thousands of rivers of oil" offered to the Lord. He had seen people who were so zealous that they would sacrifice their own children to expiate sin. But he recognized the emptiness of this zeal when there was no real love behind it.

Nominal modern Christians often wrongly interpret this text. They would have us believe this passage means that God does not require much of man, that a sentimental good-will-toward-one's-fellow-men attitude—a sort of year-round Christmas spirit—is all that matters. Such an approach to this text falls far short of its real meaning.

Actually there is no higher or more difficult achievement than real love for God and man, for the reason that it is in constant competition with the self-love that is so prominent in human nature. It is easier—much easier—to observe forms and adhere to laws than to feel genuine, selfless love.

How many Christians are there who really walk humbly with their God? D. Elton Trueblood tells of a large class in an American university that was asked to rearrange the Ten Commandments in order of importance. More than 90 per cent of the students put the first two commandments last. (*The Predicament of Modern Man,* p. 54.) The idea of placing God first in life, of being sensitive to His guidance and under the control of His Spirit, is not a popular concept even in Christian circles.

So Micah presents us with a real challenge. Centuries later Jesus said the same thing—in different words—in His definition of the two great commandments: "Thou shalt love the Lord thy God with all thy heart. . . . Thou shalt love thy neighbour as thyself." On these two commandments, He said, "hang all the law and the prophets." This is the foundation of a meaningful Christian faith.

HABAKKUK RECOVERS HIS FAITH

Although the fig tree shall not blossom, neither shall fruit be in the vines; the labour of the olive shall fail, and the fields shall yield no meat; the flock shall be cut off from the fold, and there shall be no herd in the stalls: yet I will rejoice in the Lord, I will joy in the God of my salvation. Hab. 3:17, 18.

Translated into modern idiom, Habakkuk's confession of trust in God might read something like this, "Although the stock market is dropping, and I have lost my job; the creditors are on my track and the mortgage payments are overdue; my health is slipping and the future looks dark, *yet I will rejoice in the Lord, I will joy in the God of my salvation."*

How is such calm trust developed? In Habakkuk's case it came through hard experiences. He was much upset by life as he observed it. Unprincipled fellow church members were oppressing those weaker than themselves. Arrogant pagans were attacking God's people. Circumstances were all upside-down and God seemed to be doing nothing about it. Habakkuk became very critical. "Wherefore" he demanded of God, "lookest thou upon them that deal treacherously, and holdest thy tongue when the wicked devoureth the man that is more righteous than he?"

Then he said, "I'll wait and see what God will say." He didn't have long to wait. The Lord answered, "The just shall live by his *faith."* God made it plain that He knew all about the problems that perplexed the prophet, and would solve them all in His own good time. "The Lord is in his holy temple," God said; "let all the earth keep silence before him."

An old Scottish saint was once in deep distress because he could not understand the providences of God. Recalling his experience, not unlike that of Habakkuk, he said, "Fool that I was, not to know that the messages of God are not to be read through the envelope in which they are enclosed."

Paul quoted God's statement to Habakkuk concerning faith as the foundation of his gospel. "The just shall live by faith" solves some of the most perplexing problems of life.

MALACHI BATTLES INDIFFERENCE

Return unto me, and I will return unto you, saith the Lord of hosts. But ye said, Wherein shall we return? Mal. 3:7.

The prophet Malachi tackled an almost impossible task—that of reforming people who refused to admit that they needed reforming. Their constant refrain was, "You don't mean that there is anything wrong with *us.*" Seven times in the book Malachi presented his people with a great truth or a great challenge, and in each case the answer was an evasion of the issue.

When Malachi quoted God as saying, "I have loved you," they responded, "Wherein hast thou loved us?"

When the prophet quoted God as accusing the priests of despising His name, they replied, "Wherein have we despised thy name?"

When he accused them of offering polluted bread upon the altar they protested, "Wherein have we polluted thee?"

When he told them that they had wearied the Lord with their words they said, "Wherein have we wearied him?"

When God pleaded with them to return to Him, they yawned and said, "Wherein shall we return?"

When he reminded them of their dishonesty with God they protested, "Wherein have we robbed thee?"

And finally, when he told them that they had spoken against God, they insisted, "What have we spoken so much against thee?"

God gave His people all kinds of warnings, any one of which would have saved them from disaster. But God's warnings are like reflector-studded highway signs at night—we can see them only if our own lights are on. Malachi's generation failed because the people insisted that they were in good spiritual health, when they should have heeded God's diagnosis of their ills. They were too sure of themselves.

When the light of divine truth shines on our lives do we, like Malachi's people, respond, "Who, *me?*" or do we take seriously the messages of God, confess our sins, and accept the salvation Christ has provided? Are we sensitive to the divine influences that seek to redirect our lives, or do we insist on doing as we please?

207

WITNESSES

Ye shall receive power, after that the Holy Ghost is come upon you: and ye shall be witnesses unto me both in Jerusalem, and in all Judaea, and in Samaria, and unto the uttermost part of the earth. Acts 1:8.

The Christian gospel has always been communicated by "witnesses." A Midwestern business house has the motto, "One man tells another." This is the best advertising a store can have, and the most effective way to propagate a faith. Bishop Gerald H. Kennedy tells the following story:

"The Fiji Islands were called originally The Cannibal Islands. They were inhabited by fierce and treacherous tribes whose main object was to kill and devour their enemies. John Hunt, a young Methodist missionary, went there many years ago. As a young man in England he was studying for the ministry and had just agreed to go to Africa as a missionary. He was engaged to a young woman who was willing to go with him, and what was more difficult, had obtained her mother's consent. Then the missionary society called him one day and told him that they wanted him to go to Fiji. John Hunt was willing but he wondered what Hannah would say. So he wrote her a letter and told her the change of plans and then waited for her answer. His friend saw how nervous he was and upset. Finally, John told him that he was unsure of Hannah. Then the letter came and with a shout John burst into his friend's room with the news. 'It's all right,' he said. 'She says she will go with me anywhere.' "—*Fresh Every Morning,* p. 50.

Such stories could be multiplied infinitely. Young people have been the shock troops of the movement. Vast multitudes of Christians have been the source of supply. The willingness to do anything or go anywhere has been the ground of success.

Despite secularism there are still people willing to witness, even at great personal sacrifice. Men and women of all faiths are working in remote corners of the earth telling the story of Jesus. Nothing— TV, radio, literature—obviates the need for dedicated men and women who will go anywhere.

THE ONE HUNDRED AND TWENTY

These all continued with one accord in prayer and supplication, with the women, and Mary the mother of Jesus, and with his brethren. Acts. 1:14.

The crucifixion, the resurrection, the ascension were past. Jesus' followers returned to Jerusalem from Olivet, and assembled in an upper room. The eleven disciples were there, Jesus' mother and brothers were there, and other assorted believers—"the number of names together were about an hundred and twenty" (verse 15).

Only one hundred and twenty in a world full of people, and how unpromising a lot they were! They had no influence, no prestige, no money. What could they do—a tiny minority in a big, unfriendly world? The one thing they could do was obey their Master's command on the Mount of Ascension, "Ye shall be witnesses unto me both in Jerusalem, and in all Judaea, and in Samaria, and unto the uttermost part of the earth" (Acts 1:8).

And witness they did. In a few days Peter was preaching a ringing sermon at Pentecost: "This Jesus hath God raised up," he exclaimed, "whereof we all are witnesses" (Acts 2:32). This first major experiment in witnessing multiplied the group to twenty-five times its original size.

From that day until this the strength of the church has been in its witness to the wonderful acts of God through Jesus Christ. Its enemies have tried to stifle that witness by persecution, intimidation, and scorn. But despite all opposition there are still dedicated Christians, young and old, willing to stand up and be counted.

Not many years ago the young woman chosen national queen at the Atlantic City beauty pageant witnessed to her faith in Christ, before the judges and spectators and the vast television audience. It was not easy, but it reflected the spirit that has kept the gospel of Christ alive in the world. The one hundred and twenty were not all preachers. Some of the most effective witnessing has been done by people upon whom the hands of ordination have never been placed. The tradesman, the businessman, the physician, the housewife—all may add their witness to the love of God through Jesus Christ our Lord.

PETER COMMENTS ON THE TREACHERY OF JUDAS

He was numbered with us, and had obtained part of this ministry. Acts. 1:17.

Peter is addressing the one hundred and twenty disciples in the upper room at Jerusalem on the subject of a replacement for Judas. We can imagine the chagrin of the disciples as they contemplate the perfidy of their former associate. Peter's comment is translated in the Revised Standard Version as follows: "For he was numbered among us, and was alloted his share in this ministry." These words reflect the amazement of the disciples that one who had been so close to them and to the Lord, one who had participated in the ministry of Jesus, could sink to such a low level as to betray their Master. All the way along, they had trusted him so fully that they made him treasurer of the group. He had betrayed them as well as their Lord.

Judas' treachery is likewise hard for us to understand. How could he do what he did? The clue is found in *The Desire of Ages:* "Judas did not come to the point of surrendering himself fully to Christ."—Page 717. "He determined not to unite himself so closely to Christ but that he could draw away. He would watch."—Page 719. In other words, Judas never made a complete commitment. He always had reservations. He never fully identified himself with Christ or with the group of disciples. He wanted to maintain an attitude of detachment. He would wait and see, and his lack of commitment was the cause of his fall.

In the New Jerusalem there will be a foundation stone that might have had Judas' name engraved upon it. Perhaps that stone may remain blank throughout eternity as a reminder of the tragedy of an uncommitted life. "Still as of old, men by themselves are priced, for thirty pieces Judas sold himself, not Christ."

The uncommitted person still shrinks from risk and sacrifice; and, under pressure, is still capable of treason. The other disciples were sometimes unwise and unstable, but they were basically loyal. So, today, the sin with the greatest potential for destruction is selfish disloyalty. Every Christian needs to weigh carefully the genuineness of his commitment.

ONLY ONE WAY

Neither is there salvation in any other: for there is none other name under heaven given among men, whereby we must be saved. Acts 4:12.

Many things in life can be done in various ways. We are quite free to choose our life's vocation, our spouse, where we shall live, and the political persuasion with which we shall identify. Of course, there are limits imposed on all of these choices, but within the limits of Christian principles there remains a variety of options.

But in other areas in life there are no choices. Andrew Jackson is quoted as saying, "It is a mighty poor mind that can't think of more than one way to spell a word." This observation may be comforting to some of us, but the fact remains that *most* words can only be spelled correctly in one way.

If an argument arises over the distance between two points, the matter cannot be left to choice or settled by compromise. Careful measurement or reliance upon acceptable authorities remains the only solution to the problem.

In the spiritual area there are those who would have us believe that religion is a matter of choice. According to them, each person is faced with a multitude of options—he may be an infidel, an agnostic, or a believer; he may join any one of 250 or more denominations; it really doesn't matter which course he chooses. According to this philosophy, all roads lead to the same destination.

When Peter declared that Jesus Christ is the only way of salvation, he thereby ruled out myriads of competing systems that have made their bids for the allegiance of mankind. Choosing a faith is not like selecting an automobile—an experience in which we can go from showroom to showroom, knowing that in a few months all of the models will change. The truth of God is unchanging.

In the days of the early church, Christianity had many competitors. There were Judaism, Mithraism, emperor worship, Gnosticism, and many more. Voices were calling from every direction, and many of them were attractive voices. But "there is none other name under heaven given among men, whereby we must be saved."

211

A PRAYER MEETING AND AN EARTHQUAKE

When they had prayed, the place was shaken where they were assembled together; and they were all filled with the Holy Ghost, and they spake the word of God with boldness. Acts 4:31.

In this instance prayer got results! An earthquake, a revival, and an evangelistic mission followed a prayer meeting. Why does prayer often seem so futile? Dr. John Sutherland Bonnell contributes the following suggestions in his chapter, "Does Anything Happen When You Pray?"

"Count Leo Tolstoy, in his book *My Confession,* declares that 'a man often believes for years that his early faith is still intact, while at the same time not a trace of it remains in him.'

"As an illustration of this, he quotes the testimony of a friend. Thirty years earlier this friend knelt in prayer at his bedside while on a hunting expedition with his brother. . . . When he had completed his prayers, his brother, who had been watching him, remarked, 'Ah, so you still keep that up.' Not another word was said on the subject, but it was enough to demolish the habit of prayer which he had maintained throughout his life. 'His brother's words,' said Tolstoy, 'were like the push of a finger against a wall ready to tumble over with its own weight.'

"Nothing remained of his early faith except an empty form. When once he had admitted this to himself, he couldn't continue with his prayers.

"Tens of thousands of modern people find themselves in a plight similar to this. Prayer has become for them a meaningless ritual, altogether divorced from reality. Nothing ever happens when they pray. They never expect anything to happen, and according to their faith, or more truly their lack of faith, it is done unto them."—*The Practice and Power of Prayer,* pp. 41, 42.

What a contrast between the progress of those early Christians and our feeble petitions today. The reason the church back there prayed so effectively was that its members believed so implicitly. They expected their Lord to act and they were not disappointed. Such a faith would revolutionize the church today.

BARNABAS ENCOURAGES THE CHURCH

Joses, who by the apostles was surnamed Barnabas, (which is, being interpreted, The son of consolation,) a Levite, and of the country of Cyprus, having land, sold it, and brought the money, and laid it at the apostles' feet. Acts 4:36, 37.

The Christian church was young and struggling, and many of its members were in need. There was no welfare society, no government aid, no relief agency where help could be secured. But there were some well-to-do men in the church like Joses, who sold their property and donated the proceeds to a common fund.

Joses became so noteworthy for his liberality and influence that he soon was nicknamed Barnabas. The Revised Standard Version translates his name as "Son of encouragement." To what kind of man would his friends bestow such a title?

When Saul was converted and the Christians in Jerusalem were afraid to accept him, Barnabas was there to reassure them and to urge them to consider Saul as a brother. What would have happened to Saul had there not been a Barnabas to help him find his way into the fellowship of the church?

Paul didn't want to accept Mark back, when he lost his nerve and abandoned the first missionary journey, but Barnabas insisted on giving him another chance. He showed confidence in young Mark by taking him as his own companion on a second journey. Perhaps we owe the Gospel of Mark to the "Son of encouragement" who helped a young man find himself.

When the new church at Antioch needed help, Barnabas paid them a visit and "exhorted"—literally, "encouraged"—them. He helped them to feel that their faith was worth while.

Everywhere he went, people were happier and stronger because of his influence. His warm, magnetic spirit made drooping spirits rejoice and lagging feet quicken their pace. He made people feel that serving Christ was worth while. He was spoken of as "a good man, and full of the Holy Ghost and of faith."

May his tribe increase!

213

ANANIAS AND SAPPHIRA MISREPRESENT CHRIST

Peter said, Ananias, why hath Satan filled thine heart to lie to the Holy Ghost, and to keep back part of the price of the land? Whiles it remained, was it not thine own? and after it was sold, was it not in thine own power? why hast thou conceived this thing in thine heart? thou hast not lied unto men, but unto God. Acts. 5:3, 4.

What! An untruthful, deceitful schemer in the very first Christian church of which Peter was pastor? How could Ananias and Sapphira act as they did in a church that had experienced Pentecost, and that was led by men like Barnabas and Stephen and the disciples of Jesus? May it be that the sad record of this couple was preserved to demonstrate that the church has always been embarrassed by members who were less than fully committed?

A farmer's apple orchard had a row of sour apple trees next to the road. In answer to questions regarding this fruit, the farmer said, "If you will come inside, you will find we grow a different quality."

Perhaps every church—even Peter's—has been cursed with fence-row Christians. The "sour apple trees" invariably seem to be on the outer fringe, where every passer-by is aware of their existence. Church members who are unkind, who lie and cheat, who are undependable, who are immoral, always seem to get publicity. Only a few of the thousands of converts of Peter's day are named in the book of Acts— and among the few who got the headlines were Ananias and Sapphira.

To those who are disturbed by the sour apples in the church we would repeat the farmer's comment, "If you will *come inside* you will find we grow a different quality." The real quality of the membership of the church was not reflected by the Ananiases and Sapphiras. The true nature of the church was revealed by the unnamed hundreds who sold their possessions and brought an honest contribution; by the sincere believers who risked everything for Christ; by the dedicated leaders who often gave their lives for their faith.

We must never forget that Ananias and Sapphira did not get by with their duplicity. God vindicated His honest followers.

JEALOUS LEADERS IMPRISON APOSTLES

Then the high priest rose up, and all they that were with him, (which is the sect of the Sadducees,) and were filled with indignation, and laid their hands on the apostles, and put them in the common prison. Acts 5:17, 18.

The word here translated "indignation" is more accurately rendered "envy" or "jealousy." It does not, however, denote that the high priest and his associates were quietly brooding or sulking. They were expressing their jealousy in a most indignant manner.

Why were these religious leaders so upset? Simply because multitudes of people were rejoicing in their new-found faith in Christ. Hundreds were being healed, and victims of evil spirits were being freed. Such enthusiasm and rejoicing had never been seen before. It was threatening their security.

Why didn't these religious leaders get in on the act themselves? Why should they be so angry and jealous? They should have been delighted at the good fortune of the sick and oppressed in finding deliverance. The answer is in verse 13: "Of the rest durst no man join himself to them: but the people magnified them."

The people were free to accept the new faith; the high priest and his friends were not. The traditions of their past bound them completely. They were too deeply committed to their contemporary world. The least token of recognition of the Teacher of Galilee and His followers would bring upon them rejection and derision from their peers. This was more than they could accept.

So they had to resort to violence in the vain hope that they could stamp out the religious movement they dare not approve or join. Their comfortable slavery to tradition was being challenged. Too cowardly to open their minds to a new concept of God and truth, they could only persecute the apostles of a disquieting message.

This drama has been enacted over and over again. Prison doors have closed on millions of its hapless victims. Fortunately, there is an angel of the Lord who, under some circumstances, opens these doors and sets jealousy's victims free.

215

COURAGE VERSUS PRUDENCE

Peter and the other apostles answered and said, We ought to obey God rather than men. Acts 5:29.

Peter and the other apostles were carrying on an active Christian mission in Jerusalem. The sick were being healed, unclean spirits were being cast out, and many were accepting the new faith. The religious leaders became alarmed and threw the apostles into prison, but they served a short term indeed. "The angel of the Lord by night opened the prison doors, and brought them forth, and said, Go, stand and speak in the temple to the people all the words of this life" (Acts 5:19, 20).

The apostles responded despite the danger. The religious leaders became more incensed and frustrated than ever. Summoning them before the council, the high priest stormed, "Did not we straitly command you that ye should not teach in this name? And, behold, ye have filled Jerusalem with your doctrine, and intend to bring this man's blood upon us" (verse 28).

At this dramatic point Peter and the other apostles took their position—"We ought to obey God rather than men"—and repeated again their testimony regarding the risen Christ.

Their courage was rewarded with a beating and a stern command that they should not speak in the name of Jesus. They departed from the council, "rejoicing that they were counted worthy to suffer shame for his name. And daily in the temple, and in every house, they ceased not to teach and preach Jesus Christ" (verses 41, 42).

Mark Twain is reported to have said that America has three unspeakably precious things: freedom of speech, freedom of conscience, and the prudence never to practice either. Peter and his associates had no freedom, but they had the courage to risk everything for their faith. A little more courage and a bit less prudence might be a great asset in spreading the gospel in today's world. What would happen if thousands of Christians scattered throughout the world were as invincible as Peter? The apostles could not be stopped for they knew whom they had believed. Their contact with their Lord motivated them to complete dedication.

216

REQUIREMENTS OF LEADERSHIP

Wherefore, brethren, look ye out among you seven men of honest report, full of the Holy Ghost and wisdom, whom we may appoint over this business. Acts 6:3.

In appointing a board of deacons, the early church recognized how important it is to find honest men. All other qualifications for office were quite meaningless if the fundamental requirement of honesty was missing.

Some people have a superficial understanding of the real meaning of honesty. Two women boarded a bus. In the jam of passengers, one overlooked paying her fare. When she noticed the oversight, she said to her friend, "I'll go right up and pay it." Her friend replied, "Why bother? You got away with it!" "I've always found that honesty pays," the woman said as she went down the aisle to pay her fare. When she returned to her seat she exclaimed, "See, I told you honesty pays. I gave the driver a quarter and he gave me change for fifty cents!"

A much deeper grasp of honesty was revealed to me in the following experience. During World War II, I had occasion to visit with a chaplain at the Navy headquarters in Boston. On learning of my church affiliation, he told me an interesting story. A sailor in the Pacific area had stolen some expensive equipment from his ship. While on shore leave on the West Coast, he was converted and joined the Seventh-day Adventist Church. Immediately, at the risk of severe discipline, he wrote a letter of confession to the commanding officer of the ship where he had served. The officer gave the letter to the chaplain with whom I was speaking, and he had carried this letter with him all over the world as an example of the power of the gospel to change men.

A person may be a Christian, and be poor, uneducated, and without influence, but he cannot be a real Christian and be dishonest. The Christian pays his debts, tells the truth, meets his obligations, never deceives. He can be trusted under all circumstances, and he will not yield to any temptation to compromise his integrity. He will never play an insincere role to gain influence. At any cost he will adhere to the principles of Christian integrity.

217

STEPHEN MAKES THE ULTIMATE SACRIFICE

Stephen, full of faith and power, did great wonders and miracles among the people. Acts 6:8.

When the early Christian church found it necessary to select a board of deacons, the first on the list was Stephen, "a man full of faith and of the Holy Ghost." In a unique way this man followed in the footsteps of his Lord.

Jesus was known for His marvelous works. Of Stephen it was said that he "did great wonders and miracles among the people." Unfortunately, we have no record of these deeds.

Of Jesus it was said, "Never a man spake like this man." Of Stephen it was said that his enemies "were not able to resist the wisdom and the spirit by which he spake." What powers of persuasion he must have had!

Jesus was dragged before the Sanhedrin. Stephen was brought before the same body, consisting largely, no doubt, of the same men. The same technique—calling false witnesses—was followed and the accusations were similar. Stephen was truly traveling the same road as did his Master. When the high priest said to Stephen, "Are these things so?" Stephen may have remembered the story of another occasion when probably the same high priest said to Jesus, "What is it which these witness against thee?"

At the end of the road for Jesus was a cross. For Stephen it was a rain of pelting rocks. As the weapons were doing their work, he, like the Master, said, "Lord, lay not this sin to their charge."

The genius of the Christian faith is that it has produced men like Stephen—men so devoted to their Lord that they are willing to take the ultimate risk for Him. An innumerable company of martyrs have followed Stephen's example and been strengthened by his faith.

The real results of that day's tragedy did not come from the unfinished sermon Stephen preached, though it was a masterpiece. Stephen lived on in the career of a spectator—Saul of Tarsus, who could never be the same again after watching this good man die. If Stephen had crumpled under the terrible pressure of that tragic day, might the church have been denied Paul?

SIMON OFFERS A BRIBE

When Simon saw that through laying on of the apostles' hands the Holy Ghost was given, he offered them money, saying, Give me also this power, that on whomsoever I lay hands, he may receive the Holy Ghost. Acts 8:18, 19.

Simon had been prominent in his community. As a sorcerer he had influenced many people "from the least to the greatest." Year after year his hold had strengthened on the lives of the inhabitants of the city of Samaria.

One day a competitor for the loyalty of the people came to Samaria. His name was Philip, and he was preaching the gospel of Jesus of Nazareth. The people responded with enthusiasm, and many manifestations of the grace of God were seen. Among Philip's converts were many of Simon's followers; and, strangely enough, Simon joined them. The record says he "believed," "was baptized," "continued with Philip," and "wondered." Apparently the gospel of Jesus had taken a firm hold on his life.

Hearing of this successful evangelistic effort in Samaria, Peter and John came to pay the new believers a visit. As a result of their visit, Philip's converts received the Holy Ghost. This was more than Simon could stand. Immediately he went to the apostles with a bag of money in his hand. He wanted to buy the power to cause people to receive the Holy Ghost. Peter pointed out with much emphasis that the Holy Ghost is a gift, and that Simon was mistaken in thinking that he could purchase it. Some things cannot be bought or sold.

Struck with fear because of his inappropriate request, Simon begged Peter to pray that he not be punished for his brashness. We have no record as to what eventually happened to this man, and we may wonder why this strange story appears in the Bible.

May we not consider Simon a type of the person who responds with enthusiasm to every new idea that seems to possess the prospect of personal advantage. Here was a new bandwagon—why not climb on and see where it was going? And if a well-placed bribe could put him in the driver's seat, so much the better.

SAUL MEETS HIS LORD

And he trembling and astonished said, Lord, what wilt thou have me to do? And the Lord said unto him, Arise, and go into the city, and it shall be told thee what thou must do. Acts 9:6.

Never was a greater change made in a man's life than in the case of Saul. In one short hour he was transformed from a zealous persecutor to a servant of the Christ whom he had persecuted. Nothing was ever the same for Saul again.

This notable conversion teaches us several lessons: First, the church's greatest exponent of salvation by faith began his Christian life by asking the question, "Lord, what wilt thou have me to do?" Saul never lost this sense of responsibility, although he recognized that it was only by grace through faith that he or anyone else could be saved. Second, God did not reveal to Saul his mission, but sent him to Damascus where He prompted another Christian, Ananias, to find Saul and reveal to him his duty.

From that day to the end of his life Saul was a part of the church, working with, and for, his fellow church members. Apparently this was the way God intended it to be. Finally, Saul did not seek a faraway place in which to begin his Christian ministry. "Straightway he preached Christ in the synagogues, that he is the Son of God." The synagogues where he preached were in Damascus, the very city where he planned to arrest the Christians and carry them bound to Jerusalem.

There is a thrilling strength about Saul. When he saw Christ, he accepted Him, and when he was commissioned to preach Christ, he obeyed. He made no excuses, nor did he show concern for his personal safety. When he was forced to leave Damascus, he went to Jerusalem, whence he had come, and there "he spoke boldly in the name of the Lord Jesus." Even the coolness of his fellow Christians did not diminish his ardor, and the results of the vision lasted until the end of his life.

Of Saul, or Paul, as he was later called, it has been said, "Three cubits in stature, he reached the sky." What an example of fearless personal commitment to his Lord!

PETER LEARNS A LESSON REGARDING PREJUDICE

Peter opened his mouth, and said, Of a truth I perceive that God is no respecter of persons: but in every nation he that feareth him, and worketh righteousness, is accepted with him. Acts 10:34, 35.

Peter had grown up with the prejudices of his day. To him, it was not right to identify himself with Gentiles because they were "unclean." In order to change Peter's viewpoint, God gave him a vision of a sheet let down from heaven containing all manner of animals. Peter heard a voice, "Kill, and eat." In his dream he replied, "Not so, Lord; for I have never eaten any thing that is common or unclean." Again the voice said, "What God hath cleansed, that call thou not common." To reinforce the lesson it was repeated three times.

Peter revealed that he learned the lesson well when he told Cornelius, "You know how that it is an unlawful thing for a man that is a Jew to keep company, or come unto one of another nation; but God hath shewed me that I should not call any man common or unclean."

One of the most disruptive forces in the world is prejudice. How often men have been judged, not by their real worth, but by their nationality, their creed, or their pigmentation.

"Some years ago Dr. Charles Drew developed a method of blood-plasma transfusion that has saved numberless lives. Many a man owes his life to this discovery and all of us are in debt to it. Dr. Drew was traveling in the South one time and became involved in an automobile accident which severed a large blood vessel. He was refused admittance at the nearest hospital because he was a Negro, and he died because he could not receive the help of his own medical discovery."—GERALD H. KENNEDY, *Fresh Every Morning*, p. 87.

This is a graphic illustration of evil prejudice. How different from the teaching of Jesus who, in the parable of the good Samaritan, made clear that every person in need is our neighbor! Human nature is such that prejudice can creep upon us without our recognizing it. Whenever we find ourselves becoming narrow, parochial, or prejudiced we are on dangerous ground.

PETER ESCAPES FROM PRISON

As Peter knocked at the door of the gate, a damsel came to hearken, named Rhoda. And when she knew Peter's voice, she opened not the gate for gladness, but ran in, and told how Peter stood before the gate. And they said unto her, Thou art mad. But she constantly affirmed that it was even so. Acts 12:13-15.

King Herod had killed James, the brother of John, and his next victim was to be Peter. His first step was to place Peter in prison under heavy guard. The night finally came when the officers of the king were to bring Peter forth for execution. The voice of the troublemaker was about to be silenced.

Suddenly a light shone in the prison. The chains fell from Peter's hands, and a messenger of God led him through the iron gate to freedom. He made his way to the home of John Mark and knocked at the gate.

Inside the house a group of Christians was praying for Peter's release. In fact, the church had been praying earnestly for days, and their prayers were probably most fervent on this very night when they thought he was to be taken to his death. No doubt they had been praying for hours. Their prayers were interrupted. A girl named Rhoda began shouting, "Peter's at the gate! Peter's at the gate!" Someone responded, "You're crazy!" But she insisted that she had seen him. Someone else remarked, "It is his angel." The loud knocking continued outside. Finally the group crowded toward the gate, and there he was! The Scripture says, "They were astonished."

For what had they been praying? Peter's release. Why, then, should they have been so skeptical and so amazed when he appeared? Would we be equally surprised if some of our prayers were answered? Do we pray merely because we think we ought to pray for certain things—because other people are praying for them—or do we pray with expectation of an answer? Perhaps if we expected more, we would receive more. The depth of our prayer experience is proportional to our confidence in the God to whom we pray. And while we are aware that God will not *always* see fit to give us what we ask, we should not consider it strange when He does.

TROUBLE BETWEEN PAUL AND BARNABAS

Barnabas determined to take with them John, whose surname was Mark. But Paul thought not good to take him with them, who departed from them from Pamphylia, and went not with them to the work. And the contention was so sharp between them, that they departed asunder one from the other. Acts 15:37-39.

It is disturbing to see two great, good men arguing sharply about an issue, but it sometimes happens. In this case Paul could see no light in continuing the employment of an intern who had "chickened out" when things got hard. Barnabas argued that this young man should have another chance. No compromise could be found, so the two men separated, Barnabas taking Mark and Paul taking Silas.

In the retrospect of later experience, it is obvious that Barnabas was right. Paul later admitted that Mark was a profitable servant of Christ. But while we grant this fact, we must not be too hard on Paul. He was a man of indomitable will. He could stand imprisonment, flogging, hunger, hardship of every kind; and it was hard for him to accept a person who was not able to endure the hardships of first-century evangelism in the Roman Empire. Paul was a man in whom the tides of emotion ran high. He was highly motivated himself, and had scant patience with a person who showed signs of weakness.

Dr. Harry Emerson Fosdick once remarked, "One man may have a calm, equable temperament that need never be ruffled; another may have to say, as Dr. Tyng did to one who rebuked him for asperity, 'Young man, I control more temper every fifteen minutes than you will in your whole lifetime.' One man may be an Erie Canal, another a Mississippi River, and an Erie Canal has no idea how many ways a Mississippi River has of going wrong."—*On Being a Real Person,* pp. 59, 60.

God has ways of mellowing His servants who, like Paul, are too severe. Let us leave these people in God's hands. Later it was Paul who said, "Charity suffereth long, and is kind." Perhaps as he penned these immortal words he recalled his sharpness with a tinge of regret.

PAUL AND SILAS SING IN JAIL

At midnight Paul and Silas prayed, and sang praises unto God: and the prisoners heard them. Acts 16:25.

In response to divine initiative, Paul and Silas had gone to Macedonia to preach the gospel. Their first stop was Philippi, and their first converts were Lydia and her household.

Things seemed to be going well until, one day, Paul commanded a "spirit of divination" to come out of a girl who had been, till this moment, a professional fortuneteller. Her employers brought about the arrest of Paul and Silas, a mob assembled, and the prisoners were beaten and placed under maximum security in the local prison.

An apparently promising evangelistic mission, begun under the explicit direction of God, had crashed. Other prisoners had died in those foul dungeons. Paul and Silas had no friends in Philippi except Lydia, and it was doubtful if her influence would bring about their release. Also, they had been beaten unmercifully, and the stocks were uncomfortable. It might have seemed to them as if their mission had collapsed.

But what was their reaction? A strange sound was heard at midnight. What were the words that echoed through the stone corridors of the prison? Prayer. What were the melodies that disturbed the other prisoners' restless sleep? Christian hymns! Nothing like this had ever been heard in that prison.

How could they do it? They didn't know that in a few moments an earthquake would shake open the doors of their prison. They didn't know that the harsh jailer would confess Christ that night. All they knew was that God had sent them to Philippi, that their lives were in His hands, and that they were ready to accept any experience that might come to them.

Herein is one secret of happiness. People who really know that God is leading them are not subject to uncertainty, panic, and depression. Of course there is false assurance—that is another story. But the experience of Paul and Silas teaches every Christian that confidence and happiness are possible, even under the most distressing circumstances.

PAUL'S COURAGE

When they heard of the resurrection of the dead, some mocked: and others said, We will hear thee again of this matter. Acts 17:32.

Paul's address to the philosophers of Athens on Mars' Hill is one of the greatest examples of Christian courage in all history.

"Paul on Mars' Hill at the very center and abode of Grecian culture, assuring representatives of the leading schools of thought in the most enlightened city of the world, that a crucified Jew came out of his grave, and that God has appointed that Jew to be the judge of mankind, is the highest exhibition of heroism which the Book of Acts records. Paul's act that day was one of the most daring strokes ever struck by man in the entire history of the human race. It takes more courage for an educated man of refined sensibilities to affront the intelligence of a cultivated audience than to give offense to ignorant peasants whose powers of reasoning are undeveloped, and whose intellectual judgments are of little account. The fury of the mob in Lystra was no such test of courage as the cold ridicule of the critical scholars in Athens. The contemptuous laugh of those lords of culture Paul never forgot. He never went back to Athens. He wrote no letter to the Athenians. For weeks after his Athenian experience, he was weak in body and depressed in spirit, but his courage was unabated. He determined to go on preaching that Jesus is the Messiah, that men crucified him, and that God raised him from the dead. Here is a courage like unto the courage of the Son of God."—CHARLES EDWARD JEFFERSON, *The Character of Paul,* pp. 185, 186.

Paul's work in Athens did not result in the establishment of a church—Athens wasn't that kind of city; but one of the judges who listened that day became a Christian. This, in itself, was phenomenal.

Those who endeavor to witness for Christ before the learned, the influential, and the sophisticated can emulate Paul's tact and courage. And in every culture persons like Dionysius the Areopagite have responded to the claims of Christ. They are hard to find and harder to reach, but God loves them and He has commissioned His church to preach His gospel to them.

8   225

PAUL ALARMS FELIX

After certain days, when Felix came with his wife Drusilla, which was a Jewess, he sent for Paul, and heard him concerning the faith in Christ. And as he reasoned of righteousness, temperance, and judgment to come, Felix trembled, and answered, Go thy way for this time; when I have a convenient season, I will call for thee. Acts 24:24, 25.

What a scene! Felix, known for his cruelty and lust, and the young adventuress, Drusilla, sitting in judgment on Paul! A greater contrast in characters would be hard to imagine.

The New English Bible rendition of the text makes the progress of the interview clear:

Sending for Paul, Felix "let him talk to him about faith in Christ Jesus. But when the discourse turned to questions of morals, self-control, and the coming judgment, Felix became alarmed and exclaimed, 'That will do for the present; when I find it convenient I will send for you again.'"

As long as Paul confined his remarks to the story of Jesus, Felix and Drusilla were willing to listen. Perhaps they smiled incredulously when Paul presented Jesus as the divine Son of God. No doubt they were curious to learn more about the prophet of Galilee who had made such a stir in their part of the world. They listened, as anyone might listen, to a fascinating tale, soon to be forgotten.

But then Paul pointed his finger at the guilty pair and said, "Christ's gospel demands pure morals and self-control. Christ's gospel includes a coming judgment when you will stand before God and answer for your deeds." It was at *this* point that Felix became alarmed and terminated the interview. He wanted to hear no more.

Like Felix, many people are willing to listen to the story of Jesus as long as it makes no demands that require change or sacrifice. It is true that salvation is by God's grace and man's faith, not by good deeds. But the saved person gladly accepts the responsibility of living in harmony with the revealed standards of the Christ who saved him. Redemption implies responsibility.

PAUL APPEARS BEFORE AGRIPPA

Agrippa said unto Festus, I would also hear the man myself. To morrow, said he, thou shalt hear him. And on the morrow, when Agrippa was come, and Bernice, with great pomp, and was entered into the place of hearing, with the chief captains, and principal men of the city, at Festus' commandment Paul was brought forth. Acts 25:22, 23.

There is a Chinese proverb which says, "Great men never feel great; small men never feel small." It is interesting to visualize the occasion described in our text. The procession that entered the audience hall that day was made up of military and civil leaders in Caesarea in addition to Agrippa, Bernice, and Festus. It was "with great pomp" that this group of small men assembled to listen to a great man in chains.

Paul's speech that day to his pompous listeners was a simple recital of his experience. He recalled his early life as a Pharisee, and as a persecutor of the Christians. He described his conversion and his commission to be a "minister and a witness" for Christ. He recounted his experiences as a minister of Christ's gospel, including the bitter opposition of the Jews.

When interrupted by Festus who shouted, "Thou art beside thyself; much learning doth make thee mad," Paul maintained that he was speaking "words of truth and soberness." Then Paul challenged King Agrippa to believe; and the king replied, perhaps sarcastically, perhaps seriously, "Almost thou persuadest me to be a Christian." Paul answered with sincere concern, "I would to God, that not only thou, but also all that hear me this day, were both almost, and altogether such as I am, except these bonds." Never had these proud officials met such a prisoner.

"Agrippa and Bernice possessed power and position, and because of this they were favored by the world. But they were destitute of the traits of character that God esteems. . . . The aged prisoner, chained to his soldier guard, had in his appearance nothing that would lead the world to pay him homage. Yet in this man . . . all heaven was interested."—*The Acts of the Apostles,* p. 434.

COMPLETE DEDICATION

I was not disobedient unto the heavenly vision. Acts 26:19.

General Booth of the Salvation Army was once asked the secret of his success. He is said to have replied:

"I will tell you the secret. God has had all there was of me. There have been men with greater brains than I, men with greater opportunities; but from the day I got the poor of London on my heart, and a vision of what Jesus Christ could do with the poor of London, I made up my mind that God would have all of William Booth there was."

Complete dedication is a theme of the Scriptures. From Abraham to Paul, we witness a succession of men who gave themselves without reservation to the service of their God. And the more complete the dedication, the greater the man.

The Lord Himself stated the principle—"Thou shalt love the Lord thy God with *all* thy heart, and with *all* thy soul, and with *all* thy strength, and with *all* thy mind" (Luke 10:27).

Is such obedience and dedication possible for modern man, or is this experience merely a romantic tradition of the past? Many people in the world today are willing to demonstrate for *causes*. People demonstrate by the thousands for causes—good or bad. Occasionally persons douse themselves with gasoline and strike a match to their clothing for causes. People contribute fortunes for causes—from blank-day calendars to higher education.

Less numerous are the people today who will commit their lives and their all to Christ. There are a few such—they may be found in mission fields, in churches, in schools, and in the common walks of life. They generally do not achieve fame, because our present culture seems more impressed by a draft-card burner than by a committed Christian. But they keep alive the Christian tradition of obedience to the heavenly vision, of commitment to a *person,* rather than merely to a *cause.*

A visitor asked Albert Schweitzer why he forsook a brilliant career to become a missionary. His answer was simple but eloquent: "I did it for Him." This is what we mean by dedication.

A BRAVE PREACHER

King Agrippa, believest thou the prophets? I know that thou believest. Then Agrippa said unto Paul, Almost thou persuadest me to be a Christian. And Paul said, I would to God, that not only thou, but also all that hear me this day, were both almost, and altogether such as I am, except these bonds. Acts 26:27-29.

A monument in the middle of the city of Oxford in England memorializes the martydom of Hugh Latimer, a great English reformer who was for a time royal chaplain to King Henry VIII. On one occasion he began his sermon to the king in this manner:

"Latimer, Latimer, thou art going to speak before the high and mighty king, Henry VIII, who is able, if he thinks fit, to take thy life away. Be careful what thou sayest. But Latimer, Latimer, remember also thou art about to speak before the King of Kings and Lord of Lords. Take heed that thou dost not displease Him."

Standing before King Agrippa, Paul was in a comparable situation to Latimer. How did he use this opportunity? First, he gave the king his testimony regarding his own experience. He recalled the days when he persecuted the Christians. "I verily thought with myself, that I ought to do many things contrary to the name of Jesus of Nazareth" (verse 9). Then he told of the light that illuminated his pathway on the way to Damascus, and of his commission to preach Christ to the Gentiles. As to his response, he said, "Whereupon, O King Agrippa, I was not disobedient unto the heavenly vision" (verse 19). Then he affirmed his belief in the truth most repulsive to his listeners—the resurrection of Jesus from the dead. It was at this point that Festus shouted, "Paul, thou art beside thyself; much learning doth make thee mad" (verse 24). Paul did not softpedal this testing truth.

Our passage reveals that Paul appealed to Agrippa and all his other hearers to accept Christ as he had done. This, also, was an indication of courage, but his boldness was not offensive. Agrippa would have set him free had he not appealed to Caesar.

Paul's sermon before Agrippa is an example of restrained and courteous witness in a difficult situation.

PAUL ADVISES A SEA CAPTAIN

When the south wind blew softly, supposing that they had obtained their purpose, loosing thence, they sailed close by Crete. But not long after there arose against it a tempestuous wind. Acts 27:13, 14.

Paul was on his way to Rome to appear before Caesar. The ship on which the prisoners were being transported arrived at a place called Fair Havens on the southern coast of the island of Crete. The safe months for sailing had passed, and Paul advised the centurion in charge of the ship to winter at Fair Havens, but it was finally decided to attempt to make a more commodious port farther west.

Finally the sailing day came. "The south wind blew softly," the sun was shining, the sea was calm. Everyone was eager to go except Paul, who had more accurate sources of information than the local weather bureau could supply. Despite his warning the decision was made to proceed with the voyage.

So they lifted anchor and set sail, but they were scarcely out of sight of shore when a terrific northeaster struck them. They couldn't return, nor could they reach the other harbor. They were helpless in the grip of the storm. For days they were tossed about like a cork. Their cargo and ship were destroyed, and they barely escaped with their lives.

How like life! God reveals to man many principles to direct him as to how he should order his life. A time comes when he is faced with the question, Should I obey God's counsel or my own judgment? To obey seems irrational because the south wind is blowing so softly, the sky is so blue, the sea is so serene. His judgment tells him it is perfectly safe to disregard the counsel of God—so he does what seems right under the circumstances.

But before long his situation ethics prove unsound. The results of disregarding God's counsel become evident. The storm rages, and it is too late to change course.

As in Paul's case, God may save even though man disobeys—but at what a cost in misery, fear, and risk! It pays to disregard the soft south wind and heed the voice of God.

PAUL WITNESSES FOR GOD

*There stood by me this night the angel of God, whose I am,
and whom I serve, saying, Fear not, Paul; thou must be brought
before Caesar: and, lo, God hath given thee all them that sail
with thee. Acts 27:23, 24.*

For many days the ship on which Paul was being transported to
Rome as a prisoner had been tossed about by a tremendous storm.
Even the tackling of the ship had been thrown into the sea; neither
sun nor stars had been seen for many days, and the exhausted men
were ready to give up the battle.

Then a man whom the crew and prisoners had learned to respect came forward. Shouting above the roaring of the sea and the
creaking of the ship, Paul announced that there would be no loss of
life—only of the ship. Good news, but how did *he* know? The answer soon came—"There stood by me this night the angel of God."

This experience proclaims with certainty that we do not live in
a one-story world. There is a God whose angels alighted on the
rolling deck of a ship in distress and delivered a message to a man.
This was no impression or hunch on Paul's part—it was a real experience. He knew whereof he spoke because he had been in contact
with Heaven before. A familiar voice had spoken.

Paul took advantage of this dramatic situation to witness to his
relation to the God, "whose I am, and whom I serve." He was not his
own—he belonged to God. The word translated "serve" is probably
more correctly translated "worship." Paul wanted all men to know
that he was a worshiper of God. Then, to make his testimony more
emphatic, he added, "Be of good cheer: for I believe God, that it shall
be even as it was told me" (verse 25).

Never was Paul greater than when he addressed those 275
fatigued, hopeless men. He was revealed as a man who knew God,
who belonged to God, who worshiped God, and who believed God.
What a contrast between this great man and the modern Christian
who reduces God to a philosophical abstraction, who finds nothing
for God to do. No "ultimate reality" or "ground of being" will take
the place of the God whose angel spoke to Paul in the storm.

COURAGE IN CRISIS

He thanked God, and took courage. Acts 28:15.

A few years ago it was my privilege to see the Appian Way, the old Roman highway Paul traveled as a prisoner to Rome. Somewhere along that highway Paul, encouraged by the arrival of a group of fellow Christians, "thanked God, and took courage."

It is conceivable that his courage reached an all-time low as he saw the city of Rome in the distance. In that city were enemies who had power to put an end to his ministry and to take his life, but in that city was also a challenge to bear witness on behalf of the Lord whom he loved and served.

"At Harvard one evening, a freshman named William Prescott walked into a room where some of his classmates were still enjoying themselves after dinner. One hurled a heavy crust of bread across the room just as Prescott entered. He was struck squarely in the eyes, and fell to the floor. The best oculists in Boston could save only a dim part of the sight of one eye. He completed his course as best he could, then tried work and travel in turn, but found that the eye grew worse rather than better. Five years after he had entered college dreaming of greatness, his only exercise was to walk by the hour, with outstretched arms, in a room so dark that not even the furniture was visible. But suddenly, in 1820, William Prescott announced that he intended to become a historian. In a darkened study Prescott sat for six hours every day, listening and memorizing, while assistants read to him from reference books. Then he dictated, paragraph by paragraph, and when his first volume was finished, it told the story of Spain during the reign of Ferdinand and Isabella. . . . When he died after thirty-nine years of work, he had written sixteen thick volumes of such character as to bring him world-wide fame."— JACK FINEGAN, "Thank God and Take Courage," in Charles F. Kemp, *Life-Situation Preaching,* p. 159.

There was a similarity between Prescott and Paul. Paul, too, reacted to a discouraging situation by giving of his best, and from the city which was his prison came letter after letter, to be later preserved in the Bible. Courage made him a giant.

A SLAVE OF JESUS CHRIST

Paul, a servant of Jesus Christ, called to be an apostle, separated unto the gospel of God. Rom. 1:1.

The early verses of the first chapter of Romans serve, in part, to identify the author. Paul had every right to assert his position as the greatest Christian of his day but he chose to begin his letter by calling himself a slave. The word "servant" as translated in our King James Version is not strong enough—the original word literally means "bondservant"—slave. This term was especially meaningful in a culture built on the institution of slavery.

The idea of slavery to Christ had interesting implications. Paul recognized that Christ had purchased him at a great price. He was also aware of the necessity of complete commitment to the One who owned him. He accepted this responsibility gladly, and in every case he gave priority to the demands of his Master. In the ninth verse of this first chapter of Romans, Paul says it again: "For God is my witness, whom I serve with my spirit in the gospel of his son . . ." For Paul, Christianity included service without reservation.

This attitude on the part of a Christian toward his Lord is not too prevalent in our day. The modern emphasis on liberty and self-expression does not produce a favorable climate for the concept of complete dedication. Many professed Christians refuse the idea of any kind of authority. Neither God, nor the Bible, nor Christ speaks to them with any finality. Their norm is human experience and they refuse to accept the idea of Christ as their Master. They greatly admire Christ but they hesitate to follow Him. They are willing to accept Him as their example but not as their Lord. Slavery implies obedience, and this idea has no place in their philosophy.

If Paul had not been "a servant of Jesus Christ," he would never have been "called to be an apostle" and he could never have been "separated unto the gospel of God." Dedication comes first—apostleship follows. The world is in desperate need of men and women who are willing to be slaves of Christ, who are willing to make their own interests and plans secondary and His primary. Of such is the kingdom of heaven!

CHRISTIANS IN ROME

To all that be in Rome, beloved of God, called to be saints: Grace to you and peace from God our Father, and the Lord Jesus Christ. Rom. 1:7.

What was it like, being a Christian in Rome in A.D. 58? The ruler of Rome was Nero, a cruel and extravagant monarch. Paul's letter to the church at Rome was written before the worst part of Nero's reign, but it was not long until the dissolute emperor arranged for the assassination of his own mother, and "launched on the course of combined frivolity and tyranny that made his name a synonym for evil."

The Rome of Paul's day was a city of approximately one million people. Their interests included the theater, gladiatorial combats in the amphitheater, commercial and political life, and the worship of the Roman pantheon. Approximately half of the population were slaves.

In this deteriorating culture existed the Christian church with its high ethical standards, its dedication to Jesus as Lord, and its rejection of the sensual life of the day. No contrast could be greater than the contrast between the Christian and the ordinary citizen of Rome.

In 1849 a young man of twenty moved to London to follow an evangelistic career. He was appalled by the condition of the lower classes in London, and he set out to reach the most degraded of them. Early in his ministry he organized a company of converted criminals. In 1878, William Booth's movement became known as the Salvation Army, and soon it spread to other large cities of the world. Like the faith of the early Christians at Rome, the faith of Booth's followers became known throughout the whole world.

From the time of Paul until the present, Christians have witnessed for their Lord in the great centers of population. There are still Christians in Rome, in Paris, in London, in Moscow, in New York, in Tokyo. Invariably, these Christians contrast sharply with the environment in which they live. They are "strangers and pilgrims" in the fullest sense, and God honors their witness.

234

"BOTH YOURS AND MINE"

I long to see you, that I may impart unto you some spiritual gift, to the end ye may be established; that is, that I may be comforted together with you by the mutual faith both of you and me. Rom. 1:11, 12.

Paul is writing to the Romans, a church he had never visited. For some time he had wished to make a trip to Rome, but circumstances prevented him. Although at the time of writing this letter he was faced with the immediate need of traveling to Jerusalem, he still had not given up his desire to see Rome.

And why did he wish to take this long journey? The Revised Standard Version translates his reasons thus: "That I may impart to you some spiritual gift to strengthen you, that is, that we may be mutually encouraged by each other's faith, both yours and mine." With his usual tact, springing from his love for his people, Paul suggested that their visit might bring encouragement both to them and to him. He did not assume that his visit would benefit only the members in Rome. He expected to be blessed as well.

As a pastor I have had the experience of calling on persons who were very ill or who had experienced some great misfortune, and finding them so cheerful and optimistic that they encouraged me! I recall a young man who lost his eyesight, an active man who was confined to a wheel chair with a crippling disease, a medical student who was paralyzed from the waist down by an accident, a minister who was stricken with cancer. Each of these people, and many others like them, has actually inspired others who witnessed their faith. The most eloquent witness sometimes comes from the most unexpected sources.

And should not the sharing of faith be a mutual thing? Should the church look only to its ministers for faith; or, should Christians—laymen and ministers alike—encourage one another? "Bear ye one another's burdens," Paul says in another instance. Our experience makes us particularly effective in helping someone else who may be going through a similar experience. And when we are in perplexity, usually someone not far away is equipped to help us.

235

PAUL PAYS HIS DEBT

I am debtor both to the Greeks, and to the Barbarians; both to the wise, and to the unwise. So, as much as in me is, I am ready to preach the gospel to you that are at Rome also. Rom. 1:14, 15.

James Stewart, the great Scottish preacher, asks the following searching question: " 'Shall I, as a Christian, be content to pursue the religious quest as a private hobby, and to develop my own spiritual life; or shall I concern myself personally for those outside, and take upon my heart deliberately the whole world's need for Christ?' " Dr. Stewart answers his own question as follows: "No man, with the New Testament in his mind, can have a moment's hesitation about the answer. 'What I live by,' declared St. Augustine, 'I impart.' "— *Heralds of God,* p. 10.

Paul expressed the same sentiment graphically when he declared himself "a debtor" to all men—Greeks, barbarians, wise, unwise. Witnessing for Christ was not an option but a responsibility. As he was bound to pay his financial obligations, so was he forced by duty to preach the gospel to all men whatever the risk. He fulfilled this obligation at the cost of comfort, acceptance, freedom, and life itself!

To pay this debt in the modern world is not an easy assignment. To talk religion is often unpopular. It is acceptable to be enthusiastic about sports, hobbies, politics, art, careers, travel, and scores of other interests and activities, but not religion. It is considered proper to try to persuade men to be Democrats, Pall Mall smokers, Cadillac owners, and beer drinkers—but not Christians. This reticence to discuss the most important issue in life makes Christian witnessing difficult.

The Christian must learn to recognize, behind the seemingly impenetrable façade of many modern people, a longing for a relationship with God. We can never pay our debt to these people until we know them well enough, and they know us well enough, that we can communicate to their hearts the saving gospel of Christ. Only under the guidance of the Holy Spirit can this dialog be effective.

We owe a great unpaid debt to our Christless contemporaries. May God give us wisdom to know how to fulfill this obligation.

GOD'S KINDNESS

Despisest thou the riches of his goodness and forbearance and longsuffering; not knowing that the goodness of God leadeth thee to repentance? Rom. 2:4.

The word translated "goodness" is often rendered "kindness," and many versions so render it in this instance. Paul says it is the kindness, forbearance, and patience of God that lead men to repent.

This truth is not always rightly understood. For centuries it has been taught that repentance is brought about by terror. God has been pictured as a revengeful tyrant, and man is supposed to react by repenting in order that he might "save his soul."

The doctrine of an ever-burning hell was inspired by this false philosophy. Hold people over the pit of hell so that they feel the flames and smell the brimstone, and they will repent of their sins! But it is the *kindness* of God that leads to repentance.

This concept of God's kindness as the motivating force in repentance is at the center of the gospel. "God so loved . . . that he gave" is the Biblical revelation of the kindness of God. And it is His gift of love, Jesus Christ, who draws all men unto Him.

Just as a wayward child repents of his evil ways only when he feels the impact of his parents' love, so the only force that will melt the heart of a rebel against God is love. Force will not do it, power will not do it, logic will fail; but the melting power of kindness can change the direction of a life.

One of the most wonderful descriptions of God's kindness is found in the forty-third chapter of Isaiah: "Fear not," God says: "for I have redeemed thee, I have called thee by thy name; thou art mine. When thou passest through the waters, I will be with thee; and through the rivers, they shall not overflow thee: when thou walkest through the fire, thou shalt not be burned; neither shall the flame kindle upon thee. For I am the Lord thy God, the Holy One of Israel, thy Saviour."

This kind of love leads to repentance. It is hard to resist such tender concern. If only Christians could communicate this love to the world, how many more would accept Jesus as their Lord!

237

RESPONSIBILITY

[God] will render to every man according to his deeds: to them who by patient continuance in well doing seek for glory and honour and immortality, eternal life. Rom. 2:6, 7.

"Certainly this doesn't sound like Paul," someone protests. "Did not Paul teach that man is saved by faith, not by works? Is not the grace of God the source of salvation, not good deeds?" At first glance this point of view seems out of place in Paul's teaching, but closer study reveals the reason for his statement.

The fact is that God *will* judge man according to his deeds, and He *will* reward "patient continuance in well doing." But what is the basis of these "deeds"? Are they a means to salvation? No. Salvation is only through God's grace. Can they be performed without divine aid? No. Man is unable to keep the law.

What actually happens is this: God's grace devised a plan whereby man might be saved. This plan involved the death and resurrection of His Son. Man accepts this provision by faith. Having done this, he is a child of God, a candidate for immortality. At this point the man who has been redeemed realizes what a debt of gratitude he owes his Redeemer, and he endeavors to express that gratitude in worship and obedience. Obedience reflects his love and dedication, and enriches his life. He could never have achieved Christian character without the help and the motivation of the grace of God.

When the day of judgment comes, this man who accepted God's grace is living, or has lived, an exemplary life. For years, perhaps, he has practiced "patient continuance in well doing." In response God says to him, "Well done, thou good and faithful servant," knowing that, but for His grace, the man would never have become a "good and faithful servant."

Conversion brings responsibility; responsibility results in Christian living; and the Christian life, lived by the grace of God, justifies God's action in bestowing immortality. In this sense it may be rightly said that God will render to every man according to (not "because of") his deeds. The redeemed life, though not yet perfect, reveals the power of God to change men as well as to save them.

"MUCH MORE"

If, when we were enemies, we were reconciled to God by the death of his Son, much more, being reconciled, we shall be saved by his life. Rom. 5:10.

The expression "much more" aptly summarizes the fifth chapter of Romans. Five times the phrase is repeated, and in other instances the thought is implied. The idea is that however accusing the law may be, grace is always able to pardon; however depraved our past may have been, our future may be glorious; however formidable the devil may have been, Christ is more than his equal. The "offense" was tragic, but the "gift of grace" more than compensates. Our text also implies that though reconciliation by the death of Christ is important, salvation by His life is "much more" so.

"Much more" presents a hopeful, optimistic gospel. The Christian need not limit his attention, either to the tragedies and failures of his own life or to the collective life of mankind. That which supersedes tragedy is "much more" meaningful than tragedy. Neither should the Christian limit his attention to the cross, important as it is. The resurrection, the ascension, the heavenly ministry, and the Second Coming reveal the consummation and the sequel of that for which the cross was a necessary introduction.

This being true, though Christian experience recognizes the cross, it must not overlook the empty tomb. The enmity of the past may not be altogether forgotten, yet the guidance of the Spirit in the present and the hope of the future must ever be clearly in mind. The Christian life is a steadfast climb heavenward. Real Christian experience does not lose its meaningfulness as the years go by, but becomes "much more" significant as we come to understand life better.

Verse 15 of this chapter says that the gift of grace has "abounded" to many. In the experience of some Christians, religion does not seem to "abound." It is like filling a cup from a faucet that merely drips, or wringing water from a cloth that is nearly dry. Life holds "much more" for us than we realize, if we accept the privileges available to us through Jesus Christ our Lord.

PAUL CONFESSES INNER CONFLICT

That which I do I allow not: for what I would, that do I not;
but what I hate, that do I. . . . For the good that I would I do not:
but the evil which I would not, that I do. Rom. 7:15-19.

How accurately the apostle describes the inner struggle that most of us know all too well! All of our lives we have been taught high standards, but we have never learned how to reach them.

> "Within my earthly temple there's a crowd:
> There's one that's humble—one that's proud,
> There's one that's broken-hearted for his sins,
> And one that, unrepentant, sits and grins;
> There's one that loves his neighbor as himself,
> And one that cares for naught but fame and pelf.
> From such perplexing care I would be free,
> If I could once determine which is me."
>
> *—Selected*

It would be most distressing to leave this great human problem unresolved. After developing at length the conflict he himself had experienced, Paul exclaims, "Wretched man that I am! Who will deliver me from this body of death?" (Rom. 7:24, R.S.V.). Then he answers: "Thanks be to God through Jesus Christ our Lord!"

Paul saw in Christ the remedy for this conflict. He goes on to say, "There is therefore now no condemnation for those who are in Christ Jesus. For the law of the Spirit of life in Christ Jesus has set me free from the law of sin and death" (Rom. 8:1, 2, R.S.V.). The inner tension is at rest. A new power has taken possession of the life.

The unification of the personality with Christ as a center is one of the great blessings of the Christian faith. One reason men like Paul were able to accomplish so much was that their resources were not wasted on inner conflict. The full power of their integrated personalities could be focused on the great objectives of their lives. A personality in conflict is like traffic trying to go both ways on a one-way street. Only confusion results. Like Paul, let us look to Jesus Christ, our Lord as the unifying principle of our lives.

244

THE UNIVERSE ON TIPTOE

For the earnest expectation of the creature waiteth for the manifestation of the sons of God. Rom. 8:19.

J. B. Phillips has translated this text in a very striking way: "The whole creation is on tiptoe to see the wonderful sight of the sons of God coming into their own." A similar thought is expressed in *Testimonies to Ministers,* page 119: "The universe is looking upon the controversy that is going on upon the earth. At an infinite cost, God has provided for every man an opportunity to know that which will make him wise unto salvation. How eagerly do angels look to see who will avail himself of this opportunity!"

Some contemporary philosophers have much to say about the meaninglessness of life. Many have grown utterly cynical because they can see no cosmic significance in the human drama. Agnostic about that which cannot be perceived by the senses, they have no appreciation of the supernatural and no hope beyond this life.

What a contrasting view our text presents: "The whole creation is on tiptoe"—like a crowd at a race, stretching their necks to see the participants on the track. And for what are the celestial spectators watching? Before them is being enacted "the wonderful sight of the sons of God coming into their own." The plan of salvation is of intense interest to the universe, and no point of the entire drama is more breathtaking than when those whom God has saved finally reach the finish line.

One of the themes of the teachings of Jesus is the happiness that results from the salvation of sinners. In the parable of the lost sheep the shepherd returned from his successful search rejoicing. "And when he cometh home, he calleth together his friends and neighbors, saying unto them, Rejoice with me; for I have found my sheep which was lost. I say unto you, that likewise joy shall be in heaven over one sinner that repenteth" (Luke 15:6, 7). The same joy followed the finding of the lost coin and the return of the prodigal.

The salvation of a lost person or of a lost world is always cause for rejoicing. "The whole creation is on tiptoe" to acclaim the winners in the final great day. Life does have meaning!

245

GOD IS ON OUR SIDE

If God be for us, who can be against us? Rom. 8:31.

Dr. John Sutherland Bonnell tells the following story from his pastoral experience:

"A young woman came into my study in Winnipeg. She was poorly dressed and quite evidently discouraged. Her story was a sad though not an unfamiliar one. Her father was ill; her brothers unemployed. She was the sole wage earner in the home. Her health was failing. She was exceedingly nervous. Oftentimes she had lacked sufficient food.

" 'To crown it all,' she said, 'I fear that I shall lose my position, which is all that stands between my family and destitution. Even the employees in the office are talking about my appearance and I am constantly making mistakes in my work.'

"Her trembling hands and twitching lips revealed the fact that the case was critical. Before she left the church that young woman had found God. Her face was lighted up with new hope. Again and again she affirmed, 'If God be for me, who can be against me?'

"Twelve months later a young woman came to the church for an interview. She was simply but tastefully dressed. Her face was radiant. 'Do you remember me?' she asked. I had to confess that I did not. Then with a quiet smile, she said, 'If God be for me, who can be against me?' Instantly I recognized the one who had come to me in deep distress a year before. But the spirit of defeatism had vanished. She told me a thrilling story. Her unshakable faith in God had enabled her to triumph over every difficulty and had infused fresh courage into others in her home who had given up the battle."—*Fifth Avenue Sermons,* pp. 111, 112.

Many of us are confronted with formidable difficulties. We may struggle against seemingly insurmountable odds. Our own limitations, lack of resources, unsympathetic associates, poor health—all or any of these problems may beset us. And God has not promised to protect us from these things. But we can all rest confident in the assertion, "If God be for us, who can be against us?" With God on our side we can accomplish that which would otherwise be impossible.

PAUL'S ENTHUSIASM

Nay, in all these things we are more than conquerors through him that loved us. For I am persuaded, that neither death, nor life, nor angels, nor principalities, nor powers, nor things present, nor things to come, nor height, nor depth, nor any other creature, shall be able to separate us from the love of God, which is in Christ Jesus our Lord. Rom. 8:37-39.

Paul's life had been transformed by "the love of God, which is in Christ Jesus our Lord." He had seen the lives of hundreds of other people changed, as was his own. It was the divine love that gave meaning to life and provided hope for eternity. Is it any wonder that Paul wrote with such enthusiasm?

And yet we scarcely experience a one-point elevation of blood pressure when we are confronted with this marvelous fact of the love of God. We have heard about it so long that we take it for granted. And to discuss it with enthusiasm, as Paul did, would scarcely be the in thing to do in the sophisticated twentieth century.

What would life be like if we would but release the brakes and express wholesome emotions of gratitude, appreciation, and praise. This story is told of a freight train brakeman: "On his very first run the train came to a steep grade which the engineer had difficulty negotiating. Upon reaching the summit, the engineer turned to his new brakeman and said, 'We had a hard climb, didn't we?' 'We sure did,' said the brakeman, 'and if I hadn't put on the brake we would've slipped back!' "—*Halford Luccock Treasury*, p. 326.

When Paul wrote our text he wasn't traveling with the brakes on. He was expressing supreme excitement over a great idea, and he was using the most graphic words at his command. With literary extravagance he marshals "death," "life," "angels," "principalities," "powers," "things present," "things to come," "height," "depth," on one side of the balance, and "the love of God" on the other. There is no question as to which way the scales tip.

Let us catch some of Paul's enthusiasm. We get carried away with things of much less importance. Why not go all out for Christ's gospel? Why keep the brakes on when we are trying to climb?

247

PAUL EXPRESSES CONCERN FOR HIS COUNTRYMEN

I say the truth in Christ, I lie not, my conscience also bearing me witness in the Holy Ghost, that I have great heaviness and continual sorrow in my heart. For I could wish that myself were accursed from Christ for my brethren, my kinsmen according to the flesh. Rom. 9:1-3.

"From old China comes a beautiful story as told by Madame Chiang Kai-shek that surely Jesus would have used in a parable had it happened in His day. A Chinese rice farmer on a hilltop farm felt a heavy earthquake that swiftly withdrew the water from the ocean shore line a little distance away. He knew from previous experience that it meant a returning tidal wave that would flood the lower valleys. His neighbors were down there, all oblivious to their danger. They must be gathered quickly to his hilltop. Without hesitation he set a torch to his rice barns, which were dry as tinder. Then as the flames devoured the buildings he rang the fire gong hanging beneath the eaves. The plan worked. His neighbors saw the smoke and rushed up the hill to help him. Then from their vantage point, they watched the tidal waters cover the fields they had just left. On the monument they erected for him they inscribed, 'He gave us all he had, and did it gladly.' "—H. M. TIPPETT, *My Lord and I*, p. 379.

Such was the attitude of Paul toward his countrymen who rejected Christ. He would have been willing to be "separated from Christ" (marginal rendering) if by so doing he could save his fellow Jews. His attitude toward his countrymen, although they were hostile toward him, was one of sacrificing love and deep concern.

Such an attitude revealed Paul's Christlikeness, for it was such a love and concern that motivated the Son of God "who, being in the form of God, thought it not robbery to be equal with God: but made himself of no reputation, and took upon him the form of a servant, and was made in the likeness of men: and being found in fashion as a man, he humbled himself, and became obedient unto death, even the death of the cross" (Phil. 2:6-8).

The church today needs this concern more than it needs money, power, or prestige.

248

"OFFER YOURSELVES"

I beseech you therefore, brethren, by the mercies of God, that ye present your bodies a living sacrifice, holy, acceptable unto God, which is your reasonable service. Rom. 12:1.

Many of the Christians to whom Paul wrote had known the old Jewish system of offerings. Some of them had themselves taken lambs to the Temple as an evidence of their dedication to God. Their new-found Christian faith asked them to do something in place of the old ritual—"Offer yourselves as a living sacrifice to God, dedicated to his service and pleasing to him" (T.E.V.).

What does it mean for a person to offer himself as a living sacrifice to God? First of all, it means that he accepts Christ as Lord, thereby surrendering control of the life to Him. Some want Christ as Saviour but are not willing to accept Him as Lord. Complete dedication involves placing Him in the driver's seat and letting Him plan the itinerary for our lives.

Several implications arise from this type of dedication. It means that we make God first. It rules out a type of Christianity that only has room for an occasional polite bow to God. It is contrary to the practice of many who give God what little may be left after they have showered the blessings of life on themselves. It contradicts the idea of giving our younger years to the world and our old age to God. It stands in contrast to the one-day-a-week Christianity that considers religion the cake of life rather than the bread of life.

A young missionary was killed by a savage Indian tribe. Not many months later, his wife ventured into the very territory where he had lost his life. Her purpose was to try to bring the gospel to the people who had robbed her of her husband. This is a classic example of the type of dedication described in our text—a level of dedication that is rarely seen.

The book of Revelation describes a company of people surrounding the throne of God, dressed in white robes. Regarding these people, it is said: "These are they which came out of great tribulation, and have washed their robes, and made them white in the blood of the Lamb" (Rev. 7:14). This is the destiny of dedicated people.

249

THE GREAT QUESTIONS

Be not conformed to this world: but be ye transformed by the renewing of your mind, that ye may prove what is that good, and acceptable, and perfect, will of God. Rom. 12:2.

Phillips illuminates the meaning of this great passage as follows: "Don't let the world around you squeeze you into its own mold, but let God remold your minds from within, so that you may prove in practice that the plan of God for you is good, meets all his demands and moves toward the goal of true maturity."

This passage deals with what goes on in the depths of our souls. It pictures a Christian, emancipated from the degrading influences of the world, susceptible to the shaping influences from God, moving toward the goal of Christian maturity. How can we tell if we are enjoying this experience?

"If you want to know," says Dr. Inge, "what you really believe, ask yourselves two questions. First, if I had a fairy godmother who promised to grant me three wishes, what would those wishes be? and second, what are the things, if any, that I would die rather than do?" —ROBERT J. MCCRACKEN, *Questions People Ask,* p. 77. These questions illuminate the thought of our text. If I could have anything I choose, would my choice reflect conformity to the world? Would I choose property, power, pleasure; or would my choice reflect the renewing influence of the Spirit of God? Would I choose that which would glorify God and bless humanity? Would my choices reflect childishness or maturity? And, second, have I matured to the point where there are things I would die rather than do? And what are those things? There are plenty of people who are willing to give their bodies to be burned. Some take great risks in the service of ideologies, good and bad. But how many would die rather than disregard the will of God?

Our religion is often superficial. We join the church, attend meetings, and adhere to certain regulations. However, we allow ourselves to be conformed to the spirit of the world. We lack spiritual maturity and depth. Let us ask ourselves Dr. Inge's questions—What do we want most? and, For what would we die?

IMITATION LOVE

Let love be without dissimulation. Rom. 12:9.

"Let us have no imitation Christian love," is the way Phillips translates this passage. Another version reads, "Let love be genuine" (R.S.V.). Still another says, "Love in all sincerity" (N.E.B.). What do we mean by imitation love?

An imitation is something that closely resembles something else generally considered to be of greater value. Many things, all the way from ice cream to diamonds, have been imitated. Currency, works of art, and valuable papers have been forged—to enrich the forgers.

Love is imitated by the politician who endeavors to persuade people that he is concerned about *them,* when actually he is concerned only for their votes. Love is imitated by millions of people who have never learned the difference between love and lust. Love is imitated by the unscrupulous businessman who makes his victims believe that he is genuinely interested in their welfare, when he is only seeking profit. Love is imitated by the zealous Christian worker who is more interested in statistics than in souls. Love is imitated whenever we feign a concern that we do not feel.

We must also remember that Paul is not talking about a mere feeling of friendliness and good will. Our text uses the word that refers to the highest type of regard one may have for another—Christian love. This attribute enables us to love even people whom we do not like. Real love is the motivation that makes us always put the other person's interest ahead of our own, that makes us genuinely aware of the feelings and needs of other people. A counterfeit of this type of love is a serious menace.

In days past some argued that it was an act of love to persecute a heretic because suffering might compel him to recant and thereby save his soul. Such reasoning was false, for even God, who is perfect in love, does not compel. It is imitation love that smothers, cajoles, and endeavors to control. Imitation love invariably claims to be the real thing. Every person can well afford to ask himself some searching questions: Do I *really* love my family; do I *really* love my fellow men; do I *really* love God; or is my love a sham?

251

GOOD AND EVIL

Abhor that which is evil; cleave to that which is good.
Rom. 12:9.

This would be an appropriate motto for our generation, for we are living in a time when people are looking for something good in that which is bad, and for something bad in that which is good.

In the first case, there seems to be no criminal so vile but that someone will have a tear to shed for him—yet the same sympathizer has not an ounce of sympathy for the criminal's victim. The smuttiest magazines and books have their defenders, even among educated and sophisticated people. Godless theologians and philosophers are tolerated by people who claim to be Christians. The drug-addicted, irresponsible sex pervert is often treated with great deference.

On the other hand, society's sharpest criticisms are reserved for "Puritans," "reformers," and "squares." People who live respectable lives, worship God, pay their bills, and make a contribution to society, are sneered at and often termed "hypocrites." The church is under constant criticism by people who forget that despite its weakness it remains one of the strongest bulwarks of civilization. The "establishment" is under constant fire. This term is applied to almost any aspect of organized, well-ordered society. Government is resisted because it endeavors to regulate the behavior of its citizens. It is time for thinking people to listen to Paul and "hate what is *evil*" and "hold fast to what is *good*" (R.S.V.). Someone has crawled into the show window and changed the price tags. Good is minimized, despised, rejected. Evil is praised, defended, coddled. When will Christians stand up and be counted and take their stand on the side of the values endorsed in God's Word and proved by centuries of human experience?

It may seem smart to reverse the price tags, but it is far from safe. A clear distinction must be maintained between good and evil.

In another part of Romans, Paul repeats the same idea. He says, "I want to see you experts in good, and not even beginners in evil" (Rom. 16:19, Phillips). As strange as this sounds to the modern ear, it is part of the Christian philosophy of life.

ENERGETIC CHRISTIANS

Not slothful in business; fervent in spirit; serving the Lord.
Rom. 12:11.

The New English Bible reads, "With unflagging energy, in ardour of spirit, serve the Lord." The passage suggests that all of life's varied activities are part of our service to God. The meaning of this text is reflected in the following quotation: "God's servants are to be 'not slothful in business; fervent in spirit; serving the Lord.' Listlessness and inefficiency are not piety. When we realize that we are working for God we shall have a higher sense than we ever had before of the sacredness of spiritual service. This realization will put life and vigilance and persevering energy into the discharge of every duty."—*Testimonies,* vol. 9, p. 150.

History provides us with examples of the relationship between Christian faith and energetic, effective living. In October, 1685, Louis XIV of France revoked the Edict of Nantes that had given some of the Protestants in his realm a measure of protection. As a result, more than three hundred thousand Huguenots left France. Some found homes in Holland, England, Ireland, America, Switzerland, and Germany. A large number died in prisons and galleys. Many of the weaker ones gave up their faith. What was the result of this purge? One historian tells the story as follows: "It [the persecution] destroyed a vast number of the most conscientious, enterprising, industrious, and intelligent citizens—the wealth-producers of the nation. It drove into exile a vastly greater number of the very ablest, wealthiest, most enterprising, and most religious members of the commonwealth, thereby depriving France of a large amount of capital, enterprise, skill in manufacturing and in commerce, and of professional learning and experience, and at the same time and in equal measure enriching the nations that received them and raising up competitors in lines of manufactures and commerce in which France had held the supremacy."—A. H. NEWMAN, *A Manual of Church History,* vol. 2, pp. 486, 487.

Dedicated Christians will reveal great energy and success in the practical affairs of life, doing so "in the light of eternity."

HOPE

Rejoicing in hope. Rom. 12:12.

"Let hope keep you joyful" is the way *The New English Bible* translates this verse. Much of the mental depression that makes business for the psychiatrists results from the lack of hope in the heart.

C. S. Lewis has said, " 'Hope is one of the theological virtues. This means that a continued looking forward to the eternal world is not, as some modern people think, a form of escapism or wishful thinking, but one of the things a Christian is meant to do. It does not mean that we are to leave the present world as it is. If you read history, you will find that the Christians who did most for the present world were just those who thought most of the next. It is since Christians have largely ceased to think of the other world that they have become so ineffective in this. Aim at Heaven and you will get earth thrown in. Aim at earth and you will get neither.' "—Quoted by BILLY GRAHAM in *World Aflame,* p. 202.

In Romans 15:13 Paul repeats the same idea, "Now the God of hope fill you with all joy and peace in believing, that ye may abound in hope, through the power of the Holy Ghost." This is a dependable formula in Christian living.

Hope has a way of remaining after every other support is gone. In an art gallery in London is a masterpiece entitled *Hope.* A girl is seated upon a globe, blindfolded, and in her hands she holds a lute, of which all the strings but one are broken. The girl is touching that one string with her hand, and her head is bent toward it, earnestly waiting to catch the sound from that one remaining string. So it is with hope. After all of the other strings are broken, hope remains; and for the Christian this hope is not an idle dream.

Peter is known as the apostle of hope. In the beginning of his first letter to the church he says, "Praise be to the God and Father of our Lord Jesus Christ, who in his mercy gave us new birth into a living hope by the resurrection of Jesus Christ from the dead!" (1 Peter 1:3, N.E.B.). Every hope the Christian cherishes results from the resurrection of his Lord. To take the resurrected Christ out of the life of the Christian would be like taking the sun out of his sky.

DON'T GIVE UP

Patient in tribulation. Rom. 12:12.

Paul was speaking out of personal experience when he suggested that Christians should be patient in tribulation.

Recall, for example, the occasion when Paul's enemies stoned him and dragged him out of the city thinking him dead (Acts 14:19). There he lay, surrounded by a little group of followers. No doubt they were weeping as they considered the loss of their leader. All of a sudden the supposed corpse showed signs of life. "He rose up, *and came into the city.*" They dragged him out of the city, but he walked back. He didn't leave until the next day!

Perhaps the most revealing of the records of Paul's suffering was his statement, "Five times received I forty stripes save one. Thrice was I beaten with rods" (2 Cor. 11:24, 25). Of all forms of punishment devised by man, beating was one of the cruelest. Many victims did not survive one flogging. Surely a normal man, having been beaten once, would see to it that it never happened again, whatever compromise or concession he might be called upon to make. But not Paul! Eight times he went through this ordeal, but he kept on preaching. Could one be more patient than this in tribulation?

It is one thing to submit to troubles we can in no way prevent, like sickness, famine, or bereavement; but Paul's tribulations were different. All he had to do to stop all of this trouble was to change his job. He could have been a tentmaker, a scholar, a scribe, a lawyer, or any one of a score of other honorable pursuits, and lived a quiet life. But Paul patiently accepted beating, imprisonment, stoning, privation, danger, and finally execution, because he believed so deeply in his Lord.

Nor was Paul a man who craved martyrdom. He allowed himself to be let down over the wall of Damascus in a basket when danger threatened. He avoided his enemies whenever possible. He never unnecessarily invited persecution. But when his loyalty to his Lord was at stake, he patiently endured whatever came his way. One version translates this text, "Do not give up if trials come" (Jerusalem Bible). This would be a good motto for every Christian.

255

KEEP ON PRAYING

Continuing instant in prayer. Rom. 12:12.

The unfamiliar King James Version terminology means simply, "Keep on praying."

Numerous things cause people to quit praying. Some of us get so busy we fail to take time to pray. In the morning our tasks are calling us, and when evening comes we are too weary. To all who are busy, Paul says, "Keep on praying."

Some people quit praying because the sinfulness of their lives comes up before them when they kneel before God. Not wanting to be reminded of their shortcomings, they don't care to get too close to God. To all who are slipping into sin, Paul says, "Keep on praying."

Others cease to pray because they don't see that praying does any good. They have prayed for things they failed to receive. They feel that God has forgotten them, so they quit praying. To all who have been disappointed by unanswered prayers, Paul says, "Keep on praying."

Some have become confused by intellectual problems. Simple faith in a prayer-answering God has become difficult for them. It seems naive to believe that the Creator of the universe would be interested in an individual. They find themselves trying to formulate a philosophical concept as a substitute for God. To all who are swayed by doubt and disbelief, Paul says, "Keep on praying."

Some have been so successful in gaining the good things of life —property, position, friends, security—that they feel no need of anything more. Communion with God, they think, is an experience for the less fortunate. Their own cup of satisfaction is full. In their universe there is nothing for God to do. To the self-satisfied and successful, Paul says, "Keep on praying."

No one ever gave better advice in so few words. Neither busyness, nor sinfulness, nor disappointment, nor doubt, nor self-sufficiency can destroy the need for prayer. When prayer is understood as communion with God no one is too good to pray, too busy to pray, too bad to pray, or too intelligent to pray. The counsel, "Keep on praying," fits the need of every man.

PAUL'S WELFARE PROJECT

Distributing to the necessity of saints; given to hospitality.
Rom. 12:13.

One of the most ambitious projects of Paul's life had to do with "distributing to the necessity of saints." The Christians at Jerusalem were in need, and Paul conceived the idea of raising funds from his Gentile churches to relieve their distress.

Writing to the church at Corinth, Paul directed that the members there take up a weekly offering to be held until he should come. He indicated that he had given the same instructions to the churches in Galatia. He planned that the churches should approve persons to take this money to Jerusalem, and he indicated that he might accompany them. In the fifteenth chapter of Romans, Paul revealed his plan to visit Rome on his way to Spain, but added, "Now I go unto Jerusalem to minister unto the saints. For it hath pleased them of Macedonia and Achaia to make a certain contribution for the poor saints which are at Jerusalem" (verses 25, 26). Later in the chapter he asks the Romans to pray "that my service which I have for Jerusalem may be accepted of the saints" (verse 31).

Paul's concern for the needs of the Christians at Jerusalem is commendable, but his insight into what this gift might do for the Christian church of his day was remarkable. Probably never before in the history of his age did Gentiles contribute to the needs of Jews. No such love or concern was common in that time. Paul's gospel was "the power of God unto salvation to every one that believeth; to the Jew first, and also to the Greek" (Rom. 1:16). He was anxious that the interests of Jewish and Gentile Christians be knit together. How better could it be done than to have Gentiles contribute to the needs of their Christian brothers and sisters at Jerusalem.

Paul was speaking from personal experience when he talked about "distributing to the necessity of saints." He could not rest as long as there were hungry Christians. His project set an example for the church through the ages. He demonstrated that Christian love remembers the brother who is in need, regardless of nationality and political differences.

A HARD COMMANDMENT

Bless them which persecute you: bless, and curse not.
Rom. 12:14.

This is a hard thing to do; it was as hard for Paul as for anyone else. Some time after he wrote these words to the Romans he was in Jerusalem appearing before the chief priests and all their council. He began his defense by saying, "Men and brethren, I have lived in all good conscience before God until this day" (Acts 23:1).

At this point the high priest, Ananias, commanded someone who stood close to Paul to slap him on the mouth. Hearing the command, Paul shot back, "God shall smite thee, thou whited wall: for sittest thou to judge me after the law, and commandest me to be smitten contrary to the law?" (verse 3). The bystanders reminded Paul that he was talking to the high priest, and he apologized, "I wist not, brethren, that he was the high priest: for it is written, Thou shalt not speak evil of the ruler of thy people" (verse 5). Even Paul found it hard to tolerate injustice.

There was but one person who never failed to be kind, thoughtful, and gracious to his persecutors, and that was Jesus. It was Jesus who said, "Love your enemies, bless them that curse you, do good to them that hate you, and pray for them which despitefully use you, and persecute you" (Matt. 5:44). Paul learned this principle from Jesus, and even though he found it hard to follow, he succeeded admirably in living up to it throughout a long life of tensions. In his letter to the Corinthians he said, "Being reviled, we bless; being persecuted, we suffer it" (1 Cor. 4:12). He had plenty of opportunities to put this rule into practice.

As an old man, Peter recalled this trait in the life of Jesus. He said of his Master that "when he was reviled, [He] reviled not again; when he suffered, he threatened not" (1 Peter 2:23). Peter was not naturally the sort of person to suffer indignities meekly, but he developed that grace. He, too, was tested often on this point. It takes real fortitude to remain gracious under pressure and persecution. But we serve the same Lord as did Peter and Paul, and we can achieve this level of Christian love in the same way they did—through Christ.

EMPATHY

Rejoice with them that do rejoice, and weep with them that weep. Rom. 12:15.

Much has been said and written about the importance of empathy —the ability to feel with other people—to identify with them in their joys and sorrows. This is a basic aspect of love.

If a friend of ours has unusual good fortune—if he comes into possession of wealth, if he is given a position we would like to have had, or if he achieves fame because of his ability and skill—do we rejoice with him? Of course we congratulate him and outwardly express pleasure at his success, but how do we feel inside? Do we wonder why this good fortune could not have come our way? Do we rationalize that, after all, he is not as deserving of acclaim as people think? Do we find ways to cast aspersions on his accomplishments and thereby discount them in the eyes of others? Are we really big enough to rejoice, wholeheartedly and genuinely, when someone else receives blessings for which we have longed? When we reach this point in our experience, we have attained a significant degree of spiritual maturity.

And have we learned to weep with those who weep? A friend loses a loved one. Do we try to persuade him that it is perhaps for the best? This type of reasoning he cannot understand. Do we try to divert his mind to other interests? The ability to cast aside grief comes only with the healing process of time; it cannot be forced. Do we remind him how much worse off someone else may be? This provides scant comfort. We will be of most help if our level of empathy is such that we can sincerely weep with him. A smiling face can never compare under these circumstances with a sympathizing tear.

Most of us probably find it easier to "weep with them that weep" than to "rejoice with them that do rejoice." We lend a hand to the unfortunate—to do so makes us feel good inside. But how sensitive we are when others surpass us!

Real empathy can never be achieved by the person who is wrapped up in himself. One must be responsive to the experiences of others; he must be in touch with the world about him.

PAUL DEFINES CHRISTIAN CHARACTER

Be of the same mind one toward another. Mind not high things, but condescend to men of low estate. Be not wise in your own conceits. Recompense to no man evil for evil. Provide things honest in the sight of all men. If it be possible, as much as lieth in you, live peaceably with all men. Rom. 12:16-18.

"Henry Ward Beecher was buying a horse and the owner was describing the animal.

" 'This horse is perfectly sound,' he said. 'He can go any gait—walk, pace, trot or gallop. He will stand without hitching and work any place you put him—on the off side or the near side—buggy, plow, or wagon. He is perfectly gentle, though full of spirit; goes when you want him to go and stops when you say "whoa." He has no bad habits; will neither bite nor kick; comes when you call him and does not run off when he sees anything strange.'

"Beecher looked admiringly at the animal and said wistfully, 'Ah, I wish that horse were a member of my church.' "—Quoted in *Religious Digest,* May, 1940, p. 84.

Perfect horses and perfect church members are both hard to find, but Paul had certain helpful, concrete suggestions concerning standards of character for mature Christians. An analysis of our Scripture passage reveals the following tests of a genuine Christian way of life:

1. *Harmony.* The real Christian earnestly desires to get along with his fellow men. He loves peace and is a man of good will. He, too, is "perfectly gentle, though full of spirit."

2. *Humility.* Arrogance and status-consciousness are out of bounds for the Christian. He does not think of himself more highly than he ought. He will work "on the off side or the near side."

3. *Honesty.* The Christian is, above all, a man of integrity. At any cost he avoids duplicity and misrepresentation.

These characteristics recommend the Christian's faith to the world. And these marks of real greatness are attainable through the grace of the same God who caused them to be realized in the life of Paul. He was able to speak as he did because he knew the extent to which God can transform a life.

MAGNANIMITY

If thine enemy hunger, feed him; if he thirst, give him drink: for in so doing thou shalt heap coals of fire on his head. Rom. 12:20.

"In the course of the Armenian atrocities a young woman and her brother were pursued down the street by a Turkish soldier, cornered in an angle of the wall, and the brother was slain before his sister's eyes. She dodged down an alley, leaped a wall, and escaped. Later, being a nurse, she was forced by the Turkish authorities to work in the military hospital. Into her ward was brought, one day, the same Turkish soldier who had slain her brother. He was very ill. A slight inattention would insure his death. The young woman, now safe in America, confesses to the bitter struggle that took place in her mind. The old Adam cried 'vengeance'; the new Christ cried, 'love.' And, equally to the man's good and to her own, the better side of her conquered, and she nursed him as carefully as any other patient in the ward. The recognition had been mutual and one day, unable longer to restrain his curiosity, the Turk asked his nurse why she had not let him die, and when she replied, 'I am a follower of him who said, "Love your enemies and do them good," ' he was silent for a long time. At last he spoke: 'I never knew that there was such a religion. If that is your religion tell me more about it, for I want it.' "— HARRY EMERSON FOSDICK, *Twelve Tests of Character,* pp. 166, 167.

This story of a half century ago illustrates perfectly the meaning of our text. The burning conscience of a person who is being treated well by someone he has mistreated is appropriately compared to coals of fire. Nothing will melt the heart of a wrongdoer like sincere love manifested toward him by one he has wronged.

This principle is not only found in Paul's writings and in the Sermon on the Mount, it is an Old Testament concept as well. In fact, Paul quotes our text from Proverbs 25:21, 22. The author of Proverbs adds a phrase at the end that Paul does not quote: "and the Lord shall reward thee." There is something about the magnanimous, forgiving spirit that brings God's blessings on its possessor. The rewards of forgiveness are far greater than the rewards of revenge.

261

A CURE FOR EVIL

Be not overcome of evil, but overcome evil with good.
Rom. 12:21.

A neighbor once told me how to take care of a new lawn. "Keep it watered, mowed, and fertilized," he said, "and eventually the grass will crowd out the weeds."

In the same manner, good can crowd out evil in the life. A group of teen-agers are terrorizing their community by vandalism and petty crime. A youth worker becomes acquainted with them and gets them busy in some worth-while enterprise. The former practices cease, not because of force or threats, but because evil has been overcome with good. This is the best way to solve delinquency.

A certain man was once on his way to Damascus to crush out the new Christian church in that city. He met his Lord, was baptized, and joined the group he formerly hated. He then became busy in the service of his new Master. Old evils disappeared from his life. New loyalties displaced old prejudices. New interests took the place of old hatreds. In Christ, he became a new man. Evil had been overcome with good.

Certain types of cancer are treated by radiation. The patient is exposed to tremendous bombardments of rays that destroy cancer tissue and thus permit the normal functioning of the body. The gospel of Jesus is like this. When evil is exposed to the "power of God unto salvation," it withers and dies. Where sin once grew and flourished, good takes its place.

This text tells us that good is sufficiently stronger than evil to overcome it. This is good news in a world where evil seems to have gained the ascendancy. But in due time the inherent strength of good will be revealed, because it is of God. Evil will shrivel and die in the scorching heat of divine judgment.

It is a law of life that the best way to banish evil thoughts is to think good thoughts; the best way to prevent unkind, unchristian words is to speak good words; the best way to avoid evil deeds is to be busy doing good. This is not salvation by works, but the result of God's grace. It is God's way of cultivating Christian character.

TAMPERING WITH ROAD SIGNS

Love worketh no ill to his neighbour: therefore love is the fulfilling of the law. Rom. 13:10.

During the fall of 1967 an elderly couple in Salt Lake City, Utah, decided to visit some of the National Parks in the southern part of their State. Loading their 1959 Rambler, they set out eagerly on what might have been a pleasant vacation. Little did they know how close they would come to tragedy!

Their routing included a short cut by unimproved roads. They followed the signs carefully, but eventually found themselves many miles from human habitation, with their car stuck in the sand. After spending a night in their car they started to walk. They were lost for a week with very little food and water. After walking for forty miles —in the wrong direction—they were found by a searching party.

What was the reason for the near tragedy? *Someone had turned a sign around and had caused them to take a wrong turn.* From then on they were confused. They were following the best directions they knew, but were lost. Our text says that "love worketh no ill to his neighbour." Just about the worst thing a person could do to his neighbor would be to turn the road signs around and cause him to lose his way. Yet this is often done.

How about the author who scraps divinely revealed principles of morality, and causes his reader to believe that it is safe and right to indulge in immoral conduct?

How about the teacher who plants seeds of disbelief in the minds of his students, influencing them to forsake God and the Bible and follow the cult of secularism?

How about the preacher who tells his congregation that God does not mean what He says—that they can live contrary to revealed truth and still get by somehow?

All of these, and many more, are tampering with life's road signs and doing irreparable harm to their neighbors. Divinely revealed principles given for our guidance cannot be safely ignored. If we confuse others by giving them wrong directions, we are certainly violating the principles of Christian love.

263

NO PROVISION FOR FAILURE

Put ye on the Lord Jesus Christ, and make not provision for the flesh, to fulfil the lusts thereof. Rom. 13:14.

One of the rules of Alcoholics Anonymous is that those who are trying to break the alcohol habit should keep absolutely away from liquor. Occasional indulgence ruins the program. The same idea is followed in various programs for breaking the tobacco habit. One wanting freedom must make no provision for failure.

Many Christians, young and old, would save themselves many problems if they would make final decisions on questions of right and wrong. Why should a person have to go through a process of decision making every time he meets a temptation? If I have made a once-for-all decision that I will not do certain things, I am scarcely aware of temptation when it comes. I have made no provision for failure.

For example, as a child I made a decision against motion picture theaters. For nearly a half-century since I made that decision I have lived in a world where motion picture theaters, movie stars, and theatrical productions are part of the culture. They have occupied no place in my life because I shut the door of my mind against them decades ago. I have not had to go through the anguish of deciding whether some highly advertised production is good or not. My personal boycott of Hollywood and that for which it stands had been complete and final. No doubt I have missed a few things that are good, but I know I have missed much that is bad.

One of the problems of the contemporary fad known as situation ethics is that it recognizes no absolute commitments. Every new situation faces the person with a new decision: "Shall I lie or not?" "Shall I steal or not?" "Shall I commit adultery or not?" How much less complicated the life where such questions are settled once and for all!

If we make "provision for the flesh, to fulfil the lusts thereof," be assured "the flesh" will take advantage of such provision. The first part of the text reveals how such defense against evil can be achieved. "Put ye on the Lord Jesus Christ." Let Him be your armor.

THE PRICE OF PEACE

Let us therefore follow after the things which make for peace, and things wherewith one may edify another. Rom. 14:19.

What are "the things which make for peace"?

Once I knew a man who had formed a fine habit. Whenever he heard someone say something kind or complimentary about another person, he took it upon himself to see that the person concerned learned about it. Many people are ready to repeat unkind gossip. Why not be just as avid about passing along words of kindness? This kind of thing makes for peace.

There are people—may their number increase—who always have a kind word, an expression of appreciation, or a bit of encouragement. They make people feel taller and cleaner for having been with them. They do not deal in insincere flattery, but can always think of the right thing to say to make the sun shine a little brighter. These people make for peace.

Some people never return evil for evil. Regardless of how badly they may have been treated, they do not retaliate. Their ego is not easily shattered, and they are not overly concerned if someone criticizes them. People of this type make for peace.

What is meant by the "things wherewith one may edify another"?

To "edify" means "to build up." It is easy to tear down other people. We can do it by criticizing them, by ignoring them, by belittling them. A cutting remark or a sneer can tear people apart. An expression of confidence or a word of sincere appreciation can build them up. Did you ever meet a person who made you feel that your opinions and your efforts were really important? Such people "edify"—build up —their associates.

Sometimes, in order to make peace and build up other people, we have to make sacrifices. We may have to deny ourselves some right or privilege in order not to offend the sensibilities of others. Paul expresses his willingness to restrict his own liberty in order to respect another's conscience. While Paul does not say, "Peace at *any* price," he is willing to pay a high price for peace. This is the spirit of the One who said to go the second mile, and to turn the other cheek.

MAKING CONSCIENCE BEHAVE

Happy is he that condemneth not himself in that thing which he alloweth. Rom. 14:22.

This interesting text deals with the problem of making conscience behave. Some people worry themselves sick over moral trifles. Other people seem to have no conscience at all. Conscience can be a great bulwark of righteous living, or conscience can cause an inquisition. Lecky, in his *History of European Morals,* says: "Philip II. and Isabella . . . inflicted more suffering in obedience to their consciences than Nero and Domitian in obedience to their lusts."— Quoted in HARRY EMERSON FOSDICK, *On Being a Real Person,* p. 134.

We can develop a reliable conscience by following the example of Jesus. It didn't hurt Jesus' conscience to eat with unwashed hands, to pluck heads of grain on the Sabbath, to keep company with sinners, or to forgive renegades. These activities shocked His contemporaries, but reflected His concepts of right and wrong.

It did offend Jesus greatly to see people refuse to accept their responsibility for aged parents, and then rationalize their neglect. It offended Jesus to see people taking advantage of the helpless and making long prayers in church. It offended Jesus to see people insensitive to human need, and He was positively repelled by hypocrisy.

"Conscience makes some men harsh as whips and implacable as executioners; it leads others to be wise, understanding, sympathetic, magnanimous, merciful. It led one minister in the early days of his pastorate to excoriate a misbehaving lad brought to him for counsel so that he raked the boy fore and aft with withering indignation. It led that same minister, years later, with the same kind of boy before him, to go back into the lad's life with a physician's sympathetic insight, trying to see where the trouble came from and to help set it right. In the latter case a letter came afterwards from one of the boy's closest friends: 'You would hardly recognize even his physical aspect, he is so changed.' "—*Ibid.,* pp. 153, 154. Conscience is a voice within that says, "Do right," but it doesn't define right. Only by studying God's Word do we learn what right is.

PAUL THE PIONEER

Yes, so have I strived to preach the gospel, not where Christ was named, lest I should build upon another man's foundation. Rom. 15:20.

Paul had the difficult assignment of preaching the gospel of Christ to the Gentile world of his day. He had not established the church at Rome, yet he was deeply concerned about that important congregation. As he brought his letter to the Romans to a close, he divulged his plan for visiting them on a projected trip to Spain, and explained why he had not done so previously. He had been so busy raising up churches in places where Christ had not been preached that he just hadn't had time to visit Rome.

Paul was by nature a pioneer. He didn't go from church to church to build on the foundation other men had laid, but he went to cities where there were no churches, preached in the synagogue until he was thrown out, continued his work wherever he could find an opening, and persevered until a church was established. He was not reaping where others had sown. He was both sower and reaper.

Paul reminds us of the early missionaries who went to Africa, to the Orient, and to the South Seas without budget, without the backing of mission boards, and without prospects of furlough. These men went in faith, not knowing whether they would ever see homeland and loved ones again, and many of them did not. They were utterly dependent on their ability to adjust to unfamiliar circumstances.

Some seem to think the day of pioneering is past. It is true that mission work in steaming jungles is not what it used to be. But the modern world still has frontiers where pioneers are needed.

Vast portions of the population of nearly every country never darken the door of a church. They never pray nor do they read the Bible, and their children receive no religious training. How are we going to reach all of these people? Where are the pioneers who will move into these areas of modern life and devise ways to appeal to them? Where are the young men who will not ask for all the comforts of urban life, but who will be pioneers willing to work for those who know not Christ?

267

CONTAGIOUS SPIRITUALITY

I Tertius, who wrote this epistle, salute you in the Lord.
Rom. 16:22.

Paul dictated his letters to secretaries who wrote on wax tablets. The "shorthand" was then transcribed to papyrus, and the letter was sent by the slow transportation of the ancient world to its destination. The secretaries, or amanuenses, relieved Paul of the manual labor connected with his literary efforts.

But Paul also contributed something to the lives of his secretaries. At the close of the Epistle to the Romans, Tertius, the amanuensis, inserted his greeting to the church at Rome. The fascinating thing about his greeting was the phrase, "in the Lord." Paul used this phrase, or its equivalent, 169 times in his letters. It was his way of expressing his relationship to Christ. His Master meant so much more to him that he could find no better words to express his oneness with Christ than to use the phrase "in the Lord."

This deep spirituality could not help influencing others, and is it not natural that his secretary felt its impact? Should we be surprised that when Tertius sent his greeting, he appended the phrase that he had heard—and written—so often, "in the Lord"?

We can only guess at the identity of Paul's other secretaries. Some conjecture that Timothy may have helped with 1 and 2 Thessalonians, Philippians, and Colossians. It has been suggested that Luke may have helped with 2 Timothy. But whoever the writers may have been, it seems certain that they, too, must have caught the enthusiasm of the apostle for Jesus.

One of the greatest opportunities for Christian witness is in the on-the-job situation. How many Christians succeed in making a spiritual impact on their associates, their bosses, their secretaries? Usually this isn't done by argument. If our witness is effective, it is usually the appeal of a life so dynamic, so warm, so enthusiastic, so outgoing, that the observer decides he would like to be "in the Lord" also. This kind of evangelism is within the reach of all. There is no substitute for the influence of a really Christlike life.

CONTENTIONS

It hath been declared unto me of you, my brethren, by them which are of the house of Chloe, that there are contentions among you. Now this I say, that every one of you saith, I am of Paul; and I of Apollos; and I of Cephas; and I of Christ. 1 Cor. 1:11, 12.

There was trouble at Corinth. The church, established by Paul, was torn apart by factions. There was a "Paul party" who declared their allegiance to the founding apostle. There was an "Apollos party" whose members preferred the talented Greek Christian. Others were of the "Cephas party," and they stoutly maintained that Peter was their hero—he had been one of the twelve. Finally, another group disavowed all human leaders and called itself the "Christ party." This factionalism was compromising the witness of the church. Hostility was taking the place of love, and the example and teaching of the Master were being forgotten.

Paul was severe with these offenders. He said to them, "Ye are yet carnal: for whereas there is among you envying, and strife, and divisions, are ye not carnal, and walk as men?" He pointed out that the real foundation of the church was Jesus. "Let no man glory in men," he said, "for all things are your's; whether Paul, or Apollos, or Cephas, or the world or life or death, or things present, or things to come; all are your's; and ye are Christ's; and Christ is God's" (1 Cor. 3:21-23).

Many a church has made the same tragic error as did the church at Corinth. Every pastor can tell of churches with hostile cliques vying with one another for influence and power. Many an evangelistic effort has failed because the people of the community have known of the troubles of the church, and have lost confidence in its message. Many a minister has grown weary trying to patch up difficulties within the church when he might have been bringing Christ to the world. Many a young person has left the church because all he could see was wrangling and arguing. There was once a church in which the middle aisle separated two hostile factions. Year after year people who professed to be Christians glared at each other across that aisle. There will be no such middle aisle in heaven.

269

PAUL'S CONCERN FOR THE CONSCIENCE OF OTHERS

If meat make my brother to offend, I will eat no flesh while the world standeth, lest I make my brother to offend. 1 Cor. 8:13.

In dealing with the problem of eating meat offered to idols, Paul took the position that an idol actually was "nothing," and that to eat food offered to an idol was therefore not a question of principle. However, Paul also recognized that many in Corinth had sacrificed much in order to forsake idol worship, and that to them eating food offered to idols was a serious compromise with heathenism. Paul uses the term "weak" five times in this chapter to describe these people and their position, concerned lest anyone cause them to stumble. He claimed the "liberty" to eat that which was offered to idols, but he refused to assert that freedom lest "the weak brother perish, for whom Christ died."

Commenting on Paul's attitude, S. D. Gordon has written:

"There is a very simple law to follow here. It is Paul's law. He got it from the Holy Spirit. It is *the law of love*. It speaks thus:

"Whatever dulls the sensitiveness of my spirit towards God, or takes the fine, tender edge off my thought of Him must be ruled out, for He is my Lord.

"Whatever injures or weakens my body, or affects my mastery of it, must be ruled out, for it is the temple of my Lord.

"Whatever affects hurtfully the earnestness and clearness of my witness to Jesus Christ before others must be ruled out, for it was His parting wish that I be a witness for Him to all men.

"Whatever lessens in any way, even through prejudice or mis-understandings, the results of my service must be ruled out, for to influence men for Him is to be the passion of my life.

"Whatever may cause my brother to stumble in his Christian life must be ruled out, for that would grieve Jesus."—*Quiet Talks on Personal Problems*, p. 224.

This is not a popular attitude, but it truly is the law of love. This type of "situation ethics" impels the Christian to go beyond the demands of law, because of the demands of love.

PROTECTION FROM TEMPTATION

There hath no temptation taken you but such as is common to man: but God is faithful, who will not suffer you to be tempted above that ye are able. 1 Cor. 10:13.

Life is filled with temptations to do wrong. Natural tendencies toward evil are constantly encouraged by the degrading influences of environment. Thus untold millions succumb to the lure of dishonesty, immorality, and other self-destroying sins.

But according to our text, man is not forced to yield to the downward pull. Forces working for him are greater than those working against him, if he will use them. What are these forces?

One of the most important of these protections against temptation is conscience. "When Theodore Parker, the great New England preacher, writer, poet, and advocate of freedom, was a little child, he saw in the garden a tortoise, and lifted his hand to strike it; but something suddenly checked his arm, and he heard a voice within him say, 'It is wrong.' When he went back to the house he asked his mother who it was that said it was wrong to strike the turtle. Taking him up in her arms, his mother said to him, 'Some men call it conscience, but I prefer to call it the voice of God in the soul of man. If you listen and obey it, then it will speak clearer and clearer and will always guide you right. But if you turn a deaf ear and disobey, then it will fade out little by little and leave you all in the dark and without a guide. Your life depends on your hearing this voice.'"—CLARENCE E. MACARTNEY, *You Can Conquer*, p. 39.

It is true that conscience may be warped so it will not be a safe guide. Basically, however, the sense of right and wrong has been given to man as a defense against temptation. Many a person far from home and friends has resisted the downward pull of sin because of the upward pull of a God-implanted conscience.

Another mighty defense against temptation is prayer. For a person who has formed the habit of talking to God, a few moments of prayer in a crisis may save years of regret and remorse. Under the white light of sincere prayer, sin loses its glamour. God responds when we call Him, and gives us strength to stand firm.

271

LOVE AND TONGUES

Though I speak with the tongues of men and of angels, and have not charity, I am become as sounding brass, or a tinkling cymbal. 1 Cor. 13:1.

Paul was dealing with the problem of speaking in tongues. We do not fully understand the meaning of this phenomenon in the early church, but we know that: (1) The gift of tongues at Pentecost enabled people to understand Peter's preaching in their own language. (2) The gift of tongues was perpetuated in the early church and is listed as one of the gifts of the Spirit. (3) Some in Corinth, and perhaps elsewhere, abused this gift by disorderly babble that could not be understood.

"There is something more important than tongues," we hear Paul saying. "One might speak all the languages of men and the languages of angels, but still be ineffective in the eyes of God and man. The thing that really matters is love." Paul had learned this lesson through experience. Only when he became a Christian did he know the meaning of love.

Why is love greater than tongues? The ability to speak in unknown tongues may never warm a heart or save a soul. The messages communicated may be messages of hate. The possession of a gift of the Spirit may stimulate pride that makes real Christian service impossible. But when the life is filled with Christian love, communication in one's own language or in any other tongue will edify and bless. To communicate is a blessing or a curse, depending on the spirit of the communicator.

"Sounding brass"—the blare of a trumpet, "tinkling cymbals"—the clash of metal against metal. What are these compared to a quiet word expressed in love? A word of sympathy to a person in distress; a word of encouragement to someone for whom life has lost its meaning; a word of appreciation for small deeds of kindness; a word of concern about another's welfare—these are the proofs that love is the greatest thing in the world. No oratory can match it, no experience of "speaking in tongues" can equal it. Love stands supreme.

LOVE, PROPHECY, AND FAITH

Though I have the gift of prophecy, and understand all mysteries, and all knowledge; and though I have all faith, so that I could remove mountains, and have not charity, I am nothing.
1 Cor. 13:2.

How near to ideal is the person who has everything this text describes! Only a few people have had the gift of prophecy. When we think of this gift we think of people such as Moses, Isaiah, Daniel, and John. It is an honor to be God's mouthpiece.

Understanding and knowledge are also wonderful. We think of the philosophers, scholars, and scientists of the world—men such as Isaac Newton, Louis Pasteur, and Albert Einstein. These men have contributed much to life.

There are also men of great faith—religious leaders such as Augustine, Luther, and Albert Schweitzer, who have taught the world some things about God.

But, says Paul, suppose I qualify on all three counts. Suppose I am a prophet, suppose I also have a great mind, and suppose, through experience and study, I have come to the place where I am renowned as a man of faith, what more could anyone ask? These accomplishments are all like foothills to the mountain peak of love.

Why is love superior to prophecy, knowledge, and faith? Simply because to prophesy without love may frighten people but not convert them; to have knowledge without love may impress and inform people but not solve their problems; to have faith may build confidence and trust, but only love will produce fellowship and concern.

A lost child is not impressed with wealth, pedigree, position, or profession. Neither presidents nor kings could dry his tears. Scientists and religious leaders are alike helpless to bring him happiness. He wants his mother because she symbolizes love and security. Mother may know nothing about prophecy or knowledge or faith, but she knows how to love.

We never outgrow the need for love. Without it, all of the other blessings of life are nothing. Love gives meaning to the prophet, a heart to the scholar, and Christlikeness to the religious leader.

273

LOVE, PHILANTHROPY, AND MARTYRDOM

Though I bestow all my goods to feed the poor, and though I give my body to be burned, and have not charity, it profiteth me nothing. 1 Cor. 13:3.

How could a person bestow all of his goods to feed the poor and not have charity? The answer to this question involves the possibility of doing good things from wrong motives.

If a person demands that the press be on hand to record and advertise his good deeds, it may be that his motives are inferior to those of love.

If a person is burdened with guilt, perhaps for the way in which he earned his wealth, and gives liberally as a means of soothing his conscience, would we conclude that his motive is love?

If a person is liberal with his possessions in order to gain influence and power, if he is thinking in terms of eventual political office as a reward for his "charity," would this be love?

We cannot judge motives, and we must not impugn the motives of others; but we must look into our own lives and be sure that we are really inspired by love.

The other question suggested by the text is, How could I give my body to be burned and have such a supreme sacrifice profit me nothing? In the second century of the Christian Era there was a great craving after martyrdom on the part of some Christians. Ignatius, in his letter to the Romans, exclaimed, "Let me be eaten by the wild beasts, through whom I can reach the presence of God. I am God's wheat, and I am ground by the teeth of the wild beasts so that I may be found pure bread of Christ. Instead, coax the wild beasts to be my grave."

Paul, Peter, and John did not talk this way. They were willing to suffer, if necessary, but they did not go out of their way to encourage martyrdom. Theirs was a sensible yet loyal attitude.

Yes, a person can be so zealous that he will "give his body to be burned" yet his motive may be fanatical zeal rather than Christian love. In a frenzy of emotion one may make great sacrifices, yet fail in the basic relationships of life. There is no substitute for love.

PATIENT, HUMBLE LOVE

Charity suffereth long, and is kind; charity envieth not; charity vaunteth not itself, is not puffed up. 1 Cor. 13:4.

Paul here tells us certain very important things about love:

First, "[It] is slow to lose patience—it looks for a way of being constructive" (Phillips). The person who really loves is willing to put up with faults on the part of the person he loves. Regardless of disappointments, slights, and ingratitude, love goes on. Who has not wondered at the love of a mother for a wayward child, or the love of a wife for an unworthy husband? Love is always looking for charitable interpretations of others' actions; love is always thinking of what it can give, though no repayment may be expected; love is positive and forward looking.

Second, "It is not possessive" (Phillips). Love does not demand control of the personality of the loved one. Love is not jealous and selfish. Love thinks of the interests of the one who is loved, not of the one who loves. Much that passes for love demands that the object feed the ego of the one who professes to love. There are parents who bask in the success of their children—they mistake possessiveness for love. There are husbands and wives who mistake personal security for love. Paul seemed to have an uncanny insight into these foibles of human nature.

Third, "It is neither anxious to impress nor does it cherish inflated ideas of its own importance" (Phillips). What does this mean? It probably implies that a person who really loves is so concerned about others that he forgets himself. He is not self-conscious but outgoing. He is unconcerned about position, titles, preferment, and prestige because he is so involved in adding to the happiness and well-being of those around him.

Incidentally, people who discover this type of love are happy. They aren't particularly seeking for happiness, but it slips in through a door they didn't know they left open. In forgetting themselves, they find the real meaning of life. Like the Other Wise Man in Van Dyke's well-known Christmas story, in meeting human need, they find the Christ.

LOVE AND CHRISTIAN ETHICS

[Charity] doth not behave itself unseemly, seeketh not her own, is not easily provoked, thinketh no evil; rejoiceth not in iniquity, but rejoiceth in the truth. 1 Cor. 13:5, 6.

According to a widely accepted notion in today's world, if one only has love, standards of conduct are quite immaterial. Anything goes, if it can by some process of rationalization be called "love."

But Paul had a different idea. He said, "Love has good manners and does not pursue selfish advantage" (Phillips). What did he mean? May it be that he would have rejected the notion that love excuses disregard for the amenities of cultured society? May it be that "good manners" can be an expression of love?

Paul also challenges the "every man for himself" concept. In his opinion, the person who loves will not seek his own advantage, but rather the advantage of others. This ties love and ethics into one package. Fairness, concern for others' feelings and rights, concern for the well-being of one's neighbor—these are not mere humanistic ideals, but the results of Christian love. The person who loves is so concerned about others that he is not sensitive to imagined slights. He does not worry what people think about him, so long as he knows his conduct is above reproach.

"It [love] does not keep account of evil or gloat over the wickedness of other people" (Phillips). Morality by consensus is a grave modern heresy. If someone can prove that 51 per cent of the population are unfaithful to their marriage vows, this does not make unfaithfulness a virtue. Also, love does not take fiendish delight in enumerating other people's mistakes. Many a back-fence gossiper does not realize that he (or she) is guilty of compiling statistics of evil and gloating "over the wickedness of other people." We feel righteous when we point out the mistakes of others.

The better way is held forth in this verse—"It [love] is glad with all good men when truth prevails" (Phillips). Victory is much better news than defeat. The person who really loves, admires a person whom he recognizes as better than he.

276

NO LIMITS

Beareth all things, believeth all things, hopeth all things, endureth all things. Charity never faileth. 1 Cor. 13:7, 8.

"Love knows no limit to its endurance, no end to its trust, no fading of its hope; it can outlast anything. It is, in fact, the one thing that still stands when all else has fallen" (Phillips).

The late Dr. Clarence Macartney illustrated the permanency of love thus:

"The sacraments of human love are being celebrated about us all the time. What is more common than this? A woman is married to a man who turns out to be, in the common saying, 'no good.' He is unfaithful, he is intemperate, shiftless, at times cruel, the very caricature of husband and father. All that he means to the woman is want, shame, dread, and pain. His irregularities reach their climax in some criminal act, and the man forfeits his liberty for a season and is confined within the walls of the penitentiary. To the world, outside of that woman, he ceases to exist. His own brothers and sisters disown him and only hope never to set eyes upon him again. His old friends forget him. The years slip by. The term of imprisonment is ended. He is discharged. The penitentiary gates open for him as he steps back into the world on a bleak winter's day; and there, like an angel of mercy, stands his wife, with open arms, to welcome him back to life again.

"How can you account for it? Only thus: she loves him. Marvelous, august, enduring love! Love that beareth all things. Many waters of adversity cannot quench it, neither can all the raging floods of sin drown it."—*Macartney's Illustrations*, p. 216.

A person may lose his money, his position, his fame, his reputation; but if someone genuinely loves him, life is still worth living. There is just one value that will survive the chaos and destruction that is about to overtake this world, and that value is love. After the smoke of destruction has cleared away, the survivors will be those who have responded to God's love, and they will live in perfect love throughout eternity. Love is eternal. All else is temporary. Love succeeds when everything else fails.

CHRISTIAN MATURITY

When I was a child, I spake as a child, I understood as a child, I thought as a child: but when I became a man, I put away childish things. 1 Cor. 13:11.

This simple statement of fact—a statement that might be made by any mature person—raises the question of the meaning of maturity. What are the basic differences between the thinking, the speech, and the understanding of a child and those of an adult?

First, the adult achieves a degree of patience. The little child wants what he wants *right now!* He is not willing to wait. The adult weighs values and is willing to defer a cherished desire for a greater value. The true adult is willing to deny himself present pleasures for the sake of future success and security.

A second characteristic of maturity is the willingness to listen to people who have achieved greater maturity. Why must every generation learn the lessons of life the hard way? Why can we not stand on the shoulders of those who have lived and learned before us?

A third characteristic of maturity is the ability to have deep convictions, yet to be tolerant of those whose convictions differ from ours. Ellen White urged that those who differ with us in faith and doctrine always should be treated kindly. This spirit is especially important for those of a minority religious group. It is easy to become arrogant and unreasonable. Such attitudes are signs of immaturity.

A fourth characteristic of maturity is a keen sense of responsibility. The mature person accepts the responsibilities of his job, his family, and his community. He is more concerned about what he can do for others than he is about what others can do for him.

The greatest dimension of maturity is spirituality—not a childish religion, but a mature faith in God and dedication to Him.

In the context of 1 Corinthians 13 it is obvious that Paul was thinking of maturity in terms of love. Love should grow, mellow, and become more meaningful with the passing of the years. Someone has suggested that it is wonderful to see young love at a wedding, but it is greater to see love at a golden wedding. Maturity is the friend, not the enemy, of love.

ONLY LOVE WILL LAST

Whether there be prophecies, they shall fail; whether there be tongues, they shall cease; whether there be knowledge, it shall vanish away. For we know in part, and we prophesy in part. But when that which is perfect is come, then that which is in part shall be done away. 1 Cor. 13:8-10.

"For if there are prophecies they will be fulfilled and done with" (Phillips). Prophecy is important but it has its day. When a specific prophecy is fulfilled its primary purpose has been accomplished, except as it witnesses to the revelation of God.

"If there are 'tongues' the need for them will disappear" (Phillips). Someday the diverse languages of earth will be past and everyone will understand the language of his neighbor. There will be no more need for the gift manifested at Pentecost, which was misused by some in the apostolic church. Eternity will leave tongues behind.

"If there is knowledge it will be swallowed up in truth" (Phillips). Man's knowledge is so fragmentary that it will seem like deep ignorance when the redeemed glimpse the realities of eternal truth. Knowledge is not truth, it is only man's understanding of truth. Eternity will leave knowledge behind. "For our knowledge is always incomplete and our prophecy is always incomplete, and when the complete comes, that is the end of the incomplete" (Phillips).

What is the complete to which the apostle refers? It is love. Unlike prophecy, love is never "fulfilled" or "done with." It is not tied to the history of man's nations or ecclesiastical institutions.

Unlike tongues, the need for love will never disappear. It supersedes all languages, and it will lose none of its luster when all languages are one. Love is the same in every tongue.

Unlike knowledge, it will not be swallowed up, for there is nothing greater than can swallow it up. It is the one unchangeable, permanent value in the universe. It gives meaning to life.

When we get to heaven there will be little to remind us of our former earthly life, but one thing will carry on—the love that God has placed in the human heart will find its fullest expression. Only love will last, and it will last for eternity.

279

WHEN WE THROW AWAY THE MIRROR

Now we see through a glass, darkly; but then face to face: now I know in part; but then shall I know even as also I am known. 1 Cor. 13:12.

Phillips' translation of this text is illuminating. "At present we are men looking at puzzling reflections in a mirror. The time will come when we shall see reality whole and face to face! At present all I know is a little fraction of the truth, but the time will come when I shall know it as fully as God now knows me!"

The mirrors of Paul's day were probably not as good as ours, but even today the best way to view the landscape is not through a rearview mirror! Paul's analogy reminds us of Plato's men in a cave whose knowledge of the world was limited to the reflection of light that came in through the opening of the cave. Even the most highly gifted and the most completely educated know little of the universe. All we see are the puzzling reflections, and often they are distorted.

But the time will come when we can throw away the mirror— or, to change the figure, we can come out of the cave and see reality "whole and face to face." The greatest thrill of heaven will surely not be golden streets or pearly gates or beautiful mansions. The real satisfaction of eternity will be in possessing knowledge and insight that will banish fear and insecurity and ignorance.

A child is born in the slums and spends his childhood in a depressed neighborhood. Seldom does he get more than a few blocks from the miserable tenement he calls home. Reality to him is limited to a few blocks on the wrong side of the tracks, outdated buildings, and associates as limited in experience as himself. Then, one day, he is taken from his home and circles over his city and the surrounding country in an airplane. He sees a city he never knew, although he was a part of it. The little segment of his experience grows to a widening circle as he explores more and more of the world in which he lives.

Eternity will be like that. The limited glimpse of reality we now experience will enlarge to include the universe. How can we be so content with our little slum?

THE GREATEST

Now abideth faith, hope, charity, these three; but the greatest of these is charity. 1 Cor. 13:13.

"In this life we have three great lasting qualities—faith, hope, and love. But the greatest of them is love" (Phillips).

Henry Drummond's *The Greatest Thing in the World* has become a classic. This famous book opens with the following words:

"Everyone has asked himself the great question of antiquity as of the modern world: What is the *summum bonum*—the supreme good? You have life before you. Once only you can live it. What is the noblest object of desire, the supreme gift to covet?

"We have been accustomed to be told that the greatest thing in the religious world is Faith. That great word has been the keynote for centuries of the popular religion; and we have easily learned to look upon it as the greatest thing in the world. Well, we are wrong. If we have been told that, we may miss the mark. I have taken you, in the chapter you have just read, to Christianity at its source: and there we have seen, 'The greatest of these is Love.' It is not an oversight. Paul was speaking of faith just a moment before. He says, 'If I have all faith, so that I can remove mountains, and have not love, I am nothing.' So far from forgetting he deliberately contrasts them, 'Now abideth Faith, Hope, Love,' and without a moment's hesitation the decision falls, 'The greatest of these is Love.'

"And it is not prejudice. A man is apt to recommend to others his own strong point. Love was not Paul's strong point. The observing student can detect a beautiful tenderness growing and ripening all through his character as Paul gets old; but the hand that wrote, 'The greatest of these is love,' when we meet it first, is stained with blood."—Pages 11-13.

Is not love greater than faith because it is really impossible to have faith without love? Real faith is such an intensely personal thing that it must have its source in love. And is not love greater than hope, because it is love that causes us to continue to hope? The supremacy of love does not lower the value of faith and hope. It should be observed that the apostle recognizes all three as important.

281

THE MIRACLE OF GRACE

By the grace of God I am what I am. 1 Cor. 15:10.

Paul's immortal statement stands in complete conflict with the contemporary proverb that says, "I cannot help being what I am."

Is it true that we are completely at the mercy of heredity and environment? Are our behavior patterns entirely determined by our ancestors and our associates? It surely is true that these factors exert a great influence upon us. This cannot be denied. But are there not influences that can take precedence over heredity and environment?

The experience of many people proves that the grace of God can be an overwhelming factor in shaping our lives. Consider, for example, the author of our text. His background was that of a Jew, living in the city of Tarsus, enjoying the advantages of Roman citizenship. His environment was that of orthodox leadership of the Judaism of his day. The wildest imagination could never have conceived of Paul as a Christian. It was completely contrary to his heritage and training and to the predominate influences in his life.

But the Spirit of God was able to find a response in Paul's heart. The voice of Jesus spoke to him on the way to Damascus; and Saul the persecuting Pharisee, became Paul the apostle of Christ. It was in this context that Paul could say with complete assurance, "But by the grace of God I am what I am."

The glory of the Christian gospel is its power to take any person—whatever his inheritance—out of any environment and make him a child of God. When the roll is called in the final day of judgment, there will be among the redeemed, murderers, adulterers, liars, and every other species of sinner. These people, in the colorful symbolism of the Bible, will have been "washed in the blood of the Lamb." The grace of God will have transformed them into loyal, God-fearing men and women.

"I cannot help being what I am" may often be true of an unconverted person. He may not have the will to effect needed changes in his life. But when the grace of God moves in, miracles happen. "By the miracle of divine grace, many may be fitted for lives of usefulness."—*The Ministry of Healing,* p. 169.

THE RISEN CHRIST

If Christ be not risen, then is our preaching vain, and your faith is also vain. 1 Cor. 15:14.

"If Christ be not risen." What a fearful thought!

"Some years ago a popular English novelist wrote a book called *When It Was Dark*. The story centers about the efforts of a wealthy unbeliever to discredit Christianity. He endeavors to do this by attempting to discredit the Resurrection. . . . This man hired venal archaeologists to fake a discovery of the body of Jesus in the neighborhood of Jerusalem. On the tomb was an inscription testifying that the owner of this sepulcher stole the body of Jesus and hid it there. The novel then goes on to describe the ultimate effect of such a discovery, if accepted as truth, upon the Christian world, upon the Christian Church, and upon civilization in general. In powerful passages he shows how, gradually, the Christian Church crumbles and collapses; how men and women go back to lust, cruelty, and animalism; and how the flame of hope dies out in every human heart."—*Macartney's Illustrations,* pp. 307, 308.

The most important event in the history of the world was Jesus' emergence from the tomb on the Sunday morning after His crucifixion. This event gave significance to all that had happened before, and it gave meaning to all that would happen afterward.

The resurrection was the central theme of the Christians who carried the gospel to the world during the first century. They risked everything on their belief that their Lord had come forth alive from His tomb. In a world that scorned the idea of resurrection, they never failed to witness that the Son of God died and lived again.

Likewise, the resurrection of Jesus is the center of the Christian faith today. Upon several different occasions this resurrected Christ was seen by His disciples, ascended to heaven, continued to be the living Lord of all Christians from that day to this, and is coming again.

Let us believe with all our hearts in the resurrection, and let us proclaim this faith to the world. In this faith is our life and hope.

LIVE LIKE MEN

Watch ye, stand fast in the faith, quit you like men, be strong.
1 Cor. 16:13.

The Phillips translation renders the third phrase of this text "live like men." To be a Christian requires stability and courage. Christ calls for people who are willing to "live like men."

One important quality of a real Christian is that he is willing to assume responsibility. He does his work well. He pays his bills. He supports his family. He serves his church, his community, and his country. If misfortunes overtake him, he doesn't fold.

Despite his strength and stability, the Christian man is sympathetic to those who are weak. He does not take advantage of the ignorance or misfortune of others. He does not assume that others might succeed as well as he, were they as energetic as he. He reveals his strength in his attitude toward the less fortunate. He never lets another person down.

The real man knows the meaning of discipline. He doesn't complain about the "rat race"—he keeps up. He puts in long hours, denies himself luxuries he cannot afford, shuns indulgences that are harmful, and conforms to the best conventions of the society in which he lives. He never tries to rationalize misconduct.

The real man is not ashamed of his faith. He is willing to witness for Christ under all circumstances. He does not compromise the standards of his church. If it is necessary to quit a good job in order to be honorable or to keep the Sabbath or to answer a call to God's service, he is willing to do so. He lives the same when people are looking and when they are not.

The real man is always his best at home. He does not have a charming personality for the world outside, and a faultfinding disposition at home. If he has to choose between big money or fame and emotional and spiritual security for his family, he chooses the latter.

"Live like men." Don't be immature and unstable. Be men of whom your family and your friends can be proud. Be men whom God can approve. Be men who will "stand for the right though the heavens fall." The greatest want of the world is the want of such men.

GOD HELPS US THAT WE MAY HELP OTHERS

Blessed be God, . . . who comforteth us in all our tribulation, that we may be able to comfort them which are in any trouble, by the comfort wherewith we ourselves are comforted of God. 2 Cor. 1:3, 4.

"In New York today there is a home for boys founded by a businessman. Before he was fourteen years of age his father and mother passed away, leaving him friendless and penniless. He made his way from Vermont to Boston, where he got a job in a grocery store at $5.00 a week. His board and room cost him just $5.00. His employer looked at him one day when he came to work and said to him, 'Look here, Harry, you're going to have to do something about your clothes. Your elbows are coming through.'

"The boy reached into his pocket and pulled out a nickel. 'I've kept this ever since I started to work,' he told him. 'It's all I have. I didn't dare to spend it.'

"His employer turned away without a word, and the boy thought that he understood and was sympathetic. But when Saturday came, there was a blue slip in his pay envelope. He asked his landlady when he went home that night what it meant.

" 'It means you're fired,' she said, 'and as of this moment I want my rent in advance.'

" 'But I'll get a job,' the boy said, 'and pay you by the end of the week.'

" 'You'll do just one thing,' the woman said. 'You'll get upstairs and pack your things.'

"It was a cold New England January night. There was no place for him to go except the Boston Common. There, with his belongings in a bundle for a pillow and with his overcoat wrapped closely about him, he lay on a park bench. Thirty or forty times in the night he awoke, and every time when he awoke he made a promise that if God protected him he would devote his life to homeless boys."— CLARENCE E. MACARTNEY, *You Can Conquer,* pp. 120, 121.

At the time Dr. Macartney told the story he had, in fifty-one years, given shelter and encouragement to 46,000 boys.

EARTHENWARE JARS

We have this treasure in earthen vessels, that the excellency of the power may be of God, and not of us. 2 Cor. 4:7.

Phillips translates "earthen vessels" as "a common earthenware jar." One commentator suggests that this passage probably refers "to the ancient practice among Orientals of storing gold and silver in earthenware jars" (CHARLES R. ERDMAN, *The Second Epistle of Paul to the Corinthians*, p. 47). In the light of the custom of Paul's day this analogy is especially expressive. He invited his readers to look at him as a fragile bit of earthenware—used today and perhaps broken tomorrow. But he wanted all men to view the gospel of Christ as valuable treasure that would last forever.

Bishop Gerald Kennedy comments on this scripture as follows:

"Our nature is determined by what and by whom we serve. If we bear the sign of the King, it marks us as creatures who bear eternal treasure within earthen vessels. This came to me a few years ago when I met an elderly bishop of our church. After years of service in Africa, he retired in this country and attended the meetings of our Council. He had a tendency to wander a bit when he spoke, and there was nothing in his words of drama or excitement. And then I went to Africa myself and my eyes were opened. I learned how years ago this man and his wife had walked the trails up through the Congo jungle. I went to small villages where an old man or an old woman would inquire through the interpreter if I knew Bishop Springer. Then they would tell about how young Dr. Springer had come there years ago and told the story of his Master. It came to me that this man was full of wonder and light because he had dedicated his service to Christ. Treasure in an earthen vessel, indeed!"—*Fresh Every Morning*, pp. 57, 58.

This story doubtless reminds us of some pastor who couldn't preach very well, but who was a source of spiritual strength to his church. We have all seen the treasure of God in earthen vessels—some perhaps more "earthen" than others. And then we think of ourselves, and thank God that He *does* store His treasure in earthenware jars.

286

THE STRIP OF BLUE SKY

The things which are seen are temporal; but the things which are not seen are eternal. 2 Cor. 4:18.

"The great Indian mystic, Rabindranath Tagore, once wrote a poem in which he compared our daily life to a narrow lane overhung with high buildings, between which there could be seen above a single strip of blue sky torn out of space. The lane, seeing the sun only for a few minutes at midday asks herself—is it real? Feeling some wayward breeze of spring wafted in from far-off fields, she asks—Is it real? But the dust and the rubbish never rouse her to question. The noise of traffic, the jolting carts, the refuse, the smoke—these she accepts, these she concludes are clearly the real and actual things of life; and as for that strange strip of blue above, she soon ceases even to wonder about it, for so manifestly it is only a fancy, nothing real. This, says Tagore in effect, is precisely the truth about our ordinary mundane existence. The near things, the tangible, material things— these we accept, these we say are obviously the things that matter, they are solid, substantial fact: not recognising that it is that streak of blue above, that far glimpse of the spiritual, which is the essential reality for which every soul of man is made."—JAMES S. STEWART, "What Happens in Worship," in *Best Sermons, 1951-1952,* p. 336.

This is a lesson modern man needs desperately to learn. His senses are bombarded with so many stimuli from the material world that he becomes insensitive to the realities of a higher and better world. The noises and the pressing duties of each day crowd out communion with God.

God gave man the Sabbath in order that he might not forget the eternal values, but too often even the services of the church take on a materialistic aspect all their own. The work of the Lord overshadows the worship of the Lord, and the strip of blue sky is seldom seen, nor is the "wayward breeze of spring" often felt.

Let us lift up our heads and look beyond that which is temporal to that which is eternal. Let us tune into the messages that come to us from beyond the physical horizons of our lives. Let us live in the consciousness of God and His love and care.

287

A NEW CREATURE

If any man be in Christ, he is a new creature: old things are passed away; behold, all things are become new. 2 Cor. 5:17.

Dr. John Sutherland Bonnell, in his *Fifth Avenue Sermons,* tells of a preaching mission he conducted in a penitentiary in Western Canada. One of his inquirers was a problem to the penitentiary staff. He had been a rum runner and a bank robber, and was serving a sentence for robbery with violence.

"Just as he had won the penitent thief, Christ laid his hand upon that man and made him a new creature. On his knees, in the presence of God, he confessed his sins and found forgiveness and peace. Shortly afterwards he was reconciled to his wife and children.

"When I was leaving the penitentiary, he gave me a letter to his wife and said, 'You can make whatever use of this letter you please.' According to prison regulations, of course, it was open. I quote from it one paragraph, which I copied. Speaking of his interview with me, he wrote:

"'In his presence I made the first prayer to God that ever left my lips, and now I am able to hold my head up again before any human being, regardless of my past sins. I was always unhappy before that prayer, but I feel happy now because that prayer was for you and the children. . . . Oh! What a fool a man can become. I started with a minor sin, and how they can grow into big ones without one realizing their growing! . . . But now, although I am inside grey walls, I am a free man.'"—Page 143.

This man, according to Dr. Bonnell, became secretary of a Bible class of forty prisoners, and was said by his warden to be "worth more to me than any three guards I have in the institution. . . . One never need fear trouble while he is around" (pp. 143, 144).

There is something about Christ that can change the motivations of the most sinful person. There is a power in the cross that can soften the hardest heart. The great truth of the open tomb can give hope to the hopeless. The knowledge of a Saviour who now ministers on our behalf can give security to the insecure. The hope of the second coming of Jesus can give purpose and meaning to life.

288

PAUL ADVISES AGAINST DWINDLING

Herein I give my advice: for this is expedient for you, who have begun before, not only to do, but also to be forward a year ago. Now therefore perform the doing of it; that as there was a readiness to will, so there may be a performance also out of that which ye have. 2 Cor. 8:10, 11.

Paul is writing the church at Corinth about a special offering for the church at Jerusalem, a project close to his heart. He saw in it not only the means of meeting a need but also of bringing the Jewish and Gentile branches of the church into a closer relationship.

But a good idea must be put into action. The real thrust of this passage is made clear in the Goodspeed translation: "You were the first not only to do anything about this, but to want to do anything, and that was last year. Now finish doing it, so that your readiness to undertake it may be equaled by the way you finish it up." The church at Corinth was at the head of the line in starting the Jerusalem relief program. Their early enthusiasm was admirable. But "that was last year." Enthusiasm had wavered. Pledges weren't being paid. Goals were not being met. Two entire chapters of this letter to the Corinthian church were devoted to rekindling the fire of zeal that had nearly gone out.

Apparently human nature hasn't changed with the passing of the centuries. How many church building projects start with a shout and end with a whisper. How many student projects on academy and college campuses have to be revived several times to prevent them from expiring completely. How many students begin the school year with B's and end with C's. How many mission projects begin with vision and dwindle as selfish interests predominate. How many marriages begin with orange blossoms and end in the divorce court.

Such tendencies reveal immaturity. Really grown-up people count the cost and follow through. Thousands of people are disillusioned and unhappy in later life who might have lived happy lives had their readiness to undertake been equalled by their ability to finish. "Be thou faithful *unto death,*" says our Lord, "and I will give thee a crown of life."

10   289

RIGHT AND WRONG GIVING

He which soweth sparingly shall reap also sparingly; and he which soweth bountifully shall reap bountifully. Every man as he purposeth in his heart, so let him give; not grudgingly, or of necessity: for God loveth a cheerful giver. 2 Cor. 9:6, 7.

Dr. Halford Luccock tells of a woman who collected clothing for Korean relief. She reported that on several occasions women's coats came in with all the buttons cut off. "Evidently the big-hearted, generous givers thought the buttons were quite good and could be used again, so they took the scissors and went to work, the whole gift spoiled by a nasty snip."—*Halford Luccock Treasury,* p. 328.

Our text not only advocates giving, but suggests that the donors give bountifully and cheerfully. Phillips translates the passage, "God loves the man who gives cheerfully." There are various ways in which we sometimes "cut off the buttons" when we try to be generous.

For example, some people reserve their largest gifts for projects that will enhance their memory. A bronze plaque must prove to posterity that they have been generous, otherwise there is no enthusiasm for giving. They would much rather respond visibly to a dramatic call for funds in a big meeting than give unostentatiously as the offering plate goes by.

Other people think that giving endows them with the privilege of control. Because they pay a large tithe they feel that the church should listen to their suggestions and place them in offices of leadership. Their preacher, they feel, is subject to their wishes because they help pay his salary. If they help individuals in need, they insist on dictating the direction of their lives.

Still other people measure their Christianity by their giving. They find immense satisfaction in considering themselves superior to people who give less than themselves. Like the Pharisee, they say, "God, I thank thee, that I am not as other men are. . . . I give tithes of all I possess."

In contrast to this inadequate concept of giving, Dr. Luccock cites the Good Samaritan. "He left all the buttons on his gift coat— even sent along an extra one or two, just in case."—*Ibid.,* p. 329.

PAUL FACES THE STORM

Of the Jews five times received I forty stripes save one. Thrice was I beaten with rods, once was I stoned, thrice I suffered shipwreck, a night and a day I have been in the deep; in journeyings often, in perils of waters, in perils of robbers, in perils of mine own countrymen, in perils by the heathen, in perils in the city, in perils in the wilderness, in perils in the sea, in perils among false brethren; in weariness and painfulness, in watchings often, in hunger and thirst, in fastings often, in cold and nakedness. 2 Cor. 11:24-27.

Eight beatings, one stoning, three shipwrecks, constant danger, hunger, thirst, cold—all of these experiences Paul might have avoided had he been willing to live an ordinary life. He might even have been a Christian and escaped these hardships had he chosen to be an ordinary Christian. But, extraordinary man that he was, he could not be satisfied with a conventional life.

"Gladstone was on a holiday in Scotland, walking along a country lane, when a storm came up. The snow began to fall and the wind howled. As he walked along he noticed the sheep coming up out of the hollows and from underneath the trees, going out to stand on the bare hillsides facing the storm. A little later he met an old shepherd and said to him: 'Are not sheep the most foolish of animals? Here is a storm pending and instead of remaining in shelter they are courting the fury of the blast. If I were a sheep, I should remain in the hollow.' The shepherd replied, 'Sair, if ye were a sheep, ye'd have mair sense.' Then he pointed out that down in the hollows the drafts came, and death. Instinctively, the sheep knew that their only safety was on the hills, facing the storm."—GERALD KENNEDY, in *The Pulpit,* July, 1946, p. 148.

Paul's success was the result of his endurance. In no other way could the gospel of Christ have been carried to the Roman world. Someone had to take the beatings and stonings, brave the dangers, and endure the privations—and finally die a martyr. Paul was the man whom God could use for this hazardous and painful task because he was willing to face the storm.

PAUL OVERCOMES INFIRMITIES

He said unto me, My grace is sufficient for thee: for my strength is made perfect in weakness. Most gladly therefore will I rather glory in my infirmities, that the power of Christ may rest upon me. Therefore I take pleasure in infirmities, in reproaches, in necessities, in persecutions, in distresses for Christ's sake: for when I am weak, then am I strong. 2 Cor. 12:9, 10.

What a man! Some unnamed disease or limitation made life difficult for Paul. He asked God to deliver him, but God chose to let him suffer. Without a word of complaint Paul accepted God's refusal to heal him, and determined to let his infirmities witness in Christ's behalf.

Amazing things have been accomplished by great sufferers. Robert Louis Stevenson contracted tuberculosis when young, and struggled with this handicap all of his life. In 1893 he wrote: "For fourteen years I have not had one day of real health. I have wakened sick and gone to bed weary, and yet I have done my work unflinchingly. I have written my books in bed and out of bed, written them when I was torn by coughing, written them during hemorrhages, written them when my head swam for weakness."—Quoted in J. G. GILKEY, *When Life Gets Hard,* pp. 48, 49.

His biographer records, "When a temporary illness laid Stevenson on his back he wrote in bed one of his most careful and thoughtful essays. . . . When eye-trouble forced him into a darkened room he still wrote on in the diminished light. When after a severe hemorrhage his right arm had to be bound in a sling, he scrawled with his left hand some of the gay poems now included in his book, 'A Child's Garden of Verses.' And when the hemorrhages finally became so severe that the doctor forbade him to talk, he actually tried to dictate in the deaf-and-dumb alphabet a portion of the book on which he was working."—*Ibid.*

In the light of men like Paul and Stevenson, what excuses do we have for our failure to achieve? Are we willing to accept whatever life brings with patience and understanding? Have we learned how to "glory" in our infirmities?

PAUL'S GOSPEL

Though we, or an angel from heaven, preach any other gospel unto you than that which we have preached unto you, let him be accursed. Gal. 1:8.

In early Adventist history there was a well-known minister by the name of E. J. Waggoner, an energetic proponent of the gospel of righteousness by faith in Christ. At the General Conference of 1891 Elder Waggoner gave a series of sermons on Paul's Epistle to the Romans. In his concluding sermon he made a remark that has a bearing on our text:

"Now the question arises, Was this preaching of Paul's anything like the . . . message which is committed to us? Did his preaching differ from the preaching which we preach? If it differs, are we preaching what we ought to preach? In other words, should our preaching embrace anything more than what the apostle Paul had? If it does, then whatever it may be, we had better get rid of it as soon as we can. Now let us see why—

" 'But though we, or an angel from heaven, preach any other gospel unto you than that which we have preached unto you, let him be accursed.' "

Nearly eighty years ago Elder Waggoner recognized that there has never been any improvement made on Paul's gospel. It is the good news that God sent His Son, Jesus Christ, to the world to re- deem man—that He was crucified for our sins, and resurrected that we might have life. Paul's message was that this act of God through Jesus was the *only* way of salvation for man. Time has made no change in this great doctrine.

In different ages there may be different emphases in Christian teaching. For example, John the Baptist preached a Christ to come, and Paul preached a Christ who had come. The Reformation stressed a forgiving Christ, and today we emphasize a soon-coming Christ. But in every age the gospel is the same. The grace of God that made possible the redemption of Adam is the same grace that operates in man's behalf today. The blood that was shed on Calvary means the same to every age. Let us not try to improve the gospel.

293

PAUL'S MOTIVES

Knowing this, that our old man is crucified with him, that the body of sin might be destroyed, that henceforth we should not serve sin. Rom. 6:6.

This is Paul's classic declaration on what it meant to him to be a Christian. What did he mean when he said that he was "crucified with Christ"? He saw on the cross of Christ the "old man" that had once been Paul. He saw on that cross the pride, the arrogance, the selfishness, the hatred, the cruelty, the narrowness that had characterized his earlier life. These things did not merely vanish—they were crucified, and crucifixion was a hard death. The death of the old Paul had been painful.

But even as Jesus lived again after His agonizing death, so Paul emerged from his crucifixion experience a new creature. The Christ he once hated he now loved. The people he once sought to kill were now his brothers and sisters. The beliefs he once repudiated were now the basis of his theology. A new radiance and a transformed purpose were evident in his life. Nothing was the same anymore because "henceforth we should not serve sin." Every decision was now dictated by his faith in Jesus. Every plan was related to his overwhelming desire to witness for his Lord. His whole value system had been changed by his encounter with the living Christ. At any cost, he was willing to serve his Lord and witness for Him.

Why was Paul thus motivated?—because the Lord, whose claim he had accepted, had destroyed the body of sin. In the matchless love of Christ, Paul saw sufficient reason to give up everything that had been valuable to him before, and to dedicate his life to the dangerous work of preaching the gospel.

What are our motives for serving Christ? Are we seeking remuneration, security, or position? Are we merely being pushed or persuaded into halfhearted service? Or are we motivated by faith in the Son of God who is willing to do just as much for us as He did for Paul?

Our motive in service must always be, "I did it for Him." Nothing less is acceptable.

PAUL OPPOSES PETER

When Peter was come to Antioch, I withstood him to the face, because he was to be blamed. For before that certain came from James, he did eat with the Gentiles: but when they were come, he withdrew and separated himself. Gal. 2:11, 12.

Peter was struggling with an integration problem. He had been taught from his youth that as a Jew he should not associate with Gentiles. In order to correct his prejudice the Lord had given him the vision of the sheet filled with all manner of animal life, and he had been shown that he "should not call any man common or unclean" (Acts 10:28). In harmony with this instruction, Peter continued his new manner of life when he went to Antioch.

But one day a commission arrived from Jerusalem made up of members of the conservative party of the church. These men considered it wrong to associate with Gentiles, and doubtless were very emphatic in maintaining their position. Out of fear for their reaction, Peter reverted to his old segregationist pattern of conduct. Barnabas and other Christian Jews joined him in conforming to the practices of the hard-line brethren from Jerusalem.

This was more than Paul could take. He withstood Peter "to the face, because he was to be blamed." Paul could see that his fellow leaders, in their desire to avoid friction, "walked not uprightly according to the truth of the gospel." The issue was vital, because the Gentiles to whom Paul had been commissioned to preach the gospel could not be reached if the traditional attitudes were maintained. If Christian leaders refused to eat with Gentiles, how could they bring the gospel of salvation to them?

Paul was willing to make almost any personal sacrifice in order to preserve good will. He was willing to forgo eating food offered to idols, even though he recognized that an idol was nothing. He was willing to work without pay lest he should be considered mercenary. But when the basic principle of the equality of all men under the gospel was at stake, Paul would oppose anyone—even his friend Peter, to whom he owed so much. He revealed his greatness in his willingness to stand firm when a really important issue was involved.

PAUL DESCRIBES INVOLVEMENT

I am crucified with Christ: nevertheless I live; yet not I, but Christ liveth in me: and the life which I now live in the flesh I live by the faith of the Son of God, who loved me, and gave himself for me. Gal. 2:20.

Halford Luccock records the following experience: "Some time since I overheard a conversation between two women. . . . One woman was talking about the Church of Sainte Chapelle in Paris; she was really raving about it. The other one apparently thought little of Sainte Chapelle. The first one said in amazement, 'Didn't you think that that thirteenth century stained glass was marvelous?' 'Oh,' the other one said, 'we didn't go inside; we saw it from a sight-seeing bus.' You can't see the Church of Sainte Chapelle from a sight-seeing bus. You cannot see the Christian faith from a sight-seeing bus. You must see it from inside."—*Halford Luccock Treasury,* pp. 116, 117.

No one ever accused Paul of seeing the Christian faith from a sight-seeing bus. No one was ever more involved than he. It wasn't sufficient for him to know about or believe in the crucified Christ— the only way he could describe his involvement was to say, "I am crucified with Christ." He identified himself so completely with his Lord that he said, "Christ liveth in me." This experience so influenced his daily life that he could truthfully say that his life was lived by the faith of the Son of God.

Such identification is hard to understand in an age of detachment when few people want to become involved with God, with the church, or with their fellow men. But only as Christians become deeply involved with their Lord are they truly Christians. Such an experience includes prayer, meditation, Bible study, and witnessing. It is the opposite of the prevalent secularism, which has been defined as "living as though there were no God."

In the same sermon Dr. Luccock described the results of participation with Christ. "The person in the midst of some of life's hardest experiences along a lonely way can say, 'There are two of us, not merely one.' "—*Ibid.,* p. 118. There is no such reward for detachment. Involvement makes Christianity meaningful.

ADOPTED CHILDREN

When the fulness of the time was come, God sent forth his Son, made of a woman, made under the law, to redeem them that were under the law, that we might receive the adoption of sons. Gal. 4:4, 5.

In the fourth chapter of his Epistle to the Galatians, Paul tries to show Christians that they are more than slaves in the household of God. The people of his time understood this analogy well. The slave had no legal rights, no security, no guarantee for the future. His only hope of existence was in obeying his master's every desire.

Paul was saying that through Christ those who had been slaves of law—which was the essence of Judaism—could become adopted sons of God. This new relationship would give them the status of children, heirs, members of the family. Paul was trying to convince the Galatians that they should rejoice in this relationship of sonship rather than continue under the concept of religion as slavery to law.

"There are conscientious souls that trust partly to God, and partly to themselves. They do not look to God, to be kept by His power, but depend upon watchfulness against temptation, and the performance of certain duties for acceptance with Him. There are no victories in this kind of faith. Such persons toil to no purpose; their souls are in continual bondage, and they find no rest until their burdens are laid at the feet of Jesus."—*Gospel Workers* (1892 ed.), pp. 414, 415.

Just as there were slaves to law in Galatia, there are slaves to law today. Paul pleads that Christians accept their privileges as sons of God. This means that they call God "Father," and that they are secure in His love. As a *result* of this warm relationship they will do the things God requires.

In thousands of homes throughout the world live children who have been adopted. Their foster parents have given them their name, their home, and their love. Their rights of inheritance are the same as those of natural children. Paul uses this common relationship as an illustration of God's love in redeeming people from slavery and adopting them as His own.

UNDERSTANDING ONE ANOTHER

All the law is fulfilled in one word, even in this; Thou shalt love thy neighbour as thyself. But if ye bite and devour one another, take heed that ye be not consumed one of another. Gal. 5:14, 15.

What a great day it would be if the idea of Christian love could really grip the hearts of mankind. People need love, but on every hand they meet hostility. What a tragedy!

In the *New York Times* (Jan. 4, 1959), Dr. Howard S. Rusk cited a transcription of an interview with a twelve-year-old boy, blind since birth, who was having difficulty at school. "But then," the boy said, "it isn't the darkness that I should blame, because darkness can be either friend or enemy. If wishes could come true, I'd wish I could see. But if I had only one wish, I would not waste it on wishing I could see. I'd wish instead that everybody could understand one another and how a person feels inside."—*Minister's Manual* for 1968.

No doubt the boy was right. The greatest wish may well be the wish that everybody could understand one another. In such a case the rich and the poor would lay aside their jealousies, educated and uneducated would learn to appreciate one another, races and nations would live together in peace, and the so-called liberals and conservatives would learn to tolerate and learn from each other.

During the Civil War an officer saw two soldiers carrying what appeared to be a wounded man from the field. Knowing that this was a favorite dodge of cowards, the officer ordered them to the front. The wounded man said, "Give me your hand, Colonel," and he thrust the officer's hand into a bullet hole in his shoulder. Soon he was dead. He had paid the supreme sacrifice, but had been accused of cowardice.

How often we needlessly wound because we do not understand. How much lighter life's burdens would be if we didn't have to carry them alone. Our hostilities and suspicions rob us of much of the joy of living. Fear makes it impossible for us to love or be loved.

Isn't there a better way? Jesus said, "Thou shalt love thy neighbour as thyself." This is the alternative to frustration and loneliness.

THE FRUIT OF THE SPIRIT

The fruit of the Spirit is love, joy, peace, longsuffering, gentleness, goodness, faith, meekness, temperance: against such there is no law. Gal. 5:22, 23.

Today's English Version renders this text simply and clearly: "The Spirit produces love, joy, peace, patience, kindness, goodness, faithfulness, humility, and self-control." These results can be predicted in a life that is under the influence of the Spirit of God.

It is helpful to analyze the nature of the characteristics produced by the Spirit. Some of them have to do with a person's relationship to his fellow man—love, patience, kindness. The Spirit-controlled person has a concern for his neighbor, he is patient with his neighbor's faults, he is unfailingly kind.

Another result of the presence of the Spirit is inner security. This is described under the headings of joy and peace. The Spirit of God makes its possessors happy and serene.

Furthermore, the Christian is characterized by stability. He is not only kind and secure, he also possesses goodness, faithfulness, and self-control. He is not weak, easily influenced by the evils of his environment, undependable, or fickle. His life is untainted, effective, and disciplined.

The Spirit of God, then, is more than a source of emotional excitement. It is more than a power that makes people shout and sing and speak in unknown tongues. The Holy Spirit is the source of the most fundamental values of life—kindness, happiness, character, and competence.

The problem of many professed Christians is that they are seeking the fruits of the Spirit without the Spirit. They want the results of the gospel without the gospel. They are not willing to engage in the meditation and prayer that are essential to the reception of Christ in the life, yet they expect their lives to be Christian.

A personal experience with the living Christ, a willingness to be guided by the Spirit of God, a wholehearted acceptance of Christ as Saviour and Lord—these are the prerequisites to producing the fruit of the Spirit.

PEOPLE WHO IRRITATE

Let us not be desirous of vain glory, provoking one another, envying one another. Gal. 5:26.

Today's English Version reads, "We must not be proud, or irritate one another, or be jealous of one another." How many of the problems that afflict families, communities, businesses, churches, and society, reflect the fact that people irritate one another.

How often we have heard—or used—the expression, "He gets on my nerves!" Paul is trying to say to us, "Quit getting on one another's nerves." How can we follow this counsel in practical life? A few suggestions may be useful.

One of the most irritating species of humanity is the person who talks continually about himself. Every topic is discussed within the context of "I—I—I." His afflictions, his exploits, his ideas, his plans —these are the sum total of his wisdom.

Another person who irritates is the person who makes it obvious that he considers himself superior. He listens condescendingly, he finds fault continually, his countenance bears a trace of a sneer, he dismisses others' ideas as inconsequential, and makes fun of them at every opportunity. He uses his piety, his learning, or his skill as a platform to elevate himself above his contemporaries.

Another irritant in any group is the man who loves to argue. He bolsters his ego by achieving verbal victories over his friends (if he has any). He is always positive that he is right and he insists on having the last word.

Among the chief irritants are the persons who refuse to respect the privacy of others. They barge in unexpectedly, they ask "nosy" questions, they repeat damaging gossip.

A person may be good in the sense of being a law-abiding citizen or a church member in good and regular standing, yet be very irritating. On the other hand, a person who is less pious may have a natural or cultivated sense of rightness that will keep him from being irritating. Practical religion, according to Paul, teaches that we refrain from irritating one another.

WHAT TO DO WITH SINNERS

Brethren, if a man be overtaken in a fault, ye which are spiritual, restore such an one in the spirit of meekness; considering thyself, lest thou also be tempted. Gal. 6:1.

There are two possible ways of translating the first phrase of this verse. Some translators take it to mean "if a man be caught red-handed." Others believe the thought to be, "if a man be suddenly overwhelmed by temptation." The first idea is reflected in Today's English Version, "if someone is caught in any kind of wrongdoing." The second is reflected in the New English Bible, "if a man should do something wrong, my brothers, on a sudden impulse."

There may be an unavoidable difference of opinion as to the exact meaning of the first phrase of the text, but there can be no question about the meaning of the rest of the verse, "Those of you who are spiritual should set him right; but you must do it in a gentle way. And keep an eye on yourself, so that you will not be tempted, too" (T.E.V.).

The Bible does not teach that sin should be disregarded. Jesus said, "If thy brother trespass against thee, rebuke him," but He also said, "and if he repent, forgive him." And to make the lesson more complete, He continued, "And if he trespass against thee seven times in a day, and seven times in a day turn again to thee, saying, I repent; thou shalt forgive him" (Luke 17:3, 4). In our text, Christians are told to "restore" the wrongdoer, to "set him right," to "set him back on the right path" (Phillips). But the text emphasizes that this process of reclamation should be done gently and humbly.

How often wrongdoers are treated with coldness and contempt. It is assumed that justice is not satisfied unless they are forced to suffer. In a time when they need sympathy and warmth they are subjected to all manner of embarrassment and hostility. They are left alone with their accusing consciences, with no friend to show them the way back to acceptance and forgiveness.

Never should we forget the words of Jesus to a woman "overtaken in a fault"—"Neither do I condemn thee: go, and sin no more."

301

BURDEN BEARING

Bear ye one another's burdens, and so fulfill the law of Christ.
Gal. 6:2.

Today's English Version illustrates this text with an interesting drawing. Several people are traveling single file, each with a pack on his back. In each instance the traveler is helping carry the pack of the person in front of him.

This is a picture of the ideal relationship of one Christian to another. Each of us has an uphill climb, but with help and encouragement the trail doesn't seem nearly so steep.

The cynic might say, "Why not let every man carry his own load?" Life is a lonely experience if there is no one at hand to help lighten the burden. The worst plight imaginable is for a person to reach his declining years with neither family nor close friends. Companionship and sharing are absolutely necessary to the happiness of most people.

In our text Paul equates mutual burden sharing with fulfilling the law of Christ. This means that one way to live out the law as Jesus interpreted it is to help our neighbor bear his burdens. This illustrates the difference between Jesus' version of law observance and that of the Pharisees. While the Pharisees were placing burdens on the people that they could not bear, Jesus explained that He had come to "preach the gospel to the poor; . . . to heal the brokenhearted, to preach deliverance to the captives, and recovering of sight to the blind, to set at liberty them that are bruised" (Luke 4: 18). Christ's law of love called for lifting burdens rather than imposing them.

One of the great glories of the church as Jesus established it, was that each member should feel responsible for his brother. This was intended as a great source of encouragement and happiness. Fellow church members are often closer than members of the same family. A common faith bridges barriers of culture and race.

But in a wider sense, Christians are called upon to bear the burdens of the world. Only as the church responds to this call will it be able to draw the world to Christ.

THE HUNGER FOR APPRECIATION

I also, after I heard of your faith in the Lord Jesus, and love unto all the saints, cease not to give thanks for you, making mention of you in my prayers. Eph. 1:15, 16.

Paul customarily included a word of praise and appreciation among the greetings of his letters. To the Philippians he said, "I thank my God upon every remembrance of you" (Phil. 1:3), and to the Thessalonians he declared, "Remembering without ceasing your work of faith, and labour of love, and patience of hope" (1 Thess. 1:3).

"It was a sweltering afternoon, the end of my exhausting first day as a sixteen-year-old trainee-waitress in a busy New York drugstore. My cap had gone awry, my apron was stained, my feet ached. The loaded trays I carried weighed heavier and heavier. Weary and discouraged, I didn't seem able to do anything right. Slowly I made out the complicated check for a family with several small children who had changed their ice cream order from tutti-frutti to butter pecan and back again about a dozen times. I was ready to quit.

"Then the father smiled at me as he handed me my tip. 'Well done,' he said. 'You've looked after us real well.'

"As I smiled back at him, my tiredness vanished. And when the manager asked me later how I'd liked it on my first day, I told him, *fine*. Those few words of praise had changed everything."—JANET GRAHAM, "The Power of Praise," *Christian Herald*, May, 1968.

Sometimes we misinterpret the warning not to flatter people. In order to avoid insincere flattery, we have refused or neglected to express deserved praise and appreciation. How many homes would be happier if parents noticed the good things as well as the defects in their children. How many domestic tragedies could be averted if husbands and wives would look for things to praise in each other. How often teachers consider it their business to point out the weaknesses of a student. Would not the ultimate result be greater if they would also look for things to commend?

We are all hungry for appreciation. If we give it, we will be more likely to receive it—and we will all be happier.

WHY AM I HERE?

God, who is rich in mercy, for his great love wherewith he loved us, even when we were dead in sins, hath quickened us together with Christ, (by grace ye are saved). Eph. 2:4, 5.

Charles Ives has written a composition entitled, "The Unanswered Question." Six times the trumpet repeats a phrase that is supposed to represent man's eternal query, "Why am I here?" The wood wind answers each time with increasing confusion, representing man's futile attempts to answer this question. The seventh time the trumpet asks the question there is no answer—only the soft background of the orchestra intended to represent the movement of the heavenly bodies in space. The composer seems to be saying, There is no answer to man's question.

But a little man who lived nineteen centuries ago raises his hand in protest. He states first of all that there is a merciful God who loves His creatures. This loving God "brought us to life with Christ even when we were dead in our sins" (N.E.B.). He goes on to say that God has "raised us up together, and made us sit together in heavenly places in Christ Jesus" (verse 6). This passage indicates that the experience of the Christian with his Lord adds meaning to life. The futility of existence gives way to a thrilling sense of mission that makes life worth living.

This new meaning that Christ brings to life is destined to endure. The next verse says, "That in the ages to come he might shew the exceeding riches of his grace in his kindness toward us through Jesus Christ." The blessings of Christian commitment will never end.

Why am I here? This question has been answered by the phrase, To glorify God and to enjoy Him forever. The present life has purpose when the life is centered in God, and the hope of immortality gives each life eternal meaning.

Millions find no satisfactory answer to the question, "Why am I here?" They spend their lives in a futile search for pleasure, in an attempt to remedy the emptiness of day-by-day existence. Not so with the Christian. He really lives.

PAUL DESCRIBES THE CHURCH

Ye are no more strangers and foreigners, but fellow-citizens with the saints, and of the household of God; and are built upon the foundation of the apostles and prophets, Jesus Christ himself being the chief corner stone; in whom all the building fitly framed together groweth unto an holy temple in the Lord: in whom ye also are builded together for an habitation of God through the spirit. Eph. 2:19-22.

The Christian church was a brand-new institution when Paul wrote this letter to the church at Ephesus, and in Paul's eyes it was a wonderful fellowship. Its members possessed a sense of identity—they were no longer "strangers and foreigners" in the world—they were part of God's "household." They belonged.

This new organization, of which they were so proud to be a part, rested on the apostles, the prophets, and Jesus Christ Himself. There were many temples in the ancient world, but here was a temple made of people and built on a foundation of people. In place of cold stones and hoary traditions, the Christian church was *people*, redeemed through their Lord, Jesus Christ. These people became a dwelling place for God.

Years ago a storm destroyed a little church on the English coast. The congregation was unable to replace it, and arranged to worship elsewhere. One day a representative of the British Admiralty came to the minister and said, "If you do not rebuild the church, we will. That spire is on all our charts and maps. It is the landmark by which the ships of the seven seas steer their courses."

As this church spire guided the mariners, so the Christian church was intended as a landmark in the world. It hasn't always fulfilled this mission, but it has succeeded to the extent it has been "an habitation of God through the spirit."

There never was a time when the world needed the positive witness of Christian believers more than today. If twentieth century Christians are to fill this need, their church must be built upon the foundation of the apostles and prophets, "Jesus Christ himself being the chief corner stone."

THE INDWELLING CHRIST

For this cause I bow my knees unto the Father of our Lord Jesus Christ . . . that he would grant you, according to the riches of his glory, to be strengthened with might by his Spirit in the inner man; that Christ may dwell in your hearts by faith. Eph. 3:14-17.

In this scripture Paul is praying to God that his people might be strengthened inwardly by the Spirit, and that Christ might dwell in their hearts. This was a noble, gracious prayer. What does it mean, and how can it be answered?

Constantly in sermons and devotional literature, Christians are confronted with the idea of the indwelling Christ. It is expressed in different ways; for example, "Christ in the heart," and "Christ within." What is the meaning of these oft-repeated figures of speech?

Essentially they mean that Christ controls the life. The Christian has learned to know Christ as his redeemer, his friend, and his hope. He seeks through prayer and meditation the guidance of Christ in the decisions of his life. He acquaints himself with the character of Christ, and he asks God to transform him that he may be like Christ. He accepts the redemption provided by Christ, and he loves and worships his Lord in profound gratitude and appreciation. He seeks to witness to others as to what the grace of God has done for him through Christ. His hopes, his purposes, his ideals, his motivations, are so saturated with Christ that it is equally correct to speak of him as being "in Christ," or of Christ being "in him."

The Bible uses the analogy of marriage to describe this relationship. The church, which is the aggregate of its individual members, is called "the bride of Christ." In an ideal marriage there is a strong identification of each party with the other. What brings pain or pleasure to one likewise brings pain or pleasure to the other. There is complete loyalty and devotion, each trying to bring happiness to the other.

The Christian recognizes the living Christ as his unfailing friend. He is the divine counselor, and through His Spirit He is always available. The old hymn expressed it well: "No, never alone." This relationship can be fully appreciated only by experience.

THE DIMENSIONS OF GOD'S LOVE

That ye, being rooted and grounded in love, may be able to comprehend with all saints what is the breadth, and length, and depth, and height; and to know the love of Christ, which passeth knowledge, that ye might be filled with all the fulness of God. Eph. 3:17-19.

"There's a wideness in God's mercy,
    Like the wideness of the sea;
There's a kindness in His justice
    Which is more than liberty.

.   .   .   .   .

"For the love of God is broader
    Than the measure of man's mind,
And the heart of the Eternal
    Is most wonderfully kind.

"If our love were but more simple,
    We should take Him at His word,
And our lives would be all sunshine
    In the sweetness of our Lord."

—F. W. FABER

God revealed His immeasurable love to mankind through Christ, a love wide enough to encompass the whole universe, deep enough to include every level of human experience, long enough to span the eternities, and high enough to include both God and man in its grasp.

This love was not only expressed at the cross, but finds its way into the everyday relationship between a man and his God. A person who comprehends this love enjoys a security that is unassailable. He realizes that there is One who shares his joys and sorrows, and is sensitive to his anxieties and dreams. He realizes that there is a purpose in life beyond the mere physical aspects of earthly existence. He believes that he is personally of value to a God who loves him and who is concerned about his temporal and eternal future. May we know for ourselves this boundless, limitless love!

307

"TO LOVE AND TO CHERISH"

Nevertheless let every one of you in particular so love his wife even as himself; and the wife see that she reverence her husband. Eph. 5:33.

"When the Titanic was speeding across the Atlantic Ocean in April, 1912, on her maiden voyage, suddenly and without any warning the deadly spur of a submerged iceberg tore into her hull, and ripped it open under the water for a distance of three hundred feet. More than twenty-three hundred people had come face to face with death. All the lifeboats and rafts could accommodate only eleven hundred. On the passenger decks, from the bottom to the top, there was heartbreaking bravery and some quite understandable cowardice. The last distress signal was fired in vain. An officer stood by the rail and urged the women and children forward. 'Ladies,' he said insistently, 'you must get in at once. There's not a minute to lose. Hurry. Get in. Get in.' He seized the arm of little old Mrs. Isidore Strauss of New York and pushed her toward the lifeboat. She looked appealingly at the officer and glanced toward her husband; but the officer cried, 'The men must stand back. Women and children first. Hurry on, lady, hurry on.' Without a moment's hesitation, Mrs. Strauss stepped away from the lifeboat, spurning the opportunity of rescue, and, going to the side of her husband, from whom she had never been separated from the time of their marriage, she took his hand, and twenty minutes later, locked in each other's arms, they went down into the cold water of the Atlantic. As they had been joined together in life, in death they were not divided."—J. S. BON-NELL, *Fifth Avenue Sermons,* pp. 80, 81.

Love is often manifested in depth under more prosaic circumstances. It is the young wife who works hard to help her husband reach his educational objectives or get ahead in business; it is the young husband who, during his army service, refuses to be untrue to his wife; it is the couple who are deeply sensitive to each other's needs and wishes, and each of whom constantly endeavors to enhance the happiness of the other; it is in these ways that love is most often revealed.

"A SENSE OF WHAT IS VITAL"

Approve things that are excellent. Phil. 1:10.

Modern speech translations make the thought of this text vivid: "Enabling you to have a sense of what is vital" (Moffatt); "that you may learn to prize what is of value" (Knox); "and may thus bring you the gift of true discrimination" (N.E.B.); "so that you will be able to choose what is best" (T.E.V.).

The ability to distinguish between what is best and what is of less value is most desirable. Musicians and artists take great pride in their ability to discern what is superior in their fields. The connoisseur is a respected person in any area of human activity. Surely no one needs a finer sense of discrimination than the Christian—because he is dealing with the ultimate values of life.

The context of our passage reveals how the Christian can attain this sense of what is vital: "This I pray, that your *love* may abound yet more and more in knowledge and in all judgment; that ye may approve things that are excellent." It has often been said that love is blind. On the other hand, nothing gives such insight as love. A man may seem to lack promise, but the love of a mother or sweetheart or wife who believes in him may unlock hidden resources that will result in successful and meaningful living. Let us look for the best in people, and let us try to inspire them to live up to their potential.

In the area of personal ideals we must also have a sense of what is vital. "You can always tell a man's quality by noting the things to which he is alive; people constantly reveal their spiritual rank by their responsiveness. Real music does not stir them; some cheap and tinsel tune does. The glories of God's out-of-doors awakens no response, but they are keen for the hectic excitement of a gambler's chances around tables undeserted all day long. The benedictions of a pure heart seem tame to them; they love the perversions of a vicious life. Speak to them of great books, and they are dull; tell them the last unwholesome jest, and they are all animation. They are alive to the low; they are dead to the high."—HARRY EMERSON FOSDICK, *Twelve Tests of Character,* pp. 57, 58.

May we, through love, achieve a sense of what is vital.

"TO LIVE IS CHRIST"

For me to live is Christ, and to die is gain. Phil. 1:21.

Very few people have achieved the degree of dedication Paul describes in this passage. Many, through necessity, make a reasonably good adjustment to life. They may resent the frustrations and irritations of daily existence, but they manage to "muddle through" with a minimum of complaint. But these same people find themselves completely unprepared when they come to the end of life's road. When they are young they refuse to think of death. When they grow old they are unready to come to terms with the inevitable.

Paul lived life to the hilt. He preached, he traveled, he wrote. He knew the joy of success and the pain of failure. He was gracious when he was well supported and patient when he was in poverty. He knew the warmth of human friendship and the bitter opposition of enemies. His life was as eventful, exciting, productive.

When he finally found himself in a dungeon awaiting death he did not panic. Calmly he said, "I am now ready to be offered." "I have fought a good fight." He considered death gain because he saw beyond the executioner's block a "crown of life." The man who had said "to die is gain" revealed the sincerity of his statement when he finally faced the end. "The apostle was looking into the great beyond, not with uncertainty or dread, but with joyous hope and longing expectation. As he stands at the place of martyrdom he sees not the sword of the executioner or the earth so soon to receive his blood; he looks up through the calm blue heaven of that summer day to the throne of the Eternal." —*The Acts of the Apostles,* pp. 511, 512.

A man who had once been a Christian became highly successful and very well known through America, but in the process of becoming famous he jettisoned his religion. He was invited to speak at a Christian college, and in the course of his remarks he enunciated several fine principles of living. Afterward, a friend of earlier days congratulated him and commented, "You are not far from the kingdom." He answered, "I *have* a kingdom." For this man, to live was not Christ. His "kingdom"—fame and prestige—will not prepare him ever to say, "To die is gain."

JESUS EMPTIED HIMSELF

Let this mind be in you, which was also in Christ Jesus: who, being in the form of God, thought it not robbery to be equal with God: but made himself of no reputation, and took upon him the form of a servant, and was made in the likeness of men: and being found in fashion as a man, he humbled himself, and became obedient unto death, even the death of the cross. Phil. 2:5-8.

This is one of the great passages of the Bible. In vivid strokes it pictures the sacrifice Jesus made to become man's Saviour. First, we see Him "in the form of God, . . . equal with God." No higher state could be imagined. He was co-Creator of man and of the universe; He had shared the throne with His Father from all eternity. In a very real sense He and the Father are one.

He stepped down from the throne of the universe to a peasant's cottage in Galilee, and took upon Himself all of the limitations of humanity. Literally, He emptied Himself. Jesus did not give up His divine nature, but He did give up the glory to which His divine nature entitled Him, and which, indeed, had been His before the incarnation. In order to save men He "was made in the likeness of men."

As if this were not enough, He took one more long step down the ladder. He emptied Himself again; "he was humbler yet, even to accepting death, death on a cross" (Jerusalem Bible). He could descend no further; He could give up nothing more; He could, in no more meaningful way, reveal His identification with mankind.

"Jesus might have remained at His Father's right hand, wearing His kingly crown and royal robes. But He chose to exchange all the riches, honor, and glory of heaven for the poverty of humanity, and His station of high command for the horrors of Gethsemane and the humiliation and agony of Calvary."—*Testimonies,* vol. 4, p. 121.

This sacrificial love seems indescribable—it is so far beyond the usual experience of humanity. Yet Paul says, "Let this mind be in *you.*" Jesus was not only working in our behalf, He was also setting us an example. Are we willing to empty ourselves for the sake of others? Are we able to love one another as He has loved us?

GOD EXALTS HIS SON

God also hath highly exalted him, and given him a name which is above every name: that at the name of Jesus every knee should bow, of things in heaven, and things in earth, and things under the earth; and that every tongue should confess that Jesus Christ is Lord, to the glory of God the Father. Phil. 2:9-11.

Prior to this passage, Paul described Jesus as emptying Himself, or stepping down from the throne of the universe to die for man. In this passage Paul reveals God glorifying His Son and exalting Him before the universe. This scripture, with the verses preceding it, seems to have been an early Christian hymn of praise to Christ. One translator has put these well-known words in the following metric form:

"For this reason God raised him to the highest place above,
And gave him the name that is greater than any other name,
So that all beings in heaven, and on earth, and in the world below
Will fall on their knees,
In honor of the name of Jesus,
And all will openly proclaim that Jesus Christ is the Lord,
To the glory of God the Father" (T.E.V.).

What a privilege it would have been to listen to the early Christians praise their Lord in this hymn! They were mightily moved by the great truth that Jesus Christ is Lord, and they wanted everyone to know that they accepted His lordship. Separated by only a few years from the cross, they grasped the great truth that He had been highly exalted, and that, one day, all the universe would acknowledge His sovereignty. "Adam was created in the image of God, but he lost that image because he wanted to grasp equality with God. Unlike Adam, the Heavenly Man, who in his pre-existence represented the true image of God, humbled himself in obedience and now receives the equality with God he did not grasp."—OSCAR CULLMANN, *The Christology of the New Testament,* p. 181.

Again the great truths of the gospel cause us to bow our heads in awe and reverence. Again we hear the words of Paul, "Let this mind be in you, which was also in Christ Jesus."

A WHOLEHEARTED CHRISTIAN

I trust in the Lord Jesus to send Timotheus shortly unto you, that I also may be of good comfort, when I know your state. For I have no man likeminded, who will naturally care for your state. For all seek their own, not the things which are Jesus Christ's. Phil. 2:19-21.

Among all of the available people, there was one—only one, whom Paul could recommend without reservation as pastor for the church at Philippi. Everyone else seemed more concerned about his own interests; Timothy was primarily concerned about things pertaining to Jesus Christ.

If Paul, with his keen, penetrating insight into human motives, were among us today, what would his verdict be? How many ministers and other religious workers would he find who are *primarily* concerned about Jesus Christ, and *secondarily* concerned about themselves? If this test were applied to the laity of the church, what would the result be? In other words, how seriously do we respond to the claim of Christ on our lives, and how successful has God been in eliminating selfishness from our characters?

Dr. Elton Trueblood has said: "Twentieth century man, if pressed for an answer, admits that he believes in a moral order, that he believes in religion, and that he believes in the Christian religion, but there he stops. He is trying to live in the midst of the world storm, not as an adherent of paganism and not as an opponent of the Christian faith, but as one who adheres to that faith in the most vague and tenuous manner conceivable. *He claims to be a shareholder in the Christian corporation, but the stock has been watered almost to the vanishing point and is held, moreover, by absentee owners."—The Predicament of Modern Man*, p. 69.

This level of Christianity will never save the world or the church. Some people's faith has been described as a slight inoculation that prevents them from catching the real thing. Jesus insisted that His followers should love God, "with *all* thy heart, and with *all* thy soul, and with *all* thy strength, and with *all* thy mind" (Luke 10:27). May God raise up more completely committed men like Timothy.

"STEADFAST TREAD HEAVENWARD"

Brethren, I count not myself to have apprehended: but this one thing I do, forgetting those things which are behind, and reaching forth unto those things which are before, I press toward the mark for the prize of the high calling of God in Christ Jesus. Phil. 3:13, 14.

This is one of the most encouraging passages of Scripture for the ordinary Christian who finds himself struggling with life's problems. How often we look at ourselves and deplore our shortcomings. At such times it helps us to hear Paul say, "Yet, my brothers, I do not consider myself to have 'arrived' spiritually, nor do I consider myself already perfect" (Phillips). Paul realized that even though God had done much for him, there was more to be done.

But Paul was not content to deplore his shortcomings. He was not satisfied with his imperfections. He added, "But I keep going on, grasping ever more firmly that purpose for which Christ Jesus grasped me. My brothers, I do not consider myself to have fully grasped it even now. But I do concentrate on this: I leave the past behind and with hands outstretched to whatever lies ahead I go straight for the goal—my reward the honor of my high calling by God in Christ Jesus" (Phillips).

Commenting on this verse Ellen White says, "Let the angels of heaven write of Paul's victories in fighting the good fight of faith. Let heaven rejoice in his steadfast tread heavenward, and that, keeping the prize in view, he counts every other consideration dross. Angels rejoice to tell his triumphs, but Paul makes no boast of his attainments. The attitude of Paul is the attitude that every follower of Christ should take as he urges his way onward in the strife for the immortal crown."—*The Acts of the Apostles,* p. 562.

In the Christian's life, the summit cannot be reached this side of eternity. "So long as Satan reigns, we shall have self to subdue, besetting sins to overcome; so long as life shall last, there will be no stopping place, no point which we can reach and say, I have fully attained."—*Ibid.,* pp. 560, 561. As long as this climb is shared by men like Paul, we need not lose our courage.

314

CITIZENS OF HEAVEN

Our conversation is in heaven; from whence also we look for the Saviour, the Lord Jesus Christ. Phil. 3:20.

The word "conversation" had a different meaning in the seventeenth-century King James Version from what it has now. Literally, the word translated "conversation" is derived from a verb meaning "to be a citizen." The New English Bible translation is, "We . . . are citizens of heaven"; Goodspeed says, "But the commonwealth to which we belong is in heaven"; and Moffatt translates the passage, "We are a colony of heaven."

This is a challenging idea. Anyone who has traveled outside his native country knows what a thrill it is to see his own flag, to hear his own language, to eat familiar food. He also may learn how it feels to encounter hostility to his homeland. For example, it is distressing for an American abroad to see "Yankee, go home" signs scrawled on fences and walls along the highways.

This experience illustrates the life of the Christian. His citizenship is in heaven. The church to which he belongs is a colony of heaven. The world in which he finds himself lives according to principles and customs that differ from his own. He lives constantly with the tension of being a stranger in a foreign land. He never can feel completely at home, because the Lord whom he serves is so different from the gods of the world in which he lives.

Some people try to resolve this tension by being hostile to their world. This is not the answer. The Christian is placed in the world to be a blessing. His Master told him to be the salt of the earth, the light of the world. While he cannot accept all of the ways of the world, he must maintain his love for its people.

Others try to solve their dual citizenship by neglecting the claims of Christ their Lord. They try to come to terms so completely with their environment that they rationalize the demands of their primary citizenship in heaven. This is treason. Happy is the person who can accept his dual role; who can be an exemplary citizen of heaven and at the same time, a loyal citizen of whatever nation or community happens to be his earthly home.

TWO PEOPLE WHO COULDN'T GET ALONG

I beseech Euodias, and beseech Syntyche, that they be of the same mind in the Lord. Phil. 4:2.

Paul does not identify these two people, but obviously they were not "of the same mind." Perhaps their differences were theological, or perhaps they just didn't like each other. There may have been a family feud of long standing, or possibly one was selected for church office and the other was passed by. Some commentators suggest that they were husband and wife.

Whatever the cause may have been, the church at Philippi bore a less effective witness because two of its members couldn't get along. The worship of God was less meaningful, the young people were less loyal to the church, the evangelism was less appealing.

Bishop Kennedy quotes these lines:

> "To live with the saints in Heaven
> Is bliss and glory;
> To live with the saints on earth
> Is—often another story!"
> —*Atlantic Monthly,* October, 1928, p. 459.

O the tragedy of divided churches! How often ministers wear their lives away trying to keep peace among members. How often church board meetings resemble a labor-management conference. How often the youth of the church become utterly disillusioned because of the undignified squabbling of their elders.

To all church members everywhere comes the call to "be of the same mind in the Lord." We are entitled to varying viewpoints, individuality, and divergence of opinion, but we cannot afford the luxury of hostility.

There is a fable about an ox and a colt that met at a waterhole and had a disagreement as to who should drink first. The argument became so hot that they finally squared off for mortal combat. They changed their minds about the battle when they looked up and saw vultures flying overhead. Every church that finds itself split and torn by dissension should remember the vultures flying overhead.

DON'T WORRY—PRAY

Be careful for nothing, but in every thing by prayer and sup-plication with thanksgiving let your requests be made known unto God. Phil. 4:6.

The admonition "Be careful for nothing" is variously translated: "Have no anxiety about anything" (R.S.V.); "Don't worry over any-thing whatever" (Phillips); "There is no need to worry" (Jerusalem Bible).

Psychologists and psychiatrists have given much helpful counsel regarding worry, but in our passage the apostle adds something essen-tial that is often overlooked—"in all your prayers ask God for what you need" (T.E.V.). Paul proposes prayer as a remedy. On this point Leslie D. Weatherhead has some helpful advice:

"We must not only pray to be free from anxiety, but try to un-derstand and remove its cause. No man prays about his teeth. He goes to a dentist. . . . Twenty minutes on an operating table would do more for a patient suffering from, say, appendicitis, than a week of prayer. . . . The aim of praying is unity with God and not merely the regaining of one's health."—*Prescription for Anxiety,* p. 102.

Paul not only advises that we take our anxieties and worries to God but also suggests that we do so "with thanksgiving." Norman Vincent Peale tells of a woman whose life had been full of fear and worry. Peale advised her to pray, and she found help as she followed his counsel. She said, "Every night I begin my prayers by listing all the things for which I am grateful, little things that happened dur-ing the day which added to the happiness of my day. I know that this habit has geared my mind to pick out the nice things and forget the unpleasant ones."—*The Power of Positive Thinking,* p. 59.

In all the centuries from Paul to Peale, intelligent, thankful prayer has been a great remedy for worry. If we can realize that our God is just as concerned about our problems as we are; if we can understand that He is eager that we be happy and successful; if we can remember that He is by our side and hears our prayers, we will find little reason for prolonged, destructive anxiety. We can trust Him to work things out in ways that will be best for us.

THE CASE AGAINST REALISM

Finally, brethren, whatsoever things are true, whatsoever things are honest, whatsoever things are just, whatsoever things are pure, whatsoever things are lovely, whatsoever things are of good report; if there be any virtue, and if there be any praise, think on these things. Phil. 4:8.

Much contemporary literature is created in harmony with the principle known as realism—the principle of depicting life as it exists without any attempt at idealization. Pursuant to this concept, much literature is filled with blasphemy, filth, cruelty, and sordidness. This deluge of literary sewage is defended on the basis of realism—life must be depicted as it is!

It is true that the Bible reports the sins and foibles of its characters. No attempt is made to hide the weaknesses of David, the mistakes of Abraham, or the instability of Peter. But in the Bible, reports of human weakness are always incidental to the great themes of salvation, honesty, justice, purity, and praise. The Bible reaches its peak of greatness, not in the uncovering of evil, but in the revelation of One whose life was absolute honesty, purity, and love.

There is still much good to occupy the mind. Beauty remains in nature, art, and music—to the extent that it has not been defaced by man. There is literature that possesses dignity and worth. There are unselfish people who live decent lives and love their fellow men. There are mothers and fathers who love their children, and children who respect their parents. There are citizens who become involved in their communities and try to make the world a better place in which to live.

Above all, God is still on His throne. Christ still mediates for repentant sinners. Eternal life is still the last and best hope of man.

Why read books and look at pictures that portray vice and cruelty when we have the alternative of thinking on things that are "true," "honest," "just," "pure," "lovely," "of good report"? Why should we live in life's smog when the pure air and blue sky are available to us? While we must not shut our eyes to all the sordidness of life, we need not feast our eyes on it.

THE SOURCE OF COMPETENCE

I can do all things through Christ which strengtheneth me.
Phil. 4:13.

A study of the men and women of the Bible reveals ordinary people doing extraordinary things. How did such unlikely persons succeed in accomplishing so much of noteworthy consequence? The answer is found, in part, in our text. It was Christ who transformed Peter the fisherman, and Saul the Pharisee into dynamic evangelists of the Christian gospel. A power entered their lives far beyond their own ability, and they were able to change the course of the world.

Many people—some of them professing Christians—live lives of anxiety because of feelings of inadequacy. They are not what they would like to be, and they do not accomplish what they would like to accomplish. Psychologists tell us that we should learn to accept ourselves as we are. This is true to a degree; but we also ought to take into consideration the power of Christ to make us better and more competent than we are. This is one of the by-products of being a Christian.

"A charming story is told of the painter and sculptor Sir Hubert von Herkomer, who founded the Herkomer school of painting at Bushey in 1883. His aged father, who had brought his son at the age of eight from their Bavarian home, was persuaded to spend the last years of his life with his distinguished son. The father, also a sculptor, asked for clay that he might while away the evenings in modeling. But, what with age and enfeeblement and failing sight, the old man would put aside his work at night almost in despair. He could not make it what he wanted to make it. The actuality was so distressingly far below the vision that the old man would go to bed quite sad. But after the father had gone to bed, his son would go and work secretly at the clay. In the morning the father would look at his work of the previous evening and, never knowing that another hand had touched it, would exclaim with delight: 'Why, it isn't as bad as I thought!' "—LESLIE D. WEATHERHEAD, *The Significance of Silence*, p. 142.

Yes, there is "another hand" that touches our work, smooths out the rough spots, and makes beautiful that which is commonplace. This other hand can touch our lives to the extent that we have faith.

319

FAITH IN THE FUTURE

When Christ, who is our life, shall appear, then shall ye also appear with him in glory. Col. 3:4.

"While a company of people were having dinner together, one man in the party, who had spent many summers in Maine, fascinated his companions by telling of his experiences with a little town named Flagstaff in the months before it was to be flooded as part of a large lake for which a dam was being built. All improvements and repairs in the whole town were stopped. What was the use of painting a house if it were to be covered with water in six months? Why repair anything when the whole village was to be wiped out? So, week by week, the whole town became more and more bedraggled, more gone to seed, more woebegone. Then he added by way of explanation: 'Where there is no faith in the future, there is no power in the present.' "—*Halford Luccock Treasury,* p. 420.

Many people in our world have lost faith in the future because of the threat of atomic annihilation. They live in the shadow of the great mushroom cloud they fear will someday destroy civilization.

Dr. Luccock continues: "We should not minimize the seriousness of the hour or pretend that it is not dangerous. But if we are Christians we must not leave God out of our world. For the final question is not what Russia is going to do, but what *God* is going to do. Our world has not slipped out of God's pocket. It is still in his shaping hands."—*Ibid.,* p. 421.

To the believer in the return of Christ, this faith in the future has an additional dimension. The Adventist not only believes that the future is secure in Christ but also that Christ will come and solve the problems that disturb the happiness of the world. Certainly the Adventist should not be like the people of Flagstaff, neglecting the present life in their anticipation of the next. Jesus counseled His followers, "Occupy till I come." The Adventist Christian will give his best to minister to the needs of this world, knowing that his Lord will soon come and finish the job of remaking that which has been damaged by sin. This is the Christian's hope.

PAUL'S CHALLENGE TO THE JEWS

Thou therefore which teachest another, teachest thou not thyself? thou that preachest a man should not steal, dost thou steal? thou that sayest a man should not commit adultery, dost thou commit adultery? thou that abhorest idols, dost thou commit sacrilege? thou that makest thy boast of the law, through breaking the law dishonourest thou God? Rom. 2:21-23.

Earlier in his letter to the Romans, Paul called attention to the sinfulness of the contemporary culture. The world of Paul's day, as described in the graphic language of the Phillips translation, was "filled with wickedness, rottenness, greed and malice; their minds became steeped in envy, murder, quarrelsomeness, deceitfulness and spite. They became whisperers-behind-doors, stabbers-in-the-back, God-haters; they overflowed with insolent pride and boastfulness, and their minds teemed with diabolical invention. They scoffed at duty to parents; they mocked at learning, recognized no obligations of honor, lost all natural affection, and had no use for mercy" (Rom. 1:29-31).

But Paul in his concern about Gentile sins was not about to overlook the wrongdoing of the Jews. With their strict regulations governing ethical conduct, they abhorred the waywardness of the Gentile world. Yet they were not blameless. Despite the façade of their laws, their traditions, and their profession, they were sinful too. There was dishonesty, impurity, and sacrilege. These sins were probably less obvious and gross than in the surrounding world, but they were there, and however well disguised they may have been, their presence could not be denied.

Paul's challenge is relevant to the church today. "Thou that makest thy boast of the law, through breaking the law dishonourest thou God?" It happens every day in the best of circles. Paul recognized only one remedy for this illness—the righteousness of God received through faith in Christ. No one since Paul's day has found a better answer. Only the grace of God can transform either the abandoned sinner or the insincere legalist, and this grace is mediated through the ministry of our Lord. The gospel is the only remedy for sin.

239

ALL THINGS WORK TOGETHER

We know that all things work together for good to them that love God, to them who are the called according to his purpose. For whom he did foreknow, he also did predestinate to be conformed to the image of his Son, that he might be the firstborn among many brethren. Moreover whom he did predestinate, them he also called: and whom he called, them he also justified: and whom he justified, them he also glorified. Rom. 8:28-30.

We have all read with appreciation the first verse of this passage—the promise that all things work together for good. But sometimes we interpret it superficially because we do not read the rest of the passage, which explains *how* all things "work together" for the Christian.

First, there is the *foreknowledge* of God. This world is not without a ruler. The all-seeing eye of God sees the past, the present, and the future.

Second, God predestined certain people to be saved. Who are these favored people? The Epistle to the Romans answers the question—*those who believe in Christ.* Faith is the divinely appointed criterion of salvation.

Third, God calls. His grace works through men, through nature, and through direct revelation in inviting sinners to accept the claims of Christ, and He never gives up!

Fourth, God justifies. In other words, He forgives man's sins and makes available to him adequate help for living the Christian life. He accepts man into His family, on the basis of his faith.

Finally, God glorifies. This world is not all. Salvation includes immortality, which He promises to bestow at the second coming of our Lord.

A review of these steps indicates what Paul means when he says that "all things work together for good to them that love God." He does not mean that in this life everything will necessarily "come out all right." He means that God has set up a plan that will save all who love God. This assurance provides security for every Christian.

GOD'S PRESENT BLESSINGS

Being justified by faith, we have peace with God through our Lord Jesus Christ: by whom also we have access by faith into this grace wherein we stand, and rejoice in hope of the glory of God. And not only so, but we glory in tribulations also. Rom. 5:1-3.

Paul has explained the great truth of salvation by faith. He has made it clear that men are not saved on the basis of national origin; Jew and Gentile are alike eligible. He has also emphasized that they are not saved by works, because man is, by nature, incurably sinful. He has also stressed that law cannot save—"indeed it is the straightedge of the Law that shows us how crooked we are" (Rom. 3:20, Phillips). He has extolled the grace of God that provides righteousness as a free gift—righteousness that will forgive man's past sins and make it possible for him to live a Christian life. All of these blessings, Paul declares, are available through faith, which is simple acceptance of divine forgiveness and divine power. Our text points out the results of this thrilling experience—peace with God, access to grace, and the ability to accept adversity.

First of all, the Christian who has been justified by faith has peace with God. Everything is right between him and his God. God is his friend, and he is God's friend. There are no unconfessed and unforgiven sins to mar this friendship, and no indifference or spirit of rebellion stands between the saved person and his God.

Second, the Christian has constant access to grace. Grace is God's love for sinners. Access to this grace is like having an unlimited bank account. In his human weakness the Christian finds constant forgiveness and strength and victory as he looks to God in faith.

Third, the Christian is able to face life's problems. He may be mistreated, he may be hounded by bad fortune, health and happiness may pass him by, but his faith in God causes him to grow under the discipline of suffering and misfortune. Paul goes on to point out that these hard experiences result in patience, experience, and hope.

So the blessings of faith in God are not reserved to a distant eternity. They enhance every day of a Christian's life.

241

"THE HEROISM OF GOING ON"

Not only so, but we glory in tribulations also: knowing that tribulation worketh patience; and patience, experience; and experience, hope. Rom. 5:3, 4.

"Up in the Highlands of Scotland, a little group of people were talking about heroism: they were saying that everybody had sooner or later to practice some kind of heroism. A young man turned to an old woman, she looked so ordinary and so serene; he did not know that life had been for her a series of tragic things. 'And what kind of heroism do you practice?' he said, with an obvious air of thinking that he did not believe that there could be any kind of heroism in a life like hers. 'I?' she said. 'I practice the heroism of going on.' "—*The Minister's Manual,* (Doran) 1968, p. 5.

According to our text, tribulation in a Christian's life "worketh patience." This is simply another way of saying that the Christian practices the heroism of going on. He doesn't go to pieces when trouble comes. He may have to fight an uneven battle with circumstances, alone, but with faith he faces the future.

Our text also tells us that "patience" results in "experience." Some people are able to face the future—for a time. But when the future becomes the present, and day after day brings a monotonous succession of uninteresting duties, they find that they lack the resources to cope with life. They may resort to liquor, or dope, or some other expedient in their futile attempt to add meaning to a life from which meaning has fled. But for the Christian, patience develops experience. According to the R.S.V., "endurance produces character." The heroism of going on does not diminish with the passing of the years. Out of privation, humdrum, disappointment, and pain comes a life marked by poise, sympathy, and resiliency.

Finally, "Character produces hope" (R.S.V.). People who react negatively to life lose their basis for hope beyond this life; but those who are willing to be refined and matured by trouble have every reason to anticipate immortality. Eternal life is not a refuge for the incompetent, but fulfillment for those who have lived patiently and meaningfully.

242

PAUL LEARNS TO ADJUST

I have learned, in whatsoever state I am, therewith to be content. I know both how to be abased, and I know how to abound: every where and in all things I am instructed both to be full and to be hungry, both to abound and to suffer need. Phil. 4:11, 12.

Modern psychology has high praise for the well-adjusted individual. It is a mark of maturity when a person can come to terms with his environment in such a way that he is free from inner conflicts. Sometimes, unfortunately, this adjustment is sought through surrender of moral standards and religious principles. There is a difference between adjustment and surrender.

Paul is an outstanding example of adjustment at its best. He made no concessions to the hostile world in which he lived. Very often the world's wrath was expressed in the form of imprisonment, beatings, and betrayal. He had no security—physical, financial, or social. He was intimately acquainted with hunger, pain, and danger. Yet he was able to face his unfriendly environment with his head high, with a constant song of thanksgiving on his lips, and with the pronouncement, "I have learned, in whatsoever state I am, therewith to be content." Such an attitude is no ordinary accomplishment.

It is said that George V of England was once asked to write an inscription on the flyleaf of a Bible, and these were the words that he penned: "The secret of finding happiness is not to do what you like to do, but to learn to like what you have to do." The story is told of a physician who spent most of his adult life adjusting to tuberculosis. After many frustrating years he wrote, "To cease to rebel, to stop fighting back, to be content with half a loaf when you cannot have a whole one—these are hard lessons but all of us must learn them. I have found that the great word is Acquiescence."—J. G. GILKEY, *When Life Gets Hard,* p. 78.

Paul tells us that it is not only necessary to know how to be abased; one must also know how to abound. Some people wilt under adversity; others cannot stand prosperity. The wedding vow reads, "In prosperity and in adversity . . ." We must learn to adjust to both and be defeated by neither.

11   321

THE MINISTER'S REWARD

What is our hope, or joy, or crown of rejoicing? Are not even ye in the presence of our Lord Jesus Christ at his coming? For ye are our glory and joy. 1 Thess. 2:19, 20.

Someone has said that the ministry is a miserable profession but a great calling. Paul certainly learned this through experience. Life held constant sorrow, pain, and trouble for him; but all of these tribulations were overshadowed by his joy in watching his converts grow up into Christ. Favorable reports regarding the spiritual prosperity of his people filled Paul with great happiness. On the other hand, troubles in the churches caused him great suffering.

Paul identified himself with his people, and in so doing he became the great example for Christian pastors. In the third chapter of 1 Thessalonians he says, "For now we live, if ye stand fast in the Lord" (verse 8). This is the spirit of the true shepherd of the flock.

"His patient kindness in dealing with his churches is one of the most beautiful phenomena which the New Testament has to show. He looked upon his converts as his children. All of them belonged to him. Timothy was his son, and so also was Titus, and so also was the poor slave Onesimus. All the men were his brothers and all the women were his sisters, and he, because of his age and spiritual knowledge, was a father to them all. . . . No matter how obstreperous and exasperating his converts were, he meekly continued his work. He makes his thoughts comprehensible to pagan minds, he makes his doctrines credible to Jewish minds, he softens the prejudices of the bigoted, and shows the emptiness of popular superstitions, he allays unreasonable fears, and inspires flagging hopes, he respects foolish scruples, and administers strength to the faint-hearted, he tones down the conceited, and holds in check the autocratic, and works day and night to rescue those who because of their ancestry and inherited dispositions and habits, keep slipping back into the sins of the world around them."—CHARLES EDWARD JEFFERSON, *The Character of Paul*, pp. 225, 226.

Paul's attitude is relevant for the layman, as well as the ministry. Such a spirit would bring a wonderful unity into the church.

"NEVER STOP PRAYING"

Pray without ceasing. 1 Thess. 5:17.

Obviously this admonition does not mean that a person should spend all of his time in prayer. It has been well said that he who does nothing but pray will soon cease to pray. The message of this text is that we should never discontinue the practice of prayer. What are some things that may cause us to cease praying?

Sometimes we neglect prayer because we become preoccupied with other duties and activities. When the day's work is done there is no time or energy left for God. Fatigue brings indifference and unconcern.

In other instances we cease to pray because our prayers do not seem to get off the ground. God seems far away, and our prayers seem monotonous and superficial. We have lost our sensitivity for the presence of God because "the world has been too much with us." Like the ancient mariner in Coleridge's poem:

> "I looked to heaven, and tried to pray;
> But or ever a prayer had gushed,
> A wicked whisper came, and made
> My heart as dry as dust."

Again, we cease praying because our hearts are filled with doubt. We question the love of God, the reliability of the Scriptures, eternal life, divine guidance. One after another, we forsake the foundations of Christian faith, and soon we have no one to whom we can pray.

"The darkness of the evil one incloses those who neglect to pray. The whispered temptations of the enemy entice them to sin; and it is all because they do not make use of the privileges that God has given them in the divine appointment of prayer. Why should the sons and daughters of God be reluctant to pray, when prayer is the key in the hand of faith to unlock heaven's storehouse, where are treasured the boundless resources of Omnipotence?"—*Steps to Christ,* pp. 94, 95.

"Never stop praying" is another way of translating this text (Phillips). We must not stop praying if we are to be successful Christians.

323

PAUL'S ATTITUDE OF THANKSGIVING

In every thing give thanks: for this is the will of God in Christ Jesus concerning you. 1 Thess. 5:18.

Someone has said, "An ungrateful man is like a hog eating acorns under a tree but never looking up to see where they come from." Surely this could never be said about Paul!

One of the most impressive characteristics of the apostle Paul was his thankfulness under all circumstances. On the deck of a storm-battered ship, Paul called the crew and the prisoners together, and "he took bread, and gave thanks to God in presence of them all" (Acts 27:35). Some Christians met Paul on the Appian Way, on the final lap of his journey to Rome, "whom when Paul saw, he thanked God, and took courage" (Acts 28:15).

Time and again he thanked God for the Christian believers. Even to the church at Corinth—a quarrelsome, unregenerate crowd—he wrote, "I thank my God always on your behalf, for the grace of God which is given you by Christ Jesus" (1 Cor. 1:4). To the church at Rome he wrote, "I thank my God through Jesus Christ for you all, that your faith is spoken of throughout the whole world" (Rom. 1:8). To individual Christians he expressed thankfulness, as in Romans 16:3, 4: "Greet Priscilla and Aquila my helpers in Christ Jesus: who have for my life laid down their own necks: unto whom not only I give thanks, but also all the churches of the Gentiles."

Four times in the Corinthian letters he exclaims, "Thanks be to God!" The first is in 1 Corinthians 15:57: "Thanks be to God, which giveth us the victory through our Lord Jesus Christ." The second is in 2 Corinthians 2:14: "Thanks be unto God, which always causeth us to triumph in Christ." The third is in 2 Corinthians 8:16: "Thanks be to God, which put the same earnest care into the heart of Titus for you." And, finally, 2 Corinthians 9:15: "Thanks be unto God for his unspeakable gift."

Of Paul one author says, "The beauty of his gratitude is timeless, and to the last syllable of recorded time, men will come to him to hear the music of a thankful heart."—CHARLES EDWARD JEFFERSON, *The Character of Paul,* p. 262.

WEAK LOYALTIES

Therefore, brethren, stand fast, and hold the traditions which ye have been taught. 2 Thess. 2:15.

"A while ago there was somehow smuggled out of Red China a confidential document. It was a copy of the report a Chinese communist intelligence officer made on a group of captured American soldiers. This is what his report said [of the American soldier]: 'He has weak loyalties to his family, his community, his country, his religion, and his fellow soldier. His concept of right and wrong is hazy. He is basically materialistic, and he is an opportunist. He is ignorant of social values. There is little or no understanding, even among university graduates, of United States political history and philosophy; of freedom's safeguards and how they operate.' "—GORDON W. MATTICE, "Why Stick to Moses?" *Sermon Builder,* May, 1968.

This report, if authentic, certainly does not apply to all American servicemen but it does, no doubt, describe the viewpoint of many. It reflects a certain lack of conviction and loyalty that afflicts a large segment of society, and when a person discards convictions, loyalties, and commitments, he loses basic elements of manhood.

"He has weak loyalties to his family." Family solidarity is a sign of emotional maturity. A real man never forgets his father and mother, and loves his wife and children so much that he will be loyal to them although he is on the other side of the world from them.

"He has weak loyalties to . . . his community, his country, . . . his fellow soldier." The sense of belonging brings meaning to life. Patriotism reflects appreciation for the blessings of citizenship.

"He has weak loyalties . . . to his religion." Even a Communist despises a man who pretends to have a religion but does not take it seriously. To suffer for one's religion seems strange to the modern generation. Religion is considered an optional accessory.

Much of the weakness sensed by the Communist critics has resulted from an effort on the part of young people to discard the traditions they have been taught. Family solidarity, patriotism, religion, are considered old-fashioned. Paul's counsel is vital to our survival.

325

A VOICE FROM A DUNGEON

For the which cause I also suffer these things: nevertheless I am not ashamed: for I know whom I have believed, and am persuaded that he is able to keep that which I have committed unto him against that day. 2 Tim. 1:12.

There are some experiences in life that stir one's soul—to see one's own flag in a strange land; to watch a happy couple march down the aisle of the church; to listen to "Pomp and Circumstance" at a commencement; to see new Christians baptized; to participate in the worship of God. I am sure you can think of other thrilling experiences.

As a Christian it stirs me to the depths to visualize Paul in the Mamertine prison in Rome, or one like it. Awaiting execution, he was able to compose words like our text, words that have rolled across the ages like a continuing peal of thunder.

"I know whom I have believed," he said. Literally, "I know Him whom I have been trusting." How did he know his Lord? He remembered the confrontation on the Damascus road; he remembered the many times when Christ had revealed Himself to him; he remembered the results of his life of evangelism.

"And am persuaded that he is able to keep that which I have committed unto him," he continued. The Greek text of Paul's statement can validly be translated, "He is able to guard that which he has committed unto me." Paul is speaking of the gospel, and expressing his assurance that, come what may, God will protect His gospel. Paul expected to die soon, but he didn't expect the gospel to die with him.

Finally, he concludes with the wonderful phrase, "until that day." Look at the sweep of this text. First he looks backward—"whom I *have* believed"; then he states his present conviction, "I *am* persuaded"; finally he peers into the future, "until *that* day." Paul's was no narrow, existential faith, ignoring the past, and uncertain of the future. His theology embraced past, present, and future.

Regarding Paul, Chrysostom said, "Three cubits in stature, he touched the sky." Never was he taller than when he wrote this marvelous text! It has brought courage and hope to millions.

"FAITH AND . . ."

And the grace of our Lord was exceeding abundant with faith and love which is in Christ Jesus. 1 Tim. 1:14.

This is the first of a series of unique statements found only in Paul's letter to Timothy. They have been termed the "Faith and . . ." texts. In each case, faith is connected with some other Christian virtue.

In the first instance it is "faith and love." As Paul pointed out in 1 Corinthians 13, faith is inadequate without love. Here, in his letter to the young pastor at Ephesus, he repeats this emphasis.

In the nineteenth verse of the same chapter Paul says, "holding faith, and a good conscience." In order for a person to enjoy a "good conscience" his conduct must be acceptable. He must accept his responsibility to honor God in word and act, and to shoulder his duty as a man among men. This, also, adds a vital ingredient to faith. Real faith results in the kind of life that develops a good conscience.

In 1 Timothy 2:7 the apostle uses the expression, "faith and truth" (R.S.V.). To believe implies something worthy of being believed. The Christian faith consists of revealed truth about God, about Christ, and about man. This truth is attested to by evidence, and can be grasped by man's mind. Faith develops and grows as man considers God's revelations of Himself.

Chapter four, verse six, presents another combination: "faith and . . . good doctrine." Doctrine means teaching. This expression confronts us with the idea that faith is complemented by sound teaching, by communication of Christian truth in propositions that can be grasped and remembered. For example, Jesus said, "I will come again." This is good doctrine, and has echoed through the ages with authority and hope.

Paul was a great teacher of faith; but he recognized that faith needs love, a good conscience, truth, and good doctrine. None of these things take the place of faith—they make it more meaningful. Is it not appropriate that these "faith and" texts were written to a pastor? Dealing as he was with a church, Timothy could recognize the need of all of these virtues.

MAINTAINING RESPECT

He must have a good report of them which are without.
1 Tim. 3:7.

This text refers particularly to church leaders, but it applies to all Christians. It is right and proper that all who profess Jesus Christ as Lord should be respected by those outside the church.

Inasmuch as the Christian is likely to be an object of prejudice because of his religion, he must be an unusually admirable person in order to overcome this initial handicap. Prejudice feeds on the weaknesses of its victim. If people can point out the inconsistencies of the professed Christian, they will take delight in doing so.

While traveling on the highway, my wife and I stopped at a roadside restaurant. It was obvious that the proprietors were religious people. Free religious literature was available at several places in the restaurant. Gospel hymns were being played as background music. A card on each table suggested prayers before eating.

This display of religious symbols immediately placed the management of the restaurant on trial before every customer. The average person's response would be somewhat as follows: "Is this place clean?" "Is the food good?" "Is the service good?" Anything wrong with the restaurant would be interpreted as an indication of something wrong with the religion. In this case, the owners passed the test.

Our religion is judged by how well we do our ordinary work. A church is judged, not so much by the architecture of its building, as by the effectiveness of its professional men, the integrity of its businessmen, and the faithfulness of its ordinary laborers. Any observable flaw in these areas not only reflects on the person concerned but is interpreted by "them which are without" as a reason for rejecting the church.

After all, is it not logical that the world should expect Christians to be superior to the rank and file of men? Christianity talks about "salvation" and "conversion" and "sanctification." Its tradition places great emphasis on ethics, insisting that people should be honest, pure, and kind. This profession demands that the Christian order his life in such a way that no one can scornfully say, "See how he lives."

PAUL COMMENDS THE CHURCH

These things write I unto thee, hoping to come to thee shortly: but if I tarry long, that thou mayest know how thou oughtest to behave thyself in the house of God, which is the church of the living God, the pillar and ground of the truth. 1 Tim. 3:14, 15.

Writing to Timothy, Paul was concerned that the young preacher be able to conduct himself well as a pastor and leader of the church. He impressed the seriousness of this responsibility upon Timothy by reminding him that the church is not an ordinary institution, but "the church of the living God, the pillar and ground of the truth."

Paul recognized the importance of the church. His conception of Christianity always included a corporate body with its leaders, its services of worship, its traditions, its beliefs, and its activities. While man is saved as an individual, he serves and worships God as a member of a body comparable to the human body insofar as the interrelation of its members is concerned.

"A little girl who had recently moved to a new city became lost in a holiday crowd. A policeman found her crying on the street corner. She told him her name but did not know where she lived. Since her father had been in the city such a short time, his name was not in the telephone book or city directory. The policeman was baffled; but as he talked with the child, she said, 'If I could find the church, I would know my way home.' He inquired about the appearance of the church, knew at once which one she meant, and took her there. She stood on the steps, pointed down the street, and said, 'This is the way.' Soon she was home."—WALKER DUDLEY CALVERT, *Remember Now,* p. 51.

From Timothy's day until now the church, at its best, is like that. As "the pillar and ground of the truth," it shows people their way home. Its worship puts them in touch with God, and its work keeps them in contact with their fellow men. Its doctrines interpret life's meaning and give a foundation for hope. Its great men and women reveal that the church's gospel can remake and inspire men.

The church has its weaknesses, but it is still "the church of the living God."

THE MYSTERY OF GODLINESS

Without controversy great is the mystery of godliness: God was manifest in the flesh, justified in the Spirit, seen of angels, preached unto the Gentiles, believed on in the world, received up into glory. 1 Tim. 3:16.

Many scholars believe that the latter part of this verse was a hymn sung by the early Christians, and some modern speech translations arrange it in metric form. Today's English Version renders it thus:

"He appeared in human form,
    Was shown to be right by the Spirit,
    And was seen by angels.

"He was preached among the nations,
    Was believed in the world,
    And was taken up to heaven."

If one had been present at a Christian worship service in the first century, it is altogether possible that he might have heard the congregation sing this hymn.

Note that the object of praise was Jesus. The name "Jesus" is the implied subject of each of the six lines of the poem. First, they sang of His incarnation. They knew about the mystery of Nazareth and Bethlehem, and they believed that their Lord was God in human flesh. Theirs was no merely human Christ.

Second, they sang of His vindication. The Spirit of God even spoke to the heart of the centurion who nailed Jesus to the cross and inspired him to say, "Truly this was the Son of God."

Third, He was seen of angels. They ministered to Him in the desert and in the Garden of Gethsemane. They saw Him leave the tomb, and they were there when He ascended to heaven.

Next, His followers spread His message to the world, and millions accepted it. They were fascinated by the story of a Saviour who died, was resurrected, and had been taken back to heaven. Here was a leader who had love, life, and power. They would follow Him. They had caught a glimpse of the mystery of godliness.

A CHALLENGE TO YOUNG AND OLD

Let no man despise thy youth; but be thou an example of the believers, in word, in conversation, in charity, in spirit, in faith, in purity. 1 Tim. 4:12.

The Phillips translation of this familiar text says, "Don't let people look down on you because you are young; see that they look up to you because you are an example to them in your speech and behavior, in your love and faith and sincerity." Writing to Timothy, a young minister, Paul did not endeavor to smother his youthful zeal, but he appealed to him to merit the respect of those who were more mature. Paul did more than this; he implied that those who are older should not "look down" on young people who are earnestly seeking to excel.

So this is not only a challenge to young people, but to older people as well. The resources of youth should be respected, both by youth themselves and by their elders.

"Let not young souls be smothered out before
They do quaint deeds and fully flaunt their pride.
It is the world's one crime, its babes grow dull,
Its poor are ox-like, limp and leaden-eyed;
Not that they starve, but starve so dreamlessly;
Not that they sow, but that they seldom reap;
Not that they serve, but have no god to serve;
Not that they die, but that they die like sheep."

—*Selected*

The struggle between youth and age in today's world reminds us constantly that both sides need to do some clear thinking. It is well for every youth to remember that he will one day be old, and for every older person to remember that he once was young. For every hotheaded youth who says, "Never trust anyone *over* thirty" there is a coldhearted adult who replies, "Never trust anyone *under* thirty." Both are wrong. Only in the atmosphere of mutual trust can the heritage of the past be transferred to young hands. United, youth and age must work together to meet the needs of the world and to witness for the gospel of Christ.

331

RESPONSIBILITIES OF PROSPERITY

Charge them that are rich in this world, that they be not high-minded, nor trust in uncertain riches, but in the living God, who giveth us richly all things to enjoy; that they do good, that they be rich in good works, ready to distribute, willing to communicate; laying up in store for themselves a good foundation against the time to come, that they may lay hold on eternal life.
1 Tim. 6:17-19.

This passage can be understood best by noting its background. Paul was writing to Timothy, pastor of the church at Ephesus. Ephesus was one of the most influential churches in Asia, having been established by Paul during his more than two years in that city. Apparently this church had reached the place where some of its members were wealthy, a situation not common during the first century of Christianity.

With the growth of an affluent group in the church, came problems. There was a temptation to pride and self-sufficiency, and a tendency to forget that all good things come from God. Paul suggested that Timothy remind these well-to-do people that they should use their riches to bring happiness to others. In this way they would "store up for themselves a treasure which will be a solid foundation for the future" (T.E.V.).

This passage reveals how similar human nature is in all ages and cultures. The problems of prosperity are identical in the first century and the twentieth, and the solution to these problems is the same. The concept of stewardship makes a person's sense of responsibility to God increase as his wealth increases. Thus the inroads of pride and selfishness are effectively curbed.

In Jesus' time it was the poor widow who gave of her living, and the wealthy who contributed ostentatiously that which cost them little. Today it is largely the accumulated gifts of large numbers of ordinary people that support the work of God. True, there are people of wealth who heed Paul's advice and are "generous and ready to share with others" (T.E.V.), but too often affluence makes people less sensitive to human need.

PAUL EMPHASIZES ENDURANCE

Endure hardness, as a good soldier of Jesus Christ. 2 Tim. 2:3.

Soldiering was a rugged life in Paul's day. Travel was difficult, food and supplies were uncertain, and battles were savage encounters with swords and spears. Paul frequently refers to the rigors of the army as an example of the experience of Christians. At the close of his own life he said, "I have fought a good fight" (2 Tim. 4:7).

Does this mean that Paul felt it necessary and desirable that a Christian should be in constant conflict with his environment? In his first letter to Timothy he asked the church to pray for those in authority, "that we may lead a quiet and peaceable life in all godliness and honesty" (1 Tim. 2:2). Paul did not love fighting and hardship for their own sake. He loved peace and quiet, but if it became necessary to be a soldier for Christ, he was willing to do so. And he never complained about his lot.

The important consideration for the Christian is that he be where he belongs, regardless of whether it be a peaceful valley or a battlefield. "One of the well-known institutions of the city of Philadelphia is Leary's Bookstore on Ninth Street. It has been there many years. Right next to it is Gimbels' [*sic*] large store. Gimbels wanted the land on which Leary's stood, and offered a fabulous price a few years ago. Leary's Bookstore refused. Then Gimbels increased the offer greatly. Leary's still refused. Finally one of the men of Gimbels said to the owner of Leary's, 'You are crazy not to take this offer. You could be on Easy Street.' Leary's replied, "We don't want to be on Easy Street. We just want to stay on Ninth Street.' And they did."— HALFORD LUCCOCK, "What's Ahead for Religion?" *Christian Herald,* September, 1953, p. 150.

Most of us in the twentieth century know little about enduring for Christ. We live comfortably, we are not persecuted, our faith is seldom challenged. Life holds for us many privileges and opportunities. This is good, so long as we remain willing to "endure hardness" if conscience and duty demands. We must remain good soldiers, whether we have a plush assignment at home or are sent to the front lines of the battlefield.

THE THANKFUL APOSTLE

Giving thanks always for all things unto God and the Father in the name of our Lord Jesus Christ. Eph. 5:20.

Paul's spirit of thankfulness is evident in his letter. Over and over again he expressed his appreciation for his brethren and for the gospel. His heart overflowed with thanksgiving.

Several years ago a cartoon appeared in an American newspaper illustrating a significant truth regarding man's thankfulness. The cartoon was arranged on four levels: on the top level was depicted a plainly dressed couple sitting at a table in a poorly furnished house with meager and ordinary food on the table. The room was lighted by an open wick. Both heads were bowed. The second level of the cartoon pictured the couple, dressed in better clothes, with improved furnishings and more plentiful food in a room lighted by a candle. Their heads were partly bowed. In the third scene food was excellent, clothes and surroundings were cozy and comfortable. The room was lighted by a kerosene lamp. Only the woman's head was bowed. The final picture depicted luxury in every detail of life with blazing electric lights illuminating a table loaded with good things. Neither head was bowed.

Those who celebrated the first Thanksgiving Day in the United States seemingly had little to be thankful for. Their number had been decreased by disease and death; their crops were not plentiful; enemies surrounded them; and another hard winter lay ahead. Yet they joined in giving thanks to God for the blessings He had bestowed upon them.

A well-known song says, "Come, ye thankful people, come." Thankful people, like Paul, seem to be thankful under all circumstances, and unthankful people find something about which to grumble, despite all blessings. Thankfulness is a state of mind. "It is one of the miracles of the world, that the people to whom the least has been given, and upon whom the heaviest burdens have been rolled, are often the most appreciative of the richness of life, and most thankful to God for his goodness."—CHARLES EDWARD JEFFERSON, *The Character of Paul,* p. 264.

THE GENTLE TOUCH

The servant of the Lord must not strive; but be gentle unto all men, apt to teach, patient, in meekness instructing those that oppose themselves. 2 Tim. 2:24, 25.

Three words in this passage present different aspects of the idea of gentleness: the first, translated "gentle" is the word used by Greek writers as characterizing a nurse with trying children, or a teacher with uncooperative students, or the attitude of parents toward their children. The idea is kindness, love, gentleness. The second word is translated "patient." Literally, the original word means to "endure bad." One translator renders it, "putting up with what is bad." The word implies forbearance and longsuffering. The third word is translated "meekness." It means a gentle condition of mind and heart, an inner grace of the soul. It does not suggest weakness, but strength.

This passage describes the Christian, not as a battler for truth, arguing with everyone who opposes; but as a teacher of truth, instructing his opponents with gentleness and patience. This was the spirit of Jesus. Regarding the Master, we read:

"His tender compassion fell with a touch of healing upon weary and troubled hearts. Even amid the turbulence of angry enemies He was surrounded with an atmosphere of peace. The beauty of His countenance, the loveliness of His character, above all, the love expressed in look and tone, drew to Him all who were not hardened in unbelief."—*The Desire of Ages,* p. 254.

Once there lived a man named George Fox. In a time of violence and corruption he decided that gentleness was the only answer to men's problems. At the age of twenty he went out to teach the ways of peace to a war-crazed world. He was arrested sixty times and spent much of his life in loathsome prisons. It is reported that at one time or another, fifteen thousand of his followers, known as Quakers, were in jail. A violent world resented an apostle of gentleness.

Today's world likewise considers gentleness as visionary and impractical. It is the privilege of the Christian to prove to a skeptical culture that the gentle touch actually has power.

335

"MASTERS OF THEIR OWN SOULS"

I am now ready to be offered, and the time of my departure is at hand. I have fought a good fight, I have finished my course, I have kept the faith. 2 Tim. 4:6, 7.

Not often does a man in a dungeon facing death by beheading speak with such calmness and self-possession. In Paul's entire final letter there is no hint of vindictiveness, no trace of hysteria, no evidence of fear. With complete trust he faces his future.

"A Christian of the third century, in a letter to his friend Donatus, gives a remarkable testimony to the influence which the gospel of Christ exerted upon the lives of men in that day. Here are his words:

"'If I should ascend some high mountain, you know what I would see—armies fighting, brigands on the highways, pirates on the seas, men murdered in the amphitheater to please the applauding multitudes. But in the midst of this I have found a quiet and holy people. They are persecuted, but they care not. They have found a joy a thousand times greater than any pleasure. These people are the masters of their own souls. They are the Christians, and I am one of them.'"—WALTER DUDLEY CAVERT, *Remember Now*, pp. 22, 23.

Why could it be said that these early Christians were "masters of their own souls"? Where did they find inner fortitude adequate for all situations? The answer was not in themselves, but in the Christ whom they served. Paul expressed it well: "I can do all things through Christ which strengtheneth me" (Phil. 4:13). In this text the word translated "strengtheneth" literally means "to make powerful inwardly." It was the energizing influence of Jesus that made the early Christians "masters of their own souls."

There is a strong modern tendency to consider man the victim of his genes and his environment. Deviant behavior of all sorts is excused because of the person's inheritance and surroundings. This philosophy gives little encouragement to the development of men who will master themselves. But real faith in Christ adds a new dimension to life. No longer is man a helpless victim of circumstances. Through Christ he finds a power to master circumstances.

ALONE BEFORE NERO

At my first answer no man stood with me, but all men forsook me; I pray God that it not be laid to their charge. Nothwithstanding the Lord stood with me, and strengthened me; that by me the preaching might be fully known, and that all the Gentiles might hear; and I was delivered out of the mouth of the lion. 2 Tim. 4:16, 17.

"Among the Greeks and Romans it was customary to allow an accused person the privilege of employing an advocate to plead in his behalf before courts of justice. By force of argument, by impassioned eloquence, or by entreaties, prayers, and tears, such an advocate often secured a decision in favor of the prisoner, or failing in this, succeeded in mitigating the severity of the sentence. But when Paul was summoned before Nero, no man ventured to act as his counsel or advocate; no friend was at hand even to preserve a record of the charges brought against him, or of the arguments that he urged in his own defense. Among the Christians at Rome there was not one who came forward to stand by him in that trying hour."— *The Acts of the Apostles,* pp. 492, 493.

This was neither the first nor the last time a good man was forsaken by all of his friends in his hour of extreme need. It is easy to champion a cause that seems to be winning; it is not hard to defend a cause that seems to have a fighting chance; but friends are few when things seem hopeless.

However, Paul did not crumple under the stress of the unequal conflict. He preached such an eloquent sermon in his own defense that even Nero was impressed. "He feared the apostle's God, and he dared not pass sentence upon Paul, against whom no accusation had been sustained. A sense of awe restrained for a time his bloodthirsty spirit."—*Ibid.,* p. 496.

Instead of sentencing Paul to death, Nero sent him back to his dungeon. A temporary victory had been won; Paul had given his testimony again before the Gentiles; and he had time to write another immortal letter, his second Epistle to Timothy. He had been "delivered out of the mouth of the lion."

A PECULIAR PEOPLE

Who gave himself for us, that he might redeem us from all iniquity, and purify unto himself a peculiar people, zealous of good works. Titus 2:14.

Titus was in charge of the church in Crete, an island in the Mediterranean Sea. Crete was not a good place for the development of a Christian church. The culture there was decadent, as Paul himself pointed out: "One of them, yes, one of their prophets, has said: 'Men of Crete are always liars, evil and beastly, lazy and greedy.' There is truth in this testimonial of theirs!" (Titus 1:12, 13, Phillips). It became Paul's task, with the help of the Holy Spirit, to make liars into truthful men, beastly people gentle, lazy people industrious, and greedy people generous.

Paul reveals how this miracle was to be accomplished. Of Jesus Paul says, "He gave himself for us, that he might rescue us from all our evil ways and make for himself a people of his own, clean and pure, with our hearts set upon living a life that is good" (Phillips). The sacrifice of Jesus made possible the transformation of the Cretans into clean, pure people who were determined to live Christian lives.

The expression "a peculiar people" in our passage is better translated "a people of [God's] own" (Phillips), or "marked out for his own" (N.E.B.). The Greek word translated "peculiar" does not imply a queer people, but a selected people, a people with a destiny.

One of the often mentioned problems of people today is loss of identity. Many find themselves with no sense of belonging, no meaningful experience of loving or being loved, and no purpose to live for. The loss of identity causes depression, which the victim may try to remedy by drugs, pleasure, or suicide.

The Christian who really understands his faith has no identity problem. He has been marked out by a God who loves him, who guides him in his daily life, and who will eventually grant him eternal life. Feeling this sense of destiny, he is motivated to be "zealous of good works." He rises above the level of the culture of which he is a part because he has reasons for living and striving that the non-Christian cannot understand.

THE LIMITS OF FREEDOM

This is a faithful saying, and these things I will that thou affirm constantly, that they which have believed in God might be careful to maintain good works. These things are good and profitable unto men. Titus 3:8.

What is the "faithful saying" to which Paul refers? The answer to this question is found in the preceding verses, which emphasize the grace and mercy of God as the source of man's salvation. Verse 5 says, "Not by works of righteousness which we have done, but according to his mercy he saved us," and verse 7 continues, "That being justified by his grace, we should be made heirs according to the hope of eternal life." In the writings of Paul salvation always comes from God.

But, with his usual insight Paul recognizes that those who are recipients of God's grace have a responsibility—"to maintain good works." Grace does not excuse them from living the kind of lives of which God approves. In fact, belief in God *results* in a life of profitable and well-directed effort.

This great truth reminds us that there can be no such thing as complete freedom. No one who has a job is free. No one who has a country is free. No one who has a home is free. Likewise, no one who serves God is free. But this does not bring unhappiness.

Imagine a mother who gives many hours each day to the care of her infant child. She can no longer go and come as she pleases. Her life is built around the needs and demands of her baby. One day the child dies. Is the mother happy to regain her freedom? Not if she really loved her child. She would give anything she possesses to have her liberty curtailed again by the presence of her child.

So it is in the realm of our relation to God. Being a Christian restricts our freedom to think and do as we please. But these restrictions are a small price to pay for the security, the hope, the love, the meaning, that God brings into our lives.

What kind of God would expect nothing of the beings He had created? God would not be God if He did not look for loyalty, faithfulness, love, and responsibility in His children.

PAUL URGES CHRISTIANS TO WORK

Let our's also learn to maintain good works for necessary uses, that they be not unfruitful. Titus 3:14.

The message of this passage is often missed because of the way in which it is translated. *The New English Bible* makes it clearer: "Our own people must be taught to engage in honest employment to produce the necessities of life; they must not be unproductive." The significance of the statement becomes clearer when we note that Paul is writing to Titus, who was in charge of the church on the island of Crete, and that Paul had already quoted a Cretan writer as having referred to the people of that country as "lazy gluttons" (Titus 1:12, N.E.B.). In an environment where people were not industrious Paul urges Christians to work hard.

Channing Pollock has said, "The unhappiest people I know are the idle people. I've seen them all over the world, chasing sunshine and currying favor with head waiters. I have seen them at home, and at Algiers, and Palm Beach, and along the Riviera, planning silly little social diversions, worried sick over some fancied slight, petting their palates and stocking their wardrobes, trading scandals, nursing imaginary ills, going in for the pleasures of childhood or adultery, and bored stiff."—CHANNING POLLOCK, *The Adventures of a Happy Man* (2d. ed.), p. 67.

Paul presents this ideal in a practical context: "Our people must be *taught* to engage in honest employment." If this has not been their pattern of life, *teach* them, Paul insists. In modern times, when much is being said about poverty, the following counsel is in harmony with Paul's advice: "Families live in hovels, with scant furniture and clothing, without tools, without books, destitute both of comforts and conveniences and of means of culture. . . . These people must be educated from the very foundation."—*The Ministry of Healing,* p. 192.

Labor is not the solution to all of the world's problems, but an appreciation of the dignity of work would greatly help to stabilize society.

THE GOSPEL CHANGES MEN

I beseech thee for my son Onesimus, whom I have begotten in my bonds: which in time past was to thee unprofitable, but now profitable to thee and to me. Philemon 10, 11.

Paul is writing to Philemon, a substantial member of the church at Colosse, regarding Onesimus, a slave of Philemon who had stolen his master's goods and escaped to Rome. While at Rome, Onesimus somehow got in touch with Paul. "In the kindness of his heart, Paul sought to relieve the poverty and distress of the wretched fugitive, and then endeavored to shed the light of truth into his darkened mind. Onesimus listened to the words of life, confessed his sins, and was converted to the faith of Christ."—*The Acts of the Apostles,* p. 456.

When this change took place, Onesimus was partly free. He had a new loyalty, new enthusiasm, and a new hope for the future. But there was also a new conflict in his soul. What about Philemon? What about the money he had stolen? It was easy to rationalize that Philemon had plenty of money and slaves, and that Paul needed him. It was also easy for him to speculate on what might happen if he returned.

Onesimus sought counsel from Paul, and Paul "counseled him to return without delay to Philemon, beg his forgiveness, and plan for the future" (*ibid.*). There was only one solution, so Onesimus made the long trip and faced his master. There is no record of what happened, but the very fact that the letter Paul sent to Philemon has been preserved would substantiate the tradition that Onesimus was forgiven and freed. In any case, he had a free conscience.

Of many lessons in the story, one of the most striking is that *God changes men.* He had changed Paul from a persecutor into a Christian. He had changed Philemon from a pagan into a lay leader of the church. He had changed Onesimus from a dishonest renegade into a faithful believer. The greatest evidence of change in all three of these men was the love that came into their hearts. Old prejudices, hostilities, and customs melted away. A new Christian regard for others changed their attitudes and relationships.

341

THE LIVING CHRIST

*Who being the brightness of his glory, and the express image
of his person, and upholding all things by the word of his power,
when he had by himself purged our sins, sat down on the right
hand of the Majesty on high.* Heb. 1:3.

"After he had made men clean from their sins, he sat down in
heaven at the right side of God" (T.E.V.). This is one of the most
overwhelming concepts to be found anywhere in the Bible. This passage describes, not only a Lord who solved the sin problem by His
incarnation, life, death, and resurrection, but a Lord who lives and
reigns with God. "The Son of God shines with the brightness of God's
glory; he is the exact likeness of God's own being, and holds up the
universe with his powerful word" (T.E.V.).

This tremendous truth is not taken as seriously as it should be.
A columnist tells of the visit to the United States of His Holiness
Maharishi Mahesh Yogi, a Hindu exponent of transcendental meditation, who at the time had won for himself a considerable following
in the Western world. The columnist reports a conversation with
the Maharishi: "His tactful reply to my question, 'How do you view
Jesus Christ, his death and his resurrection?' drew a hearty laugh
from the audience. 'With all admiration,' he said, and joined in the
laughter."—*Christianity Today,* June 7, 1968. One who shares the
glory of God and sustains the universe is entitled to more than "admiration"; yet there are many professed Christians whose reaction to
Christ is not much more profound than that of this Hindu philosopher.

Our passage stresses another truth characteristic of the Epistle to
the Hebrews. We must not confine our thinking regarding Jesus to
the past tense. He is a present reality. He *lives,* not just for those
who accept Him, but He is sustaining the universe with His powerful
word whether or not anyone accepts Him. If we recognize Him, He
lives. If we reject Him, He lives.

To John the revelator the same risen Christ said, "Don't be
afraid! I am the first and the last. I am the living one! I was dead,
but look, I am alive for ever and ever" (Rev. 1:17, 18, T.E.V.).

A living faith in the living Christ is the hope of Christianity.

CONTRARY WINDS

We ought to give the more earnest heed to the things which we have heard, lest at any time we should let them slip. Heb. 2:1.

This is the first in a series of warnings in the Epistle to the Hebrews. In Hebrews 1:1 we read that "God . . . *spake* in time past unto the fathers by the prophets." In verse 2 we learn that the same God "hath in these last days *spoken* unto us by his Son." What did God say through the prophets and through His Son? It was the message of salvation, of forgiveness of sins, of the love of God and the lordship of Christ—the message we call the gospel.

In view of what God had *said,* through the prophets and through His Son, the warning of our text takes on added meaning: "Therefore we ought to give the more earnest heed to the things which we have *heard.*" God has spoken—we ought to listen carefully. We should neither disregard nor forget what we have heard.

The peril of failing to respond to "the things we have heard" is made vivid by a figure of speech—"lest at any time we should let them slip." A more literal translation is, "lest we drift away from it" (R.S.V.). The picture is that of "a ship that a contrary wind causes to drift past its harbor so that it is prevented from reaching its destination. . . . A strong current or wind was threatening to make these Jewish Christians drift away from the harbor of 'salvation.'"— R. C. H. LENSKI, *Interpretation of Hebrews,* pp. 63, 64.

This figure of speech was especially apt in the days of sailing vessels, but the meaning is still clear. "Drifting" in this text does not picture a small boat lazily carried with the current toward the brink of a waterfall, or a craft bobbing about on the water, but a boat diverted from its destination by contrary winds.

How sobering this text! We have "heard" a message that has made our duty abundantly clear. We understand the issues and the final results. But there are constant counter-influences, or contrary winds, that tend to divert us from our course—materialism, secularism, selfishness, laziness, and many others. The warning of the text is not to allow these contrary winds to cause us to miss our destination.

OVERWHELMING EVIDENCE

How shall we escape, if we neglect so great salvation; which at the first began to be spoken by the Lord, and was confirmed unto us by them that heard him; God also bearing them witness, both with signs and wonders, and with divers miracles, and gifts of the Holy Ghost, according to his own will? Heb. 2:3, 4.

The Epistle to the Hebrews was probably written about thirty-five years after the crucifixion and resurrection of Jesus. With the passing of time, once-ardent followers of Jesus were drifting away. This trend may have been particularly prevalent among the Jews because of the extreme hostility of Judaism toward Christianity. It became necessary to warn these people of the peril of losing interest and confidence in the great message of salvation.

This message was originally "spoken by the Lord." The teachings of Jesus during His ministry were the sources of the gospel—His sermons, His parables, His interviews, His proverbs. This source of truth was incontrovertible. Nothing like it had ever happened in the history of the world. In these teachings Jesus explained God, Himself, His mission, His atonement, His church, His concern for the world; and these explanations were clear.

Our text goes a step further, "And was confirmed unto us by them that heard him." When the Epistle to the Hebrews was written, many who had heard Jesus in person were still alive. Some of the Gospels had been written. From these reliable, living, firsthand sources the Christians of the first century could receive confirmation regarding the message of Jesus.

But this was not all. The integrity and divine origin of the message regarding Jesus was further attested by miracles and gifts of the Holy Spirit. Those early Christians had seen their leaders delivered from prison, they had seen the sick healed, they had witnessed marvelous conversions. All of these manifestations of the Spirit of God were eloquent proof of the reliability of the gospel.

How shall *we* escape if *we* neglect so great salvation? We have even more convincing evidence than they.

344

JESUS IDENTIFIES WITH MAN

Verily he took not on him the nature of angels; but he took on him the seed of Abraham. Wherefore in all things it behooved him to be made like unto his brethren, that he might be a merciful and faithful high priest in things pertaining to God, to make reconciliation for the sins of the people. For in that he himself hath suffered being tempted, he is able to succour them that are tempted. Heb. 2:16-18.

The objective of the gospel is the forgiveness of sins and the salvation of the sinner. God determined to spare no effort to bring about this result. The Incarnation, according to this text, was part of the divine plan, prompted by the desire to provide a "merciful and faithful high priest . . . to make reconciliation for the sins of the people." Why was the Incarnation necessary to make such a reconciliation possible? Because the Reconciler must Himself suffer temptation in order to help the tempted.

This picture of God forever makes false the idea of a vengeful God seeking the punishment and destruction of His creatures. He revealed His matchless love by coming to this world in the person of Jesus to identify with man.

Parents are told to identify with their children. This requires thought and effort, but is not impossible because every parent was once a child. Teachers are advised to identify with their students. This, too, is sometimes difficult, but every teacher was once a student. But God had never been man. He had never felt the frustrations and weaknesses of humanity—until He became man.

As a result of this identification it is possible for us to approach God and say, "Lord, You know what I am going through. You not only made me, but You once lived here on earth. You can help me meet my problems." In response to such a prayer, an understanding God gives just the strength and insight needed to meet temptation.

God's love for us is more than sympathy—the ability to feel *for* us. He possesses what is often termed *empathy*—the ability to feel *with* us. This marvelous love gives us personal security and enables us to project this same love to others.

345

SOURCES OF DOUBT

Take heed, brethren, lest there be in you an evil heart of unbelief, in departing from the living God. Heb. 3:12.

This, the second of six warnings in the Epistle to the Hebrews, is against unbelief. In the earlier part of the chapter reference was made to the familiar story of the rebellion of the Hebrews during their forty years in the wilderness. Because of their unbelief an entire generation was denied the "rest" prepared for them in the Promised Land. After reminding his readers of this chapter in their history the author says, "Watch, brethren, lest perhaps there shall be in any one of *you* a wicked heart of unbelief in apostatizing from the living God" (author's translation).

This passage reveals three aspects of the problem confronting the Jewish Christian church. First, there was apostasy, at least the danger of apostasy. Feeling the pull of their old traditions, Christians were looking back to the religion in which they had been brought up. Second, this apostasy resulted from unbelief—literally, "nonfaith." They were in danger of renouncing their faith in Jesus as their Saviour, and depending on works and outworn traditions. Third, this lack of faith was accompanied by evil in the hearts of the apostates.

In all ages there have been apostates from the church—backsliders, they are often called. People leave their faith for a variety of reasons. Some are like the little girl who fell out of bed, and explained to her mother that she "must have gone to sleep too close to where she got in." Apostasy often results from lack of understanding, motivation, and experience on the part of the professed Christian.

But in many instances, apostasy results from "an evil heart of unbelief." It does not result from lack of information or from intellectual doubts, but is motivated by sin in the life, and known sin cannot coexist with Christian ideals. Impurity, dishonesty, and selfishness are the source of the doubts submitted as respectable reasons for apostasy. Many who blame the sins of others and intellectual doubts for their faithlessness would be more truthful if they were to admit that their unbelief is the result of "an evil heart."

CHRISTIAN SECURITY

We which have believed do enter into rest. Heb. 4:3.

The third and fourth chapters of the Epistle to the Hebrews have a great deal to say about "rest."

Chapter 3, verse 11, quotes Psalm 95:11: "Unto whom I sware in my wrath that they should not enter into my rest." This expresses God's reaction to the rebellion of Israel at Kadesh Barnea. The "rest" they were denied was a home in the Promised Land. In Hebrews 4, verse 1, the writer applies this lesson to Christians: "Let us therefore fear, lest, a promise being left us of entering into his rest, any of you should seem to come short of it." Here, "rest" is used to describe the blessings and security of the gospel. For centuries Israel had wandered in a wilderness of legal exactions and human tradition. The gospel of Christ promised them rest.

How could a Christian find this rest? Our text answers the question: "We which have *believed* do enter into rest." The way to salvation is faith. Accepting the provisions of God's grace guarantees spiritual security, here and hereafter. Included in this package are forgiveness of sins, ability to live the Christian life, and eventually eternal life.

Continuing the argument, Hebrews 4 presents the Sabbath of Creation as a symbol of this rest. On the Sabbath God rested from all of His works. "There remaineth therefore a rest to the people of God. For he that is entered into his rest, he also hath ceased from his own works, as God did from his." The conclusion: "Let us labour therefore to enter into that rest, lest any man fall after the same example of unbelief."

The lesson of these passages is moving. Ancient Israel did not receive the "rest" promised them, because they refused to believe. They never knew the security that comes from faith in God. Rather, they depended on works.

Augustine said, "Our heart is restless until it finds rest in Thee." Every Sabbath should speak to us of the complete security that comes as a result of faith.

347

HIDING FROM GOD

The word of God is quick, and powerful, and sharper than any twoedged sword, piercing even to the dividing asunder of soul and spirit, and of the joints and marrow, and is a discerner of the thoughts and intents of the heart. Neither is there any creature that is not manifest in his sight: but all things are naked and opened unto the eyes of him with whom we have to do. Heb. 4:12, 13.

The "word of God" in our text refers to God's message, His gospel, whether communicated through the Bible or in another way. This message "judges the desires and thoughts of men's hearts" (T.E.V.). Did you ever have the experience of finding yourself boiling with rage, and into your mind flashed a scripture—for example, "Vengeance is mine; I will repay, saith the Lord"? Or, did you ever find yourself challenged inwardly by the Beatitude, "Blessed are the pure in heart: for they shall see God"? Or did the admonition, "Provide things honest in the sight of all men" ever cause you to consider an action? The "word of God" truly is living, and powerful, and sharp. It is God speaking to our consciences, trying to lead us in the way of right thinking and right living.

"There is nothing that can be hid from God. Everything in all creation is exposed and lies open before his eyes; and it is to him that we must all give account of ourselves" (T.E.V.). Parents and teachers have all dealt with children who, when questioned regarding their conduct, would carefully study their questioners and admit only that which they were quite sure was already known. We can't hide our misdeeds when standing at the judgment bar of God!

A keen sense of the omniscience of God is important in every life. I may be in a strange city where no one knows me—but God sees me. I may have thoughts that I have never shared with anyone, but God knows them in detail. I may fool my family, my colleagues, my pastor, my community, even myself, but I cannot fool God. So why try?

A transparent life, lived in honesty and forthrightness, with nothing to hide and no fears of disclosure, is the only life worth living.

THE AVAILABLE CHRIST

He is able also to save them to the uttermost that come unto God by him, seeing he ever liveth to make intercession for them. Heb. 7:25.

This is a glorious truth, filled with meaning and comfort for every believer. Do we feel weak and needy? Are we tempted and tried? Have we hopelessly tangled the threads of life? Do we stagger under a burden of guilt? The Hebrew Christians of New Testament times apparently had these experiences too. Accustomed as they were to a priesthood, Jesus was represented to them as a high priest, and it was said regarding Him:

"Seeing then that we have a great high priest, that is passed into the heavens, Jesus the Son of God, let us hold fast our profession. For we have not an high priest which cannot be touched with the feeling of our infirmities; but was in all points tempted like as we are, yet without sin. Let us therefore come boldly unto the throne of grace, that we may obtain mercy, and find grace to help in time of need" (Heb. 4:14-16).

Their Christ was more than a historic character who had walked across the world's stage. He was more than a longed-for Messiah to come. He was a *present, living* priest and king.

Jesus is no less available now than He was then. In the heavenly sanctuary, Jesus is shedding upon His disciples the benefits of His atonement (see *Early Writings,* p. 260). And because of these benefits, we have the assurance of acceptance with God, of sins forgiven, and of eventual immortality. "The intercession of Christ in man's behalf in the sanctuary above is as essential to the plan of salvation as was His death upon the cross. By His death He began that work which after His resurrection He ascended to complete in heaven."— *The Great Controversy,* p. 489.

In practical life this means that in time of temptation, sorrow, or disappointment we can call upon our Saviour for strength and He will respond immediately to our appeal, if it is made in faith. It means that failure need not defeat us, for there is forgiveness awaiting our sincere request for it.

349

WHAT IS JESUS DOING NOW?

We have such an high priest, who is set on the right hand of the throne of the Majesty in the heavens; a minister of the sanctuary, and of the true tabernacle, which the Lord pitched, and not man. Heb. 8:1, 2.

The Christian faith is built on the historic Jesus. His incarnation, His life and teachings, His death, resurrection, and ascension—these are the foundation stones of the Christian religion. Christianity also projects itself into the future. The coming of Jesus and eternal life are legitimate expectations for the follower of Christ.

But it is possible for any of us to become so identified with the past and future aspects of our faith that we forget the *now.* Our text helps us to remember that we *have* (present tense) a high priest who ministers in our behalf *today.*

What is the nature of Christ's ministry for us today? First of all, through the Holy Spirit He is our constant companion and guide. He hears our prayers and responds to our unexpressed desires. He gives meaning and purpose to our lives, often patching together the broken pieces that result from our folly and waywardness. He also forgives our sins—an important function of a priest. We can approach Him directly, without the need of an earthly mediator, and we can have His assurance that though our sins may be "red like crimson" they shall be washed "as white as snow." 1 John 2:1 says "we *have* an advocate." He is constantly making effective in our behalf the atonement He completed for us on the cross.

We can see why we are encouraged, "Let us therefore come boldly unto the throne of grace, that we may obtain mercy, and find grace to help in time of need" (Heb. 4:16). Jesus is in the business of dispensing grace and mercy *now,* and He has sufficient to meet every need. We are also reminded that "He *is* able also to save them to the uttermost that come unto God by him, seeing he ever *liveth* to make intercession for them" (Heb. 7:25).

"He lives" is the victorious shout of the Christian, from the resurrection morning on throughout eternity. This is the central theme of the Christian faith.

HAVE FAITH IN GOD

Without faith it is impossible to please him: for he that cometh to God must believe that he is, and that he is a rewarder of them that diligently seek him. Heb. 11:6.

Millions of people in our world today deny the existence of God as a personal Being. Some of these people, who consider themselves atheists, avow that modern man no longer needs God. Others, who classify themselves as agnostics, claim that they cannot know whether or not God exists. Still others call themselves Christians, insisting that they are followers of Christ, but deny the reality of the Father of whom Christ spoke so often.

But the Word of God insists that "anyone who comes to God must believe that he exists" (N.E.B.). Failure to recognize God has some very serious results, as J. B. Phillips points out:

"Since in the humanist view a man's life is entirely restricted to his consciousness of living on this planet, and since God is totally denied, a conscientious humanist renders himself impotent in many crucial situations. Thus, since there is no life beyond this one, humanism can offer no hope to those who are severely handicapped. Since there is no God, it can offer no external power to guide and strengthen a man who is defeated by his own emotional conflicts. Humanists are themselves prisoners of a closed-system and, since they believe in it so tenaciously, they have no gospel of any kind to offer to the weak and struggling, and can offer neither hope nor security beyond the ills and accidents of this present stage of existence."—*God Our Contemporary,* p. 21.

Such a viewpoint seriously impoverishes and disfigures human life. To the person who believes in God, life has purpose and meaning. He thinks in the larger context of eternity. It is not surprising if the unbeliever concludes, "Let us eat and drink; for to morrow we shall die."

Our text not only asks us to believe that God exists, but that He "rewards those who search for him" (N.E.B.). God is our Friend, our Father, our Hope. Let us learn to love Him with our whole heart, soul, and mind.

OUR DEBT TO THE SAINTS

Seeing we also are compassed about with so great a cloud of witnesses, let us lay aside every weight, and the sin which doth so easily beset us, and let us run with patience the race that is set before us. Heb. 12:1.

The "cloud of witnesses" mentioned in this text includes the men of faith mentioned in the previous chapter—Abel, Enoch, Noah, Abraham, Isaac, Jacob, Joseph, Moses, David, and many others. What do these saints say to us ordinary people who are striving to serve the same God they served so well?

"Remember that we stand today in a picture gallery, surrounded by the portraits of the saints. In that hushed and holy atmosphere we can almost hear them speaking to us, sternly at first, 'Are you really one of us?' they ask. 'Do you belong to our company, so that one day your portrait will hang here, or have you simply come to watch and admire?' We drop our heads in shame, at the same time wondering if these saintly characters, secure in their frames, know what a tough time we are having. They know right enough; they can read our thoughts. 'You didn't start this thing,' they tell us. 'You are only taking up the fight which has been going on for centuries, but do you in your day want to be responsible for the Christian warfare ending in defeat?' 'It is more difficult in our day,' we protest. 'More difficult?' retort the saints. 'You should get to know us better. We can tell you something about difficulty.' 'You are not real,' we protest. 'We are very real,' they reply."—LEONARD GRIFFITH, *God's Time and Ours,* p. 210.

This is the appeal of our text. In view of the faithfulness of those who have gone before, "let *us* lay aside every weight, and the sin which doth so easily beset *us,* and let *us* run with patience the race that is set before *us.*"

Einstein is quoted as having said, "Many times a day I realize how much my own inner and outer life are based upon the labours of my fellow-men, both living and dead, and how earnestly I must exert myself to give in return as much as I have received."—*Ibid.,* p. 207.

352

LONELINESS

I will never leave thee, nor forsake thee. Heb. 13:5.

This is one of the most valuable promises of the Bible because it fulfills one of man's greatest needs—the need of companionship.

Loneliness is a sad experience. It often occurs in a big city where there are thousands of people on every side. Loneliness is not the state of being isolated from people, but it is rather the depression that comes upon us when there is no one near who cares.

How often the tragedy has been re-enacted. A young man or woman leaves his childhood home, possibly in the country or a small town. In his new environment the patterns of life are different. Parents, relatives, and old friends are far away. Inhibitions break down. Loneliness results in the formation of unwise friendships and participation in unwholesome activities. Eventually the character that has been built over a period of years is shattered, or at least eroded. Sometimes early training checks the person in his downward course, sometimes not. His downfall results from his willingness to pay too great a price for companionship.

It is here that sound religious experiences come to grips with the problem. A lonely boy in Egypt was tempted by a beautiful woman. His response was, "How can I do this great wickedness and sin against God?" Regardless of geography, no one ever says good-by to God. The person who is sensitive to the presence of God and who knows how to talk to Him may still be lonely for human companionship but is not likely to allow his loneliness to cause him to seek companionship at any price.

One great remedy for loneliness is to take an interest in others. Someone has remarked that it is not often that you see a lonely doctor or a lonely minister. Participation in any kind of activity intended to help others is almost a sure cure for loneliness.

The experience of youth in a strange environment is not the only manifestation of loneliness. The aloneness of old age is another. When the ordinary experiences of life cease, and the rapidly moving world leaves the older person behind—here, again, the promise is especially precious, "I will never leave thee, nor forsake thee."

LEGALISTS

Faith, if it hath not works, is dead, being alone. James 2:17.

The Bible clearly teaches that men are saved by God's grace through faith. It is emphasized time and again that man is not saved by works. Why, then, does James place so great an emphasis on works? Apparently there were those in James's day who said, "We are saved by faith. We don't want to be legalists. We are not going to be concerned about works anymore." It was to meet this fallacy that James wrote his Epistle.

There are still some who have a false concept of legalism. If a person is careful about keeping the Sabbath, they call him a legalist. If he is careful about what he eats and drinks, he is a legalist. If he is careful about where he goes or what he reads, he is labeled a legalist. If he is particular about his tithe and offerings, he is a legalist. The same people, however, who express concern about legalism usually expect others to pay their debts—to them, at least—and they would hardly approve wholesale disregard of civil law.

There is an undesirable legalism. It may consist of adhering to the letter of a law, but violating the principle upon which the law is based. For example, a person who wouldn't think of stealing your purse might overcharge you in a business deal. That is legalism. Or a person may think he can be saved by adhering to a code of ethics. This is the sort of legalism Paul battled in his letters to the Romans and to the Galatians.

But being careful about observing the laws of one's country or one's God or the standards of one's church is not necessarily legalism. It is a wholesome acceptance of James's teaching that faith without works is dead. Faith in Christ will cause the Christian to want to be like his Master. This will result in an abundance of good works, not performed to secure merit, but as a by-product of the new birth.

It has often been observed how much the Epistle of James resembles the Sermon on the Mount. Jesus said, "Not every one that saith unto me, Lord, Lord, shall enter into the kingdom of heaven; but he that doeth the will of my Father which is in heaven" (Matt. 7:21).

PURITY

The wisdom that is from above is first pure. James 3:17.

This passage goes on to name several other characteristics of "the wisdom that is from above." It is said to be "peaceable, gentle, easy to be intreated, full of mercy and good fruits, without partiality, and without hypocrisy." But it is noteworthy that the wisdom to which James refers is *"first* pure."

This is a hard standard to maintain in today's world. The Biblical, Christian sanctions against loose living have been generally shorn of their authority, even by churchmen; and no effective check on the natural impulses of man has taken their place. One of the great enemies of morality has been the motion picture theater. Billy Graham quotes the editor of the Tulsa *Tribune:* " 'Can anyone deny that movies are dirtier than ever? But they don't call it dirt. They call it "realism." Why do we let them fool us? Why do we nod owlishly when they tell us that filth is merely a daring art form, that licentiousness is really social comment?' "—*World Aflame,* p. 19. An article in the entertainment section of the Riverside, California, *Press* for July 14, 1968, authored by a film critic of the *New York Times* News Service, makes the following candid observation: "It has always been one of the major functions of movies to arouse lust, and to educate young people in the manners and fantasies of romantic love."

The Christian who believes that "the wisdom that is from above is first pure" has a responsibility to protest any institution in his culture that militates against purity. He cannot condone filthy literature, the sex-obsessed products of Hollywood, pornography, the modern dance, extreme styles of dress, and other factors of contemporary life that encourage sensual thoughts and action.

The Christian must not only condemn that which is impure, but he must maintain high ideals regarding sex and marriage that are in harmony with the Scriptures. The integrity and meaningfulness of the Christian home must be protected, however loose the practices of the world may become. "The wisdom that is from above is first pure."

355

MORE THAN A MAN

Who, when he was reviled, reviled not again; when he suffered, he threatened not. 1 Peter 2:23.

Looking back across the years the aging Peter recalled vividly his Lord's patience and forbearance. Peter himself had learned these graces from Jesus, as have thousands of His followers.

Dr. Norman Vincent Peale tells the following story:

"The saintly Wesley one day was preaching in a downtrodden section of London. . . . Over at the edge of the crowd, two ruffians appeared. They said to one another: 'Who is this preacher? We'll show him. What right has he to come here, spoiling our fun?' They reached down and took a stone in each hand and belligerently elbowed their way through the crowd until they came within hailing distance of the preacher. Then they drew back their arms with the stones, ready to hurl them on his face, when as Wesley was talking about the power of Christ to change the lives of sinful men, a beauty spread over his face, that great old light never seen on land or sea, and transformed him with its effulgence. They stood transfixed, their arms poised in air. One turned to the other with a note of awe in his voice and said, 'He ain't a man, Bill; he ain't a man.' The stones fell from their hands onto the ground, and as Wesley spoke, their hearts were softened. Finally, when the sermon had been completed, the great preacher made his way through the crowd, which parted respectfully to permit him to pass. One of the ruffians very timidly reached out his hand to touch the hem of the preacher's garment and as he did so, the attention of Wesley was drawn to him and his companion. He put out his two hands and placed them on the heads of these two ruffians and said, 'God bless you, my boys,' and passed on, and as he did so, one ruffian turned to the other and said, with even more awe in his voice; 'He *is* a man, Bill; he *is* a man. He's a man like God.' "—*You Can Win* (1938 ed.), p. 72, 73.

The graces of patience and kindness still characterize Christians as more than men. These graces are particularly valuable in a world full of violence and hatred. They identify the Christian with his Lord.

OUR ADVOCATE

My little children, these things I write unto you, that ye sin not. And if any man sin, we have an advocate with the Father, Jesus Christ the righteous. 1 John 2:1.

There is scarcely a text in the Bible that we need to read more often than this one. We have come to take sin for granted, to assume that it is something like the common cold—a malady we cannot escape and must therefore accept. John would have us realize that sin is a serious matter, and that we should do everything in our power, and with God's help, to avoid it.

However, if John had stopped at this point Christians would have had valid reason for discouragement. Any well-balanced person is sufficiently cognizant of his own weaknesses and mistakes to know that there must be some provision for human weakness, and this provision is Christ.

This does not mean that we can sin with impunity and expect Christ to "fix" our continued violations of God's law. It does mean that "Jesus makes up for our unavoidable deficiencies."—Ellen G. White, Letter 17a, 1891. Jesus does not excuse our sins, but if we are sincere He forgives them.

In this passage, and in several instances in the Epistle to the Hebrews, Christ is spoken of as our advocate or mediator. For example, "Wherefore he is able also to save them to the uttermost that come unto God by him, seeing he ever liveth to make intercession for them" (Heb. 7:25). But if God loves man, why does Christ have to play the part of a mediator between man and God?

We are certainly not correct in picturing Christ as pleading with God to love and accept repentant sinners. "There is joy in heaven over one sinner that repenteth." Rather, we might imagine Christ saying to the Father, "What can we do to help this man?" All of the resources of heaven are available to guide the sinner into the ways of God.

Our Advocate is not trying to change the mind of a severe judge, but is utilizing the resources of the universe to ensure the eternal life of His clients. He is more than an advocate—He is our friend.

"WHAT DO PEOPLE DO WHEN THEY HAVE NO FAITH?"

This is the victory that overcometh the world, even our faith.
1 John 5:4.

" 'What do people do when they have no faith?' This question, or rather exclamation, came from one who was not known to me. She belonged to that large number who come and go in the congregations of a church situated in the heart of a city. . . .

"In brief, this was her story. . . . She came of a proud religious family. Married early in life, she had a number of years of idyllic happiness. Then one day she suddenly 'awoke to utter misery and despair.' Her husband had been caught in one of those strange infatuations in the heat of which honor, duty, self-respect, consideration, kindness, and thoughts of eternal life itself are withered. . . .

"After this shipwreck she took stock of what was left. 'I had two children, some experience in business, and, *thank God,* my faith.' Thus she began to rebuild her life, hiding her grief and conquering her bitterness, taking a useful place in the world and in the church and bringing up her family in the nurture and admonition of the Lord. She could not say she was happy in the former sense, but she was content. She had fought her way through to victory. Looking back over her own experience, she asked, 'What do people do when they have no faith?' "—CLARENCE E. MACARTNEY, *You Can Conquer,* pp. 56, 57.

What *do* people do when they have no faith? The alternatives to faith are several. The woman in this story might have given way to bitterness and despair, lashing out at Providence for her ill fortune. She might have broken down completely, making it necessary for someone else to bring up her children. She might have sought solace in drugs, or drink, or dissolute living. She might have surrendered to self-pity, making herself a burden to her associates.

All of these alternatives would have fallen far short of solving her problem. When she chose faith, she did not find an immediate remedy for her heartache, but she did find a way to make the best of a bad situation. Her faith made it possible for God to help her solve her problems.

LOVE GROWN COLD

I have somewhat against thee, because thou hast left thy first love. Rev. 2:4.

Sixty miles from John's island prison of Patmos was the city of Ephesus. John had spent many years pastoring the church Paul had established there. Now he had a message for it from his Lord.

"I know thy works, and thy labour, and thy patience," said Jesus, "and how thou canst not bear them which are evil: and thou hast tried them which say they are apostles, and are not, and hast found them liars: and hast borne, and hast patience, and for my name's sake hast laboured, and hast not fainted." Yes, Ephesus was a good church. The members worked hard. Their missionary reports were excellent and they always raised their goals. They had a welfare program, and they were constantly baptizing new members. The place was a beehive of activity.

Also, it was an enduring church. They met persecution and economic discrimination bravely. They bore up under religious prejudice. They were orthodox. They were rigid in their church discipline, and they hated heretics. What more could any pastor ask?

But something was wrong. "Thou hast left thy first love." They were like a husband and wife who continued to be faithful to each other but from whose experience all deep tenderness and affection had disappeared. As a legally successful marriage can be a failure, so an outwardly prosperous church can lack the main ingredient that every church should possess.

"At the first the experience of the church at Ephesus was marked with childlike simplicity and fervor. . . .

"But after a time the zeal of the believers began to wane, and their love for God and for one another grew less. Coldness crept into the church."—*The Acts of the Apostles,* pp. 578-580.

The future of the church today depends not on its work, not on its endurance, not on its orthodoxy. All these it will possess in abundance if it has the first requirement, *love.* This love will solve church problems, enhance the church's witness, and give meaning to its worship.

359

FAITHFUL UNTO DEATH

Fear none of those things which thou shalt suffer: behold, the devil shall cast some of you into prison, that ye may be tried; and ye shall have tribulation ten days: be thou faithful unto death, and I will give thee a crown of life. Rev. 2:10.

This was God's message, through John, to the church at Smyrna, a church that was suffering much persecution. God did not promise them that suffering would be removed—He said, "Fear none of those things which thou shalt suffer." Before them were imprisonment, torture, hunger, death; but they were to meet these horrors without fear, because God would be with them and ultimately grant them a crown of life.

In northern California are large groves of redwood trees, some of which are said to be among the oldest living things on earth. These mighty trees sometimes attain a diameter of more than thirty feet, and a height of more than three hundred feet. They seem so big and strong that nothing could affect them. But a strange thing has happened in recent years. Emphasis on fire prevention has resulted in keeping brush fires from burning out the thick underbrush. Flood control has kept the rivers from overflowing and depositing silt around the base of the trees. This protection, in some areas, is proving to have an adverse effect on the life and growth of the redwoods. Great trees that were healthy before they were protected from fires and floods are now dying.

This is a parable of what often happens to Christians. When the fires and floods of opposition and persecution are removed, the Christian may begin to lose his vitality. Ideally, the Christian should grow and thrive under peace and prosperity. Ideally, redwood trees should not need fires and floods. But in the real world of real people and real trees, it seems that hardships contribute to growth and vigor.

"Faithful unto death." This is a great Christian motto. Sometimes it is just as hard to remain kind, loving, and Christian until the angel of death takes us by the hand in old age, as to meet death for one's faith in the prime of life like the martyrs of old. To be faithful may not be dramatic, but faith must endure until the end.

"I KNOW WHERE YOU LIVE"

To the angel of the church in Pergamos write: These things saith he which hath the sharp sword with two edges; I know thy works, and where thou dwellest, even where Satan's seat is: and thou holdest fast my name, and hast not denied my faith. Rev. 2:12, 13.

Among the public buildings in Pergamos were temples dedicated to Athena and Demeter, and a massive altar to Zeus. Truly this city was a stronghold of paganism. But the Christian church in Pergamos had other problems than those connected with a pagan environment. Within the church were those who taught false doctrines that led to lawlessness and immorality. No wonder Pergamos was described as a place "where Satan's seat is."

To these Christians struggling with paganism without and apostasy within, Jesus said, "I know where you live" (N.E.B.). He was not unmindful of the problems of their environment.

Does our Lord know where we live? "He is not ignorant of the fact that the Christian Church is set in the non-Christian world, and that it feels on all sides the continuous pressure of heathen influence. Christians are constantly aware that the pagan neighbours who surround them have different ideas, a different religion, a different philosophy. Their little boat is being tossed about by the winds and waves of strange doctrines. Their fortress is bombarded by the gunfire of alien cults. They feel besieged, beleaguered."—JOHN R. W. STOTT, *What Christ Thinks of the Church*, p. 52.

If you find yourself working on a job where you are constantly nauseated by the obscenity and profanity that fills the air, remember —God knows where you live and He will give you grace to witness even in such surroundings.

If you are called upon to associate with people who repudiate faith and morals, disbelieve the Bible, and mock your concern for religion, remember again—God knows where you live.

Even in Pergamos, Christians served their God and survived. However unfriendly or unfavorable the environment, the Christian's inner resources will enable him to rise above his surroundings.

FALSE INTOLERANCE

I know thy works, and charity, and service, and faith, and thy patience, and thy works; and the last to be more than the first. **Rev. 2:19.**

Jesus is speaking through John to the church at Thyatira. What a wonderful church this must have been! They had works, love, faith, and patience; and they seemed to be getting better from year to year. One author compares Thyatira to "a beautiful garden in which the fairest Christian graces blossomed."—JOHN R. W. STOTT, *What Christ Thinks of the Church,* p. 69.

But in spite of all these wonderful virtues there was weakness in Thyatira. "Yet I have this against you: you tolerate that Jezebel, the woman who claims to be a prophetess, who by her teaching lures my servants into fornication and into eating food sacrificed to idols" (Rev. 2:20, N.E.B.). Their problem was too much tolerance. But is not tolerance a virtue?

Yes, tolerance is a virtue, within certain limits. It is praiseworthy to be tolerant of people whose opinions differ from ours and whose manner of life may vary from that to which we are accustomed. It is Christian to be tolerant of the weaknesses of others and to try to help them achieve success. Such tolerance is a sign of maturity.

But tolerance has its limits. The church at Thyatira was tolerating a character whom the text calls "Jezebel," a woman who claimed to be very religious but who was immoral and idolatrous. The leaders of the church should have faced the issue and expelled her.

The church at Ephesus would have taken care of this woman in short order, but Ephesus lacked love. Thyatira possessed love but tolerated this evil person. It is possible today for well-meaning Christians who have love for their fellow men to err in the direction of too little concern about evil. As unpleasant as it may be, there come times when a person and a church have to stand up and be counted. Wickedness cannot be ignored indefinitely.

How can we recognize the line between too much and too little tolerance? Human weakness pleads for tolerance; human depravity demands action. May God help us to tell the difference!

"COULD YOU SPARE FIVE MINUTES OF CHRISTMAS?"

"Now Christmas comes—solstice in the long year—a chiming of fleet hours; the verdant wreath adorns the snowy door of winter, and the evergreen bears unaccustomed fruit.

"It is the Day of days. For twenty-four blessed and embellished hours, the floodgates of affection and generosity are opened and the thoughts of men turn kind. For twenty-four hours, some special benison descends on fallow hearts. For eyes that will see, the sometimes gloomy landscape of the material world makes way for far horizons of the spirit, where all things are possible. For ears that will hear, there are voices that speak with the tongues of angels.

"Of all the gifts of Christmas, the gift of the very day—one thousand four hundred and forty minutes—is at once the most precious and most common. It is a gift bestowed on all—young and old, high and low, just and unjust, wise and foolish, ill and well—and the use we make of it may enrich us beyond dreams of avarice; or render us very poor indeed.

"Could you spare five minutes of Christmas to embrace its honest meaning? Could you spare five minutes to give a soft answer, turn the other cheek, do unto others as you would be done by? Could you spare five minutes to protect the weak, defend the persecuted, comfort those who mourn, and love your neighbor as yourself? Could you spare five minutes to feed the hungry, invite the stranger, cherish a child? Could you spare five minutes to tender mercy, give without hope of receiving, and forgive those who know not what they do? Could you spare five minutes to cast out fear, choose between good and evil, and let your light shine? Could you spare five minutes from one thousand four hundred and forty to take the glibness out of Peace on Earth, Good Will to Men?

"So now Christmas comes, and with it again the age-old opportunity to begin anew, to reach at least slightly beyond the confining boundaries of self, to emerge from concerns determined by greed and prejudice, to depart the cheerless abode of cynicism and disdain, to cease the aimless drifting toward paths of ease. Could you spare five minutes to care?"—Editorial, *McCall's,* December, 1960.

NOMINAL CHRISTIANS

I know thy works, that thou hast a name that thou livest, and are dead. Rev. 3:1.

A nominal Christian is a Christian in name only. Such was the problem at Sardis. The people in that church were known as Christians but they were gradually losing their Christianity, and God sent them this warning: "I know what you are doing; I know that you have the reputation of being alive, even though you are dead! So wake up, and strengthen what you still have, before it dies completely. For I find that what you have done is not yet perfect in the sight of my God. Remember, then, what you were taught and how you heard it; obey it, and change your ways. If you do not wake up, I will come upon you like a thief, and you will not even know the hour when I come. Rev. 3:1-3, T.E.V.

This warning comes to nominal Christians from the first century to the twentieth. What are the characteristics of such Christians?

"Now the correct word for this behaviour is hypocrisy. It is a Greek word in origin and meant literally to play a part on a stage, or to act in a drama. So hypocrisy is makebelieve, to assume a role which is not real. It is the 'let's pretend' of religion.

"And hypocrisy can permeate the whole life of a church. It can invade our worship. We can have a fine choir, an expensive organ, good music, great anthems and fine congregational singing. We can mouth hymns and psalms with unimpeachable elegance, while our mind wanders and our heart is far from God. We can have pomp and ceremony, colour and ritual, liturgical exactness and ecclesiastical splendour, and yet be offering a worship which is not perfect . . . in the sight of God."—JOHN R. W. STOTT, *What Christ Thinks of the Church,* pp. 87, 88.

The nominal Christian has no vital personal experience with Christ, he has no deep motivation to serve Christ, and he is satisfied with his condition. He wants to be a church member, and gives the church token support. He attends services when convenient, and often states that he "could never be anything else but" the particular brand of Christianity he accepts. But nominal Christianity will not save.

OPEN DOORS

I know thy works: behold, I have set before thee an open door, and no man can shut it; for thou hast a little strength, and hast kept my word, and hast not denied my name. **Rev. 3:8.**

What was the Lord saying to the church at Philadelphia in this passage? What did He mean by "an open door"? Was He not assuring the Philadelphians that great opportunities were before them, and no one could deprive them of these opportunities?

He goes on to explain the nature of these "open doors." First, He promised the Philadelphians that He would make "the synagogue of Satan"—their enemies—"to come and worship before thy feet and to know that I have loved thee." What an opportunity for service, what a vindication of the church, when their enemies become their admirers.

Then the Lord says to the Philadelphians, "I will also keep you from the ordeal that is soon to fall upon the world" (verse 10, N.E.B.). God is opening another door, a way of escape from the persecutions and troubles surrounding them. And, finally, the Lord promises the Philadelphians a home in the New Jerusalem with all of its privileges and blessings. This is the greatest door of all.

Why were such amazing promises given this church? They had kept His word, they had not denied His name, they had kept His "command and stood fast" (N.E.B.). God recognized the faithfulness of this church by giving them every imaginable incentive and reward.

In the sequence of the seven churches, Philadelphia is next to the last. To them the Lord says, "Behold, I come quickly: hold that fast which thou hast, that no man take thy crown" (verse 11). To a church living near the second advent of Jesus, the message to Philadelphia is particularly timely. We can learn from this message that the Lord of us all, who holds the key of our destiny in His hands, stands by an "open door" beckoning us to enter and live full, effective lives in this world, and to prepare for eternal life.

How tragic it would be for any of us to ignore this "open door" and go our own selfish way. Many doors stand open before us, but Christ stands by only one—the gateway to service and salvation.

URGENCY

I counsel thee to buy of me gold tried in the fire, that thou mayest be rich; and white raiment, that thou mayest be clothed, and that the shame of thy nakedness do not appear; and anoint thine eyes with eyesalve, that thou mayest see. Rev. 3:18.

The Laodiceans lived in a fertile valley traversed by important trade routes. Their city boasted a banking center, a thriving textile business, and a medical school where special attention was given to the cure of eye disease. The Christians there apparently succumbed to materialism, and were "lukewarm" about their religion.

To this church Christ spoke with severe warning. He reminded them that although their material assets were plentiful, their spiritual wealth was negligible. He said: "In fact, though you do not know it, you are the most pitiful wretch, poor, blind, and naked" (N.E.B.).

It is amazing how relevant this message is to the present time. For years prophetic interpreters have said that Laodicea represents the final church before the return of Christ. A contemporary writer comments as follows: "Perhaps none of the seven letters is more appropriate to the twentieth-century church than this. It describes vividly the respectable, sentimental, nominal, skin-deep religiosity which is so widespread among us today."—JOHN R. W. STOTT, *What Christ Thinks of the Church,* p. 116.

The city that boasted of its wealth was told to buy "gold tried in the fire"; the manufacturers of fine clothing were warned to purchase white raiment; the dispensers of ophthalmic ointment were asked to anoint their eyes with eyesalve that they might see. Ellen White explains the symbolism: Gold represents faith and love; white raiment refers to "purity of character, the righteousness of Christ"; and eyesalve describes the ability to discern between good and evil (*Testimonies,* vol. 4, p. 88).

We have all seen the painting of Jesus standing at the door, knocking. This picture is based on His message to the Laodiceans. It is not a gentle rapping at the door, but an urgent pounding. The church is in danger, and Jesus has come to rescue it.

"AND WORSHIP HIM"

I saw another angel fly in the midst of heaven, having the everlasting gospel to preach unto them that dwell on the earth, and to every nation, and kindred, and tongue, and people, saying with a loud voice, Fear God, and give glory to him; for the hour of his judgment is come: and worship him that made heaven, and earth, and the sea, and the fountains of waters. Rev. 14:6, 7.

The first angel's message is more than an announcement of the hour of judgment. It is a proclamation of the everlasting gospel, the good news of salvation through God's grace.

Do we really know what it means to worship? Often we go to services in the house of God with little sense of reverence and awe. We act as if we were in a common auditorium attending a secular gathering. As Ellen White said many years ago, "An enemy has been at work to destroy our faith in the sacredness of Christian worship." —*Testimonies,* vol. 5, p. 496.

Several years ago I visited Westminster Abbey. A printed sheet, prepared for visitors, contained the following suggestions:

"You are entering a famous church which contains the memorials of many generations of men. You cannot help being a 'sightseer' in such a place, and we welcome you.

"But, first and foremost, the Abbey is a House of God, where worship has been offered continuously for nearly 900 years. . . .

WE ASK YOU
as you walk around
to remember that you are on holy ground
to behave with reverence
to speak quietly
and do not forget to look up often
if you wish to see the glory of the Church."

Are we not well advised to "look up often" to see the glory of any church? "True reverence for God is inspired by a sense of His infinite greatness and a realization of His presence."—*Prophets and Kings,* p. 48.

ARE WE READY?

He which testifieth these things saith, Surely I come quickly.
Amen. Even so, come, Lord Jesus. Rev. 22:20.

This is the next to the last verse of the Bible. It presents a promise of Christ, "Surely I come quickly," and John's response, "Even so, come, Lord Jesus." Christ's promise represents the hope of the world. John's response should be the reaction of every Christian to the greatest fact of our time, the fact that Jesus is coming again. But we can only say, "Even so, come, Lord Jesus," if we are ready.

"When former President Eisenhower was vacationing in Denver a number of years ago, his attention was called to an open letter in a local newspaper, which told how six-year-old Paul Haley, dying of incurable cancer, had expressed a wish to see the President of the United States. Spontaneously . . . the President decided to grant the boy's request.

"So one Sunday morning in August, a big limousine pulled up outside the Haley home and out stepped the President. He walked up to the door and knocked.

"Mr. Donald Haley opened the door, wearing blue jeans, an old shirt, and a day's growth of beard. Behind him was his little son, Paul. Their amazement at finding President Eisenhower on their doorstep can be imagined.

" 'Paul,' said the President to the little boy, 'I understand you want to see me. Glad to see you.' Then he shook hands with the six-year-old, and took him out to see the presidential limousine, shook hands again and left.

"The Haleys and their neighbors, and a lot of other people, will probably talk about this kind and thoughtful deed of a busy President for a long time to come. Only one person was not entirely happy about it—that was Mr. Haley. He can never forget how he was dressed when he opened the door. 'Those jeans, the old shirt, the unshaven face—what a way to meet the President of the United States,' he said."—BILLY GRAHAM, *World Aflame*, pp. 206, 207.

Are we ready for a surprise visit, not from a President, but from the Lord Himself?

VALEDICTORY

The God of peace, that brought again from the dead our Lord Jesus, that great shepherd of the sheep, through the blood of the everlasting covenant, make you perfect in every good work to do his will, working in you that which is wellpleasing in his sight, through Jesus Christ; to whom be glory for ever and ever. Amen. Heb. 13:20, 21.

Another year has drawn to a close. Perhaps no more appropriate scripture could be suggested than these words that bring to a close the message of the Epistle to the Hebrews.

The God whom we serve and love is the God of peace, regardless of how much war and turmoil there may be in the world whenever and wherever these words are read. The most tranquil lives will be those that are dedicated to Him.

And always it must be remembered that God raised our Lord Jesus from the dead. This is the most important single fact of the Christian faith. We worship a risen Saviour.

And the Lord is our shepherd. He leads us beside still waters and through the valley of the shadow. His presence is ever near, and His concern for us never falters.

All of this was purchased for us at great cost—namely, "the blood of the everlasting covenant." Salvation is not cheap.

But the redeeming power of God has a very practical application. It is intended to "equip you thoroughly for the doing of his will!" (Phillips). The redeemed person is a changed person with new motives and new standards of life. His greatest ambition is that he may do the will of God.

The inspired apostle brings his valedictory to a close by wishing the greatest blessing any pastor could wish for his flock. "May he effect in you everything that pleases him through Jesus Christ, to whom be glory for ever and ever" (Phillips). Would that God could look upon each of us at the close of this year and say, "Everything pleases Me." Let us resolve that, through Christ, we will come nearer and nearer to the fulfillment of this dream. Here is a challenge for better days—and years—ahead.

Scripture Index

371

372

Acknowledgments

The following copyrighted works are quoted by permission of the authors and/or publishers.

Bonnell, John Sutherland. *The Practice and Power of Prayer*. Westminster Press, 1954.
————. *Fifth Avenue Sermons*. Harper & Row, Publishers, Incorporated, 1936.
Brown, Charles Reynolds. *Yale Talks*. Yale University Press.
Buttrick, George Arthur. *Jesus Came Preaching*. Charles Scribner's Sons, 1931.
Cavert, Walter Dudley. *Remember Now*. Whitmore & Stone (Abingdon Press), 1944.
Chappell, Clovis G. *The Cross Before Calvary*. Abingdon Press, 1960.
————. *The Sermon on the Mount*. Abingdon Press, 1930, renewal.
————. *Sermons on Biblical Characters*. Harper & Row, Publishers, Incorporated, 1922, 1950.
Davies, Horton. *Varieties of English Preaching, 1900-1960*. Prentice-Hall, Inc., Englewood Cliffs, N.J., 1963.
Ford, Leighton. *The Christian Persuader*. Harper & Row, Publishers, Incorporated, 1966.
Fosdick, Harry E. *The Meaning of Service*. Association Press, 1950.
————. *On Being a Real Person*. Harper & Row, Publishers, Incorporated, 1943, 1965.
————. *What Is Vital in Religion*. Harper & Row, Publishers, Incorporated, 1955.
Glover, T. R. *The Conflict of Religions in the Early Roman Empire*. Beacon Press, published as a Beacon Paperback in 1960.
Gordon, Samuel Dickey. *Quiet Talks on Personal Problems*. Fleming H. Revell Company.
Gossip, Arthur J. *The Hero in Thy Soul*. Charles Scribner's Sons, 1936.
Gross, Ronald (ed.). *The Teacher and the Taught*. Dell Publishing Co., Inc., n.d.
Graham, Janet. "The Power of Praise," *Christian Herald* (May, 1968), in *The Reader's Digest*, 1968. The Reader's Digest Association, Inc.
Griffith, Leonard. *God's Time and Ours*. Abingdon Press, 1965.
————. *The Eternal Legacy of the Upper Room*. Harper & Row, Publishers, Incorporated, 1964; Hodder & Staughton Limited, London, original publishers, 1963.
Kemp, Charles F. *Life Situation Preaching*, quoting Robert J. Macracken, *Questions People Ask*. Bethany Press, 1963.
————. *Life Situation Preaching*, quoting Jack Finegan, "Thank God and Take Courage." Bethany Press, 1963.
Kennedy, Gerald H. *Fresh Every Morning*. Harper & Row, Publishers, Incorporated, 1966.
————. "No Permanent Victory," in *The Pulpit* (July, 1946). Christian Century Foundation, 1946.
————. *With Singleness of Heart*, quoting Charles Fiske, "The Bishop's New Spectacles," in *The Atlantic Monthly* (Oct., 1928). The Atlantic Monthly Company.
Lenski, R. C. H. *Interpretation of the Epistle to the Hebrews and the Epistle of James*. Augsburg Publishing House, 1938, 1966.
Luccock, Robert E. (ed.). *Halford Luccock Treasury*. Abingdon Press, 1963.
Macartney, Clarence E. *Great Nights of the Bible*. Abingdon Press, 1943.
————. *The Greatest Texts of the Bible*. Abingdon Press, 1965.
————. *Macartney's Illustrations*. Whitmore & Stone, 1945 (Abingdon Press).
————. *You Can Conquer*. Pierce & Washabaugh, 1954 (Abingdon Press).

Newman, A. H. *Church History,* vol. 2. The Judson Press, n.d.
Packard, Vance. *Status Seekers.* New York: David McKay Company, Inc., 1959.
Peale, Norman Vincent. *The Power of Positive Thinking.* Prentice-Hall, Inc., 1954.
————. *Faith Is the Answer.* Abingdon Press, 1940.
————. *You Can Win.* Abingdon Press, 1938.
Pollock, Channing. *Christian Heritage* (May, 1968).
Rutledge, Archibald. *It Will Be Daybreak Soon.* Fleming H. Revell Company, 1938.
Shuler, Robert P. *What New Doctrine Is This?* Robert P. Shuler, Jr., 1946.
Sizoo, James. *Way of Faith.* Harper & Row, Publishers, Incorporated, 1935.
Sockman, Ralph W. *The Higher Happiness.* Pierce and Smith, 1950 (Abingdon Press)
Stewart, James S. *Heralds of God.* Charles Scribner's Sons, 1946.
Stott, John R. W. *What Christ Thinks of the Church.* William B. Eerdmans Publishing Company, 1958.
Trueblood, Elton. *The Predicament of Modern Man.* Harper & Row, Publishers, Incorporated, 1967.
Weatherhead, Leslie D. *Prescription for Anxiety.* Pierce & Washabaugh, 1956 (Abingdon Press).
————. *The Transforming Friendship.* Abingdon Press, n.d.
————. *The Significance of Silence.* Whitmore & Stone, 1945 (Abingdon Press).
————. *That Immortal Sea.* Abingdon Press, 1953.
————. *This Is the Victory.* Abingdon Press, 1941.
Whitesell, Faris D. *Great Expository Sermons,* quoting J. H. Jowett. Fleming H. Revell, 1964.
Williamson, Robert L. *Effective Public Prayer.* Broadman Press, 1960. *Christianity Today.* Interview between Carl F. H. Henry and Kenneth Scott Latourette, October, 1967.

Bible Translations

The Holy Bible: Revised Standard Version. Thomas Nelson & Sons. Copyrighted 1946 and 1952 by the Division of Christian Education of the National Council of the Churches of Christ in the U.S.A., and used by permission.
Smith and Goodspeed, *The Complete Bible: An American Translation.* Copyright 1939 by the University of Chicago.
A New Translation of the Bible, by James Moffatt. Harper & Row, Publishers, Incorporated. Copyright by James Moffatt 1954. Used by permission of Harper & Row, Publishers, Incorporated.
The Jerusalem Bible. Copyright © 1966 by Darton, Longman & Todd, Ltd. and Doubleday & Company, Inc. Used by permission of the publishers.
Good News for Modern Man: The New Testament in Today's English Version. Copyright American Bible Society 1966. By permission.
The New English Bible, New Testament. © The Delegates of the Oxford University Press and the Syndics of the Cambridge University Press 1961. Reprinted by permission.
The New Testament in Modern English. The texts in this book credited to Phillips are from *The New Testament in Modern English,* © J. B. Phillips 1958. Used by permission of The Macmillan Company.